Tennesseans and Their History

Tennesseans

and
THEIR HISTORY

Paul H. Bergeron • Stephen V. Ash • Jeanette Keith

The University of Tennessee Press • Knoxville

Copyright © 1999 by The University of Tennessee Press / Knoxville.
All Rights Reserved. Manufactured in the United States of America.

Cloth: 1st printing, 1999.
Paper: 1st printing, 1999; 2nd printing, 2004; 3rd printing 2007; 4th printing, 2016.

The paper in this book meets the requirements of American National Standards Institute / National Information Standards Organization specification Z39.48– 1992 (Permanence of Paper). It contains 30 percent post-consumer waste and is certified by the Forest Stewardship Council.

Frontispiece: Right: A typical Tennessee yeoman's homestead. East Tennessee Historical Society, Knoxville. *Harper's New Monthly Magazine*, November 1857. Left, clockwise: Excavated trade objects from Overhill Cherokee sites. McClung Museum, University of Tennessee, Knoxville; Wartime Chattanooga. East Tennessee Historical Society, Knoxville; Knoxville race riot, 1919. McClung Historical Collection, Knox County Public Library, Knoxville; Crowd on Tennessee Day at Centennial Park, Nashville. Official History of the Tennessee Centennial Exposition (Nashville, 1898). Special Collections, University of Tennessee, Knoxville.

Library of Congress Cataloging-in-Publication Data

Bergeron, Paul H., 1938–
    Tennesseans and their history / Paul H. Bergeron, Stephen V. Ash, and Jeanette Keith. —1st ed.
        p. cm.
Includes bibliographical references (p.) and index.
ISBN 1-57233-055-4 (cl.: alk. paper)
ISBN 10 1-57233-056-2 (pbk.: alk. paper)
ISBN 13 978-1-57233-056-6
1. Tennessee—History.
I. Ash, Stephen V.
II. Keith, Jeanette.
III. Title.
F436 .B48 1999
976.8—dc21

99-6126

To

The People of Tennessee:

Past, Present, and Future

Contents

Illustrations

Figures

Maps

Tables

Preface

TENNESSEE'S HISTORY IS ANYTHING but dull. It is full of dramatic events, colorful characters, and intriguing story lines that can match anything the greatest novelist or Hollywood screenwriter ever created in his or her imagination.

Tennessee's history is not only fascinating, but also important. Time and again over the years, the Volunteer State has been the scene of events of enormous significance. There was the bloody battle of Shiloh in 1862, the greatest battle ever fought on American soil up to that time. There was the Dayton "monkey trial" of 1925, which pitted traditionalists against modernists in a clash that captured the attention of the whole nation. There was the tragic murder of renowned civil rights leader Martin Luther King, Jr., in Memphis in 1968. These are only three of the episodes in Tennessee's past that helped to shape the history of all America; there are many others.

But Shiloh, the monkey trial, the King assassination, and the other momentous events are not the whole story of Tennessee's past. Nor are such eminent figures as John Sevier and Andrew Jackson and Austin Peay the only Tennesseans whose lives are worth studying. Tennessee's history is also a story of everyday events and common people—women as well as men, black and red and yellow and brown people as well as white people. Although these common folk never accomplished great deeds that would win them a place of honor in the annals of history, their daily lives and personal struggles are a part of our past that deserves to be remembered.

For a long time, there has been a need for an up-to-date history of Tennessee, one that takes into account the wealth of new evidence about the state's past unearthed by historians in recent years. That is why this book has been written. The authors hope that it will appeal not only to college students needing a good, basic Tennessee history textbook, but also to members of the general public looking for a lively and informative account of the state's past. If we manage in these pages both to instruct and to entertain, we shall have accomplished our purpose.

I

Tennessee's Beginnings

HOW OLD IS TENNESSEE? The answer depends upon whom you ask. A geologist defines Tennessee as a particular configuration of rocks and soils and rivers, and would tell you that its origins go back hundreds of millions of years. An anthropologist, on the other hand, envisions Tennessee as a human habitation and would say that its genesis was only a few thousand years ago, when the first Indians came. But ask a historian, who reconstructs the past mainly from written records, and you will learn that Tennessee's history (as historians define the term) is not to be measured in eons or even millennia, for in fact it goes back only a few centuries, to the time when the first Europeans arrived and recorded their experiences.

The historian would be quick to admit, however, that some understanding of the prehistoric past is essential to an understanding of the historic past. Before we begin our journey through Tennessee history, therefore, we need to look briefly at the state's natural features and at what we know about its prehistoric peoples.

The Land

More than a billion years ago, nature began creating the landmass we call Tennessee. What eventually emerged was anything but a uniform landscape; Tennessee in fact is a patchwork of no fewer than nine geologically distinct subregions. Indeed, few other states in the nation can boast of more geological diversity than Tennessee. This variegated terrain (contained within a roughly rectangular area 432 miles east to west and 106 miles north to south), in many important ways, has shaped the human experience in Tennessee.

Along Tennessee's eastern border lies a mountain range ten to fifteen miles wide, known as the Unaka Mountains. This range includes the Great Smokies and other subranges, and it in turn forms part of the vast Appalachian chain that stretches from New England to the Deep South. Rugged and tall (with peaks over six thousand feet above sea level), the Unakas

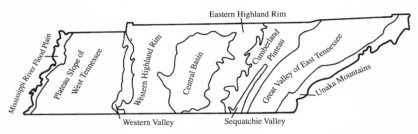

Physiographic regions of Tennessee. Edward T. Luther, *Our Restless Earth: The Geologic Regions of Tennessee* (Knoxville: University of Tennessee Press, 1977), vii.

cover 2,500 of the state's 42,244 square miles and stand like a gigantic wall separating Tennessee from the lands to the east.

Immediately west of the mountains lies the Great Valley of East Tennessee, a geologically complex subregion composed of numerous parallel ridges and valleys running northeast to southwest. Sixty miles across at its widest point, the Great Valley covers some 8,000 square miles.

Rising abruptly above the western edge of the Great Valley like another huge wall is the Cumberland Plateau. Ranging in width from forty to fifty miles, the Cumberland Plateau comprises about 4,200 square miles and towers a thousand feet above the subregions on either side of it. Though generally flat on top (except where bisected by the narrow Sequatchie Valley), it is steep and rough on both flanks.

Heading westward, one next encounters the Eastern Highland Rim of Middle Tennessee, averaging twenty-five miles in width. Joining the Eastern Highland Rim at its northernmost point is the Western Highland Rim, which is considerably wider than its eastern counterpart. Together these two subregions cover about 12,000 square miles.

The Highland Rims surround a sixth geological subregion, the Central Basin of Middle Tennessee. Roughly oval in shape, over fifty miles across, and three to four hundred feet lower than the encircling highlands, the Central Basin is at the geographical center of the state and covers some 5,500 square miles. It is the only subregion of the state that does not stretch all the way from the southern border to the northern, for it is separated from Kentucky by the conjoined Highland Rims.

West of the Western Highland Rim and about three hundred feet below it lies the Western Valley of the Tennessee River. It is a 1,200-square-mile ribbon of land, on average only a dozen miles across and straddling the river where it flows northward through Tennessee toward Kentucky.

Stretching westward from the Western Valley for eighty miles or so is the Plateau Slope of West Tennessee. Three hundred feet higher than the Tennessee River to its east and two hundred feet higher than the Mississippi River to its west, the Plateau Slope covers about 8,000 square miles. For the most part it is very flat, a legacy of its long existence as a seabed in the distant past.

The ninth and last of Tennessee's subregions, the Mississippi River Flood Plain, marks the state's western boundary. Only a few miles separate the Flood Plain's eastern edge, where it abuts the Plateau Slope along the Chickasaw Bluffs, from its western edge, which is the bank of the Mississippi River. The Mississippi Flood Plain covers about 900 square miles and, like the Plateau Slope, is quite flat.

No less important than topography in shaping Tennessee's experience are the state's natural resources, chief among them forests and soil. Nature generously supplied all of Tennessee's subregions with trees and thus offered the early settlers a ready supply of fuel and building material. In some areas, especially the Unaka Mountains, the forests were extensive enough to encourage commercial lumbering as the state developed.

Nature was a little more sparing with soil, however, at least the good, arable kinds. The best soils in the state are the phosphate-rich limestone soil of the Central Basin and the alluvial soil of the Flood Plain. Somewhat less fertile but still quite productive soils cover the Plateau Slope, the Western Valley, most parts of the Highland Rims, the valley sections of the Great Valley, and the small coves nestled within the Unaka Mountains. Early settlers tended to avoid the other parts of Tennessee, especially the relatively sterile Cumberland Plateau.

Mineral resources are abundant in Tennessee and became increasingly important as the state developed. Among the most significant are iron deposits in the Great Valley and Western Highland Rim, copper in the southernmost part of the Unaka Mountains, coal in the Cumberland Plateau, and marble in the Great Valley.

Tennessee's rivers, especially its three major ones, also have played a crucial role in its development. The Tennessee River, which originates at the confluence of two streams near the center of the Great Valley, flows southwestward into Alabama; there it turns north, reenters Tennessee, and proceeds through the Western Valley into Kentucky and to the Ohio River. The Cumberland River, originating in eastern Kentucky, flows southwestward across the state line, along the juncture of the two Highland Rims, and into the Central Basin; then it curves northwestward, slices through the Western Highland Rim, and exits the state not far east of the Tennessee River, eventually emptying into the Ohio. The great Mississippi River, originating far to the north, meanders southward along Tennessee's western border.

Nature, it seems, had decreed the division of Tennessee into three broad regions—East, Middle, and West—long before any people arrived. East Tennessee, bounded by the formidable Unaka Mountains and eastern Cumberland Plateau, would remain relatively isolated from the rest of the state and the nation for a good part of its history; the Tennessee River, though navigable within East Tennessee, was not a dependable link to the outside world because of dangerous river hazards near what is now Chattanooga and at Muscle Shoals, Alabama. Middle Tennessee, walled off from East Tennessee by the Cumberland Plateau but connected to the outside world by the readily navigable Cumberland and lower Tennessee Rivers, likewise in some respects would pursue its own destiny. And so would West Tennessee, which shares the Western Valley with Middle Tennessee but is oriented mainly toward the Mississippi. Acts of man subsequently would ratify nature's decree and reinforce the distinctions among Tennessee's three "grand divisions."

The First Tennesseans

Humans first set foot on Tennessee soil over twelve thousand years ago. They were descendants of the very first Americans, who had crossed from Asia to North America on the land bridge that linked Siberia and Alaska during the Ice Ages. These people (whom anthropologists call Paleo-Indians) perhaps should be regarded as the first visitors to Tennessee, rather than the first Tennesseans, for they were nomadic hunters with no permanent habitations. They lived in temporary camps as they followed the herds of mastodon and other game. Traveling in bands that seldom numbered more than two dozen people, they built no structures more sophisticated than lean-tos and left few traces of their existence other than campfire sites and simple stone tools.

With the passage of time, the climate warmed, the last Ice Age ended, and the flora and fauna of North America changed. Forests grew more widely; the mastodons disappeared; and deer, elk, and moose proliferated. As the environment evolved, so did Indian culture. By about 8,000 B.C., a new way of life, known to anthropologists as the Archaic tradition, had replaced the Paleo-Indian tradition.

The Archaic Indians of the Tennessee region have a better claim than the Paleo-Indians to the title of "first Tennesseans." Though still nomadic, they did not roam as far as their predecessors, preferring instead to hunt, gather, and fish intensively within a limited area. Moreover, they moved seasonally rather than daily, and this more settled existence allowed their numbers to increase and enabled them to develop a more advanced technology than their ancestors had. Among the important innovations of Archaic culture were clay hearths, bowls carved from soapstone, fishhooks fashioned from the toe bones of deer, baskets woven from reeds, and, above all, the *atlatl* (spear thrower), a device that significantly increased the range and killing power of the hunter's spear.

The culture of the prehistoric Indians of Tennessee never was static. It evolved continuously and, by 1,000 B.C. or so, had changed so much that anthropologists deem it a wholly different culture, called the Woodland tradition. Though they still went on hunting expeditions, Woodland Indians lived in permanent settlements of around one hundred inhabitants. They also developed the first real agriculture in Tennessee, raising crops such as sunflowers, squash, and corn. They were more sophisticated technologically than their predecessors, too, for they made pottery vessels and hunted with bow and arrows.

The Woodland Indians also built burial mounds for some of their dead. The body of the deceased was laid in a rectangular tomb topped with logs, which then was covered with earth. As time passed, more burials would be made in a similar fashion, one on top of the other, eventually creating a sizable man-made hill. These mounds tell us much about Woodland culture. For one thing, the mounds were reserved for the bodies of prominent individuals, suggesting a degree of social stratification unknown in earlier cultures. Moreover, they required the organized labor of many workers, indicating a relatively advanced political system. The fact that the dead often were buried with their prized possessions—copper earrings, carved stone smoking pipes, and so forth, presumably for use in the afterlife—is evidence of a complex belief system. And the fact that some of the implements and ornaments buried with the dead actually were made in other regions of North America shows that the Woodland Indians of Tennessee had developed a network of trade relations with Indians elsewhere.

Around 900 A.D., a new culture, the Mississippian tradition, appeared among Indians living along the Mississippi River. Gradually it spread eastward, as some of the original Mississippians migrated and their practices were adopted by the Woodland Indians among whom they settled. Eventually all Tennessee Indians were more or less Mississippian.

That culture was considerably more elaborate economically, politically, and socially than its predecessors. Mississippian Indians lived in large towns. These concentrated populations required highly organized agriculture and hunting to support them and some form of government to distribute their resources. Chiefs and priests formed the apex of a social hierarchy more rigidly defined than any known in the previous cultures.

Anthropologists are unsure of the connection between the early Mississippian Indians and the Indians in Tennessee at the dawn of the state's historical era in the sixteenth and seventeenth centuries A.D. But whether these latter-day peoples—the Cherokees, Chickasaws, Creeks, and Shawnees—came to Tennessee before or after Mississippian culture was established there, they were essentially Mississippian by the time Europeans first encountered them.

Those four tribes, though differing in their languages and certain other traits, had much in common. Their people all lived in palisaded hilltop towns overlooking rivers and grew their crops on the bottom lands below. Each town had a central plaza surrounded by a number of earthen platform mounds. Atop these mounds sat the public buildings, including a temple and a council house, and the homes of the elite. Clustered below the

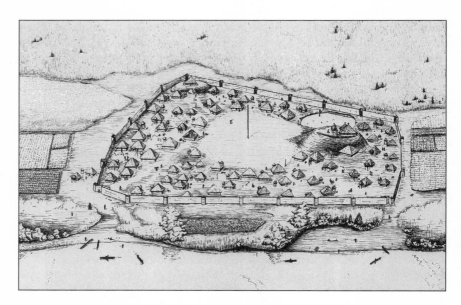

Artist's reconstruction of a Mississippian Indian town in East Tennessee, c. 1500 A.D. Artwork by Thomas Whyte. McClung Museum, University of Tennessee, Knoxville.

mounds were the homes of the common folk, structures some sixteen feet square, with walls of saplings and cane woven together and covered with mud, and roofs of thatched grass.

Gender relations in the four tribes were strictly delineated. Women's duties included farming and gathering as well as domestic chores, while men had sole responsibility for hunting, fishing, making war, and government. Moreover, only men were allowed to play the popular game of *tchung-kee* (or *chunkey*), which featured two competitors who rolled a stone disk across a playing field and tried to predict where it would come to rest, while a crowd of onlookers cheered them on and wagered on the outcome.

The government of these late-prehistoric Indians was extremely decentralized—to call it anarchic would be only a slight exaggeration. Each town nominally was governed by a chief and council of elders; but those leaders, while influential, wielded little coercive power. Decisions were arrived at by discussion and consensus among all the men of the town, meeting in the council house. Furthermore, whatever authority the town government had was checked by the power of the kinship groups known as *clans*, which had a strong claim on their members' loyalty; each tribe encompassed a number of clans, bearing such colorful names as Deer, Snake, Wild Potato, and Long Hair. There was, moreover, no real tribal government to which the towns and clans deferred. The tribe was basically a confederation of independent towns linked by language and kinship.

Green Corn Ceremony

Among the Mississippian Indians of Tennessee, the most important public event was the Green Corn Ceremony, an annual festival lasting up to eight days. It featured rituals, dancing, storytelling, feasting, and games that were intended to propitiate the gods, offer thanks for the harvest, and strengthen and purify the community. During the festival, the town's sacred fire was extinguished, then re-lit to symbolize the birth of a new year. In another event, the men of the town drank the "black drink." This bitter potion was brewed from holly leaves and served in conch shells; it induced immediate vomiting, which the tribesmen believed would purge them spiritually as well as physically.

The people of the tribes viewed the world in a particular way—a way that differed radically from the assumptions of the Europeans they eventually would encounter. For one thing, the tribes had no concept of private property, at least insofar as land was concerned; they regarded all their land as tribal land. Furthermore, they made no distinction between worldly and spiritual realms. Their gods were the Sun, the River, and other natural phenomena; and every aspect of their lives, from hunting and agriculture to healing and warfare, was shaped by mystical beliefs and organized around sacred rituals. A bad omen, for example, could delay planting or postpone a hunt; and no warrior would think of going on the warpath without first purging himself according to the priest's instructions and then fasting for the prescribed period.

Although Indian boys were taught the ways of the warrior as part of their upbringing, intertribal wars were relatively infrequent. When tribes did take up arms, it was rarely out of materialistic greed, for Indians were not acquisitive people; nor was it often a conflict over territory, for the Tennessee country was vast and the Indians few. Warfare was more likely to be instigated by young men seeking to win recognition through heroic deeds, or by clan members retaliating for an injury done to one of their own. Such wars almost always were small in scale and the casualties few.

Europeans Arrive

In the fifteenth century, Western European nations began sending out expeditions of discovery all over the globe. Eventually European explorers penetrated deeply into North America. Rarely troubled by doubts about their own righteousness, they dismissed the Indian inhabitants as unworthy heathens and grandly claimed all the "newly discovered" lands in the name of their sovereign and their God.

It is very likely—but not certain, for their written accounts are somewhat vague—that the first Europeans to enter the Tennessee country were a force of six hundred Spaniards who came in the sixteenth century, led by Hernando de Soto. Having landed in Florida, de Soto and his men passed through Georgia and South Carolina, then crossed the southern Appalachians and apparently entered East Tennessee, perhaps along the Hiwassee River, in the spring of 1540. They stayed in that vicinity for a while, welcomed by some Indians whose hospitality they repaid with abuse; and then they marched down to the area of present-day Chattanooga. After wasting weeks in a fruitless search for gold, they moved on to Alabama and Mississippi, mistreating Indians all along the way. In 1566–67, another Spanish party (under Juan Pardo) probably entered East Tennessee, tracing part of de Soto's route.

Technically speaking, Tennessee's history can be said to begin with these Spanish expeditions. But the Spanish did not follow up, and Tennessee passed the next 106 years unseen by European eyes. Moreover, when Europeans next appeared in Tennessee, in the late seventeenth century, they were not Spaniards—Spain concentrated its colonial efforts farther south—but Frenchmen and Englishmen, whose countries both were challenging Spain for control of North America.

France established bases in eastern Canada by the early 1600s and eventually sent exploring parties westward and southward to claim more land. In the spring and summer of 1673, Father Jacques Marquette, a Jesuit missionary, and Louis Joliet, a fur trader, led a canoe expedition down the Mississippi River in the name of France. They went as far as the mouth of the Arkansas River, with one of their stops along the way probably being at the bluffs where Memphis now stands. France thereafter reinforced its claims by building a string of forts and trading posts from Quebec to New Orleans.

Coincidentally, at the very time Marquette and Joliet were paddling along Tennessee's western extremity, two Englishmen were crossing Tennessee's eastern border. These two, James Needham and Gabriel Arthur, came from the English colony of Virginia, which had been growing steadily since its founding in 1607. They were not officials, but rather were private agents of one of Virginia's leading merchants, Abraham Wood, who sought to expand his trading into the trans-Appalachian country. Traveling across the mountains—a long and arduous trek on the most primitive of trails—Needham and Arthur entered the Great Valley of East Tennessee and on July 15, 1673, arrived at a Cherokee town. Needham soon headed home, but Arthur stayed on for months and learned the Indians' language.

The expedition of the Englishmen Needham and Arthur and that of the Frenchmen Marquette and Joliet are of infinitely greater significance in Tennessee history than those of the Spaniards de Soto and Pardo, for they heralded the sustained penetration and eventual conquest of Tennessee by Europeans. These expeditions also drew Tennessee into a world of international conflict from which it would not escape for a century and a half. Furthermore, the coming of the English and French marked the beginning of the end of Tennessee's native culture.

At the time when the English and French appeared, Tennessee was not inhabited extensively by Indians. The Shawnee tribe hunted in the Cumberland River area of Middle Tennessee and had a few towns there, but most of its people lived farther north, nearer the Ohio River. The Creeks (who were not really a single tribe but a confederacy of small tribes) had some towns in the Chattanooga area but lived mostly to the south, in Georgia, Alabama, and Florida. The Chickasaw tribe hunted in West and Middle Tennessee but had no permanent habitations anywhere in the state; its towns were in northern Mississippi.

The native Americans with the most significant presence in Tennessee at the time were the Cherokees. The tribe as a whole numbered perhaps thirty thousand people (it was the largest in the South), living in some fifty to eighty towns in the southern Appalachians. These towns clustered in four districts: the Upper and Middle Settlements in western North Carolina; the Lower Settlements in western South Carolina and northern Georgia; and the Overhill Settlements in East Tennessee, situated along the Tellico, Hiwassee, and Little Tennessee Rivers. Among the important towns in the Overhill district were Tanasi (from which the state derived its name), Chota, and Great Tellico. The Cherokees regarded all of East and Middle Tennessee as their hunting grounds, their claim to the latter being disputed by the Chickasaws, Shawnees, and others.

The Indians of Tennessee became important to the Europeans mainly because of the Europeans' insatiable desire for animal skins and furs. The colonizing powers subscribed to the theory of mercantilism, which valued colonies primarily for the wealth that could be extracted from them. Tennessee could not offer what the Europeans sought above all—gold and silver—but its forests were rich with deer and beaver, whose pelts were almost as desirable as precious metals. The Indians, who were expert hunters and trappers, could provide the Europeans with what they wanted; and the Europeans had much to offer the Indians in return.

White traders, French and English, became a common sight along Tennessee's Indian trails after 1673. (Both France and England claimed the Tennessee region, of course, on the basis of their "discovery" of it.) The French traders operated from posts along the Mississippi and even had one on the Cumberland by the early 1700s, at the present site of Nashville. The English traders at first came from Virginia; but as the Carolina colony (founded in 1670) developed, its traders took advantage of their somewhat easier access to Tennessee and soon overshadowed their Virginia rivals. By 1690, Carolinians were in contact with the Overhill Cherokees, and by

---

"Beloved Women" of the Cherokees

Among the Tennessee tribes, women generally were excluded from governmental affairs, but the Cherokees were an exception. All Cherokee women were allowed in council houses, and a select few were elevated to the status of Agehyagusta ("beloved woman"). The Agehyagusta had the privilege of participating in important decisions, including the decision for peace or war, and had the power of life or death over prisoners captured in war.

The most renowned of the "beloved women" of the Overhill Cherokees was Nancy Ward (Nanye'hi). "She was of queenly and commanding presence and manners," one historian has written. Until her death in 1822, she was a firm advocate of peace between Indians and whites.

1698 at least one had passed through Chickasaw country all the way to the Mississippi River. These Carolina traders generally were from Charleston; the Carolinians of the Albemarle region to the north never were as interested in transmontane trade as the Charlestonians. After the two districts became separate colonies in 1712, South Carolinians continued to dominate the trade. Virginia traders, however, achieved a partial comeback after 1740, when a new and shorter trade route was blazed from their colony into Tennessee.

Loading up his dozen or more pack horses with goods to offer the Indians—guns, ammunition, tools, jewelry, blankets, and many other items—the trader would set off for the Tennessee country in the late summer or early fall. Often he would travel in company with others, and pack trains of a hundred horses were not uncommon. Arriving at his destination after a long journey (to go from Charleston to the Overhill Cherokee district, for example, took three to four weeks), the trader would peddle his wares to the natives on credit: a musket for the promise of thirty-five deerskins, a hatchet for three, a broadcloth coat for thirty, and so forth. Then he would settle in for the winter in an Indian town, perhaps with his Indian wife, while the native hunting parties set out. In the late spring, after the hunters had returned and paid him what they owed, the trader would make the long trip home and deliver the pelts to the merchant who had provided his trade goods on credit. From there the treasures of the Tennessee forests were shipped to their ultimate destination in Europe.

Besides skins and furs, the Europeans procured another valuable commodity from the Tennessee country: Indian slaves. Knowing that the great demand for labor in the American colonies meant big profits for anyone

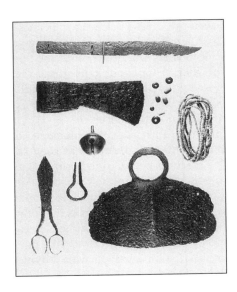

Excavated trade objects from Overhill Cherokee sites. McClung Museum, University of Tennessee, Knoxville.

who could supply workers, traders encouraged their native trading partners to sell them captives from other tribes who had been taken in battle or kidnapped in raids. Because these Indian slaves would try to escape if they remained anywhere near their homeland, usually they were shipped to the West Indies and sold to plantation owners there.

Historians speak of the "Columbian Exchange" that took place wherever Europeans and Indians came into contact. From the Indians the Europeans learned, for example, how to plant corn and make birch-bark canoes and survive in the forests; from the Europeans the Indians got firearms and metal tools. It must be said, however, that the Europeans' influence on Tennessee's Indians was, in the long run, vastly greater than the Indians' influence on the Europeans.

Native culture changed profoundly as Tennessee was drawn into the orbit of Europe. The Indians grew increasingly dependent upon the weapons and other things they bought from the Europeans, and to pay for them they had to exploit the forest resources more intensively. Their hunting and trapping became a business—an extractive industry, really—rather than just a means of subsistence, and this had the effect of depleting the game and intensifying rivalries over hunting grounds. The Europeans' demand for slaves likewise increased friction among the tribes. Strategic matters impinged upon the Indians, too, for they found themselves being recruited as proxies in the struggle among the European powers for control of North America, armed by one side or the other and cajoled into fighting for their "ally." Driven by these unrelenting commercial and international political pressures, the tribes warred against one another with growing frequency and ferocity.

These conflicts transformed the Tennessee country within a matter of decades. By 1715, the Cherokees had driven the Creeks out of East Tennessee altogether, in a war instigated by the English to procure Indian slaves; Charleston traders in fact had supplied both sides with guns, with the understanding that all captives were to be sold. About that same time, the Cherokees and the Chickasaws began forcing the Shawnees out of Middle Tennessee. By 1730 all the Shawnees' settlements were gone, and by 1745 even their hunting parties no longer ventured into the region.

That left the Cherokees as the only tribe with permanent settlements in Tennessee (though the Chickasaw hunting and war parties that roamed West and Middle Tennessee were still a force to be reckoned with). The Cherokees meanwhile were experiencing changes within their society. For one thing, their numbers declined markedly, as thousands of their people became victims of the incessant, bloody warfare or the diseases brought in by Europeans. The white man's rum also began taking a toll on the Cherokee people. Nor was alcohol abuse the only egregious aspect of white culture adopted by the Cherokees; before long, some of them were buying Negro slaves.

Not all the changes in the Cherokees' way of life were necessarily for the worse. Their agriculture, for example, benefited enormously from the introduction of metal hoes and domesticated animals. Their political structure evolved, too, becoming more centralized in response to the demand by the English for a single authority with whom they could deal. In 1721, a South Carolina official convinced three dozen or so of the Cherokee towns to name one leader to represent them in treaty negotiations. Nine years later, an envoy from England recognized Moytoy, chief of the Overhill town of Tellico, as the Cherokee "emperor." Because the English also insisted on holding the whole tribe responsible for individual transgressions, the Cherokees concluded that some kind of central judicial and legislative authority was needed. By the 1750s, a sort of tribal government was functioning, although it could not always rein in its traditionally independent towns, clans, and warriors.

Tennessee and the Struggle for Empire

The European powers never were content to share the riches of North America. Each lusted to possess the whole continent. Between 1689 and 1748, they fought three wars among themselves, all of which were, in part, contests for (and in) North America. These struggles were inconclusive, however. When the third ended, England, France, and Spain still were firmly implanted in North America, each country jealously guarding its own possessions and greedily eyeing those of its rivals.

The remote Tennessee country was not involved directly in those three conflicts; no European armies had trod upon its soil. But the final showdown was still to come; when it did, Tennessee indeed would have a role to play.

The Great War for the Empire (better known in America as the French and Indian War) began in America in 1754. By then Spain was in decline, and it was clear that the real contest would be between France and England. Each side had strengths and weaknesses. The French held Canada and much of the Mississippi Valley, but their colonial population was small—a mere ninety thousand. They were outnumbered sixteen to one by English inhabitants, whose thirteen colonies were strung along the Atlantic coast from New England to Georgia. But the English colonies lacked central direction; each in many respects remained autonomous, for London exerted minimal control. The French colonists were more unified.

Indian alliances were crucial to both sides. Trade and gift-giving were the primary means by which the rival powers sought to bind the tribes to them. The French were disadvantaged in that respect, however, for their traders and officials could not match the offerings of the more numerous and better supplied English. The French compensated for that handicap to a degree by treating the Indians respectfully—unlike the English, whose officials tended to be high-handed and whose traders often were swindlers. The Indians, for their part, often were able to gain advantage by playing the rival European powers off against each other.

One important exception to the generally shabby English treatment of the Indians had occurred in 1730, when Sir Alexander Cuming (the envoy who recognized Moytoy as Cherokee emperor) took six Cherokee men with him back to England. They were received there with great ceremony, were wined and dined in high style, met King George II himself, and were persuaded to sign a treaty. The treaty committed the Cherokee tribe not only to submit to the sovereignty of the English king, but also to trade exclusively with England and to fight on England's side if war should break out in North America. After their return home, the six remained firmly committed to the English and consistently used their influence on England's behalf. Especially prominent among them was a leader of the Overhill Cherokees named Attakullakulla, or "Little Carpenter."

Not all the Cherokees were Anglophiles, however. Some responded to the overtures of the French. One was Oconostota, the tribe's chief warrior, whose hatred of the English can be traced in part to his belief that they were deliberately spreading smallpox among his people. Oconostota himself survived an attack of the disease, but it left his face badly scarred, a circumstance that only deepened his enmity.

Another threat to the English alliance with the Cherokees appeared in 1736, in the person of one Christian Priber. An odd, idealistic German, Priber wandered into the Overhill town of Great Tellico that year and began preaching his own brand of utopianism, urging the Indians to create what he called the "Kingdom of Paradise" and designating himself its "Secretary of State." He stayed on for years and gained something of a following. The English thought him harmless at first but changed their minds af-

Fort Loudoun, c. 1758. Artwork by Doug Henry. Tennessee Department of Environment and Conservation, Nashville.

ter he began exhorting the Cherokees to renounce English sovereignty, make peace with all the other tribes, and trade with the French. In 1743, English authorities had Priber arrested as an enemy agent. He died in captivity, but thereafter a nationalistic faction of Cherokees remained faithful to his cause and skeptical of entangling alliances.

Nevertheless, the English continued to hold the loyalty of most of the Cherokee tribe, mainly because of their trading advantage over the French. The Cherokees, growing more dependent upon European goods with every passing year, could ill afford to alienate the well-supplied English. A majority of the Chickasaws saw things the same way and thus sided with the English, too. But these Anglo-Indian alliances never were secure; they were constantly endangered by French intrigue and by the knavery and arrogance of English traders and officials. As the two great powers moved inexorably toward the decisive war for North America, English authorities ceaselessly fretted about their Indian allies.

One way to bind the tribes more securely was to build forts in their territory. No one appreciated that fact more than South Carolina's royal governor, James Glen, who, from the time he took office in the 1740s, lobbied energetically for English forts in the Cherokee country. Such forts, he pointed out, would discourage French penetration and thus preserve the Cherokee districts as a buffer between the French and the English colonies; moreover, he noted, a well-garrisoned fort would be a useful instrument for controlling the native population—"a Bridle in the Mouths of the Indians," as he put it. Glen's efforts led to the construction of Fort Prince George in western South Carolina in 1753. This bolstered English influence among the Cherokees of the Upper, Middle, and Lower Settlements, but it was of no help in the distant Overhill Settlements in Tennessee.

When the French and Indian War broke out in the Ohio Valley in 1754, the issue of an Overhill fort became critical. The English called on their Cherokee allies to send a force of warriors north to fight, but the Cherokees demurred. They demanded as the price of enlistment the construction of a fort in the Overhill district where Cherokee women and children could take refuge in the event the French or French-allied Indians attacked while the men were away.

Governor Glen therefore arranged to send a fort-building expedition across the mountains. Virginia's governor agreed to send a detachment of men to help. Early in the summer of 1756, the Virginians arrived; finding the South Carolinians not present, they went ahead and built a small fort beside the Little Tennessee River opposite Chota, the chief Overhill town. But as soon as the job was finished, they all headed back to Virginia, leaving no garrison behind—to the disgust of the Cherokees, who proceeded to level the fort to keep it from falling into French hands.

The South Carolina expedition had set out about the same time as the Virginians but had been delayed when Glen was replaced by a new governor, William Henry Lyttelton. Lyttelton held up the project while he reviewed it, but he was soon convinced of its usefulness and even managed to get more money for it from the colonial assembly. He also confirmed Glen's appointment of a royal army officer, Capt. Raymond Demere, to command the expedition and an engineer, John William Gerard DeBrahm, to supervise construction.

Demere's force, consisting of 120 short-term South Carolina troops to build the fort and 80 British regulars to garrison it, set out from Fort Prince

---

Fort Loudoun

Situated on a hill where the Little Tennessee and Tellico Rivers meet, Fort Loudoun was an imposing fortification, a diamond-shaped structure three hundred feet long on each side and with a bastion at each corner. Around the fort ran a ditch three feet deep and ten across, planted with thorny honey locusts to discourage attacks by Indian warriors, who, as John DeBrahm wrote, "always engage naked." Inside the encircling ditch was a four-foot earthen parapet surmounted by an eight-foot log palisade. Firing ports for muskets were cut into the logs. In the bastions were mounted twelve cannons that had been laboriously hauled over the mountains on horseback from South Carolina.

George on September 21, 1756. Ten days later, they arrived in the Overhill district, where the Cherokees—once they were assured that a permanent garrison force was on hand—greeted them jubilantly. Despite this auspicious start, the expedition proved to be a troubled one, mainly because of the mutual antagonism of Demere and DeBrahm. The former was a hard-nosed professional military man; the latter, though an experienced engineer, was a highly eccentric civilian given to mysticism and alchemy—one acquaintance described him as "A Madman truly." Demere and DeBrahm quarreled constantly, *ad nauseam,* about everything: the location of the fort, its design and construction, the employment of the workforce, and so on. Eventually the two refused even to speak to each other, and in December DeBrahm left for South Carolina in a huff. Nevertheless, work progressed, and in July 1757 the fort was completed. It was christened Fort Loudoun in honor of the commander of British forces in America.

Raymond Demere left in August for another post and was replaced by his brother, Paul, who also was a royal army captain. The South Carolina troops departed, too, leaving the British regulars to hold the fort. Some of these soldiers eventually were joined by their wives and children, and a bustling little community soon existed within the fort, its daily routines enlivened by the frequent visits of Cherokees wanting to trade or to get their guns and tools fixed by the garrison's blacksmith. Food supply was a persistent problem, however. The troops hunted, fished, grew some corn in the surrounding fields, and traded with the Indians for other eatables, but they still had to import most of their provisions along the rough trail that stretched two hundred miles east to the nearest white settlements.

The fort's commander was the de facto Indian agent of the crown in the Overhill district. Raymond Demere had been friendly to the natives, but Paul Demere proved rude and overbearing. The Cherokees loathed him. They were, nevertheless, reassured by the presence of the fort and its garrison, and at last they consented to go off to war with the English. Soon a sizable contingent of Cherokee warriors was in the Ohio country fighting against the French and the French-allied Indians, among whom were the Shawnees.

Before long, however, the Anglo-Cherokee alliance began to dissolve. The trouble started when a number of Cherokee warriors returning home from the Ohio Valley passed through the white settlements of Virginia's frontier and there stole some horses and plundered cabins. The Virginians in turn killed some of the warriors. Indian custom demanded retaliation for these deaths by the clansmen of the deceased. All Englishmen being of the same tribe in the Cherokees' eyes, the avengers did not confine their killing to Virginians.

When some innocent South Carolinians became victims of the Cherokees' revenge, Governor Lyttelton responded by halting the shipment of arms and ammunition to the entire tribe. This was a serious blow to the Cherokees, for their hunting and self-defense depended on a steady supply of muskets, bullets, and powder. Consequently, late in 1759, Oconostota led a delegation of his people to Charleston to parley with the governor. Lyttelton, meanwhile, had decided that the Cherokees deserved further punishment and was organizing a military expedition against them. He therefore took Oconostota and his party hostage in Charleston and then led them west, along with his troops, to Fort Prince George. Before long, the governor called off the expedition and prepared to return east, but he ordered that the hostages remain confined in the fort, pending the Cherokees' surrender of the warriors who murdered the Carolinians. Eventually Attakullakulla arrived and negotiated Oconostota's release. Then both men signed an agreement with the governor promising to turn over the guilty warriors; until they did so, the remaining hostages would stay in English hands.

Oconostota, furious over his treatment by the governor, probably never intended to honor the agreement. As soon as Lyttelton and his troops returned to Charleston, the warrior chief mustered his own forces and began attacking white settlers and traders on the Carolina and Georgia frontier. Moreover, in February 1760, he led an attempt to rescue the hostages at Fort Prince George. After luring the fort's commander out on a pretext, Oconostota signaled his warriors to fire; the commander fell mortally wounded. The garrison troops thereupon murdered all twenty-three hostages. This brought the Cherokees and the English into all-out war, despite Attakullakulla's pleas for peace.

Oconostota then turned his sights on Fort Loudoun, now isolated and vulnerable. In March 1760, he and his warriors surrounded the fort, cut its supply line, and—judging it too strong to assault—took up positions out of cannon range and settled in for a siege. Inside the fort were three hundred men, women, and children, including a company of South Carolina troops sent earlier as reinforcements. Luckily for them, they had sufficient provisions stockpiled to last several months.

Governor Lyttelton was eager to relieve Fort Loudoun but had no forces to spare. He therefore called upon the governors of North Carolina and Virginia for aid. The former provided none at all; the latter ordered a force into the Overhill country, but its commander dawdled and never reached his destination. Lyttelton also called upon the British army, which obligingly dispatched 1,300 regulars to Charleston under Col. Archibald Montgomery. This force marched west into the South Carolina mountains; but there, in June 1760, it was ambushed by Oconostota. Though his casualties were not heavy, Montgomery lost heart, turned his troops around, and headed back to Charleston.

The failure of these relief expeditions doomed Fort Loudoun. Inside the fort, provisions were running low. The garrison troops and their dependents eventually were reduced to eating the horses, and by July even those were mostly gone. Attakullakulla did what he could to help; he remained nearby, visited the fort daily, and even betrayed Oconostota's plans to Captain Demere on a couple of occasions. Finally, however, his fellow Cherokees branded him an enemy and drove him off.

By August, the situation was hopeless. On the night of August 4, a number of soldiers deserted, and the next day all the rest threatened to go. On August 6, Demere called a meeting of his officers; they resolved to seek terms of surrender. The Cherokees agreed to let all the occupants of the fort depart in peace and even take their small arms, if they would give up the fort with its cannons.

On August 8, the troops lowered the flag and abandoned Fort Loudoun. Then the long column—180 soldiers and 60 dependents—began the trek to Fort Prince George, accompanied by a Cherokee hunting party that was to secure food for them along the way. They camped that evening fifteen miles from the fort. But during the night, the hunting party slipped away, and the next morning 700 Cherokee warriors attacked without warning. Twenty-six soldiers and 3 women were killed before the rest surrendered. Paul Demere now had reason to regret his unpopularity with the Cherokees. He died horribly. Wounded and then scalped alive, he was forced to dance before his captors; then his limbs were hacked off one at a time. The other captives were marched off to Cherokee towns. Some were tortured and killed, but most were held for ransom.

The Cherokees' military success was short-lived. The British army struck back in the summer of 1761, with a punitive expedition into the Lower and Middle Settlements. It was led by Col. James Grant, who had learned from Montgomery's mistakes. Grant adroitly avoided ambush as he, in his words, "burned fifteen towns, fifteen hundred acres of corn, and drove five thousand Cherokees into the mountains to starve."

The Cherokees soon realized the game was up. For a time their hopes were buoyed by the promise of a French expedition that was supposed to come up the Tennessee River and occupy Fort Loudoun; but the French were stymied by the river obstructions near Chattanooga and got no farther. Late in 1761, Attakullakulla reasserted his authority and helped negotiate a peace agreement with the English, which included the return of Fort Loudoun and the release of all hostages.

Meanwhile, England had triumphed in the struggle against France, and in 1763 the two nations signed the Treaty of Paris. France gave up virtually all claim to North America, leaving England master of that portion of the continent between the Atlantic Ocean and the Mississippi River—including, of course, Tennessee.

Fort Loudoun never was garrisoned again and soon stood in ruins, but it had served its purpose well. By binding the powerful Cherokee tribe to the English during the critical early stage of the French and Indian War, when the French were winning, the fort undoubtedly helped the English hang on until the tide of war turned in their favor.

Aftermath of War

Now that England had evicted its most powerful rival from the continent, what was to become of the trans-Appalachian region that included Tennessee? Settlers from the thirteen colonies were pressing westward, and it was surely only a matter of time before they spilled across the mountains and spread out over the rich lands beyond. This prospect worried the English authorities, who had decided in the wake of the war that they must apply a firmer hand to the unruly American colonies.

The Proclamation of 1763, promulgated by King George III in October of that year, seemed—from the perspective of London—a sensible solution to the problem. It prohibited white settlement beyond the crest of the Appalachians. This, the authorities reasoned, not only would keep the colonial population confined and thus make it more manageable, but also would limit the expense of administering the newly enlarged colonial possessions and reduce the chances of trouble with the Indians.

Had the imperial authorities been able to enforce the proclamation, Tennessee would have remained the preserve of Cherokees, Chickasaws, and Carolina and Virginia traders. But the restless and acquisitive colonists to the east were not to be restrained so easily. Well before the proclamation was made, white hunters had begun to cross into Tennessee to secure deer and beaver pelts for themselves. (This was illegal, for only traders were licensed to acquire pelts.) These "long hunters"—so called because their expeditions took them away from home for months at a time—had learned all the forest skills of the Indians and, with the supply of game diminishing, clearly threatened the Indians' livelihood. When they could catch them, the

---

Daniel Boone

The most famous of the "long hunters" was Daniel Boone. Though identified mainly with the Kentucky frontier, Boone was roaming through northeastern Tennessee as early as 1760, when he was twenty-six years old. In the early 1770s, he and his wife Rebecca lived at Sapling Grove, near present-day Bristol. In many respects, Boone fit the stereotype of the frontiersman: he was nearly illiterate, wore deerskins, and plaited his long hair. But, contrary to popular belief, he disdained coonskin caps and instead wore a hat. Like others of his ilk, he was viewed as a threat by the Indians, who on one occasion captured him and held him for days before he managed to escape. His son James was less lucky: in 1773 he was captured, tortured, and killed by Indian warriors in Powell's Valley, Tennessee.

Indians typically confiscated the long hunters' pelts and sent them home empty-handed; sometimes they killed them. But the poachers were wily and elusive and rarely got caught. The Indians consequently appealed to the English authorities, reminding them of the treaties that gave the natives exclusive use of the hunting grounds. "The white people pay no attention to the talks we have had," Oconostota complained to the British superintendent of Indian affairs in 1769. "They are in bodies hunting in the Middle of our Hunting Grounds. . . . [T]he whole Nation is filling with Hunters, and the[ir] guns rattling every way on the path."

The long hunters not only took skins and furs back to the white settlements, but also delivered information—detailed reports about the land, the trails, and the Indians beyond the mountains. That information would prove invaluable to those who, as the 1760s drew to a close, were preparing to move westward and stake out homesteads in the Tennessee country.

Suggested Readings

Arnow, Harriette Simpson. *Seedtime on the Cumberland*. New York, 1960. Reprinted, Lincoln, Neb., 1995.

Caruso, John Anthony. *The Appalachian Frontier: America's First Surge Westward*. Indianapolis, 1959.

Chapman, Jefferson. *Tellico Archaeology: 12,000 Years of Native American History*. Knoxville, Tenn., 1985.

Cotterill, R. S. *The Southern Indians: The Story of the Civilized Tribes Before Removal*. Norman, Okla., 1954.

Hudson, Charles. *The Southeastern Indians*. Knoxville, Tenn., 1976.

Lewis, Thomas M. N., and Madeline Kneberg. *Tribes That Slumber: Indian Times in the Tennessee Region*. Knoxville, Tenn., 1958.

Luther, Edward T. *Our Restless Earth: The Geologic Regions of Tennessee*. Knoxville, Tenn., 1977.

Satz, Ronald N. *Tennessee's Indian Peoples: From White Contact to Removal, 1540–1840*. Knoxville, Tenn., 1979.

Williams, Samuel Cole. *Early Travels in the Tennessee Country, 1540–1800*. Johnson City, Tenn., 1928. Reprinted, Nashville, Tenn., 1970.

2

Frontier Times

IN 1768 OR 1769, no one can be certain of the exact dates, the first permanent white settlers moved into upper East Tennessee, the land of the Cherokees. Usually they arrived in groups, typically families, to plant settlements. Most came from either the Virginia or the North Carolina colony, believing that one or the other of those governments had legal claim to the territory.

Why did these people move into this scarcely known region? Unfortunately, there is no precise or definitive answer to this question, but there are several valid possibilities. There seems to be little doubt that "push-pull" forces were very much in evidence. Some persons were "pushed" out of their settings in the adjacent colonies by legal or financial difficulties they faced; they sought a new chance in a different place. Perhaps discontent with the colonial governments, such as that exhibited by the North Carolina "Regulators," stirred individuals or groups to move away from their familiar surroundings. Historians disagree, however, about the significance of the Regulator movement as a motivation for settlement in the Tennessee country. Still other frontier settlers may have been "pushed" toward the new lands by an internal restlessness, an urge to move on, a belief that one should not stay in any one place for any great length of time.

Pulling some late-eighteenth-century settlers to Tennessee may have been the challenge of "conquering" a new area. Stories and reports concerning the richness of the transmontane lands doubtless served as sufficient stimulation for many daring souls. Those persons interested in land speculation—and they were more numerous than we sometimes realize—could hardly wait to venture forth and mark out claims (greed might not be too harsh a term for what pulled them). After the initial group of settlers crossed into the new region, friends and families left behind often were captivated by the desire to join them. Whatever the motivation, it was strong enough to overcome migrants' fears of a difficult passage into the new region, the Indian menace, possible deprivation and physical suffering, separation from loved ones, or any number of other powerful concerns.

North Carolina Regulators

In the 1760s, some North Carolina citizens became disgruntled with unfair taxation practices, including their collection, and with the unfair representation of local governments in the colony. They organized formally in 1768 and issued a set of "Regulations," but the governor ignored them. Two years later, riots broke out in some of the counties; in response, the colonial government cracked down on anyone even suspected of rioting. Subsequently, Governor Tryon called out the militia to suppress the Regulators, which it succeeded in doing at Alamance in the spring of 1771. This defeat not only ended the movement, but also caused hundreds of Regulators to move westward into present-day Tennessee.

Wilderness Calling: Watauga

Within a very short time, a veritable flood of white settlers swept into upper East Tennessee to make their homes there. Quickly four distinct settlements emerged in the new region. Because of its location, the so-called North Holston "colony" (present-day Bristol) had an experience somewhat different from that of the other three settlements. Established by Evan Shelby, who built a store immediately, this enclave was thought to be clearly located within the territorial claims of Virginia. To the southeast of North Holston was the Watauga or Sycamore Shoals settlement (present-day Elizabethton), evidently the first of the four gatherings of settlers. William Bean and James Robertson were its early leaders. Southwest of the North Holston settlement was the Carter's Valley group (situated between present-day Kingsport and Rogersville). John Carter of Virginia was its founder. Like Evan Shelby, he built a store (the entrepreneurial spirit seems to have been transported successfully to the new frontier). The fourth and southernmost settlement was the one established by Jacob Brown at the Nolichucky River (present-day Erwin). Thus, hundreds of white settlers invaded the Cherokee lands and did so with relative ease, at least initially.

Aiding the seemingly smooth transition were the negotiations which had taken place between the Cherokees and British officials in 1770. The Lochaber Treaty drew new boundary lines in an effort to prohibit the incursion of white settlers south and west of those lines. Instead, the treaty had the opposite effect; that is, whites eager to move from Virginia and North Carolina believed that now they could do so without worrying about Indian titles to the land. In reality, the treaty's demarcations showed that only a very small northeastern corner of present-day Tennessee legally

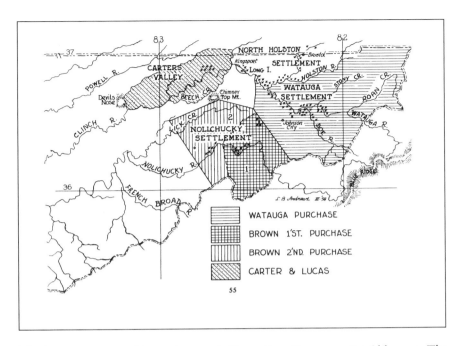

The four permanent white settlements in Upper East Tennessee. Pat Alderman, *The Overmountain Men* (Johnson City, Tenn.: Overmountain Press, 1970), 55. Used by permission of the Overmountain Press.

could be settled by whites. Misunderstandings about the treaty, deliberate or unintentional, encouraged white movement into the region.

The following year, however, British officials authorized an actual survey of the boundaries. John Donelson of southwestern Virginia headed the surveying team, assisted by a British agent named Alexander Cameron and by the Cherokee chief Attakullakulla. They discovered that only the North Holston settlement lay within the region ceded to the British by the Cherokees in the Lochaber Treaty. The ramifications of this revelation could not be exaggerated, for potentially they spelled disaster for the newly established white enclaves. In fact, Cameron immediately ordered the Carter's Valley, Watauga, and Nolichucky settlers to vacate the Indian lands. Suddenly, the realization that they were residing outside the legal jurisdiction of either Virginia or North Carolina threatened these hardy pioneers with perils they had not anticipated.

Yet the resourceful frontier leaders proved themselves equal to the new challenge. They would not be embarrassed by mere directives from a British official; they would circumvent legal niceties. Accordingly, representatives of the three settlements banded together to form a quasi-government in the wilderness, the Watauga Association. They also sent emissaries to the Cherokee chiefs in order to negotiate a new arrangement. James Robertson and others convinced the Cherokees to permit the white settlers to lease the lands for a specified period of time, in exchange for various goods. With this bold move, the pioneer leaders showed their creativity, as well as their disregard for treaty provisions and historic Indian land claims.

The articles of agreement by which the Watauga Association was established were lost long ago to the ravages of time and neglect. Therefore, we know very little about the details of the actual governing institution, except that apparently a five-member legislative-judicial council existed, as well as the usual sheriff, clerk, and minor officers. In short, the Watauga framers drew upon their previous experiences in Virginia and North Carolina. Having created a semblance of government and having concluded land arrangements with the Cherokees, the frontier leaders of the three settlements were ready to resume the more usual chores of farming, hunting, trading, and generally carving a niche for themselves in the wilderness. For approximately three years thereafter, these little communities expanded and prospered, relatively speaking. Their situations changed in 1775, however.

In the spring of that year, the American Revolution erupted in far-away New England. Eventually, word of these events reached the Tennessee country. The North Holston settlers, secure in being part of Virginia's Fincastle County, had less reason to worry than did the pioneers at the other three locations. These latter folk, feeling quite vulnerable, first formed a revolutionary committee of safety; then, in the fall months, they organized themselves as the "Washington District." A special Committee of Thirteen, headed by John Carter, took charge of running things.

Finally, the associated people of Watauga sought annexation by either Virginia or North Carolina. Indeed, on July 5, 1776 (the day after the signing of the Declaration of Independence in Philadelphia), they sent a petition to North Carolina. In that document they pleaded to "be considered as we deserve, and not as we have (no doubt) been many times represented, as a lawless mob." Basic apprehensions gripped them—namely, that their settlements "might become a shelter for such as endeavoured to defraud their creditors." No noble patriotism for these folk! However, they added later in the petition their desire to be annexed "in such manner as may enable us to share in the glorious cause of Liberty."

Whatever their motivations, economic or otherwise, their plea was heard by the North Carolina revolutionary leaders. (Virginia apparently never responded.) These men recommended that the Wataugans elect representatives to a proposed November meeting in Halifax which would frame a constitution for North Carolina. The transmontane residents chose five men, four of whom (John Sevier, John Carter, John Haile, and Charles Robertson) actually attended and subsequently signed the state's new constitution.

Having thus participated in North Carolina's new experiment in government, the Wataugans seemed eager to be incorporated therein. Consequently, in 1777, when North Carolina called for legislative elections, the transmontane folk chose John Carter as senator and John Sevier and Jacob Womack as members of the House of Commons. Once convened, this body designated the settlements across the mountains, excluding the North Holston enclave, as Washington County. Revolutionary, indeed, had been the accomplishments in the short span of two years.

Watauga's Relations with Indians

Remarkably, there was very little overt conflict between the Cherokees and the early white settlers. In fact, the Indians repeatedly made concessions, as noted earlier. This experience contrasts sharply with that of frontier settlements elsewhere, such as the Cumberland group in Middle Tennessee. Examining Watauga's story in the latter half of the 1770s, however, reveals a changing scene; indeed, a treaty-war-treaty cycle seems apparent.

An amazing treaty negotiation took place in the Tennessee country in early 1775. Judge Richard Henderson of North Carolina engineered the deal, which was rooted in a crass desire for land. He and friends formed a land company, called—in grandiose fashion—the Transylvania Company. Henderson held informal talks with various Cherokee leaders to notify them of his desire to purchase vast tracts of land. He even invited them to inspect in advance the household of goods (valued at ten thousand pounds) that he had set aside for this purpose. The judge found the Cherokees

---

Nancy Ward

Born at the Cherokee town of Chota in about 1738, Nanye'hi was a member of the Wolf clan. She accompanied her husband, Kingfisher, into battle against the Creeks; when he was killed, Nanye'hi took his place and became one of the "War Women of the Cherokee." A few years later, when she married the white trader Bryant Ward, Nanye'hi became Nancy Ward.

During the Cherokee war of 1776, Nancy saved the life of William Bean's wife, who had been taken captive. From the whites, Nancy Ward learned how to make butter and cheese and subsequently helped the Cherokees develop dairy operations. By the time of her death in 1822, Ward, the last of the "Beloved Women," operated an inn along the road that ran from Georgia to Nashville.

Signing of the Sycamore Shoals Treaty, March 1775. Pat Alderman, *The Overmoun-tain Men* (Johnson City, Tenn.: Overmountain Press, 1970), 25. Used by permission of the Overmountain Press.

eager partners; indeed, they began arriving at the designated treaty grounds at Sycamore Shoals in January, far in advance of the date proposed.

Several considerations account for the willingness of the Indians to ne-gotiate a land sale. One obvious fact, sometimes overlooked, is that they had a history of negotiating with white leaders. Moreover, the Cherokees probably did not comprehend fully the implications of shifting the bar-gaining focus from trading privileges and boundaries to land purchases. Further assisting the environment in 1775 was the palpable weakness of British officials, the usual allies and sometime protectors of the Cherokees. By this time, these agents were in a disadvantaged position and could not be counted upon. No wonder Henderson was eager to proceed with his plans; he was a shrewd judge of timing.

Some reports indicate that nearly twelve hundred Cherokees gathered at Sycamore Shoals for the treaty conference, a remarkable turnout. Discussions commenced on March 14 with Henderson's speech to the assembled audience of Indians and whites. He unveiled his breathtaking plan to purchase most of present-day Kentucky and all of Middle Tennessee—approximately twenty million acres, according to some calculations. Amiable speeches from several Indian chiefs followed; but young Dragging Canoe, son of Attakullakulla, voiced a strong protest against the purchase agreement. He rightly warned of further encroachments by whites upon Indian lands. His disturbing words brought the negotiations to a temporary halt. But Henderson and his allies did some skillful behind-the-scenes lobbying, and by March 17 the chiefs were ready to endorse the treaty.

On that date, three of them—Attakullakulla (who disagreed with his son), Oconostota, and Savanucah—signed Henderson's purchase proposal. Meanwhile, white settlers who witnessed this incredible transaction decided to join in the Sycamore Shoals spirit of land-grabbing and asked the chiefs to permit a purchase of the lands that the pioneers previously had been leasing. Evidently in an expansive mood, the Indian leaders agreed to this request. All in all, it was quite a day for white land companies and settlers! From these negotiations flowed many results, not least of which was the Cumberland settlement a few years later. It should be noted that the colonial governors of both Virginia and North Carolina denounced Henderson's Sycamore Shoals deliberations; indeed, the latter aptly labeled the Transylvania group "an infamous Company of land Pirates."

Be that as it may, the following year armed conflict broke out for the first time between the Cherokees and the settlers of upper East Tennessee. This was a direct consequence of what now had become the full-scale American Revolution. British agents in the region first urged the Cherokees to remain neutral, but by the spring of 1776 they reversed that policy and offered to support the Indians in any plans for aggression against the white settlers. Indeed, in May these officials demanded that the pioneers vacate their homes and move either north of the Donelson line or south to British Florida. The response of the Wataugans was twofold: immediately they built new defenses at the settlements, and they sought aid from either North Carolina or Virginia. Meanwhile, the increasingly hostile Cherokees decided to attack.

In July, they launched a three-pronged offensive against the white settle-

---

Catherine ("Bonny Kate") Sherrill Sevier

Born in North Carolina in 1754, Catherine moved with her family to the Tennessee country shortly before the outbreak of the Cherokee war of 1776. In fact, she was almost killed in the Indian attack upon the Watauga fort. Catherine and several other women were outside the fort milking cows when the assault began. Hearing the alarms, the women ran toward the fort; according to legend, John Sevier saved Catherine by reaching down and pulling her up over the walls to safety. Four years later he married her, soon after the death of his first wife.

Catherine immediately assumed responsibility for rearing Sevier's ten children, and eventually she gave birth to eight more children of her own. Catherine managed the household so that Sevier could pursue his political ambitions. After her husband's death, Catherine moved to Overton County, where the family had large grants of land. She died on a visit to Alabama in 1836.

ments. Dragging Canoe directed the assault upon a portion of the North Holston settlement located at Long Island. But whites fought back vigorously and repelled the invaders, even inflicting a serious wound on Dragging Canoe himself. Chief Savanucah ("The Raven") led the campaign against the Carter's Valley settlement. Whites fled in advance of the Cherokee arrival, so the Indians easily burned and plundered the region. Old Abram of Chilhowee directed the attack against the third site, Watauga or Sycamore Shoals. The Cherokees laid siege to the fort there for at least two weeks but were unable to defeat the white pioneers. Afterwards the Indians retreated to their towns along the Little Tennessee River.

Unfortunately for them, neighboring states soon sent military assistance to the white settlers in the Tennessee country. More than two thousand troops arrived from North Carolina, Virginia, South Carolina, and Georgia, congregating at Fort Patrick Henry in the North Holston region. Led by Gen. Griffith Rutherford of North Carolina, these soldiers marched toward the Cherokee towns in September 1776 and met little or no resistance. Quickly they destroyed several of the sites; the Indians then had no choice but to sue for peace.

Treaty negotiations eventually were held at Fort Patrick Henry (Long Island) in the summer of 1777. Both North Carolina and Virginia sent special commissioners to fashion an agreement with the Cherokees. Eventually, separate peace treaties were negotiated with both states. Signed in July, these documents specified formal cession of lands, with the new boundaries legalizing all four of the original white settlements. Grandiose rhetoric was plentiful during such deliberations. The North Carolina commissioner, Waightstill Avery, proclaimed, "We are about to fix a line that is to remain through all generations,

---

King's Mountain Campaign, 1780

As a part of his southern campaign in the American Revolution, Lord Cornwallis sent Maj. Patrick Ferguson into the northwestern reaches of South Carolina. Meanwhile, transmontane settlers became increasingly involved in military actions east of the mountains. Approximately nine hundred men congregated at Sycamore Shoals in late September to commence their search for Ferguson's troops. On October 7, the frontiersmen met the British at King's Mountain, where they assaulted Ferguson's entrenched troops and encircled them. With Col. John Sevier leading the attack at the center, the patriots quickly gained the upper hand and forced the surrender of the British. This heroic victory rightly has been called the turning point of the Revolutionary War in the South.

and be kept by our Children's children." The new lines survived less than ten years, however. Both treaties pledged, too, that "hostilities shall forever cease between the said Cherokees and the people" of Virginia and North Carolina. All sides violated this promise in less than two years. Yet, for the moment, one treaty-war-treaty cycle had been completed.

Having already experienced organized military action, white leaders in the Tennessee country waited for new opportunities. In 1780, the burgeoning southern campaign of the American Revolution offered just such possibilities. Tennessee pioneers participated in several different military engagements in the Carolinas, the most notable being the Battle of King's Mountain in October. The defeat of the British there was significant and heroic, especially for John Sevier. Pioneers from the transmontane lands played a critical role in the outcome of that battle. In just a few short years, they would wage a different kind of fight against the parent state of North Carolina.

Wilderness Calling II: Cumberland

Scarcely nine years after first arriving in upper East Tennessee, certain prominent leaders determined to push toward the Cumberland River area of Middle Tennessee. And thereby hangs a tale—initially a story of three men consumed by land schemes. Not surprisingly, Richard Henderson of Sycamore Shoals fame instigated the deal; after all, he did intend to take advantage of the extensive domain he had acquired. But his enthusiasm for the Kentucky lands lessened in 1778, when Virginia invalidated his claims in that region. He was not the sort of man to be easily discouraged, though; immediately he enlisted James Robertson and John Donelson to explore and settle the Cumberland area. They had to act quickly, before North Carolina took steps to void Henderson's monopoly on those lands.

The first order of business, of course, was to reconnoiter the prospective region. Robertson eagerly agreed to do so, and in the summer of 1779 he led an exploring party there, going by way of the Cumberland Gap into Kentucky and then more or less following the course of the Cumberland River until reaching the French Lick (at the site of present-day Nashville). He returned to the Watauga region with enthusiastic reports about what he had just seen and experienced. Probably no one was more excited than Henderson and Donelson. There was adventure (and land) enough for everyone!

These three leaders recruited approximately three hundred men (including slaves), women, and children to be the "new" pioneers of the 1780s. Robertson volunteered to conduct about one hundred men (and his young son) by foot and horseback via the route he had taken months earlier. It was a daunting challenge, to say the least. Nevertheless, they quickly organized themselves, gathered supplies for the trek, and spent final fleeting moments with their wives and children. By late October or early Novem-

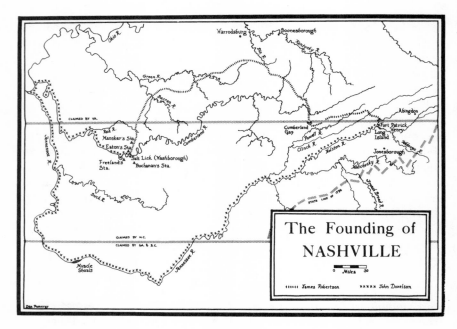

The Founding of
NASHVILLE

James Robertson and John Donelson explorations to Middle Tennessee. Map by Daniel E. Pomeroy. Used by permission of the cartographer.

ber, they set out for this promised land, led by a latter-day Moses who actually would reach the destination.

While there are scattered accounts of the journey, we do not know much about it except that the weather was quite cold and disagreeable. It was an arduous trip that took two full months to complete, but everyone survived its rigors. Different bands of Robertson's entourage arrived in the Cumberland region at slightly different intervals, but all of them discovered that the river was frozen solid; some walked or rode across it on Christmas Day of 1779. There was no time to waste, however, for immediately they had to construct some sort of shelter, hunt for fish and game, and possibly plant a few crops. These hardy souls could scarcely afford time to wonder about their wives and children, who would, it was hoped, join them in a few months.

Meanwhile, back in upper East Tennessee, John Donelson had been busy building an ark—not in anticipation of a prolonged period of rain, but in preparation for a great nautical journey. He had agreed to take about two hundred men (some of them slaves), women, and children to the Cumberland region via the river system, a route of over one thousand miles. With a keen eye for drama, he named his boat *The Adventure*; and, with a eye toward posterity, he committed himself to record the trip's events in a journal.

The Donelson voyage is launched late in 1779. Pat Alderman, *The Overmountain Men* (Johnson City, Tenn.: Overmountain Press, 1970), 51. Used by permission of the Overmountain Press.

By late December (about the time that Robertson's group arrived at the French Lick), the Donelson armada was ready to launch out into the Holston River. Some thirty to forty boats eventually joined the flotilla; they were of various sizes and descriptions. Donelson's vessel was a large flatboat capable of carrying more than forty persons (perhaps as many as thirty of whom were slaves), as well as supplies of all sorts. The expedition departed at that season of the year because the leaders were certain that the bitter cold weather would lessen the likelihood of Indian raiding parties and because the rivers were high and swift. Donelson and others who had mapped out plans for the voyage were confident that the Chickamauga Indians (a dissident group of Cherokees led by Dragging Canoe) would present no problems in the Chattanooga vicinity. Evan Shelby's attack on the Chickamauga towns in April 1779 presumably had removed this potential menace.

The journey began most inauspiciously. Donelson's armada departed three days before Christmas, but a sudden drop in the water level and other complications caused the boats to travel no more than three miles during the first two months! At that rate, years would have been required to reach the Cumberland Basin area. Less determined pioneers would have walked back to Fort Patrick Henry, the starting point, and abandoned the dream; but Donelson makes no mention of this happening. Instead, he picks up the story in late February 1780 and proceeds with an almost daily account of the tribulations that beset his party.

Fiction could not improve upon the saga of birth, death, smallpox, frostbite, shipwreck, Indian attack, and other misadventures that occurred. The first fatality was a black slave who died on March 6 from complications of frostbite. Almost as if by design, that trauma was balanced by the birth of a baby the next day, to Mrs. Peyton. But no sooner did she rejoice over this happy event than the Jonathan Jennings boat in which she was riding hit a large rock and became stuck in the swirling currents of the Tennessee River in Chickamauga country. Jennings ordered Mrs. Peyton and other passengers to lighten the boat by throwing their supplies overboard. They quickly obeyed, while Indians opened gunfire upon them. Amid this frantic scene, Mrs. Peyton mistakenly and tragically threw her newborn baby out of the boat. Others from that cursed flatboat were drowned or otherwise killed, but eventually it was freed from the rock, thanks to the heroic actions of Jennings's wife, whose dress was "very much cut with bullets." Thomas Stuart and his family were stricken with smallpox on the trip and thus were forced to keep some distance from the rest of the flotilla. The Chickamaugans captured Stuart's boat and took prisoner or killed everyone. "Their cries were distinctly heard by those boats in the rear," recorded Donelson.

By mid-March, this armada of "historic persons and the begetters of historic persons" (so the writer Donald Davidson described them) reached the vicinity of Muscle Shoals. The leaders looked in vain for evidence that James Robertson had reached the area earlier and had left signs pointing to an overland route. But mainly they looked at the menacing river and its shoals. "Here we did not know," Donelson confessed, "how soon we should be dashed to pieces and all our troubles ended at once." The "hand of Providence," however, preserved the brave pioneers for further adventures.

A week later, Donelson and his fellow travelers reached the mouth of the Tennessee River, the end of their downstream journey. Now they had to exert themselves to go the short but difficult distance up the Ohio River in search of its connection with the Cumberland. As Donelson complained, this part of the river journey was "truly disagreeable." They barely made it; in fact some persons (including one of Donelson's daughters and his son-in-law) did not, for they chose to depart and proceed downstream to connect with the Mississippi River. Once the main group reached the mouth of the Cumberland on March 24, it took them another month to arrive finally at the French Lick. Along the way, however, they met none other than Richard Henderson! He just happened to be in the vicinity marking off the Tennessee border as a special commissioner from North Carolina (and doubtless checking on his sundry enterprises in the region).

In any event, the one-thousand-mile, four-month nautical journey was over. James and John had accomplished their mission: they had led three hundred or so settlers (among them Rachel Donelson, the future wife of Andrew Jackson) to the Cumberland region.

Government and Laws

But there was more to be done, of course. For example, one week after the Donelson boats arrived, Henderson assembled everyone at the Nashborough "station" and offered them a governing document. Called the "Cumberland Compact," this was partly a land-buying contract and partly a rudimentary constitution. Approximately 250 settlers signed the document on May 1, declaring: "That as this settlement is in its infancy . . . and not included within any county within North Carolina . . . *we find ourselves* constrained from necessity to adopt this." They hoped thereby to restrain the licentious and to secure "the blessings flowing from a just and equitable government." In the process, they also agreed to pay Henderson more than twenty-six pounds per hundred acres (an excessive charge) for their land. This was in addition to agreeing to pay Henderson's appointed entry taker some twelve dollars for each entry made.

The compact provided for a governing council of twelve judges, representing the eight different settlements, or "stations." These leaders were to be elected by free men twenty-one years of age or older; no other qualifications for voting were prescribed. While the judges were invested with the usual governing powers, they could be removed, according to the compact, by "the people in general," simply by calling for new elections. In the language of the compact, the judges constituted "a *proper court* or jurisdiction for the recovery of any debt or damages"—a clear indication of some of the economic concerns of this fledgling community.

The document provided for a militia and made all males sixteen years and older subject to duty, in return for which they could purchase lands in their own name. The compact focused upon a pressing concern of the new settlers when it referred to "the frequent and dangerous incursions of the Indians, and almost daily massacre of some of our inhabitants." It further spoke of the vulnerability felt by many: "We are, from our remote situation, utterly destitute of the benefit of the laws of our country, and exposed to the depredations of the Indians." Such words would ring true again and again in the Cumberland experience.

Satisfied with his handiwork, in terms of both the new compact and the arrival of settlers, Henderson left the region, never to return. His optimism was premature, to say the least. Roaming bands of hostile Indians made the next two years particularly difficult. The sketchy evidence available indicates that the government established under the compact did not function during this special time of travail: "The manifold suffering and distresses that settlers here have from time to time undergone, even almost from our first settling; with the desertion of the greater number of the first adventurers, being so discouraging to the remaining few, that all administration of justice seemed to cease from amongst us." Of necessity, the Cumberland pioneers switched to the survival mode and abandoned the governing mode. But extant minutes from Cumberland demonstrate that, in January 1783, after a lengthy hiatus, some semblance of government once more existed. From that point on, the status of government and law began to improve, thanks in part to the actions of the state of North Carolina.

Doubtless unknown to the harried Cumberland settlers, the parent state took steps to influence and exert control over its far-flung enclaves. In 1782, for example, the state government decided to grant, to all those who had settled in the Cumberland region prior to June 1780, preemption rights to 640 acres. Moreover, in order to be able to offer land grants to North Carolina veterans, the government designated a large portion of Middle Tennessee as a military reservation; this legislation was refined the following year. Suffice it to say that land speculators benefited immensely from this measure, for they eagerly bought up grants from soldiers who, either strapped for cash or lacking a desire for wild adventure, chose to sell their bounties rather than move to the Cumberland area.

Several significant developments occurred in 1783. Out of the Cumberland settlements, North Carolina created Davidson County and established its county court. Residents subsequently chose James Robertson and Anthony Bledsoe as the men to represent them in the legislature of North Carolina. In addition, the government passed the so-called "Land Grab Act," which reopened the land offices and put on the market all lands not within the designated military reservation or the Cherokee reservation (an area south of the French Broad and Holston Rivers). For a price of ten pounds per one hundred acres, prospective buyers could claim whatever they or their subordinates could mark. Under terms of this act, which was in effect only for the period from October 1783 to May 1784, nearly four million acres were claimed. It was a bonanza for land speculators who had the funds to hire surveyors to mark vast claims in a hurry and to pay for the lands. Needless to say, this land act stirred much activity in both the Cumberland and East Tennessee regions. Henderson himself was not forgotten that year, for, although the North Carolina legislature repudiated his earlier purchase of the Cumberland River region, it offered him a consolation prize of some two hundred thousand acres in the Powell's Valley area.

In recognition of the development of the settlements in the Cumberland Basin, the North Carolina government created Sumner County in 1786 by subdividing Davidson. Two years later it established Tennessee County from portions of those two counties. The three then constituted the newly designated Mero District.

Indian Relations

Unlike the upper East Tennessee settlements, which had enjoyed relative tranquillity in their early years, the Cumberland settlements never knew peace. As both the Cumberland Compact of 1780 and the Cumberland minutes of January 1783 indicate, the lives of the white settlers were in constant peril. The easy accessibility of the stations in Middle Tennessee and their proximity to at least three different Indian tribes—Creeks, Chickasaws, and Chickamaugans—spelled potential disaster. It is not difficult to understand the bitter resentment felt by the Indians as they watched whites intrude upon their hunting grounds. Henderson's Sycamore Shoals treaty notwithstanding, these Indians had signed no treaties ceding land to the arriving whites.

Thus violence disturbed the Cumberland Basin from the earliest days. So bad was it that, from time to time, settlers abandoned various stations in order to congregate at two or three, in hopes of securing greater protection. Chickasaws attacked Renfroe's station on the Red River and killed more than twenty whites, initiating the atrocities. After Chickamaugan attacks in the fall of 1780, John Donelson, who had had his fill of such activities during his voyage months earlier, packed up and headed for Kentucky. (He later returned to the Cumberland settlements.) Throughout 1781, Chickasaws and Chickamaugans repeatedly attacked white settlers; several years later, James Robertson declared that year to have been the worst one. There were rivals, however.

Some hope arose late in 1782, when the Chickasaws, disturbed by the defeat of their British allies, began making peace overtures to the Cumberland settlements. The faction led by Piomingo blamed the British for putting "the Bloody Tomahawk into our hands." Robertson naturally favored a possible alliance with the Chickasaws as a hedge against the Creek and Chickamaugan menace. Eventually, in 1783, the Virginia governor designated John Donelson and Joseph Martin to negotiate with the Chickasaws at Nashborough. They managed to devise a treaty by which both sides promised assistance; but, interestingly enough, the Chickasaws made no land cessions. The level of Indian problems diminished somewhat for a time, only to rise again subsequently.

The years 1787–89 witnessed repeated attacks by Indians and, for the first time, an offensive against them by the white settlers. Both James Robertson and Anthony Bledsoe pleaded with the North Carolina government for assistance and protection against the Indians, but to no avail. As Bledsoe told the governor in the summer of 1787, the Creeks and Chickamaugans caused "very great spoil" to the Cumberland settlements "by murdering numbers of our peaceful inhabitants, stealing our horses." A year later, a raiding party of Creeks killed Bledsoe at his brother's station. They killed Robertson's son Charles in another attack that same year and wounded Robertson himself in a 1789 assault. Meanwhile, whites, led by

Robertson, had launched an expedition in 1787 against Coldwater, a town near Muscle Shoals occupied mainly by Creeks. Proving themselves ferocious, the whites left death and devastation in their wake. This attack brought only temporary relief; the continuing bad relations between whites and Indians persisted into the next decade.

Spanish Flirtations

Cumberland leaders were convinced that a major factor in the Indian situation on the frontier was the Spanish influence, particularly in the latter half of the 1780s. They believed that Spanish officials from Louisiana had encouraged the Creeks and Chickamaugans in their raids upon the Cumberland stations. Since North Carolina authorities refused to respond to these complaints, Robertson and others concluded that making overtures to the Spanish would be a shrewd strategy.

A second concern revolved around the economy. Beginning in 1784, Spain threatened to bar American shipping on the Mississippi River, a potential lifeline for the Cumberland settlers. When it appeared that the American government negotiator, John Jay, was willing to surrender navigational rights on the Mississippi, Cumberland leaders knew that they had to seek some sort of accommodation with the Spanish.

As part of that strategy, Robertson persuaded the North Carolina legislature to name the new district in Middle Tennessee for the Spanish governor of Louisiana, Don Estevan Miro. Flattery sometimes works, although it is more effective when the person's name is spelled correctly. *Mero* District it became, however.

Daniel Smith initiated correspondence with the Spanish governor, emphasizing the desire for more harmonious relationships with both the Indian tribes and the Spanish. Robertson followed with letters of his own to reinforce the point. Rumors circulated widely that the Cumberland people wanted some direct union with Spanish authority. Dr. James White, a former U.S. Indian agent and now a special agent for Don Diego Gardoqui, fanned the flames of those rumors—a self-serving maneuver on his part, to be sure. Governor Miro eventually offered assurances to the Cumberland leaders on both the Indian question and the navigation dispute. But it became increasingly clear that improved contacts and relations with Spanish officials would not yield the solutions sought by Robertson, Smith, and others. Only a more vigorous and effective American government could do that.

Frontier Life

Daily life on the frontier, whether in the Cumberland region or the upper East Tennessee area, was perilous and challenging, but it was also fairly simple and routine. Frontier folk, when not confronting some dramatic or dangerous predicament, struggled to provide food, clothing, and shelter. When those necessities were satisfied for the moment, then brief opportunities existed for contemplation and enjoyment.

The frequent reports of abundant wild game (such as bear, buffalo, deer, and turkey) and fish indicate that the pioneers had a wide variety of food choices. Remarkably, they even drove milk cows, hogs, and some sheep with them to the wilderness regions. In addition, they went prepared to cultivate crops and vegetables that would provide necessary foodstuffs. Farming was even more critical than hunting to survival; it was a way of life for the frontier people. Indeed, as Harriette Simpson Arnow once observed, the most precious items the pioneers transported were seeds. Shortly upon arriving, they planted corn, beans, and other vegetables. Corn quickly became the most important crop; it was the foundation of the daily diet. Corn also was highly prized and sought after in liquid form—namely, corn whiskey. It probably is no exaggeration to argue that the pioneer settlements would not have survived without whiskey, for it was the multipurpose remedy for all kinds of aches and pains, as well as a ubiquitous socializing potion.

Clothing was derived from several sources. The skins and hides of animals, such as deer, beaver, bear, and cattle, provided the basis for different types of garments. Frontier farmers planted flax, from which they produced linen, and cotton. The latter crop was grown only in small quantities in the early years, however, and was confined to the Cumberland Basin region.

The log cabin provided shelter for the pioneers. The first ones were small and fairly crude; but eventually more elaborate ones, even with glass windows, were built. The abundance of timber simplified the choice of

---

Flatboats

Probably the most common mode of river travel in the early days of Tennessee—particularly if one had to transport a number of people or a heavy load of freight—was the flatboat. The larger flatboats measured up to 20 by 100 feet. John Donelson's *Adventure* was a prime example of such boats.

A broad-bottomed, boxlike structure, the flatboat was steered by a board fastened to a pole at the rear and was steadied by oarlike sweeps (called "broadhorns") on each side. The boats thus required at least three men to operate them. Generally a roof extended over half or two-thirds of the hull. Under it were crude bunks for sleeping and a stone hearth for cooking. Flatboat traffic was one-way traffic: downstream. After arriving at their destination, the flatboats were dismantled.

building material, while the absence of sawmills dictated that logs, rather than lumber, were the simplest option. Later, native stone was utilized to construct dwellings.

Had it not been for certain items of equipment that the early settlers possessed, they could not have met the requirements for food, clothing, and shelter. Guns were an indispensable part of frontier life; they could protect against Indian attack, of course, but they also could kill wild game. No one could function without a hoe; any attempt at planting or farming required that tool. Finally, a person in the wilderness owned one or more axes, for woodcutting never stopped: logs for cabins and wood for cooking. When considering the daily lives of these pioneers, one should remember that their time was spent mostly outdoors. They had little choice.

Assisting the white settlers were black slaves. Unfortunately, information about them in this early period is scarce. We do know that the first white persons who moved into the upper East Tennessee area brought slaves with them. As was noted earlier, numerous slaves accompanied the pioneers who traveled to the Cumberland River region. On the frontier, slaves were relatively few in number and thus probably had fairly close relationships with their owners. Records from the Cumberland area indicate that slaves fought alongside their masters against Indian assaults. The laws of both Virginia and North Carolina, not surprisingly, recognized and protected slavery; as a result, the transmontane settlers were accustomed to it and made no attempt to prohibit slavery in the new regions.

It is quite difficult to uncover data about the number of slaves and slaveowners for this early period. But some tax lists for districts in Washington County provide at least limited information. For example, the 1779 list of 292 taxpayers (restricted to adult males) shows that 31 owned slaves. This same list also indicates a slave population of 102 persons, of whom a large percentage were women and children (the tax on them was less than on adult male slaves). A Washington County taxpayer list for the following year reveals a similar pattern of few slaves and very few slaveowners. How representative of actual slaveholding these lists are simply is not known. It is certain, however, that by the 1790s slavery had expanded noticeably in the Tennessee country.

Whatever circumstances of daily life the early white frontier folk confronted, sometimes they had opportunities to consider the mind and the soul. Formal schooling for children was extremely rare, of course, although two academies, Martin and Davidson, were established in the 1780s. Books, however, were in plentiful supply in most families, and they provided instruction and entertainment for youth and adults alike. William Neely, killed on the Cumberland frontier in 1780, owned several Bibles, a collection of Isaac Watts hymns, and several theology books. While Neely may have been atypical in his choice of books, he was fairly representative of the well-read pioneer.

The frontier generally was characterized by a lack of organized religion. Perhaps most settlers simply did not have time or inclination to devote to such matters. But Presbyterians made a dent in that resistance or indifference; in the early days they predominated among those pioneers who did profess a formal affiliation. The Reverend Samuel Doak arrived in upper East Tennessee in 1777 and immediately established several Presbyterian congregations. His accomplishments there were matched by those of the Reverend Thomas Craighead in the Cumberland settlements. The Baptist faith and practice, much more suited to the frontier than Presbyterianism, quickly founded churches, the first of which is thought to be the Sinking Creek congregation (1775), located in present-day Carter County. The identity of the region's first resident Baptist pastor is a matter of some dispute, with at least three claimants. Also contending for the souls of the pioneer folk were the Methodists, not formally a separate denomination until the mid-1780s. The famous circuit-rider approach to evangelizing the frontier was evident in the Tennessee country. Three such itinerant preachers were busy in upper East Tennessee by 1786, the year when the first Methodist church building was erected there. Methodism reached the Cumberland region via a circuit rider who traveled to the area from his home base in Kentucky. Bishop Francis Asbury visited the Methodists of upper East Tennessee in 1788, the first of numerous trips he made to spread the faith. Despite the best efforts of these and other devoted ministers, however, organized religion on the Tennessee frontier gained relatively few adherents. Religion's harvest time would have to wait until the turn of the century.

Independence Calling: Franklin

In the 1780s, the upper East Tennessee area became engulfed in an independence movement. By that time, the region was evolving into a more sophisticated environment. Now, for example, there were three counties—Washington, Greene, and Sullivan—and several towns, including Jonesboro, Rogersville, and Greeneville. Since at least 1782, certain leaders—particularly Arthur Campbell of southwestern Virginia—had begun to press for establishment of a separate state. Added to these facts was North Carolina's infamous "Land-Grab Act" of 1783, which stimulated tremendous activity in the western region on the part of land speculators. William Blount quickly became the prince of such men. Moreover, under the Articles of Confederation, the young national government requested that all states with western land claims surrender them to it.

The only other ingredient required to foment an authentic independence push was a recognized leader. John Sevier quickly emerged as just the man. As Donald Davidson once said of Sevier, "The times were made for him, and he was made for them." He already had been accorded hero status by the white settlers; furthermore, he was eager to promote various land-buying schemes.

A

DECLARATION of RIGHTS

MADE BY

The REPRESENTATIVES of the Free-
men of the State of FRANKLAND.

I. **T**HAT all political power is vested in,
derived from the people only.

II. That the people of this State ought to have the
sole and exclusive right of regulating the internal government and police thereof.

III. That no man, or sett of men, are entitled to
exclusive or separate emoluments or privileges from
the community, but in confideration of public fervices.

IV. That the Legiflative, Executive, and Supreme
Judicial powers of government ought to be for ever
feparate and diftinct from each other.

V. That all powers of fufpending laws, or the execution of laws, by any authority, without the confent
of the Reprefentatives of the people, is injurious to
their rights, and ought not to be exercifed.

VI. That elections of members to ferve as Reprefentatives, in General Affembly, ought to be free.

VII. That, in all criminal profecutions, every
man has a right to be informed of the accufation
againft him, and to confront the accufers and wit-
neffes with other teftimony, and fhall not be compelled to give evidence againft himfelf.

A 4   VIII.

The Declaration of Rights served as a preamble to the Franklin Constitution, 1784.
Tennessee Historical Society, Nashville.

At this juncture, the political leadership in North Carolina divided over
the question of the future of the transmontane lands. Politicians from the
eastern part of the state seemed eager to get rid of the western lands, viewing them as a nuisance. Meanwhile, land speculators who saw a separate
state across the mountains as the best way to enhance their land dealings
joined with easterners. Their alliance produced the decision by the legisla-

ture, in June 1784, to cede the western lands to the Confederation government. But the legislature enumerated four conditions for this cession: (1) land entries made earlier under North Carolina authority should continue to be valid; (2) land bounties for veterans could be located outside of the designated military reservation, if there should not be enough acreage within it; (3) slavery should not be abolished without consent of inhabitants; (4) and North Carolina laws should be enforced in the ceded lands until a new state was created. Having thus set down its requirements, the state essentially surrendered its claims to the transmontane region.

Responses from Both Sides of the Boundary

Once word reached the leaders of the western counties later in the summer, they called for an assembly to meet at Jonesboro in August. This group voted unanimously in favor of the establishment of a new state and also issued a call for a convention. Later the proposed Franklin constitution outlined the five reasons why western residents sought independence. First, consent of North Carolina seemed implied in the cession act itself; and the current legal ambiguities had "reduced us to the verge of anarchy." Second, "we are alone compelled to defend ourselves from these savages"—meaning the Indians, who had not yet received the goods promised them by North Carolina. Third, the Confederation Congress had encouraged the creation of new states. Fourth, the consensus was that the western counties should not remain aligned with North Carolina because of geographical separation, partly attributable to the "high and almost impassable mountains." Finally, the Franklin proponents argued that "our lives, liberties, and property can be more secure" in a new state. Of course, they neglected to mention the fundamental question of land acquisition by prominent speculators. It seemed best to maintain an official silence on that matter.

While Sevier and others mapped plans for Franklin and excited the region with the prospect of independence, North Carolina was convulsed by dissension over the land cession. By the fall months, the legislature prepared to reverse its earlier decision. It did just that in November 1784. In an attempt to placate disappointed Franklin adherents, however, the legislature established the western counties as the Washington District, with David Campbell as superior court judge and John Sevier as brigadier general. In rescinding its land cession, North Carolina heightened the transmontane confusion. The Franklin leaders proceeded with their December meeting, ignorant of the most recent decision of the North Carolina legislature.

The Jonesboro meeting, presided over by John Sevier, designated Franklin as the name of the new state and also elected provisional officers of the government. Not unexpectedly, the delegates chose Sevier as governor. The assembly also took a vote on the question of separate statehood; surprisingly, a substantial minority (15 of 43) voted in opposition. This was an early warning sign, but one ignored by Sevier and his main supporters. John Tipton, one of the fifteen negative votes, subsequently would become Sevier's chief nemesis.

After the Jonesboro delegates had returned home, Sevier received the message about North Carolina's November actions. Initially he felt flattered at being named brigadier general and therefore wavered in his enthusiasm for Franklin. He soon recovered, however, when friends reminded him of his political ambitions and their land speculation designs. The pursuit of independence—indeed, rebellion—must go forward.

In the spring of 1785, the conflict between Franklin and North Carolina escalated, though it remained a war of words. Letters and manifestos flew back and forth across the mountains. In late March, for example, the Franklin assembly replied to Gov. Alexander Martin's earlier letter to Sevier. Martin then issued a manifesto to the Franklinites in late April, admonishing them to "return to their duty and allegiance, and forbear paying any obedience to any self-created power and authority . . . not sanctified by the Legislature." Martin further warned that, while his state did not want to "be *driven to arms*," there might be civil war. Shortly thereafter, Richard Caswell replaced Martin as governor, but the epistolary skirmishes continued. Ironically, Caswell and Sevier were close associates, especially in land-buying activities. One gets the impression that the springtime hostilities between the two states were more imagined than real.

Franklin took a bold step toward independence in May, sending William Cocke to New York City, then the nation's capital. His special mission was to convince the Confederation government to admit Franklin as the four-

---

Payment of Franklin Taxes

The lack of a readily available currency caused the Franklin government to accept many different items as payment for land and poll taxes. Good flax linen was accorded a value ranging from three shillings and sixpence per yard down to two shillings, whereas woolen and cotton linsey carried a value of three shillings and sixpence per yard. Animal skins and furs were cherished: beaver at six shillings, otter and deer also at six shillings, but raccoon and fox at one shilling and three pence. Good distilled rye whiskey was valued at two shillings and sixpence per gallon, good peach or apple brandy at three shillings per gallon. Country-made sugar was worth one shilling per pound, while tobacco was valued at fifteen shillings per hundred.

teenth state in the Union. Cocke made a valiant effort; but the national government, being the ineffective entity that it was, could not reach agreement. Seven states in fact favored Franklin's admission, but nine were required. Obviously, if this strategy had worked, the whole story of Franklin—and of Tennessee itself—would have been dramatically different.

Several months later, the Franklin convention met again, this time to reach agreement on a permanent constitution. The November conclave, held at Greeneville, witnessed an extraordinary dispute between advocates of differing constitutions. One faction, led mainly by some Presbyterian clergymen, presented an entirely new frame of government, one that seemed more democratic. But a second faction, centered around Sevier and another group of Presbyterian divines, opposed this document and favored the provisional one adopted in December 1784. The latter faction prevailed, as the Greeneville convention accepted the constitution that was nothing more than a replica of North Carolina's governing document. Hence the "rebellious" Franklinites embraced institutions they allegedly had rebelled against.

Indian Problems

Given the unrelenting pressure of the white settlers upon Cherokee lands, it is no surprise that Sevier and the Franklin government confronted difficulties. The governor already had an established reputation as an Indian fighter, which stood him in good stead with his constituents. In the spring of 1785, he pressed the Cherokees to accept a new boundary line. The June treaty of Dumplin Creek legalized white settlement south of the French Broad River, all the way to the ridge that divided Little River from the Little Tennessee River. Franklinites ignored the fact that a portion of this newly designated area was within the Cherokee Reservation established by North Carolina two years earlier. In any event, in November 1785, the United States government negotiated with the Cherokees at Hopewell, South Carolina. In the so-called Hopewell Treaty, the lines marked by the Dumplin Creek negotiations were repudiated and replaced by the old boundaries originally set by the Long Island treaties of 1777. Oddly enough, this redrawing of lines placed Greeneville within the Cherokee region and outside of Franklin. Needless to say, neither whites nor Indians observed the Hopewell boundaries. Attacks upon whites by the Cherokees were frequent throughout Franklin, as were retaliations by whites against the Cherokees.

After continued skirmishes back and forth, Governor Sevier forced the Cherokees to meet him at Coyatee in August 1786. The resulting treaty pushed the boundary of white settlement southward all the way to the Little Tennessee River, the locale of the historic Cherokee towns. New hostilities erupted in the aftermath of this negotiation; ferocity matched ruthlessness. Sevier further enhanced his reputation as a fierce fighter against Indians.

The worst atrocity occurred in 1788, when the governor and others entrapped some Cherokees under flags of truce. They then mercilessly slaughtered the defenseless Indians. The State of Franklin gave every indication that it would take over Cherokee lands with impunity and exterminate anyone who stood in its way.

Franklin's Demise

One might argue that Franklin was doomed from the beginning—that is, that the independence movement simply could not prevail. But there is plenty of evidence that the new state managed reasonably well during its first two years. From 1786 on, however, dissenters within Franklin, as well as certain North Carolina leaders, pushed it to the brink of collapse. John Tipton stirred opposition to Sevier and to the Franklin government by spearheading the strategy to have Franklinites elected to the North Carolina legislature. In that year, Tipton achieved election as a senator, while North Carolina appointed Evan Shelby to replace Sevier as brigadier general and also created Hawkins County (thus binding the residents there more closely to the parent state).

In the following year, the divide-and-conquer policy continued. North Carolina, for example, appointed "loyal" persons to various county offices within the Franklin counties. The resulting confusion seems to have weakened support for Franklin. Moreover, in 1787, North Carolina announced forgiveness of taxes owed it by residents of the transmontane counties—another strategy to conciliate the so-called "rebellious" westerners. In the summer of that year, the Franklin leaders chose Evan Shelby as governor for a term beginning in 1788, but Shelby declined the honor. Obviously, the winds of change were blowing.

Some Franklin supporters fastened their hopes upon the constitutional convention meeting at Philadelphia in 1787. Perhaps the new national governing document would provide for Franklin. Such optimism was soon dashed, however. Instead, the framers mandated (Article IV, Section 3) that no new state could be formed "without the Consent of the Legislatures of the States concerned as well as of the Congress." At this juncture, ardent but realistic Franklinites knew that North Carolina never would agree. Hence, hopes for the new state dimmed a bit more.

Franklin still had some fight left in it, however. Indeed, early in 1788, overt hostilities broke out between the Tipton crowd and the Sevier followers. One presumably reliable version of the story claims that Washington County's Sheriff Jonathan Pugh, at Tipton's urging, seized some of Sevier's slaves as possible payment of the governor's *North Carolina* taxes! Enraged at this turn of events, Sevier assembled a band of supporters and attacked Tipton's home. Of course, Tipton wisely had gathered his own corps of marksmen. A shoot-out ensued, leaving several wounded and two dead. Quite possibly, leaders of the Cherokees and of North Carolina alike derived some satisfaction from this Tipton-Sevier imbroglio.

The governor's days were numbered, in more ways than one. His term expired in March 1788; and since there had not been a successful election, there was no replacement. Thus the Franklin government fell into serious disrepair. Samuel Johnston, the new governor of North Carolina and no lover of Franklin, sent orders for the arrest of Sevier on grounds of treason. John Tipton eagerly volunteered to serve the citation to Sevier and did so in October. The erstwhile governor surrendered without a shoot-out this time and was escorted to Morganton to stand trial. Shortly thereafter, friends and family appeared there to whisk Sevier away from the clutches of North Carolina law. Doubtless pleased to be rid of him, local authorities made no effort to chase after the Sevier entourage.

Amid such excitement, Franklin leaders (much like Cumberland leaders) were in contact with high Spanish officials. Concerns about navigation of the Mississippi and protection from the Indians were identical to those listed by the Cumberland people. Much of Sevier's actual contact occurred *after* his gubernatorial term had expired, but no matter. He hinted at a possible alliance with, or even annexation by, the Spanish; but they, although interested, were suspicious. Eventually Governor Miro sensibly nixed the deal. It was much ado about nothing.

After having dramatically arrested Sevier, North Carolina officials in November 1788 extended pardon to all Franklinites, including the ex-governor. In one more irony of history, a few months later, Greene County voters elected Sevier to the North Carolina legislature! The State of Franklin had gone out with a whimper and not a bang. Yet John Sevier, folk hero and consummate politician, was poised for even greater recognition. He seems to have had nine lives; already he had used several, but he had a few remaining. He would have to share center stage, however, with William Blount, his land-speculating ally. Together they would push the Tennessee country into territorial status and eventually into statehood.

Suggested Readings

Abernethy, Thomas P. *From Frontier to Plantation in Tennessee: A Study in Frontier Democracy.* Chapel Hill, N.C., 1932.

Arnow, Harriette Simpson. *Flowering of the Cumberland.* New York, 1963.

———. *Seedtime on the Cumberland.* New York, 1960. Reprinted, Lincoln, Neb., 1995.

Davidson, Donald. *The Tennessee: The Old River: From Frontier to Secession.* New York, 1946. Reprinted, Knoxville, Tenn., 1978.

Driver, Carl. *John Sevier: Pioneer of the Old Southwest*. Chapel Hill, N.C., 1932.

Henderson, Archibald. *The Conquest of the Old Southwest*. New York, 1920.

Williams, Samuel Cole. *History of the Lost State of Franklin*. Johnson City, Tenn., 1924.

———. *Tennessee During the Revolutionary War*. Nashville, Tenn., 1944.

3

Southwest Territory

BY THE END OF THE DECADE of the 1780s, the frontier folk of the Tennessee country seemed eager for a definite break from North Carolina tutelage and control. The saga of the "lost state" of Franklin had expressed elements of this desire, to be sure. And it is certainly fair to say that North Carolina leaders once again were poised to surrender their claims to the transmontane lands. A principal sticking point was simply that North Carolina had not yet ratified the new United States Constitution, one of only two of the thirteen states that had not done so. Finally, in November 1789, the state consented to the Constitution and thus formally entered the "more perfect" Union. That official action set the stage for the advent of the territorial phase of Tennessee's experience.

Formation Process

Daniel Smith, prominent leader of the Cumberland Basin settlements, attended the ratifying convention in North Carolina in the fall of 1789. He took advantage of that occasion to urge upon Gov. Samuel Johnston the state's cession of its western lands. Many months earlier—in January, in fact—a meeting at the Greene County courthouse had recommended that the people of upper East Tennessee petition the North Carolina legislature to surrender the western lands to the U.S. government. In August, a delegation of Cumberland region inhabitants convened at Nashville and voted to send a memorial to the North Carolina government, seeking a formal cession of the transmontane area. Thus Daniel Smith represented recognized opinion when he stressed the desire for federal, rather than North Carolina, supervision of the Tennessee country.

On December 22, one month after ratification, the North Carolina legislature voted to give up its claims to the western lands. It did so because the U.S. government had urged such a step and because the residents of the transmontane region were "desirous" of the cession. There was desire on the part of North Carolinians, too. A letter from a Wilmington resident, for example, praised the passage of the cession act thus: "We are rid of a people who were a pest and a burthen." In its act that ceded these lands, the legislature enumerated at least ten provisions. Basically, North Carolina wanted to protect property rights and land acquisitions already staked out. It stipulated, moreover, that if insufficient lands were allocated in the military reservation, additional acreage should be provided. The state emphasized that the newly surrendered western lands should be governed under terms of the Northwest Ordinance of 1787—with the major exception that Congress should pass no regulations to emancipate slaves. North Carolina further stipulated that residents of the area south of the French Broad River should be granted preemption rights. Persons living in the transmontane lands who owed debts to North Carolina should continue to be liable for the payment of them. Congress was given eighteen months to accept or reject North Carolina's cession.

But the federal government did not require that much time to reach a decision. Once President Washington conveyed to Congress copies of the state's cession act, the national legislature moved swiftly to approve it. On April 2, the president signed the congressional bill. Shortly thereafter, Congress designated the territory south of the Ohio River as the "Southwest Territory" (which included only the area of present-day Tennessee) and prescribed that it should be governed under the Northwest Ordinance. The president signed this legislation on May 26.

The federal government had an abiding interest in the presence of public lands in the new territory. Indeed, to some degree its fortunes were linked to the availability of such lands. At the outset, government leaders held unrealistically high hopes for unclaimed lands there that could be sold. They wanted badly to believe the assertions found in an April issue of the *New York Daily Advertiser,* to the effect that there were 24.5 million acres in the Southwest Territory, 8 million of which already had been sold or designated in some manner. The 16.5 million available acres should be reduced, the paper noted, by the 5 million acres considered to be barren or mountainous. But the remaining 11.5 million acres could readily be sold by the federal government. Congressional leaders listened attentively to the July 1790 speech by a North Carolina representative who boasted of at least 10 million acres available for public sale by the U.S. government. Depending upon whose calculations one trusted, these lands, it was estimated, would yield between $3 million and $6 million for the national government. With such dazzling possibilities, the new Southwest Territory merited much attention.

But eventually, in March 1791, Congress mandated that the president undertake an investigation of the lands actually available in the Southwest Territory and the Northwest Territory. Washington in turn delegated this assignment to Secretary of State Thomas Jefferson, who struggled for months trying to obtain reliable information. Finally, in November, he startled Congress with the revelation that the public land in the Southwest

Territory was nowhere near as large as the amount claimed earlier. After accounting for the dispersal of millions of acres there, Jefferson estimated that a paltry 300,000 acres remained for the federal government. (In his report, he calculated that, by contrast, at least 21 million acres were available in the Northwest Territory.) No wonder the federal government thereafter had trouble giving much support and attention to the Southwest Territory; the potential returns did not justify doing so.

Meanwhile, in the spring of 1790, Washington and others still looked optimistically upon the new territory. The immediate task facing the president was the appointment of the right person to shepherd the territory during Tennessee's apprenticeship period. The supreme irony is that Washington turned to William Blount, the man who had grabbed hundreds of thousands of acres before the federal government could have a chance at them. Blount admittedly had several advantages as he openly lobbied for the appointment. Certainly the backing of the North Carolina congressional delegation was critical. The simple fact that he was from the state that had ceded the lands was another consideration. That he, unlike John Sevier, never had been identified with or tainted by the Franklin movement or massacres of Indians added to his claims. Furthermore, Washington knew Blount personally; as a matter of fact, they recently had worked together at the Philadelphia Constitutional Convention. Doubtless there were other considerations, but Blount had the inside track from the outset; the only other viable candidate, Sevier the folk hero, was no match for the land baron.

Accordingly, on June 8, the president announced Blount's nomination. Word quickly reached North Carolina, where an eager and immensely satisfied Blount received it. He had sought the appointment to soothe his disappointment at losing the U.S. Senate election in North Carolina. Now he could exercise powers that far exceeded those of a mere senator. Close to his heart and mind, of course, were his extensive investments in western land. As he confided to a friend, "my Western Lands had become so great an object to me that it had become absolutely necessary that I should go to the Western Country, to secure them and perhaps my Presence might have enhanced there [sic] Value." Blount was eager to move to the new territory, for, as he told his partner and brother, John Gray Blount, the post of governor is "of great Importance to our Western Speculations."

Blount waited somewhat impatiently for weeks before receiving copies of the acts passed by Congress. After scrutinizing them, he made final plans to move westward and take the reins of government firmly in hand. Seeking further instructions, however, Blount decided to confer in person with the president and other officials. He therefore went to Virginia, where he visited with Washington at his Mount Vernon estate and took the oath of office before a Supreme Court justice. Afterwards, he traveled toward the Southwest Territory, a region upon which he never before had set foot, despite his massive land dealings there. Arriving on October 10, the new governor was ready to assert his authority. In a few days he moved to William Cobb's commodious home, "Rocky Mount," at the juncture of the Holston and Watauga Rivers. There he established the territorial capital, until such time as he would decide upon a permanent location.

The most pressing formal duty confronting Blount was the requirement to establish the new government throughout the territory. Since seven fully functioning county governments already existed, he had to deal with each of them right away. Beginning late in October, Blount visited the four upper East Tennessee counties (Greene, Hawkins, Sullivan, and Washington). At each location, he reconstituted the existing local governments in the name of the U.S. government and made numerous appointments, such as sheriffs, militia officers, and justices of the peace. Amid these official ceremonies, the new governor shrewdly found time to meet with John Sevier, in the hope of establishing a working relationship with him. The pair approached each other cautiously and suspiciously, but both recognized that they needed each other and therefore agreed to work harmoniously together. By the end of November, Blount not surprisingly appointed Sevier brigadier general of the Washington District militia and James Robertson, his longtime ally and land agent, brigadier general of the Mero District militia.

The necessity for reconstituting the governments in the latter district presented quite a challenge to Blount, for he would have to venture there in person. He left Cobb's home on November 27, bound for Nashville. Accompanying him were twenty-five guards, several friendly Indians, and between forty and fifty settlers who wanted to move to the Mero area. Apparently there was strength in numbers, because they made the journey without incident. Having arrived at Nashville, Blount met with leaders of

---

Rocky Mount

Built of white oak logs during the years 1770–72, the well-known home of William Cobb was located at the junction of the Watauga and Holston Rivers. A two-story house with nine rooms, it had two brick chimneys. When William Blount arrived there in October 1790, he made special note of the fireplaces and the glass windows. Rocky Mount was the seat of government for the new territory until Blount moved to Knoxville early in 1792.

The house was a favorite stopping place for many prominent travelers. In 1795, William Cobb and his family moved to Grainger County, and the house passed to Henry (Hal) Massengill Jr., the husband of Cobb's daughter Penelope. Rocky Mount remained in the Massengill family for four generations.

County Courts

At the local level, there was no more important governmental agency than the county court, comprised of justices of the peace who met quarterly each year. As a judicial body, the court heard a variety of cases and meted out fines and punishments. These could include public whipping and confinement in the stocks— wooden frames in which an offender's hands and feet could be locked. The justices levied fines for swearing, Sabbath breaking, assault, fornication, quarreling, and other offenses. Fines, along with taxes, were the two sources of income for the county governments.

The county courts depended upon sheriffs and clerks to assist them; the sheriff was the tax collector, as well as the enforcer of laws. These courts devoted a good bit of time to managing the estates of the deceased and taking care of charity cases. They also regulated ferries, taverns, and inns and provided for road and bridge construction.

---

the three county governments (Davidson, Sumner, and Tennessee). While in Nashville, Blount also had extensive conversations with Robertson, probably about possible land purchases, and with Daniel Smith, who as secretary would be second in command of the territory. Blount also would share governance with the three territorial judges: Joseph Anderson, David Campbell, and John McNairy. After completing his official and unofficial activities in Nashville, the governor headed back across the territory to Cobb's place, which he reached on December 29. All in all, he had completed an eventful and successful first ten weeks on the job.

Red and White Problems and Negotiations

The congressional act establishing the Southwest Territory specified that the governor also should function as superintendent of Indian affairs. Upon receiving word of his appointment, Blount worried about that duty, fearing that it would be "laborious and disagreeable." And so it would prove to be. As events and developments unfolded in the territory, "the Indian problem was," in the words of Blount's biographer, William Masterson, "the keystone of all policy." It simply could not be avoided, because the Indian presence forced the issue. Blount would deal not only with Cherokees, whose lands were being steadily encroached upon, but also with Creeks, Choctaws, and Chickasaws, all of whom had vested interests of one sort or another in the Southwest Territory. Initially, white settlers were optimistic that the U.S. government would bring power and prestige to the arena of Indian relations and thus usher in a time of peace and treaty negotiations. Moreover, territorial residents hoped that the national government would intervene with military force to deal with any alleged Indian aggression. But, as noted earlier, the federal government's enthusiasm for direct involvement in the Southwest Territory diminished, once the scarcity of public lands became known.

In the summer of 1790, even before Blount took command, the U.S. government invited Creek leaders to New York for negotiations. Alexander McGillivray, chief of the Creek Nation, arrived in July to participate in discussions which eventuated in the Treaty of New York (signed in August). It set new boundaries in Alabama for the Creeks, who in turn promised an end to hostilities and an exchange of prisoners. Washington administration leaders hoped thereby to lessen at least some of the problems that Blount would confront when he arrived in the territory.

Secretary of War Henry Knox, who was Blount's immediate superior on all Indian matters, directed the new governor to hold a conference with the Cherokees, because the presence of illegal white settlers south of the French Broad was a troubling point of conflict. Accordingly, in January 1791, Blount sent out a message urging Cherokee chiefs to meet with him in late May to discuss possible revisions to the 1785 Treaty of Hopewell (which had been ignored or violated by both sides). Several matters clouded the preconference environment, however: scattered white atrocities against Indians, an attempt by whites to establish a settlement at Muscle Shoals, and persistent stories of Blount's hunger for land. Nevertheless, by late May, when the governor reached the designated conference spot on the Holston River (at present-day Knoxville), nearly twelve hundred Cherokees had gathered, including forty-one chiefs.

Blount proved himself a formidable negotiator: first he dazzled the Indians with pomp and ceremony, then he aggressively presented his plan for revised land boundaries. When some of the Cherokee leaders protested, he minced no words and uttered some threats. Eventually, both parties reached agreement, albeit somewhat reluctantly, and signed the Treaty of Holston on July 2, 1791.

Most important, the treaty legitimized the white settlements below the French Broad, for it set new boundaries. On the west, the line was to follow the Clinch River; the all-important southern boundary would stretch along a line from the mouth of the Clinch eastward to the North Carolina boundary. In exchange, Blount offered an annual payment of one thousand dollars to the Cherokee Nation. This and all other provisions were enacted so that "there shall be perpetual peace and friendship between" the whites and the Cherokees. The latter solemnly acknowledged no sovereign other than the United States (a pledge demanded by the whites, who were trying to head off Spanish influence). For whites, "free and unmo-

Signing of the Treaty of the Holston, July 1791. Mary U. Rothrock, *This Is Tennessee* (Knoxville, 1963), 188. Used by permission.

lested use of a road from Washington District to Mero District, and of the navigation of the Tennessee River" was promised by the Cherokees. Evidently believing that Cherokee society should be reshaped, whites agreed to provide "useful implements of husbandry" so that the Indians could "become Herdsmen and cultivators" instead of remaining hunters. After the treaty was signed, Blount boldly entreated the Indians to sell him lands south to the Muscle Shoals vicinity. The rumors of his land grabbing appeared accurate, and the Cherokees denied his request.

Disgruntlement with the Treaty of Holston continued after everyone left the treaty grounds. Those Cherokee chiefs (including Chickamauga leaders) who had not attended or participated in the negotiations were particularly unenthusiastic. Therefore, in the fall months Indians met to air their grievances about the treaty and determined to send a delegation to Philadelphia. Perhaps because Blount was absent from the territory on a visit to North Carolina, the Cherokees opted for direct contact with the national administration. At any rate, shortly thereafter a group of Cherokees left the Tennessee country for Charleston and thence traveled to the nation's capital. Once there, they conferred with both Washington and Knox, who listened attentively to their complaints. In response, the administration increased the annual payment to $1,500, sent large amounts of goods, and appointed Leonard Shaw as special agent and James Carey as interpreter. Blount did not learn of these negotiations until the end of January 1792, when he received a letter from Knox.

Meanwhile, several other developments occurred that had a direct or indirect impact upon red-white relations in the territory. In August 1791, for example, Mero District residents sent a memorial to the U.S. president, in which they enumerated the atrocities that had been committed by Indians during the summer. More important, in November, Indian forces defeated U.S. troops in a battle in the Northwest Territory. This disaster reverberated throughout the entire nation, to be sure; but in the Southwest Territory it stirred white fears of an even greater Indian menace. Certainly, in light of this defeat, no federal troops would be made available for Blount's territory. During the governor's absence, Washington appointed three men to survey and run the Holston Treaty boundary lines; unfortunately, their mission was not accomplished for years. Finally, in December, the Spanish government appointed Luis Carondelet as a replacement for Miro, governor of Louisiana. Carondelet assumed office with the intention of stirring up Indian—especially Creek—antagonism against white settlers in the Southwest Territory. From that policy flowed months, even years, of tribulation for the people under Blount's care.

The years 1792–94 constituted a particularly challenging time for the governor and for the territory's people, red and white. During this period, hostilities between the rival groups were almost constant, relieved only intermittently by discussions and negotiations. From the white perspective, it was fortunate that the Chickasaws and the upper Cherokees (as distinguished from the lower Cherokees, or Chickamaugas) were friendly more often than not. The chief antagonists, therefore, were the Creeks and the Chickamaugas, although from time to time all the tribes engaged in attacks and raids upon white inhabitants.

Interestingly enough, the national administration was convinced that whites usually were responsible for stirring up trouble with the Indians—a not completely erroneous view. Blount and others made little headway in altering this attitude; but the governor did struggle to cultivate harmonious relations with Indian tribes. In May 1792, for example, he met at Coyatee with an immense assembly of Cherokees (some said nearly twenty-four hundred persons). There a "seasonal drinking of whiskey," as well as some gambling, took place in an atmosphere of conviviality. Blount departed the conference grounds with a belief that the Cherokees (including the Chickamauga) were friendly and with a negative opinion of Leonard Shaw, the agent. Blount next planned a gathering of Chickasaws and Choctaws at Nashville for August. When the national government made available eight thousand dollars' worth of merchandise as gifts for the Indians, Blount encountered sizable logistical problems. Eventually the goods were shipped by boat, accompanied by two militia companies. Blount and others, however, took an overland route to Nashville. After arriving there, the governor learned that very few Choctaws had elected to attend; nevertheless, he presided over a friendly conclave devoted primarily to the exchange of gifts. Perhaps the conference solidified Chickasaw support for Blount and his administration.

Typically, just as advances were made, they were offset by an outbreak of hostilities. The Mero District, which bore the brunt of most raids and attacks, in September 1792 braced itself for a major assault upon Nashville by the lower Cherokees. Although the expected attack did not materialize, the disorganized Indians launched a raid upon Buchanan's Station instead. The white defenders acquitted themselves quite well and repelled the Indians. This attack stirred whites to insist even more loudly upon an offensive against the Indians and on assistance from the national government.

In February 1793, a company of regular troops arrived in Knoxville from North Carolina, the first—and one of the few—tangible signs of support from Secretary Knox and the president. They were assigned garrison duty, however, and actually contributed little to the protection of the region. Suppliers of goods to the soldiers benefited monetarily, of course, but there seem to have been few other advantages. Knox instructed Blount to invite the Cherokees to travel to Philadelphia for a conference with the president. But even after some "eating, drinking and jocular conversation" with Cherokee leaders, Blount was unable to persuade them to make the trip. The governor nevertheless decided to go to Philadelphia without the Indians, for he had several matters to attend to. Meanwhile, James Winchester had preceded him there, carrying a memorial from the Mero District seeking federal protection and complaining "loudly," noted Blount, "of everything that deserves to be complained of."

The governor departed from the territory for Philadelphia just prior to a serious white attack upon the Cherokees. He had authorized Capt. John Beard to lead a company of militiamen to pursue Indian raiders, assuring him that "your killing of them will afford me great pleasure." Therefore it could have come as no surprise when Beard and his troops actually assaulted some Indians; the shock was that they attacked the camp of Hanging Maw, a friendly chief. The militia killed and wounded several Cherokees, much to the dismay of Daniel Smith, who was in charge of the territorial government in the absence of Blount. Retaliatory attacks by both whites and Indians followed in the immediate aftermath, but there was no general warfare.

Once in Philadelphia, Blount lobbied Knox for a general offensive against the Indians and especially for an invasion of the Creek Nation. But the secretary of war remained resolute in his insistence that the whites in the territory should adhere to a defensive stance only. The federal government—which was more concerned about the Indian situation in the Northwest—would not support any attack upon the Indians. News from Smith about various white atrocities stiffened the administration's resolve.

Before the disappointed governor returned to the Southwest Territory, further hostilities occurred. Capt. John Beard even led yet another attack upon the Cherokees. In September 1793, an Indian "army" of one thousand warriors (Cherokee, Chickamauga, and Creek) crossed the Tennessee

River and headed toward Knoxville, which at that time had only forty defenders available. The greatly feared assault on helpless Knoxville did not occur, however, primarily because the diverse Indian groups could not agree upon a strategy. Instead they turned on Cavett's Station and killed the thirteen whites there. Afterwards, in October, Daniel Smith instructed John Sevier to take six hundred men to pursue and punish Cherokees wherever he could find them. Accordingly, Sevier eagerly pushed southward all the way to the Indian town of Etowah in Georgia, burning two towns and destroying provisions everywhere. But, to the disappointment of Sevier and his men, they engaged in no decisive battle with the Indians.

Governor Blount returned to the territory in mid-October, just in time to learn about Sevier's campaign and other hostilities. David Henley, newly appointed paymaster and agent of the War Department, accompanied the governor back to Knoxville and set up an office. It was widely assumed that one of Henley's functions was to keep a keen eye on the governor and send reports back to Philadelphia. There would be plenty for him to see: Blount's land dealings, the push for a territorial legislature, and further Indian problems. For a time there was a lull in conflict with the Indians, but as the year 1794 unfolded, hostilities increased once again, particularly those instigated by the Creeks. All parts of the territory were affected, but most of the trouble occurred in the Mero District.

In the spring and early summer, representatives of two Indian tribes made trips to the nation's capital. A Cherokee delegation conferred with Knox and Washington and successfully sought amendments to the Holston Treaty. The secretary of war agreed, for example, to increase the annual payment to five thousand dollars, a substantial increment indeed. Later a Chickasaw group, led by Chief Piomingo and escorted by one of Blount's associates, also went to Philadelphia. There the president showered gifts upon them, including an annual payment of three thousand dollars. All in all, it was a profitable journey for both Cherokees and Chickasaws.

Back in the territory, however, tensions mounted, especially because of Creek and Chickamauga activities in the Mero District. White leaders there demanded an offensive against the Indians. Blount urged caution but sent Maj. James Ore of the Hamilton District to Mero with a militia detachment. Ore and his men joined an invasion force of whites that had congregated in Nashville by September 1794. James Robertson helped plan the attack upon the lower Cherokee (Chickamauga) towns of Nickajack and Running Water and secretly resigned his post as brigadier general. Ore directed the assault, which his troops carried out ruthlessly; they returned to Nashville triumphant. As soon as word of the Nickajack expedition reached Blount, he dissociated himself from every aspect of it; but unofficially he was quite pleased. Secretary Knox, irritated with the latest news from the territory, admitted his continuing frustration with Indian-white relations there. Very encouraging news came from the Northwest Territory, however, where in August federal troops won a decisive victory over the Indians at Fallen Timbers. This success would have an impact upon Blount's territory.

For the moment, though, Indian-white tribulations continued. Yet, even in the midst of these, some hopeful signs appeared. For instance, Blount met with the Cherokees (upper and lower) at Tellico Blockhouse in November. Mindful of the recent Indian defeat in the Northwest, they brought messages of peace and a willingness to exchange prisoners. Both red and white leaders agreed that Creeks represented the remaining threat.

In 1795, even the Creeks made direct peace overtures, first in April and then in October. In the latter month, Creeks joined with delegations of Cherokee, Chickasaws, and Choctaws who assembled at Tellico Blockhouse for the purposes of talking peace and exchanging prisoners. In June, Washington had appointed a three-man commission to conduct talks with the Creeks, an obvious stimulus to the cultivation of friendly relations. At long last, in the valleys of the Tennessee and the Cumberland, peace seemed a credible possibility. Due recognition must be given, of course, to the Spain-U.S. Treaty of San Lorenzo of 1795, which committed the Spanish to restraining the Indians and to accepting the 31st parallel as the northern boundary of Spanish territory. Creeks and all other southern Indian tribes realized that they no longer could look to Spanish officials for backing and encouragement.

While Blount throughout the year luxuriated in the prospects for peaceful relations with the Indians, he wrestled with new conflicts with the federal government. At the first of the year, Timothy Pickering replaced Knox as secretary of war. Pickering immediately reviewed Blount's Indian policies and found them wanting. In March he delivered a strongly worded denunciation of Blount's alleged attempts to stir up a war between the Creeks and the other Indian groups. As a result, Blount became increasingly disenchanted with the Washington administration and more determined to push the territory toward statehood.

Territorial Government

It would take more than five years as a territory before the evolutionary process finally culminated in statehood. In the early period, Blount functioned as sole authority in the territory, although in a limited way he shared governance with the three judges and the territorial secretary. He exercised substantial power, especially in the matter of appointments, and thus he built a loyal base of political support. As he later confessed, "It is a principle with me . . . not to stand between a Friend and a Benefit." A multitude of "friends" could testify to Blount's faithful adherence to this "principle." He even had direct influence over those territorial appointments made by the Washington administration.

The governor handled the chores of office, including the incessant burden of Indian problems, reasonably well. The only newspaper in the territory, the *Knoxville Gazette*, greatly assisted Blount. As a matter of fact, shortly after he received the announcement of his appointment as governor, he recruited George Roulstone, a North Carolina newspaperman, to move to the new territory. He set up shop in Rogersville and, beginning in November 1791, published his paper there (although it never carried that town's name) for eleven months before moving to Knoxville in October 1792. Roulstone and Blount needed each other. The newspaperman needed employment and a reasonably steady source of income; the *Gazette* furnished both, as did additional jobs that Blount arranged for Roulstone. The governor desired a convenient medium for communicating information and shaping opinion, particularly about his tenure as chief executive. Roulstone performed quite ably but strove to keep the paper from being totally slanted toward Blount, lest it lose all credibility. There is no question, however, that the two men "managed" the news effectively.

The governor was content to operate out of "Rocky Mount" for a time, but he considered it a temporary arrangement (maybe the Cobbs did, too). In any event, Blount decided that the permanent capital must be at a new place and therefore not at one of the already established towns. Perhaps correctly, he concluded that the capital needed to be farther south, so as to be more conveniently situated to deal with the Indians and to communicate with the Mero District. Aware of James White's fort on the Holston River, the governor selected that area for the first Cherokee treaty negotiations. Subsequently, he determined that the new capital should be established there, and in October 1791 town lots were drawn off and sold. That town, named for Blount's boss, Henry Knox, would serve for years as the seat of government.

The Northwest Ordinance, which was the instrument of government for

---

George Roulstone

A native of Massachusetts, where he was born in 1767, Roulstone started his newspaper career there but moved to Fayetteville, North Carolina, in 1789. At Blount's urging, Roulstone located in Rogersville, in the new Southwest Territory, the following year. In 1791, he began publication of the *Knoxville Gazette*. In addition, he served as the territorial government's printer and subsequently as postmaster at Knoxville. Once the state was formed, Roulstone became clerk of the senate as well as the official printer. He also operated a book-selling business in Knoxville. Roulstone died in 1804, but his widow, Elizabeth, became the new state printer and also continued the newspaper.

First issue of the *Knoxville Gazette.* Tennessee Historical Society, Nashville.

the Southwest Territory, provided for three stages of transition from territory to statehood. The second one stipulated that, once a territory had a population of at least five thousand free adult males, it was entitled to a legislature. When Blount arrived in the territory, no one had any idea how many people lived in the seven existing counties. He refused, however, to have a census taken right away, because he simply did not want to be bothered. But in the spring of 1791, he sent out a request to the counties to conduct a census, which they completed in July.

The data revealed a number of important things. It probably astounded everyone to learn that the total population of the territory stood at 35,700. The imbalanced distribution spoke volumes about the development of the different parts of the territory: the Washington District had almost 29,000 inhabitants, while the Mero District had only 7,000. Of course, the upper East Tennessee region had at least a ten-year head start on the Cumberland Basin settlements. Greene, the most heavily populated county, by itself had more residents than the three counties of the Mero District combined. The census takers ventured into the prohibited area south of the French Broad River and counted 3,600 persons—a fact that had a direct bearing upon the Holston Treaty negotiations. The slave population totaled 3,400—unevenly

[56]

Schedule of the whole number of perfons in the territory of the United States of America, South of the River Ohio, as taken on the laſt Saturday of July 1791, by the Captains of the Militia within the limits of their refpective diſtricts.

WASHINGTON DISTRICT.	Free white males of 21 years and upwards, including heads of families.	Free white males under 21 years.	Free white females including heads of families.	All other perfons.	Slaves.	Total of each county.	Total of each diſtrict.
Counties Waſhington	1009	1792	2524	12	535	5872	
Sullivan	806	1242	1995	107	297	4447	
Greene	1293	2374	3580	40	454	7741	
Hawkins	1204	1970	2921	68	807	6970	
South of Fr. Broad	681	1082	1627	66	163	3619	
MERO-DISTRICT.							28649
Counties Davidſon	639	855	1288	18	659	3459	
Sumner	404	582	854	8	348	2196	
Tenneſſee	235	380	576	42	154	1387	
							7042
	6271	10277	15365	361	3417		35691

Note. There are feveral Captains who have not as yet returned the Schedules of the numbers of their diſtriƈts, namely: In Greene County, three—in Davidſon, one—and South of French-Broad, one diſtriƈt.

September 19th, 1791.

W^m: **BLOUNT.**

Census of the Southwest Territory, 1791. *First Census of the United States* (Philadelphia, 1791), 56.

divided, with almost 2,300 in the Washington District and fewer than 1,200 in Mero. Obviously, however, the ratio of slaves to whites was much higher in the latter district than in the former. Perhaps the most significant statistic was that the territory had nearly 6,300 free adult males, far in excess of the 5,000 required for stage two. But the governor chose to ignore the legal entitlement to a territorial legislature and opted instead to govern without the encumbrance of a law-making body.

The go-it-alone attitude meant that, during the first three years of his tenure, Blount had to answer only to the national administration. The residents of the territory had little recourse, other than praise or criticism for the governor. As Indian problems mounted, so did pressures upon Blount to share governance; yet he resisted until late in 1793. In the meantime, many aspects of running the territory, in addition to handling Indian problems, demanded his attention and energy. A continuing challenge (one he relished) was the appointment of officials. In 1791, he shrewdly named William Cocke as attorney general of the Washington District and Andrew Jackson to hold that post in the Mero District. In the following year, he formally established Knox and Jefferson Counties; they constituted the new Hamilton District. In November 1792, the governor and territorial judges authorized the county courts to levy and collect taxes on polls and land—a controversial decision, to say the least.

Red-white hostilities in 1793 contributed to the new movement for a territorial legislature. Before he left for his lengthy visit to Philadelphia, Blount, aware of steadily growing criticism of his policies regarding the Indian menace, began to assert that he favored a territorial assembly. In fact, in June he sent a directive to militia commanders to conduct a survey of voters to ascertain sentiment about an election for territorial representatives. Upon his return in early October, new demands for an assembly greeted him, especially an address from the Hamilton District grand jury. Therefore, on October 19 (a scant nine days after arriving in Knoxville), Blount issued a call for elections to be held in December. All free adult males were eligible to vote, the sheriffs were to conduct the elections, and a total of thirteen representatives would be chosen. Although afterwards there were allegations of fraud and scandal in some of these December contests, Blount accepted the returns as valid, and on January 1 he called for the new assembly to meet in Knoxville in late February 1794. It was time to share the burdens of governing.

Among the thirteen men who gathered at the territorial capital on February 24 were some very familiar names: John Tipton of Washington County, William Cocke of Hawkins, John Beard of Knox, and Dr. James White of Davidson. Those assembled first listened to a sermon by the Presbyterian clergyman Samuel Carrick, whose text from the Book of Titus reputedly had been selected by Blount: "Put them in mind to be subject to principalities and powers, to obey magistrates." With those sobering words, the delegates addressed their only actual task—devising a list of ten men from whom President Washington later would choose five to serve as the council, or upper house, of the territorial assembly. Instead of adjourning, however, the representatives authored a petition to Blount and a memorial to Congress, in which they reported atrocities by Indians and begged for additional protection. This maneuver ruffled the feathers of the governor, who did not hesitate to adjourn the assembly on March 1. Afterwards, he entreated Dr. White to journey to Philadelphia with a record of the proceedings.

In the late spring, the president revealed his roster of five men chosen for the territorial council: James Winchester, Griffith Rutherford, John Sevier, Stockley Donelson, and Parmenas Taylor. These luminaries would join the representatives on August 25 for the first session of the full territorial assembly. As an indication of the elevated level of public interest in self-government, approximately two hundred persons from the Mero District who wished to participate in some manner in this historic event traveled to Knoxville. Not all remained in town until September 30, the final day of the session, for it is known that even several legislators left prior to adjournment.

A number of important items of business awaited the newly chosen public servants. Not surprisingly, one of the most far-reaching and controversial was the tax on persons and land. The council proposed a rate, favored by Blount, of 12.5 cents per hundred acres, whereas the lower house favored a rate of 25 cents. Eventually the latter rate prevailed, much to the dismay of large landowners. The assembly established a Treasury Department and various courts and created Sevier County. In addition, it chartered Blount College in Knoxville and Greeneville College in Greeneville. The legislature chose Dr. James White as territorial delegate to Congress and George Roulstone as public printer. Naturally, the assembly, whose deliberations were interrupted at least once by rumors of a pending Indian attack, adopted a memorial to Congress, pleading once again for protection and criticizing the policies that had failed to yield peace. Before adjourning, the legislators requested the governor to undertake a new census of the territory in July 1795 and also to conduct a referendum on the question of statehood. Their crowded agenda completed, the weary but satisfied members of the assembly retired to Chisholm's tavern to celebrate.

Blount College

In 1794, the territorial assembly chartered Blount College, to be located in Knoxville. The Reverend Samuel Carrick, who had founded the town's Presbyterian church, became the first and only president of the infant college. The board of trustees included the most prominent figures in the territory. Apparently a building was erected on property sold to the school by James White for thirty dollars. Early records indicate that tuition was eight dollars per session, and board was twenty-five dollars. The first and only graduate of Blount College, William Parker, completed his studies in 1806. At one point, five female students were enrolled, but, given their ages, probably they were preparatory students. The school went out of existence in 1807, when East Tennessee College superseded it.

In a March 1795 letter to his brother, Blount confided that he was "disgusted of the rascally Neglect of Congress & weary of the Duties of Office." No wonder that he decided to convene the territorial assembly in June, instead of waiting until the October date agreed upon previously. This meeting would hasten the advent of statehood. Both houses met in Knoxville on June 29 and remained in session until July 11. They quickly agreed to enact a law requiring a census and a referendum on statehood. The sheriffs were to supervise the census and poll taking, in return for which they would be compensated at the rate of one dollar for every one hundred persons counted. These tasks were to be carried out during the period of mid-September through mid-November. Believing that the census would reveal more than the 60,000 free persons required for statehood, the legislature authorized the governor to issue a call for the voters to elect five men from each county to serve in a constitutional convention. In other matters, the assembly created Blount County and chartered Washington College at Salem. Indicative of the transformed state of Indian-white relations by the summer of 1795, the legislators made no attempt to devise a memorial to Congress on the topic of the Indian menace. Instead, they praised the prospects of peace and then adjourned to await the results of the fall computations.

The new census revealed some startling facts. For the moment, the most important was the presence of some 66,650 free persons—clearly more than the requisite number. Thus, the territory, under terms of the Northwest Ordinance, now was eligible for the third stage in its journey toward statehood. The total population was 77,300, more than double that reported just four years earlier—and this despite the turmoil caused by Indian-white hostilities! The eight eastern counties accounted for 65,300 persons (two and a half times their 1791 population), whereas the Mero counties reported 12,000 (one and three-fourths times their 1791 population). The number of slaves in 1795 was 10,600—more than triple the total found in the earlier census. Approximately 80 percent of the slaves (8,150) lived in the eastern counties, with the balance (2,500) in the Mero District. Since 1791, the slave population had doubled in the Mero counties but tripled in the Washington and Hamilton districts.

The non-binding referendum on the question of statehood showed solid support for it, although only 9,000 persons registered an opinion. Of those, 6,500 (roughly 72 percent) supported statehood, an overwhelming endorsement. The Mero counties of Davidson and Tennessee voted against statehood; no poll was reported for Sumner County. All the eastern counties supported statehood, although the vote in Greene was surprisingly close. Armed with this evidence of commitment to statehood and with the data from the census, Blount, on November 28, called for an election in December of five delegates from each county to a proposed constitutional convention. That convention was to commence on January 11, 1796.

Wanted to Purchafe,

A NEGRO FELLOW, about the age of 20 or 24 years— one who can be recommended for honefty and fobriety.

Apply to the printers.
Nov. 4, 1791.

Notices about slavery in the Southwest Territory. *Knoxville Gazette*, November 5, 1791, and October 6, 1792.

TEN DOLLARS REWARD.

RUNAWAY the 4th of September laft, from the fubfcriber, living in Wythe county, about 12 miles from the Lead Mines, on Cripple Creek, a mulattoe fellow, named THOMAS, about twenty years of age, fix feet high, the little toe on the right foot grows to the next one to it, took none of his clothing with him. Whoever will apprehend faid flave, and fecure him fo that I can get him again, fhall receive the above reward.

HEZEKIAH CHENNEY.

N. B. It is probable he may make for the Cherokee nation
Oct. 2, 1792.

Framing a Constitution

Fifty-five notables, forty from the eastern counties and fifteen from the Mero counties, congregated in Knoxville a few days after the new year began. Among the more prominent were: Joseph Anderson, William Blount, Landon Carter, William C. C. Claiborne, William Cocke, Thomas Hardeman, Andrew Jackson, Charles McClung, Joseph McMinn, John McNairy, Archibald Roane, James Robertson (twenty-six years after leading a group of permanent settlers into the Watauga region and a little over sixteen years after taking a group to the French Lick), Daniel Smith, John Tipton, and James White. These men already had achieved fame or would do so in the near future. Conspicuous by his absence from the list of framers was John Sevier, although actually he attended the convention and worked behind the scenes to promote Blount's views. Sevier's son served as clerk of the convention, so the family was represented formally. Since Blount controlled the majority of the delegates, it is no surprise that they designated him president of the convention. Interestingly enough, he was the only delegate at this conclave who also had participated in framing the U.S. Constitution in 1787.

After listening to the obligatory sermon by the Rev. Samuel Carrick, the delegates got down to business. A truly remarkable accomplishment was their decision to *reduce* their per diem pay from $2.50 to $1.50, since "economy is an amiable trait in any government." A commendable attitude

Office of Gov. William Blount, Knoxville. Courtesy of Blount Mansion Association, Knoxville.

on the part of public servants, to be sure, but one seldom if ever espoused by subsequent Tennessee legislative bodies. The convention designated two men from each county to form the drafting committee and named Daniel Smith to chair that group. Borrowing heavily from other state constitutions, particularly that of North Carolina, these men quickly hammered out the document for the proposed state.

Although they disagreed on and debated certain matters, the framers had no major disputes. They considered a one-house legislature but acquiesced in the majority opinion, which favored two houses. Blount and his followers succeeded in providing for "equal and uniform" taxation of land and slaves. In other words, the actual *value* of these did not matter; one hundred acres of barren land would be taxed at the same rate as one hundred acres of rich and productive land. The constitution prescribed property qualifications for holding office (two hundred acres for a legislator and five hundred acres for a governor). The right to vote was granted to all free (white and black) adult males who owned a freehold. The legislature and governor retained the right to appoint many county and local officials. Among the more democratic features of the new constitution was the provision that men who served in the militia would elect their officers; these in turn would elect the top officers (major generals and brigadier generals).

Tradition holds that Andrew Jackson was the convention delegate who proposed "Tennessee" as the name for the new state. At any rate, the record shows that he was responsible for the clause that restricted Knoxville's tenure as state capital to the period ending in 1802. This was a ploy on the part of Mero delegates to prevent Knoxville from always dominating the political scene. Jackson and others had sharp eyes focused on the future.

Article VIII denied any clergyman the right to hold office in either house of the state legislature. It also mandated, though, that no one "who denies the being of God or a future state of rewards and punishments" could hold any office at any level of government. These clauses typified similar provisions in many state constitutions.

The final portion of the document enumerated a lengthy declaration of rights, a section contained in most constitutions. But Blount was instrumental in inserting a right not found elsewhere, one reflecting the citizens' long-time concern about the Mississippi. This statement declared free navigation of this river to be an inherent right of Tennessee citizens, one that could not "be conceded to any prince, potentate, power, person or persons whatever"—a reminder of the Spanish influence.

The convention's final day was February 6; in four short weeks, the framers had fashioned a very respectable document. They provided for legislative and gubernatorial elections to be held in March and thereby set in motion the steps necessary to consummate their efforts. The delegates saw no need to submit the constitution to the people for ratification or rejection. Instead, their concern was to hasten a copy of it to Congress before its anticipated adjournment in late spring. As the Knoxville delegates departed, they commissioned Joseph McMinn to deliver their handiwork to Philadelphia. The fate of the proposed new state soon rested in the somewhat uncertain hands of the national government.

In something less than six years, William Blount had led the territory and its people through the apprenticeship period. Never a folk hero or even a very popular leader, he nonetheless was a resourceful, strong, and persistent leader. One also must accept the reality that, during his tenure, he was heavily engaged in land speculation. Indeed, at times it seemed difficult for him to separate his private business from his governmental responsibilities. In communications with Secretary Knox, David Henley accused Blount of malfeasance in office and attempted to stir up opposition to him. There is no denying that at times the governor diverted public funds for personal use; this, like his extensive borrowing, was done to meet his almost insatiable demand for money with which to purchase lands. Blount and his brothers began to specialize in sales of immense tracts of land, an enterprise that required a cadre of conveniently located and well-connected agents. David Allison, for example, assisted with transactions conducted in Philadelphia, while Nicholas Romayne sought buyers in England for Blount's lands. James Robertson, John Chisholm, and Stockley Donelson all participated at one time or another in the governor's land-purchasing enterprises.

Seeming never to miss an opportunity to enhance his personal fortunes, Blount also attended to his political future. To this end, he built a base of support with his manifold and shrewd appointments to public office. More-over, eventually he embraced the dream that, with statehood, he could achieve the political plum denied him in North Carolina—namely, a U.S. Senate seat. In the process, he would have to accommodate John Sevier's political aspirations by dangling before Sevier the possibility of election as governor of the new state. The plan worked.

Suggested Readings

Abernethy, Thomas P. *From Frontier to Plantation in Tennessee: A Study in Frontier Democracy.* Chapel Hill, N.C., 1932.

Driver, Carl. *John Sevier: Pioneer of the Old Southwest.* Chapel Hill, N.C., 1932.

Durham, Walter T. *Before Tennessee: The Southwest Territory, 1790–1796.* Piney Flats, Tenn., 1990.

———. *Daniel Smith: Frontier Statesman.* Gallatin, Tenn., 1976.

Masterson, William H. *William Blount.* Baton Rouge, La., 1954.

Satz, Ronald N. *Tennessee's Indian Peoples: From White Contact to Removal, 1540–1840.* Knoxville, Tenn., 1979.

4

Early Statehood Years

IN THE THIRTY OR SO YEARS that followed the framing of the new constitution, Tennessee blossomed and flourished in ways hardly imaginable to those whose handiwork produced the governing document. Yet problems and difficulties often stalked the landscape. To set matters in motion once the 1796 convention departed from Knoxville, Governor Blount sent writs out to the sheriffs calling for the election of state legislators and the governor. Fast on the heels of those instructions came the elections themselves, early in March.

At the end of that month, eleven senators and twenty-two representatives gathered in Knoxville for the meeting of the first state legislature. After taking the oath of office, they elected James Winchester speaker of the senate and James Stuart speaker of the house. On the second day, they reviewed the gubernatorial election returns and announced that John Sevier had been "duly and constitutionally elected" governor. Sevier was inaugurated the next day, accompanied by the roar of sixteen cannon rounds fired in his honor.

Before their adjournment on April 23, the legislators tended to numerous business matters, many of them associated with the requirements for launching a new state government. They decided that the state could not have a county that bore the same name as the state; therefore, they split Tennessee County into two counties, Montgomery and Robertson. Several days later, the General Assembly established two counties in the eastern region, Grainger and Carter. Of much significance was the legislature's action naming William Blount and William Cocke as U.S. senators. This decision came as no surprise, of course, but Blount was immensely pleased nonetheless; finally he had his reward.

Admission of the New State

Sevier and the legislators conducted their business in full faith that they acted legitimately on behalf of the new state. Thus they were perturbed to learn of obstacles that thwarted acceptance of the state's request for statehood in the spring of 1796. They had not taken into account that this was a presidential election year and that Congress was divided, with the House being predominantly Anti-Federalist and the Senate Federalist.

President Washington forwarded the Tennessee constitution and the 1795 census returns to Congress in early April but failed to make an actual recommendation about what action he desired. The House began debate on the admission proposal in early May. The opponents—Federalists who feared that the new state would vote for Jefferson, the Anti-Federalist presidential candidate—voiced several objections. They argued that Congress, not the Southwest Territory, should have initiated the process of seeking statehood. Given that no state had yet been carved out of a federal territory, there was much confusion about the proper course of action. The skeptics furthermore asserted that Congress should have directed and supervised the census taking. And they claimed that the Tennessee constitution had been written in haste and that some of its provisions conflicted with the national constitution. Fortunately for the future of Tennessee, several strong advocates of statehood, such as Thomas Blount (brother of the former territorial governor), James Madison, and Albert Gallatin, expressed themselves quite effectively. This last debater declared simply that once the region had sixty thousand free residents, it automatically became a state.

On May 6, the House agreed to admit Tennessee as the sixteenth state. Rough sledding awaited the proposal in the Senate, however. Meanwhile, Blount and Cocke arrived in Philadelphia, eager to take their seats—a wish denied them. Parliamentary sparring in the Senate, designed to stall Tennessee's admission, predominated. The Senate committee finally insisted that the state could be admitted only after a congressionally supervised census had been taken. This stipulation obviously was designed to keep Tennessee out of the Union long enough to deny it a vote in the forthcoming presidential election. Eventually, however, the two houses of Congress ironed out their differences over the admission of the new state. On May 31, they agreed to accept Tennessee, with the proviso that the state's representation in the House would be reduced from two members to one and that the two senators would have to be reelected. The following day, President Washington signed the statehood bill. Thus June 1 and not March 28 (the day the state legislature convened) became the official birth date of Tennessee.

As soon as he received the good news, Sevier called a special session of the legislature, to meet in Knoxville on July 30. When the legislators convened, the governor announced the well-known fact that Congress formally had admitted Tennessee to statehood, "a circumstance pregnant with every flattering prospect of peace, happiness and opulence to our infant State." The General Assembly reelected Blount and Cocke as U.S. senators and established the mechanism for electing a single representative. The state's voters subsequently chose Andrew Jackson to occupy that post, in recognition of his growing prominence.

Government and Politics: To 1820

John Sevier was the undisputed leader of the new state; after all, he held the governor's office for eleven out of its first thirteen years (1796–1801, 1803–9). The two-year break in his tenure was the result of a constitutional stipulation that no one could serve more than three consecutive terms. In a sense, though, he reigned but did not rule. That is to say, Sevier, like subsequent governors, discovered that the actual powers of the governor were quite limited. Thus there is not much to report about his career as the state's chief executive, other than that he launched the new state smoothly and kept it on course. His long tenure in the governor's chair was due to his reputation as a popular hero, established earlier, and not to his accomplishments as the state's leader.

Controversy erupted from time to time during his terms, almost all of it political in nature. For example, the marriage of convenience between Sevier and Blount, which had enabled each to achieve his dream of high office, did not long endure. Indeed, the two men quickly became rivals again. Blount had built his political base wisely, but he knew that he could not compete against Sevier directly. Many of his staunchest supporters were located in the Mero District, the least populous portion of the state. Meanwhile, Sevier was "boss" of East Tennessee. In the long run, however, Blount's faction overshadowed Sevier's, for the middle area outdistanced the east in both population and wealth. Moreover, men such as James Robertson, Willie Blount, Joseph McMinn, and especially Andrew Jackson lent considerable weight to the Blount side of the rivalry. The Sevier crowd persevered as long as Sevier stayed in office but afterwards quickly diminished.

The first federal census taken in Tennessee was the 1800 poll. It revealed a total population of 106,000 residents, a tripling of population since the 1791 census and an increase of nearly 30,000 since the 1795 census. By the time Sevier left office, more remarkable records had been established. According to the 1810 census, the state's population had increased to 262,000—two and a half times the figure recorded ten years earlier. Most strikingly, Middle Tennessee for the first time had a majority of the population (61 percent), with 160,000 residents. Indeed, of the state's ten most populous counties, the top seven all were in Middle Tennessee, whereas the bottom three all were in the eastern section. More than 35,000 slaves (79 percent of the state's total) were located in the middle counties in 1810, while only about 9,300 were in the east. These statistics shed much light on the economic, as well as political, shifts in the state.

William Blount, while serving as U.S. senator, engaged in a "conspiracy" that caused trouble for him and others and temporarily jeopardized his political career. Stated simply, in late 1796 and early 1797, John Chisholm and Blount concocted a scheme whereby they, aided by British money and military assistance, would attempt to capture Spanish Florida and Louisiana. It was the sort of plot conceived by reckless and extremely ambitious men. In some measure, of course, it reflected the worsening international conditions in the late 1790s, but primarily it stemmed from the plotters' intense desire for acclaim and wealth.

Blount's own carelessness brought about the downfall of the conspiracy. Upon his return to Tennessee in April 1797, he wrote letters to prospective allies, one of whom was James Carey, residing at or near the Tellico Blockhouse. Blount revealed to him various aspects of the planned invasions of Louisiana and Florida but cautioned him against sharing this information. In fact, he admonished Carey to read the letter three times and then burn it. Unfortunately for Blount, Carey did not heed this request; instead, he passed the letter along to others. Eventually the remarkable epistle landed in the hands of David Henley at Knoxville, who gleefully arranged for it to be forwarded to the Adams administration leaders in Philadelphia.

After scrutinizing the document and mapping their strategy, these Adams men exposed Blount publicly. The implication of British involvement in the whole matter restrained them somewhat. The president nevertheless sent a message to the Senate on July 3 that disclosed aspects of the alleged conspiracy. Blount arrived in the chamber in time to hear his April letter to Carey read aloud by the clerk. The scandalized Senate immediately established a committee to investigate. Eventually, the Senate voted to expel Blount—a dubious distinction, to be sure. The House attempted to bring articles of impeachment against Blount but ultimately was thwarted by the ruling that, since he already had been expelled, he could not be impeached.

Although there was a warrant out for his arrest, Blount managed to elude the authorities and escape to Raleigh. He spent August and September there, keeping a low profile and contemplating his uncertain future. Finally, he returned to Knoxville, where something resembling a hero's welcome greeted him. In fact, legislators vowed to re-elect him to the Senate, but Blount wisely declined. The Senate's sergeant-at-arms soon arrived in town to arrest Blount, who entertained him lavishly and sent him back to Philadelphia empty-handed. Meanwhile, Blount's friends and neighbors elected him to a term in the state senate, whose members then elevated him to the post of speaker. Now it seemed that Blount at last had achieved heroic status!

But his death in March 1800 cut short his aspirations for political resurgence. His tattered mantle of leadership now passed to several men, not least of whom was Andrew Jackson. He was the individual most likely to challenge John Sevier; their rivalry had the character of a battle between "young Turks" and the "old guard." In any event, while serving briefly as a U.S. representative, Jackson sought election as major general of the state militia, a more prestigious post. But he had to compete against Sevier's candidate, who eventually won the contest in the fall of 1796. Jackson attacked the governor on the grounds that he had interfered in the major general race; few other men would have dared to challenge Sevier thus. As a sort of consolation prize, the legislature in 1797 chose Jackson to be a U.S. senator; although he accepted the office, he resigned a few months later. Jackson simply was not ready for the national political arena.

It was during his extremely brief tenure as senator, however, that Jackson learned about massive Tennessee land frauds engaged in by some prominent citizens. He reported his information to the North Carolina governor, since the scandal had involved the secretary of state's office there. At this juncture, Jackson did not reveal that John Sevier was implicated in the land frauds. Some critics later charged that only political considerations motivated Jackson's reticence.

Be that as it may, in 1802 the ambitious Jackson once again sought election to the post of major general of the state militia. This time his rival was none other than Sevier himself, now out of the governor's chair for a legally mandated respite. When the vote returns reached Governor Archibald Roane's office, he learned that the two men had the same number of votes. A friend of Jackson and an important figure in the Blount faction, Roane willingly broke the tie in favor of Jackson. Adding to Roane's motivation was Jackson's disclosure to him about Sevier's land fraud activities. Thus Jackson became major general, a post he held in addition to being judge of the state superior court. He was a man on the way up the political ladder.

But Sevier and his allies were not finished yet. In fact, Sevier announced his intention to challenge Roane for the governor's office in 1803. As the race heated up, the somewhat desperate Roane played his trump card: he revealed Sevier's involvement in the land scandal. Jackson also entered the fray when he published a communication in the *Knoxville Gazette* charging Sevier with wrongdoing. This prompted the gubernatorial candidate to respond with a strong denial. Without much difficulty, Sevier defeated Roane, despite the controversy.

There is more to the story, however. About two months after the election, Jackson arrived in Knoxville to conduct court. Sevier and he engaged in a heated exchange of words and then foolishly agreed to a mid-October duel. They indeed had a confrontation of sorts; pistols were drawn, as were canes and swords, but the occasion hardly qualified as a duel. As a consequence of his challenge of Sevier, Jackson's popularity diminished and factional rivalries increased.

In addition to Sevier, three other men occupied the governor's office during the first twenty-five years. (After Sevier's eventual retirement from the post of governor in 1809, he served without distinction in the U.S. House of Representatives until his death.) As already noted, Roane served between Sevier's sets of terms. He lost attempts at reelection in 1803 and 1805; thus Roane has the distinction, if such it be, of being the only one-term governor until Sam Houston's abbreviated career in the late 1820s.

Political leadership shifted to Middle Tennessee in 1809, when Willie Blount, half-brother of the late territorial governor, assumed the governor's

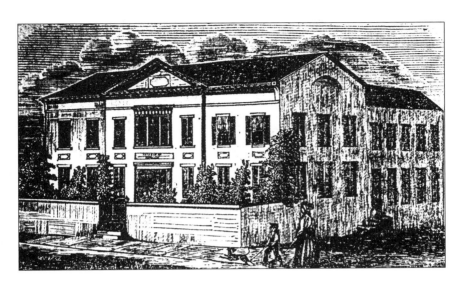

Nashville's Masonic Hall, built in 1819. It also served as the state capitol building. James Patrick, *Architecture in Tennessee, 1768–1897* (Knoxville: University of Tennessee Press, 1981), 80.

chair. Needless to say, he was a staunch member of the Blount faction. He served three terms, during which time he issued a call for Tennessee troops to fight in the War of 1812. After Blount's tenure, leadership returned to East Tennessee with the election in 1815 of Joseph McMinn of Hawkins County. As things turned out, McMinn would be the last governor from that section of the state until the mid-1850s. An ally of the Blount faction, McMinn had to confront economic troubles during his three terms as governor.

Curiously, Tennessee changed state capital locations almost as frequently as it switched governors. (Actually, the state had no *permanent* capital until after 1843.) Knoxville, of course, was the first seat of government, but in 1812 Nashville became the capital. Five years later, state leaders moved the capital back to Knoxville, but it shifted away from East Tennessee, never to return, when it located in Murfreesboro in 1819. In 1826, the government settled in Nashville and never left that city again.

The unusually mobile capital perhaps reflected something of the political and economic transformations occurring in Tennessee during the first three decades of its existence. The 1820 census told part of the story. By that date, the state's population had grown to 423,000—a remarkable 61.5 percent increase over the previous census total. Middle Tennessee swelled by 125,000 during the ten years, a figure contrasting sharply with the anemic increase of 34,000 in East Tennessee. Census takers counted 2,000 residents in the newly opened western third of the state. Middle Tennessee now could boast of having 67.5 percent of the total state population; it never would relinquish its dominance during the nineteenth century.

Public Lands Controversy

The young state wrestled with the complex and frustrating problem of competing land claims. In fact, Tennessee, North Carolina, and the United States found themselves locked in a triangular rivalry. Each asserted rights to lands in Tennessee, but, ironically, after the dispute finally ended in the 1840s, the United States departed without one acre of land or one dollar of proceeds. Actually the fight over public lands commenced in 1790, when Congress accepted North Carolina's cession of its western lands. The U.S. government agreed to honor North Carolina land claims, particularly the military warrants, but it failed to conduct any formal surveying during the territorial period. This neglect set the stage for conflict when Tennessee became a state.

Three years after statehood was achieved, Tennessee declared that Congress had no right to the vacant lands in the state, inasmuch as the national government had not stipulated such when it admitted the state. But in 1801, Congress rejected Tennessee's position, asserting that the vacant lands automatically had been transferred to the federal government. Meanwhile, North Carolina busily promoted the dispersal of military warrants to lands in Tennessee, even publishing rosters of Revolutionary soldiers so that they or their heirs could enter claims. Frightened by the conviction that a greedy North Carolina was grabbing its unappropriated lands, Tennessee sent John Overton to Raleigh in 1804 to seek some sort of compromise. North Carolina agreed to permit Tennessee to perfect all land titles in the state; this in effect would make Tennessee North Carolina's agent. But the next year Congress rejected this arrangement.

The federal government then seized the initiative in the three-way dispute, when Congress enacted the so-called Land Compact of 1806. For several years this measure served as the solution to the rivalry over vacant lands. The law drew a boundary line around all of West Tennessee and also the southwestern corner of Middle Tennessee and specified this gigantic tract of land as the Congressional Reservation. The federal government was to have exclusive authority over land claims inside this vast region. The State of Tennessee would have no rights to lands therein, nor would North Carolina—unless the demand for military warrants could not be satisfied elsewhere in the state. This law essentially acknowledged the national government's surrender of any claims to lands *outside* the Congressional Reservation. The Land Compact bestowed on Tennessee the right to handle all North Carolina land claims (basically an acceptance of the 1804 North Carolina–Tennessee agreement). It also stipulated that Tennessee must set aside one hundred thousand acres in the old Cherokee Reservation in East

Tennessee for the support of two colleges, one in the eastern and one in the middle section of the state. (Eventually East Tennessee College in Knoxville and Cumberland College in Nashville would be the two designated schools.) The Land Compact also required Tennessee to provide 640 acres in every six-mile square (outside the Congressional Reservation) for the benefit of public schools, a proviso blatantly ignored by state authorities.

As a direct consequence of the 1806 congressional legislation, the only area of the state actually thrown on the market was the old Cherokee Reservation region. No new North Carolina land warrants could be located there. Tennessee could put lands up for sale, but nearly all the lands already had been occupied and claimed by squatters, who were granted preemption rights. So any revenues would be quite limited.

In the immediate aftermath of the Land Compact's enactment, the triangular conflict abated. But within a few years, the old rivalry resurfaced, particularly after North Carolina sent surveyors into the Congressional Reservation in 1811 to locate lands. Tennessee quickly nullified these new claims. Soon, however, the state adopted a different strategy; it began to plead with the federal government to open portions of the Congressional Reservation. In 1818 Congress agreed, so that North Carolina's military warrants could be located there. Fast on the heels of this decision was the treaty with the Chickasaws, whereby they surrendered all rights to West Tennessee lands. Therefore, the state passed a land law in 1819 that provided for the systematic surveying of the Congressional Reservation lands and the establishment

---

Student Rules of East Tennessee College

East Tennessee College succeeded Blount College in Knoxville. An 1821 version of the rules of student conduct contains many fascinating points. First, every student had to show "proper tokens of Reverence & obedience to the Faculty." A student would be expelled if found guilty of "Blasphemy, Robbery, fornication, theft, forgery, duelling," or any other serious crime. Likewise, a student faced expulsion if he "shall assault, wound or strike the President, a Professor or tutor, or shall maliciously or designedly break their windows or doors." Punishment awaited those students who quarreled, lied, committed fraud, or wore women's apparel. During specified study hours, every student "shall abstain from hallowing, singing, loud talking, playing on a musical instrument and other noise in the College or the neighborhood." Even during vacation times, students were held accountable for "all vicious, scandalous and immoral conduct."

of land offices. Moreover, squatters residing there prior to September 1819 were granted preemption rights to 160 acres. Thus, tract by tract, North Carolina and Tennessee diminished the national government's hopes for lands there.

Adding to the confusion was the fact that the University of North Carolina was busily staking out claims for lands in Tennessee, especially in the newly opened portion of the Congressional Reservation. This practice actually had begun earlier elsewhere within the state, when North Carolina designated its university as the recipient of all military warrants unclaimed by veterans or their heirs. By 1821, the university had entered claims for nearly four hundred thousand acres in Tennessee. Eventually, the two states resolved their disagreements over these claims by splitting the total amount. There would be something for everyone—except the federal government.

The three-way land rivalry continued for years thereafter, however. In response to further pressure from Tennessee about North Carolina land warrants, Congress in 1823 consented to open additional lands within the Congressional Reservation. But more controversy about the vacant lands ensued. No resolution came until the 1840s, when the U.S. government finally abandoned any hope of marking and selling public lands in Tennessee. In 1841, it appointed the state as its agent for the disposal of lands, but proceeds were to go to the federal treasury. Five years later, however, the national government simply surrendered all of the remaining lands to Tennessee and allowed the state to keep all revenues earned since the 1841 law.

Meanwhile, in the eastern section of the state a different situation prevailed, for no North Carolina warrants could be located there. After extinguishing Indian claims to the region between the Little Tennessee and the Hiwassee Rivers in 1819, the state established the Hiwassee District. Tennessee hoped to sell vacant lands there for two dollars per acre, the minimum federal land price. But in 1823, Congress removed the requirement that public lands in Tennessee must be sold for the federal price; the state then introduced a graduated scale—much to the dismay of some state leaders, who desired sizable revenues from these land sales. Eventually, however, Tennessee reaped over seven hundred thousand dollars from the Hiwassee purchases. It is difficult to calculate the revenues produced from sales of other public lands or to measure the value of lands "lost" to North Carolina warrants. Suffice it to say that the young state fought a good battle; although it did not win against North Carolina, it did get the upper hand with the national government.

Indian Treaties

On the eve of statehood, as discussed in chapter 3, Indian-white relations improved, so that almost all overt hostilities ceased. Thus the young state did not have to deal with continuing red or white atrocities. Indeed, the

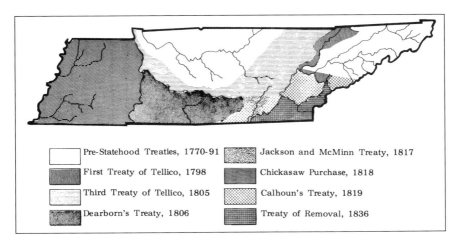

Indian treaties in Tennessee. Robert Corlew, *Tennessee: A Short History,* 2d ed. (Knoxville: University of Tennessee Press, 1990), 148.

federal government actively intervened, as it had not during the territorial period, to promote specific treaties and general peace. From the white perspective, this new approach worked remarkably well; from the Indian perspective, however, the treaties spelled doom. Ultimately, complete removal of the Indians from Tennessee lands would be the outcome.

Questions about public lands and Indian treaties were inextricably linked. Vacant lands, wherever they might be located, legally could not be sold or claimed unless Indian titles to those lands had been extinguished. This stipulation did not stop white squatters from settling on lands, of course, but it did mean that those squatters had no valid claim to them. Hence, during the years of early statehood, whites exerted considerable pressure upon the national government to engage in treaty negotiations in order to eradicate Indian claims.

Despite having been agreed upon in 1791, the Treaty of Holston boundary lines were not actually surveyed and marked until 1797. Upon completion of this project, the Adams administration sent some federal troops into Tennessee to remove white settlers who were residing illegally on Cherokee lands. Needless to say, the state legislature protested strongly. In response to that message, the federal government sent commissioners to entice the Cherokees to cede two additional tracts, both of which were in East Tennessee (one along the Clinch River and the other in the Little Tennessee River area). Cherokee leaders surrendered their claims to these lands in the First Treaty of Tellico, signed in October 1798. Thus white settlement there was legitimized.

As soon as the Jefferson administration came into office, Tennessee leaders engaged in conversations about their desire for more Cherokee cessions. Four years later, in 1805, two negotiators, Return J. Meigs and Daniel Smith, convinced the Cherokees to relinquish their somewhat shaky claims to Middle Tennessee lands north of the Duck River. The document signed was called the Third Treaty of Tellico.

During the following year, these same two negotiators conferred with both Cherokees and Creeks, with a view to extinguishing claims to lands between the Duck River and the state's southern boundary. The federal government was willing to pay the Creeks $14,000 for surrendering their claims. Meanwhile, a delegation of Cherokees went to Washington and dealt directly with Secretary of War Henry Dearborn, who offered them $10,000 for their claims. The resulting agreements were known as Dearborn's Treaty of 1806. White settlers and speculators rushed into all the areas cleared by these treaties.

Two more Cherokee negotiations were carried out subsequently. The federal government appointed Andrew Jackson and Gov. Joseph McMinn as agents to convince the Cherokees to surrender additional lands in Tennessee in exchange for lands west of the Mississippi River. The so-called Jackson-McMinn Treaty of 1817 gave the Cherokees land along the Arkansas and White Rivers in return for their lands in Georgia and in the Sequatchie Valley of Tennessee. Two years later, a Cherokee delegation visited U.S. Secretary of War John C. Calhoun, who demanded that the Indians cede additional eastern lands as compensation for new territories to the west. They agreed to give up three separate tracts, the most important of which was the area between the Little Tennessee and Hiwassee Rivers. This successful negotiation was known as Calhoun's Treaty of 1819.

One of the biggest obstacles to white settlement was the Chickasaw claims to all of West Tennessee. Although squatters pushed into the area and North Carolina land warrants were located there, no one had legal claims until Indian title could be extinguished. Accordingly, the federal government, which had a vested interest in the matter, appointed Andrew Jackson and Kentucky Gov. Isaac Shelby to negotiate with the Chickasaws. Using familiar bribery techniques, Jackson and Shelby convinced the Chickasaw leaders to give up the tribe's claims to the vast West Tennessee region, as well as parts of western Kentucky. The treaty signed in October 1818 required the national government to pay $300,000 to the Chickasaws for their land claims. This was the largest single cession of land in present-day Tennessee by any Indian tribe. The state passed a land law in 1819, and white settlers and speculators flooded into West Tennessee; two counties, Hardin and Shelby, were created that same year.

Thus, by 1819, all Indian claims to Tennessee had been eliminated, except for the extreme southeastern corner of the state, where some Cherokees lived. This was, in the words of historian Ronald Satz, "an island in an engulfing sea of white settlements." For a decade and a half, this small

Cherokee Constitution, 1827

Hoping to maintain sovereignty over their tribal domain, Cherokee leaders endorsed the strategy of following "the white man's road." This culminated in the adoption of the Cherokee constitution—the first such effort by any Indian tribe in North America. Modeled on the U.S. Constitution, the Cherokee document provided for three branches of government. The national legislative body was known as the General Council; among its duties was the selection of the principal chief (the nation's executive) and the three supreme court justices. Free male Cherokees, age eighteen and older, were eligible to vote for members of the General Council.

contingent of Cherokees continued to reside on their "island," while the push for complete Indian removal from the Southeast gathered momentum. The Cherokee nation was torn by rival factions, one (led by John Ross) resisting removal and the other (led by Major Ridge) favoring it. Eventually the federal government compelled the Cherokees to sign a removal treaty in December 1835. Known as the New Echota Treaty, it required the removal of the Cherokees to the West within the next two years. In 1838, President Martin Van Buren sent federal troops to force the Cherokees off the lands in Tennessee and Georgia. Thus began the tragic Trail of Tears. Except for a remnant of Cherokees who escaped into the North Carolina mountains and remained there, all of the Cherokees were expelled from the Southeast. Finally, all Indian inhabitants had been pushed out of Tennessee—a process that had begun with the arrival of the first permanent white settlers nearly seventy years earlier.

Economic Conditions: The Good and the Bad

There is no question that the young state prospered and grew and developed; after years of thriving, however, hard times eventually hit Tennessee. Tennessee's economy could not readily progress without banks, but the state was eleven years old before the first bank was organized and chartered. Thus the early economy was somewhat primitive in nature. Finally, in 1807, the state legislature approved the establishment of the Nashville Bank, to be capitalized at a maximum of $200,000. The state itself was authorized to purchase stock in the bank but chose not to do so. Four years later, the state government chartered the Bank of the State of Tennessee, located in Knoxville. Despite its official-sounding title, the new institution was a private bank with a maximum capitalization of $400,000. This bank opened its doors in 1812, with Hugh Lawson White as president. These were the only two banks in operation in Tennessee prior to the outbreak of the War of 1812.

Indicative of the boom times that commenced immediately upon conclusion of that war, Tennessee in 1815 approved the establishment of three new banks, two in the middle and one in the eastern section. Two years later, the legislature agreed to charter ten more banks, three in East Tennessee and seven in Middle Tennessee. Thus the state had what appeared to be a thriving banking industry—fifteen banks altogether, only two of which had existed prior to the war.

Another potential banking institution was a branch of the Bank of the United States, chartered by Congress in 1816. An interested business community in Nashville attempted to secure a branch of the national bank in 1817 but met resistance from a group who succeeded in imposing a prohibitive tax upon any bank chartered outside of the state. Evidently, leaders of some of the banks did not welcome competition from such a rival. In any event, ten years later, after economic difficulties had come and gone, the state repealed the tax on the national bank, and a branch opened in Nashville.

Middle Tennessee, more than East Tennessee, experienced notable prosperity in the wake of the war, much of it related to the high price of cotton on the national and international market. The economy in the state and elsewhere in the nation rode the crest of inflation. But in 1818, the national bank, fearful of the greatly expanding economy, inaugurated a policy of retrenchment and contraction, primarily by calling in loans around the country. The impact was immediate and devastating: businesses collapsed, cotton prices plummeted, and banks ceased specie payments. This last development allowed banks to protect themselves by refusing to redeem their paper notes with specie (gold or silver). The Panic of 1819 had arrived in full force; unfortunately, it lasted more than that one year.

Felix Grundy, a noted lawyer and former congressman from Nashville, seized the initiative by devising a plan to relieve debtors. Being elected to the state legislature in 1819 as a champion of the suffering citizens, Grundy proposed a "stay law." The legislature quickly enacted his plan. The new law provided simply that no creditor could foreclose or execute judgment against a debtor for a period of two years—unless the creditor was willing to accept depreciated paper money in payment for the debts. There is ample reason to doubt the efficacy of this legislation, given the seriously depressed economy. But there is no doubt that it was reassuring to some residents.

Soon, however, new voices emerged to insist that additional steps be taken by the state government to aid the impoverished. Governor McMinn received petitions from citizens, imploring him to call a special session of the legislature in 1820. The governor agreed to this extraordinary request and summoned the General Assembly in June. As he informed that body, the "distresses of the times are strongly marked with the character of permanence"; therefore the

Built in 1827, the Nashville branch of the Bank of the United States. Detail from 1832 Ayers map of Nashville. Tennessee Historical Society, Nashville.

government should "devise measures of alleviation." Admitting that there were leaders who opposed any action by the government, McMinn neverthe-less reminded the legislators that thousands looked to them for assistance; they must not be abandoned "in their affliction." The governor went on record in favor of a proposed state bank (or loan office).

As soon as word of such a proposal circulated, certain leaders opposed it. Chief among them were Andrew Jackson and his neighbor and friend, Edward Ward. As hard-money men, they opposed the state bank or loan office because its notes would be legal tender. Moreover, they had no faith in the plan to support the proposed bank with revenues derived from the sale of public lands in the Hiwassee District (a not unreasonable skepticism). Jackson and Ward also regretted that there was excessive concern for debtors but not much for creditors. They scoffed at the idea that issuing paper notes somehow could cure an economy already suffering (in their opinion) from too much paper currency.

All these arguments notwithstanding, the legislature enacted the state bank proposal in 1820. It authorized the bank to make loans at 6 percent interest (though few persons could take advantage of that), to issue $1 million in bank notes, and to receive state funds on deposit. Heads of other banks in the state immediately criticized their new competitor and steadfastly refused to accept notes issued by the state bank. Nevertheless, the new bank opened its doors and remained in business until its enabling legislation was repealed twelve years later. How significant a role it played in the recovery of the statewide economy is still a matter for debate.

Amid political and economic turmoil, the state's highest court in 1821 ruled the "stay law" unconstitutional. It declared the law to be an impairment of the obligation of contracts and thus repugnant to the state constitution, because it suspended the execution of judgments against debtors. Two years later, at Grundy's urging, the legislature defiantly reenacted the law—a somewhat empty gesture, given the rebounding economy. By 1825, the state began to experience the return of prosperity, and banks soon resumed specie payment. The night of economic travail was over.

The War of 1812

After several years of mounting tensions and hostilities and failed diplomacy between Great Britain and the United States, the time for war arrived. Congress, including all members from Tennessee, responded enthusiastically to President Madison's June 1812 request for a war declaration, despite the fact that the nation was wholly unprepared for war. Earlier that same year, Tennessee literally had been shaken by the famous New Madrid earthquake that struck the northwestern corner of the state. In fact, aftershocks still were occurring when the nation girded itself for war against Britain.

Tennessee residents had not been affected directly by the British orders in council, the impressment of sailors, or the attacks upon American ships on the high seas. Indeed, if this was, strictly speaking, a maritime war, there was little to stir the bellicose spirits of Tennesseans. But once they perceived it as partly an Indian war, white citizens agitated for action. Like many other Americans, they also deemed the affronts to the nation's honor and sovereignty sufficient justification for war.

In his September 1812 messages to the legislature, Gov. Willie Blount first commended the thousands of Tennesseans who had volunteered to

New Madrid Earthquake

Between December 1811 and March 1812, tremendous earthquakes struck the Mississippi Valley region; and aftershocks continued for many months thereafter. Of these earthquakes, the most intense were three that hit within a two-month period beginning in December. The third one, which measured 8.8 on the Richter scale—the strongest ever recorded in North America—had its epicenter at New Madrid, Missouri. It left its imprint upon Tennessee in the form of Reelfoot Lake, in the state's northwestern corner. The force of the earthquake either created or greatly enlarged the lake. While these quakes caused incredible destruction, they did not actually kill very many people—thanks to the sparse population in the region.

serve their state and country. Then he authorized Andrew Jackson, major general of the state militia, to assemble 2,500 men for immediate service. But his next official communication to the legislature focused upon alleged Creek atrocities recently committed against Tennessee residents. He sought money for the purchase of arms and other equipment. Thus it quickly began to appear that the War of 1812 would be partly an Indian war, a scenario familiar to many Tennesseans. The following September, the legislature passed a law authorizing more Tennessee troops and the expenditure of up to $300,000—all for the purpose of repelling an anticipated invasion of the state by the Creek Indians.

Meanwhile, in the fall of 1812, Governor Blount, in response to requests from the Madison administration, had asked Jackson to call out troops and have them ready to go to New Orleans by December. In early January 1813, Jackson and his Tennessee troops left Nashville for Natchez. Shortly after arriving there, however, the secretary of war informed Jackson that the New Orleans campaign had been scuttled and told him to disband his troops and send them back to Tennessee. Although greatly disappointed, Jackson had little choice but to follow these orders. Eventually he accompanied the troops back to Nashville and in the process gained their great admiration. Along the way, they began to call him "Old Hickory"; this sobriquet in time would become one of the most famous in American history.

For the moment, both the general and his troops believed that they would not share in the glories of war. Other Tennessee soldiers, however, sought involvement in the conflict in other locales. For example, Col. John Williams took a contingent of East Tennessee troops to Georgia for a proposed attack upon Florida, but it never materialized and they returned home. Gen. James Winchester led soldiers northward to participate in an invasion of Canada. In early January 1813, however, taken by surprise by British and Indian troops, the Tennesseans surrendered.

With their attack upon Fort Mims in Alabama in August 1813, the Creeks created the Indian war that Tennesseans had anticipated and even desired. This offered the best hope for military adventure and action. Governor Blount immediately authorized Jackson to raise 2,500 militia and volunteers in Middle Tennessee and Gen. John Cocke to raise a like number in East Tennessee. In early October 1813, Jackson took command of his "army," gathered at Fayetteville, and moved south into Alabama. A month later his troops had their first significant engagements with the Creeks, first at Tallushatchee and next at Talladega.

By the end of the year, despite successes, Jackson was short of supplies and men. Governor Blount even advised him to abandon his Alabama station and return to Tennessee. Jackson responded, however, with a strong and persuasive letter to the governor, urging more soldiers and supplies. Blount agreed and, with War Department backing, called for 2,500 new troops. By March 1814, Jackson had nearly 5,000 men under his command in Alabama. He took them to Horseshoe Bend to defeat the Creeks for the final time. Some have labeled the battle there one of the most significant of the War of 1812. Suffice it to say that Jackson eventually returned to Nashville to a hero's celebration.

The Natchez Trace

The famous road that stretched from Nashville to Natchez, Mississippi, was a significant conveyor of prominent persons, as well as murderous thieves. The mere mention of such men as Joseph Hare, Samuel Mason, and Wiley ("Little") Harpe—notorious criminals who stalked the Trace—stirred fear within all persons contemplating a trip there. But a fearless Methodist circuit rider, Lorenzo Dow, defiantly journeyed the Trace to proclaim salvation.

Certainly one of the best-known persons to meet death along that road was Meriwether Lewis, governor of Upper Louisiana and formerly a great explorer of the West. Lewis died at Grinder's Stand in October 1809, while en route from St. Louis to Washington, D.C. Reliable accounts vow that Lewis committed suicide, while other versions point to murder. Thus was another mystery added to the many that hover over the Natchez Trace.

Surrender of Red Eagle to Gen. Andrew Jackson in 1814. John Frost, *A Pictorial Biography of Andrew Jackson* (1860), 248.

But, of course, the war was not actually over, although the Indian part of it was. Commissioned a major general in the U.S. Army in the spring, Jackson returned to battle; he occupied Mobile in August and captured Pensacola in November. From there he went to New Orleans (his original destination back in 1813) to seek and find his greatest military glory. His victory over the British in January 1815 was amazing. The war was over.

Religious Stirrings

In the early days of statehood, there were wars, rumors of wars, economic panics, and political campaigns; but there was more. As a matter of fact, Tennessee became one of the most prominent scenes of the great outpouring of religious enthusiasm sometimes called the Second Great Awakening.

Immediately prior to this sudden development, however, the state was known in religious circles for its declining church membership and general indifference to religious matters.

At the very end of the 1790s, however, an outbreak of revivalism occurred in both Kentucky and Tennessee. A Presbyterian divine, the Rev. James McGready, pastored three small congregations in Logan County, Kentucky. Beginning in the summer of 1799, his members responded to his preaching with unusual emotional reactions. Similar responses next happened in a Presbyterian congregation in Sumner County, Tennessee, led by the Rev. William McGee. The fires of religious enthusiasm began to spread throughout regions of both states and would continue to do so for several years.

The year 1800 marked the beginning of a new century. It also witnessed

Typical scene at a frontier revival camp meeting. Archives and Special Collections, DePauw University, Greencastle, Indiana.

a special eruption of revivalist activities. A four-day sacramental meeting in June at McGready's Red River church attracted McGee and his brother, John McGee, a Methodist preacher. After three days of exhortation and singing, the congregation produced an emotional scene of almost uncontrollable weeping followed by shouting. This became a familiar pattern the next month, when these same clergymen conducted a meeting with another of McGready's congregations. In September, the epidemic swept through Sumner County at a sacramental service at Desha's Creek. In October, over one thousand persons attended a five-day revival at Drake's Creek. Adding to the excitement there was the presence of three prominent Methodist clergymen, among them Bishop Francis Asbury. In his journal, he referred to this meeting thus: "Fires blazing here and there dispelled the darkness and the shouts of the redeemed captives, and the cries of precious souls struggling into life, broke the silence of midnight."

The development of the camp meeting was a natural outgrowth of the revival movement, for a way simply had to be found to accommodate the huge crowds. The great outdoors became the surrogate cathedrals of frontier religion. So, when five thousand people attended, as they did at some of the meetings, there was room for them. Doubtless the greatest manifestation of religious enthusiasm occurred at Cane Ridge in Kentucky in 1801, when twenty-five thousand persons participated. Even much more modest numbers presented problems as well as opportunities. The preachers had difficulty managing such throngs. Whiskey dealers and prostitutes attended in order to traffic in their usual wares, and vandals often wreaked havoc at the site. Needless to say, in such environments much wickedness took place on the periphery, suggesting how thin was the line between religious enthusiasm and baser desires. More than one student of these camp meetings has maintained that they were as much a social as a religious institution. It does not require much imagination to comprehend that the socializing appeal of these large gatherings was tremendous.

Whether at organized camp meetings or crowded into church buildings, many people responded to the stirring atmosphere. They frequently did so in peculiarly physical ways, one of the hallmarks of that remarkable harvest time. Sometimes labeled "acrobatic Christianity," the reactions included falling, jerking, rolling, running, and even barking and laughing. Some preachers measured the success of the revivals by the number of persons who "fell" during the services. At some meetings, it appeared that a giant invisible force knocked people off their feet. On other occasions, attendees were seized by jerking sensations; it is said that some twenty thousand persons were tossed about at the Cane Ridge revival. One observer reported that the jerking caused the long, unbraided hair of strong women "to lash and crack like a whip, perfectly audible at a distance of twenty feet." Barking or laughing (the "holy laugh") broke out at some revivals as manifestations of religious enthusiasm. Such scenes were no place for contemplative or reticent souls.

Cumberland Presbyterians

The frontier revivals spawned divisions within the Presbyterian denomination. The Cumberland Presbytery (which encompassed Middle Tennessee), organized in 1802, quickly accommodated itself to the revivals by lowering the educational requirements for clergy. Over a period of several years, however, the Kentucky Synod and the General Assembly of the national church challenged such actions of the Cumberland Presbytery. Finally, in February 1810, three clergymen—Finis Ewing, Samuel King, and Samuel McAdow—met at McAdow's home in Dickson County to chart a new course by wholeheartedly embracing the revivalism of the day. Their actions resulted in the creation of the Cumberland Presbyterian Church, which enjoyed rapid growth.

As the experience of McGready and the McGees suggests, Methodists and Presbyterians cooperated in the early phase of revivalism. To do so, they had to avert their theological eyes, but the prospect of adding substantial numbers to the church rolls was a mighty persuader. The Methodists were ideally suited for the rough-hewn approach to religious faith. They embraced a free-will theology (Arminianism) well suited to revival preaching, and they had an organizational structure tailor-made for that environment. With bishops, superintendents, and, most of all, circuit riders, the followers of John Wesley were well equipped to evangelize the remote areas of Tennessee and other states. Bishop Asbury blazed an impressive trail and stamped Methodism upon the landscape.

After the initial wave of religious excitement, Presbyterians began to have doubts about their participation. After all, most of them still clung tenaciously to Calvinism, a theology that focused upon the "elect" and predestination. This simply would not fit the revival mode. Moreover, they worried about maintaining the educational qualifications of their clergy, a matter of little or no concern to Methodists. Consequently, Presbyterians steadily withdrew from the front lines of revivalism. As a matter of fact, a schism developed within the family: revival versus anti-revival factions arose. The latter group prevailed, but not before the division resulted in the establishment in 1810 of a heretical Cumberland Presbytery, which would become a separate denomination.

Baptists were slow to jump on religion's revival train. This puzzling reticence was related in part to their strong sectarian tendencies; they were uncomfortable sharing religious activities with other groups. Their answer was to stage camp meetings and revivals of their own. Their lack of ecclesiastical structure gave them tremendous freedom to participate in any way they wished, although their fierce congregationalism often precluded cooperating even with fellow Baptists. These early Baptists were more tinged with Calvinism than they later would admit to; therefore, some theological accommodation had to be worked out. But once fully engaged in the revivalism of the day, the Baptists benefited numerically, if not as much as the Methodists. The religious stirrings in Tennessee in those early days were impressive; the harvest and the laborers were more than sufficient.

Politics in the 1820s

Many competing forces, not least of which were the economic dislocations caused by the Panic of 1819 and the presidential ambitions of Andrew Jackson, ushered in a decade of particularly noteworthy political activity. The established tradition of conducting politics through factional rivalries rather than party competition continued through the 1820s. The old Sevier faction had disappeared, but the Blount contingent persevered. The latter group dominated the political scene, especially the governor's office, occupied by Willie Blount and Joseph McMinn, and therefore stayed organized and united. Gradually, however, John Overton took charge of the Blount faction and prepared it for competition in the 1820s. He soon had the valuable assistance of such men as John H. Eaton and William B. Lewis. As they assumed leadership roles, the group became known as the Overton faction.

After he left the governor's office in 1809, Sevier exerted less and less influence in state politics, which partially explains the demise of his faction. In any event, on the eve of the new decade of the 1820s, a new faction emerged. The principal leader was Andrew Erwin, who, like John Overton, was a wealthy and prominent Middle Tennessean. Erwin gathered around him incipient leaders such as Newton Cannon, John Bell, and John Williams. Most important, they became the champions of William Carroll and as such rode into power with his election as governor in 1821. These events eventually set the stage for Jackson's entry into national politics.

First, however, the governor's race demanded attention. Since McMinn could not run again in 1821, the campaign was wide open. The Erwin crowd wasted no time in pushing forward the candidacy of Carroll. Like Jackson, he enjoyed military fame; indeed, he had been Jackson's vital assistant in the Creek conflict and also at the Battle of New Orleans, and for several years he had served as major general of the state militia. Thus, he was an attractive contender in Tennessee circles. His unsuccessful business ventures proved to be no liability in the campaign; in fact, they may have enabled him to identify with people who were suffering from the effects of the economic panic. The Overton faction placed Edward Ward in the gubernatorial contest. Ward, Jackson's friend and neighbor, was a wealthy planter and had served two terms in the state senate. Jackson, torn between supporting his personal friend and backing his former military aide, opted for Ward.

Once the campaign commenced, it became apparent that there were few differences between Ward and Carroll. Neither man, oddly enough, endorsed the state's stay law or the new state bank. Carroll did insist upon the resumption of specie payments by the banks, hardly a radical position. The Erwin faction understandably placed much emphasis upon Carroll's military career. The strategy worked, for he easily defeated Ward, carrying all but two counties in the state. Inaugurated in 1821, Carroll held the governor's chair until 1835—with a two-year break in 1827–29. His twelve years as governor were quite significant, as he launched a progressive reform agenda including criminal code revision, a new state penitentiary, and an insane asylum.

Sam Houston was the man who interrupted Carroll's long tenure as governor. Constitutionally prohibited from running in 1827, Carroll pushed Houston's candidacy. Some later claimed that Carroll's support rested upon Houston's agreement to serve only one term. Be that as it may, Houston, a military hero from the Creek campaign, major general of the militia, and a U.S. representative, had no trouble defeating two rivals in the governor's race. Strange as it may seem, Houston enjoyed support from both Jackson and Carroll, a fact that disturbed the Overton and the Erwin factions. Houston's brief career as governor was a troubled one in several respects; but when his marriage to Eliza Allen disintegrated a few months after their wedding in January 1829, Houston suddenly announced his resignation as governor and mysteriously headed west to live among the Indians for a time. The remaining months of his gubernatorial term were filled by the speaker of the senate.

The Houston drama played itself out after other notable events in the political realm already had taken place. Andrew Jackson was the star of the production. The Overton people had begun to search for avenues of political enhancement after being shut out of the governor's office by Carroll's victory in 1821. They naturally turned to Jackson; he was their main hope. But at first they were not sure exactly how to utilize him to best advantage. Some of the Overton crowd began to talk boldly of a presidential candidacy for Jackson, for certainly that would benefit them on the state level. In 1822, the state legislature unanimously recommended "Old Hickory" for the presidency, thereby launching the strategy.

Jackson, it was believed, needed more political visibility. Emboldened by favorable public reaction to the idea of his presidential candidacy, the Overton leaders embraced the strategy of having the legislature choose Jackson as U.S. senator in 1823. Such a plan elicited quite a negative reception from John Williams, the strongly entrenched occupant of that post at the time. Almost in desperation, Eaton and Lewis pushed forward Jackson's name for senator at the session of the legislature, an action that produced "great uneasiness and alarm among the more timid members" (as Lewis noted). A messenger immediately rode from Murfreesboro to Jackson's home to notify him and to urge him to attend the session in person. Jackson consented, reaching the capital on the eve of the vote taking. By a ten-vote margin, the legislature chose Jackson over Williams. A few weeks later, he and Eaton, his senatorial colleague, departed for Washington.

Jackson simply marked time in the Senate chambers (he had done so back in 1797 as well), for greater things awaited him. In 1824, the presidential quest began. Unfortunately for Jackson, the field was quite crowded, with three other contenders: John Quincy Adams, Henry Clay, and William H. Crawford. Nevertheless, he acquitted himself remarkably well; America seemed ready for a military hero again. Indeed, Jackson emerged in November with the most electoral votes, but inasmuch as the vote was split among four rivals, no one had an electoral majority. Therefore, the House was empowered to make the decision. It did so in February 1825, when it chose Adams. Although greatly disappointed, Jackson accepted the verdict of Congress; that is, until Adams appointed Clay as his secretary of state. This "corrupt bargain" and intrigue stung Old Hickory as few things previously had done; hence he vowed to settle the score with those two men in 1828.

By the end of the decade of the 1820s, Tennessee stood poised to move into the national arena. The years of early statehood had slipped away; recognition and even prominence awaited a state that had come of age.

Suggested Readings

Abernethy, Thomas P. *From Frontier to Plantation in Tennessee: A Study in Frontier Democracy.* Chapel Hill, N.C., 1932.

Goodstein, Anita Shafer. *Nashville, 1780–1860: From Frontier to City.* Gainesville, Fla., 1989.

Norton, Herman A. *Religion in Tennessee, 1777–1945.* Knoxville, Tenn., 1981.

Parks, Joseph H. *Felix Grundy: Champion of Democracy.* Baton Rouge, La., 1949.

Posey, Walter B. *Frontier Mission: A History of Religion West of the Southern Appalachians to 1861.* Lexington, Ky., 1966.

Remini, Robert V. *Andrew Jackson and the Course of the American Empire, 1767–1821.* New York, 1977.

Satz, Ronald N., *Tennessee's Indian Peoples: From White Contact to Removal, 1540–1840.* Knoxville, Tenn., 1979.

5

Antebellum Politics, Economy, and Society

DURING THE ANTEBELLUM ERA—the forty years that preceded the outbreak of the Civil War—Tennessee developed at a remarkable pace. The state's population multiplied, its economy burgeoned, its culture matured, and its politics blossomed and gained national recognition. In these years Tennesseans cast off their frontier status, steered their state out of the national backwaters, and moved toward the mainstream of nineteenth-century America.

Expansion and modernization were not the only striking features of the state's political, economic and social experience in the antebellum period. Those years also saw the essentially "southern" character of the state and its people evolve and solidify. Meanwhile, intrastate sectionalism became even more pronounced, as East, Middle and West Tennessee followed paths of development that sometimes were similar but more often were disparate.

Politics proved to be one of the most significant arenas of the state's life. When Andrew Jackson was elected president in 1828, Tennessee achieved a national prominence it had not known previously. Indeed, some would say that its "golden age" of politics commenced in, and lasted through, most of the antebellum period. Jackson's sweeping victory over incumbent John Quincy Adams was quite impressive in the nation and particularly so in Tennessee. The campaign attracted 46,000 of the state's voters to the polls—approximately 50 percent of the eligible electorate (only 2,000 voted against Old Hickory). Four years later, when Jackson easily defeated Henry Clay both in Tennessee and the nation, only about 29 percent of the state's voters exercised their voting rights. Although more than one interpretation is possible, this low turnout may suggest a waning of enthusiasm for Jackson in his home state. Even so, there is no doubt that his presidency had a definite impact, not only upon the nation at large (as is well known) but also upon political developments in Tennessee.

A New Constitution

One cannot fully appreciate Tennessee's antebellum political world without taking into account the constitution devised in 1834. One of the hallmarks of the Jacksonian period across the nation was the adoption of new state constitutions. It comes as no surprise, then, that Tennessee joined this movement.

Prior to 1834, there had been several efforts to push the state toward constitutional revision. Statewide votes were held in 1819 and 1831 on the matter of calling a constitutional convention. But both times the voters rejected such a proposition. Immediately after the General Assembly reviewed the returns from the 1831 vote, however, it decreed that there should be another vote two years hence, in conjunction with the gubernatorial and legislative campaigns. The third time worked. Nearly 54,000 voters favored the call, which exceeded the required one-half of the total statewide gubernatorial vote. As one historian pointed out years ago, the valleys of northeastern Tennessee and the Cumberland Basin refused to endorse the call, but the mountainous and hilly districts supported it heavily, as did almost all of West Tennessee. In response to the favorable vote, the legislature called for an election, to be held in March 1834, to choose delegates to the convention.

Afterwards, on May 19, the sixty chosen delegates, nearly two-thirds of whom were farmers and almost one-third lawyers, gathered in Nashville. These men completed their task fourteen weeks later and adjourned on August 30 (the 1796 convention had lasted only four weeks).

Not surprisingly, revision of the taxation clause was the principal focus of conflict at the convention. Both West Tennessee and the eastern third of the state strongly advocated taxation reform. Eventually the delegates from these areas prevailed, as the convention agreed to switch from the equal taxation provision of the 1796 document to the requirement that "all property shall be taxed according to its value."

Complaints about the state's court system caused the delegates to focus upon that part of the old constitution. Eventually they provided for a state supreme court with three justices, one from each section of the state. Concerning the legislative branch, the delegates decided to apportion representation on the basis of *qualified voters*, rather than taxable inhabitants, as the first constitution had done. Moreover, the convention removed property requirements from the list of qualifications for legislators and the governor.

In like manner, the delegates eliminated property holding from suffrage requirements, thereby widening the franchise (as did most states in that period). But the voting clause got caught up in racial issues when certain delegates argued for disfranchising free black males. After a frequently interrupted debate that stretched over several weeks, the convention supported a proposal to insert the all-important word *white* in the franchise clause. By that action, the delegates regrettably narrowed suffrage rights.

Closely related to these deliberations was the topic of emancipation of slaves. The convention would have preferred to ignore the subject, but the arrival of some thirty different petitions (memorials) from sixteen counties, seeking gradual emancipation, forced the issue. The convention president appointed a special three-man committee to handle the emancipation question.

In mid-June, that committee's completed report eloquently articulated the view that slavery was a necessary evil, not a positive good. "To prove it to be a great evil," confessed the committee, "is an easy task, but to tell how that evil can be removed, is a question that the wisest heads and most benevolent hearts have not been able to answer in a satisfactory manner." The committee subscribed to the belief that the colonization of slaves, the "door of hope," was the best way to provide for the eventual abolition of slavery.

But a group of emancipation advocates charged that the committee's report was subversive of republican principles and also at variance with the Scriptures. They concluded their appeal with these poignant words: "Viewing the report (as we do) a kind of apology for slavery, we have thus raised against it our feeble testimony, in discharge of a duty we owe, not only to the memorialists, but to that degraded people whose voice cannot be heard here." One month before adjournment, the convention voted that the General Assembly should "have no power to pass laws for the emancipation of slaves." Remarkably, the vote was close: thirty-one favored the clause, while twenty-seven opposed it. The convention's decision in 1834 was one of those poignant "might-have-beens" of history.

On a far different matter, the delegates addressed the long-deferred question of the state's permanent capital. Nearly forty years after statehood, Tennessee still had only a "temporary" capital. At the convention, supporters of both Nashville and Murfreesboro vied for designation as the seat of government. Proponents of the latter city boasted that it lacked "those sources of amusement" that would "distract the Legislators from strict attention to their duty." The delegates weaseled out of the matter by stipulating in the new constitution that the legislature in 1843 should make the final decision about the permanent capital.

Completing its tasks, the convention provided for a statewide plebiscite on the constitution. In March 1835, 71 percent of those voting favored the new document. Of the state's sixty-four counties, only four (Davidson, Robertson, Smith, and Williamson) opposed it. Thus the stage was set for the political excitement that was to mark the era.

Political Rebellion in the 1830s

Tennessee, the home of President Jackson, seemed a most unlikely place for rebellion against him, yet it happened. The Nashville business community clearly was unhappy with the president's veto of the national bank recharter. While there was support in Tennessee (led by Governor Carroll) for Van Buren as Jackson's vice president in 1832, there seemed to be little sentiment in favor of Van Buren's future political plans. That is to say, some Tennessee leaders could not be persuaded to permit Jackson to place Van Buren in the presidency without challenge or competition.

It soon became apparent that the anti-Jackson element would attach itself

Hugh Lawson White, prominent political leader. Portrait attributed to Ralph E. W. Earl. Tennessee Historical Society Collection, Tennessee State Museum, Nashville.

to the prospective presidential candidacy of Sen. Hugh Lawson White. Long known as a supporter of Jackson and yet also known as a fairly independent political leader, White enjoyed immense popularity in the state (second only to Jackson himself, some claimed). The anti-Jacksonians shrewdly calculated that pushing White as a presidential contender, rather than directly attacking Jackson, was a much safer and more productive approach. Moreover, such a strategy appealed to local pride, inasmuch as Tennesseans readily embraced the notion of having one of their own seek the presidency.

There were other matters to attend to before the year of the presidential campaign arrived. For example, there was the rivalry between John Bell and James K. Polk for speaker of the national House of Representatives. Both were representatives from Tennessee, and both were Jackson men. Bell won the 1834 contest but had to court anti-Jackson congressmen to garner enough votes. In the 1835 competition, Polk, now clearly recognized as Jackson's preferred choice, defeated Bell.

Between these two speakership elections, the Tennessee congressional delegation gathered in Washington in December 1834 to determine its stance on the future presidential race. These men discussed whether they should endorse White as a candidate at this time. Division was evident within the ranks, but the majority signed a document in support of White. Such an endorsement on the eve of the 1835 gubernatorial election year helped launch the "revolt" against Jackson in his home state. That election, coupled with the presidential campaign that followed a year later, ignited the flames of political rebellion and solidified anti-Jacksonian power in Tennessee.

A scramble to secure gubernatorial candidates took place early in 1835. Newton Cannon, who had been lukewarm or hostile toward Jackson, announced his candidacy on a pro-White platform. West H. Humphreys of West Tennessee, a minor contender, likewise declared his preference for White. Meanwhile, the Jackson crowd, shaken by the developments thus far, wondered who would carry its banner. Finally, Governor Carroll stepped forward. But his candidacy was shrouded in a legal haze, because he actually was seeking a *fourth* consecutive (and hence not constitutionally permissible) term. His attempt to finesse the question by asserting that he was running for a *first* term under the new constitution proved unsuccessful.

Although the matter of Carroll's eligibility continued to bother voters, the major issue was the forthcoming U.S. presidential election. Indeed, the guber-

---

Nashville Union

Political parties in Tennessee depended heavily upon their partisan newspapers for survival and success. Therefore, it was of great concern to state Democrats in the 1830s that a strong paper be established in Nashville. Supported by several prominent party leaders, James K. Polk put together a financial package, as well as a search for an editor, and in 1835 launched the *Nashville Union*. But both the paper's finances and its editor, Samuel H. Laughlin, were in shaky condition most of the time.

Democratic leaders finally forced Laughlin out in 1837, only to deal with two short-term editors in the next year and a half. In desperation, Polk, eager to secure an effective editor in time for his gubernatorial campaign, commenced yet another search. By the end of 1838, he had secured J. George Harris, who arrived in time to be of tremendous value in the 1839 campaign and in subsequent elections.

natorial candidacies of Carroll and Cannon (to say nothing of Humphreys) became lost in a whirlwind of anxiety about the national race. Cannon proudly carried the White banner, while Carroll somewhat reluctantly held aloft the Van Buren flag. On election day in August, the voters showed that the rebellion against Jackson had arrived. More than eighty-nine thousand voters went to the polls, a figure that accounted for between 78 and 80 percent of the eligible voters, a remarkably high percentage. Cannon won the election but did not receive a majority, since Humphreys's candidacy split the anti-Jackson vote. Cannon carried both East and West Tennessee, an alliance that would become fixed in subsequent statewide elections. Carroll experienced the first political defeat of his long and effective career.

Hard on the heels of the governor's race came the presidential campaign. The national Democratic convention chose Van Buren, just as Jackson wanted. On the other hand, the national anti-Jackson forces, now labeling themselves the Whig Party, followed the dubious strategy of having three regional presidential candidates—with Hugh Lawson White from the South. The state legislature formally endorsed him.

The presidential race of 1836 was something of a rerun of the previous year's gubernatorial campaign. Since anti-Jackson leaders in the state were not yet calling themselves Whigs, their ploy was to insist that White was still a true Jacksonian. Needless to say, the president ranted and raved about this shaky assertion; in fact, he actively campaigned in his home state in hopes of averting an embarrassing defeat. Truth to tell, there were no major differences between White and Van Buren. But the pro-White campaigners intimated that their candidate might be more inclined toward government support of economic activities—an appealing strategy in certain business circles and in parts of the state already favorably disposed toward public backing of internal improvements.

Eventually, the emboldened White leaders directly challenged Jackson. They could not avoid it, because the Van Buren campaigners talked more and more about Old Hickory's accomplishments and less and less about Van Buren. Thus, John Bell and others began to focus upon Jackson's interference in state politics; he was, they declared, attempting to dictate to citizens how they must vote in November. Why, they shrewdly asked, would he push Van Buren upon the voters instead of throwing his support to native son White? This approach struck a responsive chord among many Tennessee voters.

On election day, White swept all three sections of the state and captured an impressive 58 percent of the statewide vote, the highest percentage of any presidential contender from that point forward until after the Civil War. Although White carried the state, he did not succeed nationally, where Van Buren was victorious. Tennessee had boldly rebelled against Jackson and his party and would continue to do so.

Hardly had the smoke cleared from the presidential battle than state political leaders geared up for the 1837 gubernatorial race; there was no rest for the weary. The incumbent Governor Cannon announced that he would seek reelection; meanwhile, Democrats, stunned by two consecutive state-wide defeats, looked in vain for a contender to run against Cannon. Finally, Robert Armstrong, Nashville postmaster, either decided to take the plunge or was pushed into the icy waters of political competition.

By comparison with the two immediately preceding statewide races, the 1837 canvass was quiet; indeed, the two competitors did not even campaign actively. Cannon had several advantages from the outset and never lost them. For example, the Panic of 1837 hit the country in the spring months; banks across the state immediately suspended specie payments. Naturally, Van Buren and the Democratic Party received blame for the economic turmoil. Moreover, despite his popularity based upon prior military service, Armstrong was a weak candidate. Indeed, one of his *friends* declared that Armstrong "cannot speak, and is radically defective in intelligence." With friends like this, Armstrong did not need enemies.

Amazingly enough, hordes of voters swarmed to the polls, despite the lackluster, low-key campaign. The election attracted approximately 80 to 82 percent of the eligible voters. Cannon won reelection easily; he carried all three sections of the state and garnered nearly 61 percent of the total vote.

In the aftermath of such a defeat for the Democrats, there was only one person in the state who might be able to rescue the Jacksonian party from utter ruin. That person was James K. Polk. Therefore, a year before the 1839

Sarah Childress Polk

A member of a wealthy and prominent Murfreesboro family, Sarah Childress married James K. Polk on New Year's Day, 1824. From that point on, she was vital to his political career. During Polk's years in Congress, Sarah earned a reputation as a lively and successful hostess. When her husband sought the governor's office, she managed his campaigns by arranging his schedule of speaking engagements, mailing out political literature, handling his correspondence, and, of course, sending him information and encouragement through her letters. When Polk became president of the United States, Sarah took on the immense responsibility of running the White House. Moreover, she routinely read through newspapers each day and marked the articles that she thought the president should read. Her good political instincts and admirable social graces were an impressive combination.

governor's race opened, Polk put himself forward as the Democratic standard-bearer. Polk knew that, should the state become an unredeemable bastion of Whig strength (and it was on the verge of becoming exactly that), he had no real political future. His announcement stirred hope and excitement within the state's Democratic ranks, and the party quickly united behind him.

Governor Cannon, unmindful of certain Whigs' lingering discontent with him, declared his candidacy for a third term. Cannon more than met his match in this race, however, for Polk insisted upon a vigorous and demanding four-month campaign. They canvassed the state, sometimes together and at other times separately. By mid-June, Polk already had traveled some 1,300 miles by horseback through thirty-seven counties in Middle and East Tennessee. He had given forty-three scheduled speeches (usually two to three hours each) and numerous impromptu ones. Polk understandably suffered from fatigue, but no more than his horse, which became so exhausted that it had to be replaced. After a very brief respite at Columbia, Polk resumed his extensive electioneering. Greatly assisting him was his wife, Sarah Childress Polk, who ran the campaign headquarters out of their home. Just three days before the election, Polk met up with Cannon at Rogersville. After a somewhat rowdy exchange between the Whig and Democratic camps, Polk bought a barrel of whiskey, had it rolled out into the street, and cracked it open for his followers. Once again he demonstrated some of his skills as a campaigner—much to the consternation of Cannon and the Whigs.

At great risk, considering Van Buren's low rating among Tennesseans, Polk declared himself in favor of Van Buren's reelection as president in 1840. He framed the issue so as to try to force Cannon to come out in support of Henry Clay, a man with even less support in the state than Van Buren. But Cannon continually refused to endorse Clay and stuck with the strategy of simply stating that he would not support Van Buren.

On election day, Polk emerged triumphant with 51.1 percent of the statewide vote—an astounding reversal of the 1837 outcome. The joint canvass obviously had stirred the voters, for 89 percent of them voted. Polk halted the Whig juggernaut in its tracks and rescued his party. In the process, of course, he enhanced his own future.

Whigs' Decade: The 1840s

As it turned out, Polk's victory was an aberration, for it had been preceded by three consecutive Whig (anti-Jackson) successes and would be followed by four more. The Whig presidential victory in 1840, both in the nation and in Tennessee, ushered in a particularly fruitful decade for that party. Altogether there were eight statewide elections in Tennessee during the decade; the Whigs carried six of them. In the process, the state became recognized as one of the strongest Whig states to be found anywhere—hardly solace for Jackson and his allies.

Beginning with the presidential contest of 1840, two-party politics became fixed in Tennessee; the transitional years were over. Several hallmarks of this fierce competition characterized the decade. For one thing, all the elections (with the exception of the 1840 contest) were extremely close. High voter turnout, another feature of the Jacksonian period, became commonplace in Tennessee. It began in the late 1830s, to be sure, but achieved new levels and new consistency in the 1840s. In none of the eight elections, for instance, did voter participation drop below 81 percent. In this decade, the pattern according to which presidential contests outpolled gubernatorial elections became established. For the first time in the state's political history, parties began to stage conventions—sometimes to nominate candidates and sometimes to designate the state's central committees and other key committees. By the middle of the 1840s, state party conventions had become the norm and would remain so into the following decade.

Given that women were entirely disfranchised, it is remarkable that they participated in the political process. But their involvement was particularly noticeable in the presidential campaigns of 1840 and 1844 in Tennessee. Whether waving handkerchiefs and cheering on the "log cabin" boys in the 1840 contest or actually making brief speeches at some rallies, women expressed themselves. Indeed, a group of 350 women collectively persuaded Henry Clay to be the principal speaker at the great Whig rally in Nashville in August 1840 (he had refused two previous invitations to speak there). At that tremendous gathering, Clay reportedly saw women whose dresses sported sashes declaring, "Whig husbands or none."

In 1844, the Democrats made certain that they included women, especially at the major events. For example, Polk leaders invited women to at-

---

1840 *Campaign Doggerel*

In response to the log cabins, caged coons, hard cider, and other symbols of the Whig's "Tippecanoe and Tyler Too" campaign, the *Nashville Union* (a Democratic paper) offered these lines:

Mum is the word, boys,
Brag is the game;
Cooney is the emblem
Of Old Tip's fame.
Go it, then, for cooney,
Cooney in a cage;
Go it with a rush, boys,
Go it with a rage.

tend and be part of the procession at the giant rally in Nashville in August. They also urged women to "embroider the LONE STAR on every national flag you can find." Not to be eclipsed by the Democrats, state Whigs likewise courted female participation at their Nashville rally and festival. One group of women walked in the procession carrying a large banner with the portrait of Henry Clay on it, while another contingent rode in twenty-six carriages, representing all the states in the nation. Late in the 1844 campaign, one disgusted Democrat accused the Whig ladies of being partisan politicians and praised Democratic females for "attending to their domestic duties." Meanwhile, a Whig presidential elector allegedly insulted the Democratic ladies of Bedford County, who responded with a set of condemnatory resolutions. Involvement by women continued, although evidently in less visible ways in subsequent campaigns.

With the rollicking campaign of 1840, everyone could sense that the decade would be filled with exciting activity. The national Whig Party got the jump on the Democrats by choosing William Henry Harrison ("Old Tippecanoe"). Whigs in Tennessee and throughout the nation embarked on a great adventure with mass politics. They had a further advantage in that Van Buren, tainted by economic hard times, sought reelection. Inspired by the slogan, "Tippecanoe and Tyler Too," state Whigs, under the tutelage of Ephraim Foster, girded themselves with organizational armor in preparation for battle. Their conventions and committees quickly warmed to the task of carrying the state for Harrison.

The campaign of log cabins and hard cider captivated the voters in Tennessee, as it did in the rest of the country. The famous Whig rally in Nashville, for example, attracted a vast throng of more than one hundred thousand persons. Meanwhile, a West Tennessee Democrat, trying to offset the Whig appeal, entreated Polk for a donation of several hundred dollars to assist in garnering votes for Van Buren. After all, he readily confessed, "you know that among a certain class a little liquor will go a great way." Elsewhere a Democratic presidential elector, obviously caught up in the heat and frustration of battle, shot a Whig campaigner at Somerville (fortunately, the wound was not fatal). At any rate, when the last song was sung and the last parade ended, Tennessee voters chose Harrison, who carried all three sections of the state and captured 55.7 percent of the vote statewide.

The Democratic defeat embarrassed and troubled Governor Polk, for it cast new doubts upon his political future. He attributed the Whigs' success to their "superior organization and industry," whereas another Democrat blamed the victory on "*Mobbocracy*, carried on and kept up, with Log cabins, Whisky & cider, coonskins, Tip. songs, roudy conventions and lies." Polk determined to win reelection as governor in 1841 and thereby revive his party and his standing in it. Such was not to be the case, however, for the triumphant Whigs threw caution to the winds and chose James C. ("Lean Jimmy") Jones to campaign against Polk. They found very few issues to debate and instead engaged in a quite lively and humorous joint canvass, reminiscent of the Tippecanoe campaign the previous year. Indeed, one of Polk's friends had warned the governor at the outset that the Whigs would "run Jones as the log cabin boy taken from the plough." Frustrated by Jones's practice of telling anecdotes at their joint rallies, Polk threatened to "tell what few ditties he could command," after which "he would bor-

Cartoon showing James K. Polk and James C. Jones, from the gubernatorial campaign of either 1841 or 1843. William G. Brownlow, *A Political Register . . .* (Jonesboro, Tenn., 1844), 212.

row Jones' joke book." The long campaign across the entire state took its toll on both contenders, both of whom became ill from time to time. But their joint appearances at various locales excited the voters.

Jones carried the state with 51.2 percent of the total vote of 104,000. Polk and his fellow Democrats, discouraged by the results, vowed to do better the next time.

Unfortunately for them, the governor's race in 1843 in most respects was a repeat of the earlier one. Jones and Polk squared off against each other once more. The tone of the campaign was more serious, however, for Jones attacked the Democrats in the legislature (the "Immortal Thirteen") who had blocked the election of U.S. senators. The candidates naturally debated their preferences for president. Jones took the initiative with a strong endorsement of Henry Clay; Jones gambled that Clay's popularity in the state had improved, particularly in comparison to Van Buren's. Polk steadfastly refused to state his preference, however, vowing only to support whomever the Democratic national convention put forth.

Tennessee voters elected Jones to a second term in 1843. When the race was over, the Whigs had won three consecutive statewide contests and Polk had twice gone down in defeat.

This record did not augur well for the Democrats as they approached the 1844 presidential campaign. Certain leaders revealed their unhappiness with Polk; in fact, some boldly announced their preference for Lewis Cass of Michigan as the presidential nominee. This move disturbed Polk, who continued to believe that his only hope for national office was to cling to Van Buren.

Van Buren's unexpected public announcement opposing the annexation of Texas seriously disrupted the party on the eve of its convention. Jackson immediately demanded a pro-expansionist candidate. The Baltimore convention eventually swung away from Van Buren to Polk and selected him to carry the party's banner. Democrats in Tennessee quickly set aside their feuding and committed themselves to Polk.

Although Henry Clay, like Van Buren, publicly announced his opposition to Texas annexation, the Whigs stuck with him, for they had no other candidate available in 1844. Clay's stance presented obvious difficulties for Tennessee Whigs, since the state was decidedly in favor of annexation. Nevertheless, they entered the campaign as well organized and financed as they ever had been.

Expansionism, particularly the Texas part of it, figured prominently in the statewide campaign. Democrats never tired of championing annexation; as one of their prominent leaders assured Polk, "The Texas question is a powerful lever in our hands and will give us many Whig votes." Meanwhile, Whigs struggled to find a comfortable position on the question. They were aided to some extent by Clay's subsequent moderation of his stance. Some Whig rallies in the state adopted strong pro-annexation resolutions.

The well-fought contest stirred 120,000 Tennesseans to vote. They were doubtless astounded to learn that Clay, not Polk, had won the state, albeit by a razor-edge majority of 50.1 percent, a margin of nearly 300 votes. Despite bitter disappointment at losing his own state, Polk could boast of winning the national prize.

Indicative of the attitudes of many Democrats was an editorial admonition in the *Nashville Union*: "The smallness of the majority by which we were defeated in 1844 gives to every Democrat the most perfect assurance that victory is within our power." To that end, the party summoned Aaron V. Brown, three-term congressman and Polk's close personal and political ally, to carry its banner in the 1845 governor's race.

The Whig camp was thrown into disarray when Governor Jones revealed that he would not seek a third term. Soon, however, the party tapped Ephraim Foster, former U.S. senator and party war-horse, as its candidate. Foster had voted against the Texas annexation treaty in 1844 and then against Congress's joint resolution to annex Texas. Given the climate of the day, these were sins that could not readily be forgiven.

Indeed, from the first joint debate in April until the end of the canvass, Brown and Foster wrestled with the Texas question. Just before election day, word arrived that the Texas convention had accepted the terms of the joint resolution, a revelation that strengthened Brown's cause.

Aaron Brown won the election, but it was a typically tight victory, with 50.7 percent of the statewide vote. Whigs complained, with some validity, that they lost because they did not get their people out on election day.

In 1847, Brown had another opportunity to stem the Whig tide but did not succeed. Instead, the Whigs climbed back into the driver's seat with the election of Neill S. Brown. Not surprisingly, the two Browns argued constantly about the Mexican War, which had begun the preceding year. Aaron Brown and his party strongly approved Polk's prosecution of the war. But the Whigs, on the other hand, contended that the war was unnecessary and that Polk had pushed the nation into it unconstitutionally.

Neill Brown and other Whigs shrewdly shifted to the presidential preference question, for they were eager to trumpet their enthusiasm for Zachary Taylor. At the very first joint debate, Brown announced his endorsement of Taylor for president. This immensely popular war hero helped the Whigs carry the governor's race. Neill Brown, the beneficiary of a larger turnout at the polls, squeaked by with 50.3 percent of the vote.

It came as no surprise when, a year later, the state bestowed its vote upon Taylor in the presidential contest. After all, the 1847 governor's race had been something of a preview or trial run. As soon as the national convention chose Taylor, state Whigs did not hesitate to close ranks behind him. Meanwhile, Tennessee Democrats bravely tried to put the best face on Lewis Cass's chances for success in the state.

While issues such as the Wilmot Proviso and the extension of slavery into the West were vital topics in the presidential contest elsewhere, they did not cut a wide swath in Tennessee. Whigs tried to be as nonpartisan and noncommittal as possible, in order to attract Democratic votes. They were aided in this strategy by Taylor's own refusal to take a public stand on any issue. He captured 52.5 percent of the votes; there is no question that he picked up the new voters as well as some traditional Democratic voters.

Luckily for the Democrats, the decade ended with a victory for them in the 1849 gubernatorial contest. Otherwise, they might have faded completely from the political landscape. They selected William Trousdale, who had achieved modest fame in the Mexican War, as the man to reverse their string of defeats. Meanwhile, Whigs—albeit not unanimously—went with Neill Brown again.

Indicative of the changing climate in the aftermath of the Mexican War was the state Democratic convention's adoption of a platform that rejected the Wilmot Proviso, denied the right of the federal government to interfere with slavery, and exhorted the state's citizens to resist any threats to their sovereignty and property rights. Although the Whigs submitted no platform, Brown placed himself squarely in opposition to the Wilmot Proviso and in favor of slavery. Democrats charged Brown and his supporters with being submissionists (willing to yield to national antislavery forces), whereas Whigs accused Democrats of being disunionists. Campaign debates and rhetoric never strayed far from these issues.

Trousdale won the election with 50.6 percent of the vote statewide. Credit must be given to Trousdale, who benefited from his military acclaim but who also managed to define the issues in such a way as to attract votes. Thus the Democrats had a victory at last; no one could predict what the next decade would bring.

Democrats' Decade: The 1850s

The volatile years of the 1850s, full of sectional strife and discord, shook the nation. It need not have been that way, for the decade commenced with Congress producing the famous Compromise of 1850. By this agreement, the nation sought to treat nagging questions about the expansion of slavery in the new western areas, slave trade in the District of Columbia, and the plight of fugitive slaves. Once the Compromise was adopted, Tennesseans, particularly Whigs, quickly voiced their approval—in the hope that there would be no further exacerbation of the slavery controversy.

Even while Congress edged toward a reasonable solution during its 1850 debates, however, Nashville hosted two sessions of the Southern Convention (in June and in November). Generally speaking, Tennessee was not favorably disposed toward the goals of these conclaves. Whereas Democrats took an active part in the deliberations, state Whigs avoided them and criticized the assemblies. The summer meeting occurred while the Compromise

---

Nashville (Southern) Convention

In the fall of 1849, a Mississippi convention issued a call for a southern convention to be held the following summer in Nashville. A modest-sized gathering of 175 southern delegates met in early June (while the Compromise of 1850 was being debated in Congress). The convention adopted fairly moderate resolutions upholding southern rights, particularly with regard to the territories that had not yet been admitted as states.

The gathering also stipulated that a second meeting should be held in the fall months. Accordingly, in November (two months after final passage of the Compromise of 1850), an even smaller convention of southerners assembled in Nashville. The tone and resolutions of this conclave were more radical, with talk of disunion, state sovereignty, and resistance.

---

of 1850 was being hammered out in Congress and therefore was restricted in its statements. But the November session followed by about two months the completion of the Compromise. Oddly enough, this smaller convention took a more extreme states' rights, pro-South stance. Tennessee delegates, all Democrats, voted against the conclave's final report. It was risky business at this juncture for the state's political leaders to be linked with any sort of extreme position.

A sort of uneasy tranquillity marked the years immediately following adoption of the Compromise. But that was shattered in 1854 by the famous Kansas-Nebraska Act, which reintroduced the slavery controversy into the halls of Congress and into the nation at large. In effect, this measure repealed the old Missouri Compromise line and reopened the *possibility* that federal territories north of that boundary might permit slavery. Tennessee's congressional delegation was badly divided on this legislation. Sen. John Bell opposed the bill, for instance, whereas Sen. James C. Jones supported it. The four Democratic representatives also backed it, as did two of the Whigs. But four of the state's Whig members of the House fought against it. So bitter and divisive were the debates in Congress and so destructive was the implementation of the law that the nation and the Whig Party never would be the same again. In fact, the Whigs collapsed under the weight of these burdens and disappeared as a political party. The times were changing.

Tennessee felt the impact of these events, especially after the traditional two-party alignment fragmented. The decade belonged to the Democrats, for they won five out of the seven statewide elections. Indeed, after the Whigs captured the 1851 governor's race and the 1852 presidential election, they did not win another contest. The Democrats then put together five consecutive victories, including the first presidential triumph (1856) since Jackson's reelection in 1832. The state's Democrats benefited from new and vigorous leadership in the 1850s, especially that provided by Andrew Johnson and Isham G. Harris, both of whom occupied the governor's chair.

The Whig Party disappeared after the 1853 gubernatorial campaign. But since politics, like nature, abhors a vacuum, new political parties emerged to replace the Whigs. In 1855, for example, the American or Know Nothing Party (essentially the Whig Party reconstituted) sought the Tennessee governorship, though unsuccessfully. It competed again in the 1856 presidential and in the 1857 governor's races and then vanished. In 1859, the anti-Jackson crowd in Tennessee called itself simply the Opposition Party. Remarkably, these new parties gave the Democrats strong competition, for they never received less than 45 percent of the statewide vote. Thus, even amid the significant changes of the decade, Democrats still had to fight hard to win on election day.

Insofar as the gubernatorial contests are concerned, the decade began with a Whig victory in 1851. The incumbent governor, Democrat William Trousdale, lost to William B. Campbell. The two men naturally discussed the Compromise of 1850 a great deal, with Campbell strongly embracing it as the "final settlement" of the slavery dispute. Trousdale and the Democrats supported it as a necessity to preserve the Union but expressed some hesitation. The candidates raised the usual presidential preference question but aroused no great enthusiasm. On election day, Campbell squeaked by with a very narrow victory.

Andrew Johnson quite ably ran the 1853 and 1855 campaigns and launched the Democratic sweep. He sought the post of governor in the former contest, because the Whig-dominated legislature had redrawn his congressional district so as to make it difficult for him to win. The Whigs chose Gustavus A. Henry, the architect of the redistricting measure, as their standard-bearer. Beyond the obvious disputes over that "Henrymandering" of the congressional districts, the candidates found little to debate. Johnson came very close to carrying East Tennessee, his home section, on his way to winning nearly 51 percent of the vote statewide.

He sought a second term in 1855 and again enjoyed success. This time he faced a new party, the American or Know Nothing Party, and its candidate, Meredith P. Gentry. He went on the attack immediately, castigating the anti-foreigner and anti-Catholic views of the Know Nothings. Gentry proved no match for Johnson on the campaign trail. Although Johnson complained later about the lack of unified Democratic support in the campaign, he managed to win reelection.

The following two gubernatorial campaigns were led by the victorious Isham G. Harris. Johnson announced in 1857 that he did not intend to seek a third term; instead, he had his eyes riveted upon a U.S. Senate seat (which

---

U.S. Senate Contests, 1835–1860

Until the twentieth century, the state legislature elected U.S. senators. In Tennessee, battles over Senate seats contained several noteworthy features. For example, by long-standing tradition, one seat belonged to East Tennessee and one to Middle Tennessee. This tradition was broken only in 1851, when James C. Jones of West Tennessee was elected. Only once, in 1839, did the state legislature instruct Tennessee's U.S. senators to vote for a particular measure in Congress; in reaction, both senators resigned. The fact that the legislature at that time was controlled by Democrats and the two Senators were Whig was critical. Throughout the period, the party affiliation of those occupying Senate seats varied, reflecting the results of statewide elections. By era's end, however, Democrats controlled both seats. Strangely enough, in 1841–43, Tennessee had no U.S. senators, thanks to the fact that Democrats blocked the elections.

---

he won). Harris, an emerging force in Democratic circles, seemed the obvious candidate. The slowly disintegrating American Party had difficulty enlisting a nominee but finally settled on Robert Hatton. There were no major issues in the canvass, although Harris eventually focused upon Know Nothing tenets. Not unexpectedly, Harris won a resounding victory at the polls, carrying all three sections and garnering slightly over 54 percent of the total vote.

Harris led his party to its fifth consecutive victory in 1859. This time he faced the so-called Opposition Party, which fielded John Netherland as its standard-bearer. Harris directed attention upon slavery and states' rights. Netherland protested that the Democratic Party was constantly agitating that topic, solely for political gain. Although Harris's victory in 1859 was not as decisive as the one two years earlier, he captured a respectable 52.8 percent of the statewide vote.

What about presidential politics in the 1850s? Whigs swung the 1852 election, but Democrats took the 1856 vote. In the former contest, much division existed within the state Whig ranks, prior to and after the national convention. Disagreement centered on whether Winfield Scott or Millard Fillmore should be the nominee. Most Tennessee leaders preferred Fillmore; in fact, after Scott's nomination, certain prominent Whigs defiantly refused to support him. Although he favored Fillmore, Governor Campbell reluctantly agreed to support Scott, acknowledging that he was "too old to change or equivocate & expect to go to the devil with the Whigs, but I may go along more quietly than I have in days gone by." On the Democratic side, there was little enthusiasm for Franklin Pierce but evidently no real divisions among the state's Democrats. The presidential race focused upon the Compromise of 1850. In Tennessee, however, no differences appeared, as both parties again endorsed the Compromise. Democrats raised the question of which party could best be depended upon to uphold the Compromise, while at the same time safeguarding the rights of the South.

In November 1852, while voters across the nation chose Pierce, Tennessee did not. Once more the Whig candidate emerged victorious in the state; Scott carried East and West Tennessee and secured 50.7 percent of the statewide total. The citizens could not know it at the time, but this election was the "last hurrah" for the Whig Party in Tennessee.

Four years later that party did not even exist, having been replaced by both the Republican and the American parties. The former attracted no support in Tennessee, however. The state's Know Nothings (American Party) eagerly embraced the national ticket of Fillmore and Andrew J. Donelson (a Tennessean). State Democrats quickly lined up behind the candidacy of James Buchanan, once their national convention reached its decision.

Not unexpectedly, the Kansas-Nebraska Act and the turmoil in Kansas itself were prime topics of debate in the 1856 campaign. The question of popular sovereignty attracted discussion everywhere. As the *Nashville Union and American* expressed it, the "principle contained in the Kansas Nebraska act is the only issue now before the country." Democrats declared that southern interests could be entrusted only to their party. They attacked Fillmore, asserting that he stood no chance of being elected and that a vote for him thus was tantamount to a vote for John C. Frémont and the Republicans. Know Nothing campaigners protested that Fillmore in reality was a moderate on the slavery question and undeniably was devoted to the Union.

During the campaign, there were repeated claims that Know Nothing leaders, including Donelson, were drinking too much. One observer complained that William Haskell "speaks under the influence of brandy & is always half drunk . . . yet all admire his ability." Several large rallies across the state characterized the campaign, including the Know Nothing gathering in Nashville, which attracted between 30,000 and 50,000 participants. So lively did the canvass become that, near the end of it, leaders from both parties formally agreed that, in Nashville, Wednesdays and Fridays would be reserved for Democrats, while Thursdays and Saturdays would be set aside for Know Nothings.

Following the electioneering, nearly 140,000 of the state's voters turned out to vote. They offered Buchanan 52.7 percent of the statewide vote. Hence, for the first time since 1832, Democrats won a presidential contest in Tennessee.

The state had been staunchly Democratic in the early 1830s, when Jackson occupied the presidency. But then a rebellion of sorts occurred, as political leaders and voters moved in a different direction to support an anti-

Jackson movement. That cause, eventually consolidated as the Whig Party, captured Tennessee and dominated politics throughout the 1840s. Yet the following decade witnessed another sea change, as the Whig Party collapsed and the state's Democratic Party rose up to seize control. By the middle of the 1850s, Democrats held the upper hand and would not yield. As the vigorously Democratic *Nashville Union* declared on the eve of the 1852 presidential election: "This State was never intended to be anything but democratic. . . . It is impossible that a State, whose history is identified with that of Jackson could ever really affiliate with the Whig Party." But most assuredly it did, at least until the final antebellum decade.

Tennessee's People in the Antebellum Years

In antebellum Tennessee, a high birth rate and large-scale immigration from eastern states kept the population growing. (Outmigration to the new western frontiers partially offset this increase, however, and kept the rate of growth well below that of the frontier era.) Between 1820 and 1860, the number of Tennesseans increased 162 percent, from 422,823 to 1,109,801.

As was true in all other southern states in that period, a sizable proportion of Tennessee's people were black. In fact, the black population increased at a rate even faster than that of the whites. In 1820, blacks numbered 82,844 (less than 20 percent of the state's whole population); by 1860, they numbered 283,019 (over 25 percent of the population). Of Tennessee's three racial groups, only the Indians diminished in number: in 1820 there were still several thousand in the state, but four decades later only sixty remained.

The antebellum era also witnessed significant demographic shifts among the state's three grand divisions. Throughout the frontier era, East Tennessee had held the great majority of the state's population. But by 1860, it could claim only 27 percent of the total, well behind faster-growing Middle Tennessee, which boasted 45 percent. The most spectacular growth, however, was in West Tennessee. Virtually unpopulated in 1820, forty years later it contained 304,000 people—three thousand more than East Tennessee—and almost 28 percent of the state's total.

Another important aspect of the state's development in the antebellum years was urbanization. Frontier Tennessee had hardly any towns (if they are defined as population centers of twenty-five hundred people or more) and nothing like a real city (ten thousand people or more). But by 1860, the state boasted five towns (Knoxville, Chattanooga, Columbia, Murfreesboro, and Clarksville) and two cities (Memphis and Nashville). Memphis in particular experienced dizzying growth in those years, reaching a population of nearly twenty-three thousand in 1860 and thereby surpassing Nashville, with seventeen thousand inhabitants. It is important to keep in mind, though, that, despite the substantial growth of towns and cities, antebellum Tennesseans remained overwhelmingly rural—a key element of their southernness.

Agriculture

Agriculture was the heart and soul of the antebellum economy. The majority of Tennesseans in that era made their living on farms, the majority of the state's wealth was in its farmland, and the majority of its products grew out of the soil.

As Tennesseans multiplied, they spread rapidly over the land, staking out homesteads and planting crops. Agricultural production soared as the land was cleared, fenced, and sowed. The most important products—corn, wheat, cotton, tobacco, and livestock—all saw substantial increases in the antebellum era. Cotton production, in particular, boomed in Tennessee (as in most other parts of the South): in 1821 it stood at about fifty thousand bales, in 1859 nearly three hundred thousand.

Many of the Tennesseans who toiled in the fields were black slaves, and in some cases they worked in gangs on farms extensive enough to be considered plantations—a distinctively southern form of agricultural production. By 1860, Tennessee had nearly three thousand plantations (defined as farms on which at least 20 slaves were held), each with hundreds of acres under cultivation. A few, such as G. A. Washington's "Wessyngton" plantation in Robertson County, with its 5,100 improved (i.e., cleared and fenced) acres and 274 slaves, were truly immense. The typical Tennessee farm, however, was a modest operation, consisting of a plot of fifty or a hundred improved acres and a larger amount of woodland, worked by a

Contemporary artist's sketch of a barn-raising in Tennessee in the 1850s. Artist unknown. McClung Historical Collection, Knox County Public Library, Knoxville.

farmer and his immediate family with the help of one or two slaves, or, more likely, no slaves at all.

Beginning in the 1830s, many Tennessee farmers took up the cause of agricultural improvement. Worried that traditional methods of husbandry were depleting the soil and limiting productivity, they experimented with fertilizers, crop rotation and diversification, stock breeding, conservational plowing, and new kinds of farm implements. They learned of the latest techniques and equipment through local farmers' clubs and through journals such as the *Tennessee Farmer*. In many counties they organized annual fairs where they could show off the finest products of their farms and compete for awards. In 1854, at the urging of farmers and with the encouragement of Gov. Andrew Johnson, the Tennessee legislature established the State Agricultural Bureau. The bureau sponsored farmers' clubs, county and regional fairs, and even a grand state fair, which was held near Nashville each fall beginning in 1855, on a forty-acre site that contained dozens of stables, a large exhibition hall, and an eight-thousand-seat amphitheater.

Although some farmers dismissed the idea of scientific cultivation and went on farming just as their fathers and grandfathers had, the "agricultural awakening" of the antebellum era measurably improved Tennessee agriculture. Those farmers who were willing to change their ways generally were rewarded with better crop yields and higher-quality livestock. A number of Tennessee farmers and stockmen, including horse-raiser L. J. Polk of Maury County and sheep-raiser Mark Cockrill of Davidson, earned national recognition (international recognition, in fact, in the case of Cockrill, who in 1854 won a gold medal at a world exposition in London). Tennessee's agriculture became noticeably more diversified, too, as farmers gave new crops a try.

As the state's agriculture developed in the decades before the Civil War, each grand division evolved a distinctive pattern. East Tennessee remained, on the whole, a region of small farms producing corn, wheat, cattle, and hogs primarily for family use or for barter within the community—an agricultural system little different from that of the frontier era. Plantations were very scarce, slave laborers few, and commercial agriculture limited.

In West Tennessee, by contrast, there emerged an agricultural system like that in the Mississippi River Delta districts to the south—that is, one dominated by slave plantations growing a cash crop for export. Cotton was the cash crop of choice in West Tennessee, for the plant was particularly well suited to that region's climate and soil. Most of the fleecy fiber was shipped down the Mississippi River to New Orleans, where it was loaded on ocean-going vessels and sent to the textile factories of England and New England.

Middle Tennessee occupied a kind of middle ground between the agricultural systems of east and west. A good number of plantations existed there, especially in the Central Basin, but they did not dominate the agricultural economy as in West Tennessee. Most of Middle Tennessee's agricultural output came from family farms; but those farms were more productive, more likely to employ a few slaves, and much more likely to produce for export than the ones in East Tennessee. Tobacco (grown in the northern counties of the region) and cotton (in the southern counties) were important cash crops in Middle Tennessee, but the leading export by far was livestock. The region was one of the South's primary suppliers of hogs, mules, horses, and sheep. To feed these animals, Middle Tennessee farmers and planters grew corn in great quantities and maintained extensive pastures.

Soil quality had a lot to do with the differences among the three regions. In Tennessee, as in the rest of the South, plantations tended to proliferate where the soil was rich. West Tennessee's alluvial lands and Middle Tennessee's Central Basin contained prime soil, but East Tennessee had almost none.

Transportation

Another factor behind the increasing distinctiveness of Tennessee's three grand divisions was access to outside markets, without which large-scale commercial agriculture is impossible. Rivers offered the best natural means of access, but East Tennessee was denied easy river transport because of the obstructions in the Tennessee River below Chattanooga. West and Middle Tennessee, on the other hand, were blessed with the readily navigable Mississippi, Cumberland, and lower Tennessee Rivers.

The Steamboat Comes to Nashville, 1819

In 1818, a young Nashville merchant and future governor named William Carroll became part owner of the steamboat *General Jackson*. Along with his fellow investors, he made plans to bring the vessel from New Orleans to Nashville, which had not yet been visited by any steamboat. But the first attempt, in the spring of that year, was a disappointment. The boat got snagged in river obstructions several miles down the Cumberland from Nashville, and its cargo had to be unloaded and hauled to the city by wagon.

The next try almost failed, too, as low water grounded the vessel twenty miles from the city. But eventually the river rose, and the *General Jackson* made its way to Nashville, arriving there on March 11, 1819. A witness described the scene: "The whole population, men, women and children, collected on the bank of the river, and loud cheers rent the air. . . . The first ship that crossed the Atlantic, and touched the shores of America, was not an object of more wonder to the astonished natives, than was this steamboat to the people of Nashville."

Those rivers became even more important to Tennessee's economy with the advent of the steamboat. This newfangled contraption first appeared on the Mississippi River in 1811, though none visited any Tennessee town for some years thereafter. Finally, on March 11, 1819, the aptly named *General Jackson* steamed up the Cumberland to Nashville. A few days later, it headed back to New Orleans with a load of Tennessee tobacco.

Steamboats represented a great leap forward in transportation. They were faster and more maneuverable than the flatboats Tennesseans had long relied upon to send goods downriver; and they were much faster and more capacious than the keelboats, laboriously poled against the stream, which previously had been the only means of bringing goods into Tennessee by river. Steamboats could go from Nashville to New Orleans in just seven days and return in seventeen. They soon became a common sight on the Cumberland: by the 1840s, one might see fifteen docking in Nashville in the space of a week. Steamboats helped that city grow and prosper, and they did the same for Memphis, which emerged as an even busier river port than Nashville after West Tennessee was settled.

East Tennesseans welcomed no steamboat until 1828, when an intrepid river captain piloted the *Atlas* up the Tennessee River, through the dangerous Muscle Shoals, and past the notorious "Suck" and "Boiling Pot" near Chattanooga. On March 4, the boat arrived in Knoxville, where the mayor made a speech lauding the occasion as "the commencement of a new era in the commercial affairs of East Tennessee." He was wrong, though. The *Atlas* did not herald East Tennessee's participation in large-scale interregional trade. In the succeeding years, few other steamboat captains dared to make the hazardous upriver journey, and most of the goods that went into or out of East Tennessee continued to take a slow, difficult, and costly trip by wagon.

Concerned about their economic future, many East Tennesseans began calling for "internal improvements" that would facilitate trade with the outside world. They were joined by other commercially minded citizens, including many West and Middle Tennessee farmers who lacked easy access to the rivers.

Some believed that the solution was better roads. The 1830s saw a spate of road building in Tennessee, most of it by private companies with some state financial aid. The "turnpikes" these companies built were good, graded roads, surfaced with gravel or macadam, and ditched to prevent washouts. The companies charged tolls—so much per person, per wagon, per head of livestock—in order to recoup their costs and make a profit.

As it turned out, Middle Tennessee and especially Nashville benefited most from the turnpike boom. The majority of the roads constructed were in the middle region of the state and led to the capital, thus reinforcing the city's regional economic predominance. In any event, turnpikes were not really the answer to Tennessee's transportation needs: even on first-class roads, overland travel was slow, cargoes necessarily small, and the cost of shipment high. At best, turnpikes were useful as feeder lines to nearby river ports.

What, then, was the answer? For a time Tennesseans talked excitedly about canals, which were being built throughout the North. No canal ever was dug in Tennessee, however, for, by the time Tennesseans began marshaling their resources for big transportation projects, their fancy had been caught by the latest marvel of the age—the railroad.

Many Tennesseans caught railroad fever in the 1830s, but the temperatures of East Tennesseans ran highest. "Rail-roads are the *only hope* of East Tennessee," one Knoxvillian declared. On the Fourth of July, 1831, there appeared in Rogersville the *Rail Road Advocate*, the first newspaper in the nation devoted exclusively to promoting the iron horse. Five years later, several hundred railroad enthusiasts convened in Knoxville and endorsed a plan to tie

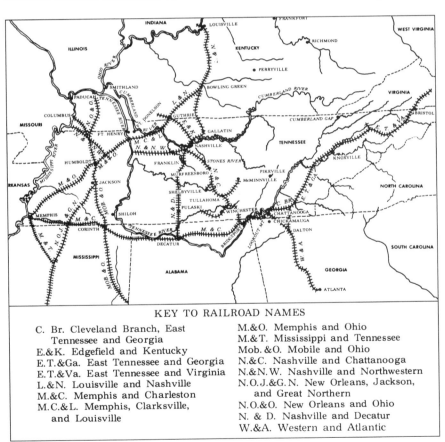

KEY TO RAILROAD NAMES

C. Br. Cleveland Branch, East Tennessee and Georgia
E.&K. Edgefield and Kentucky
E.T.&Ga. East Tennessee and Georgia
E.T.&Va. East Tennessee and Virginia
L.&N. Louisville and Nashville
M.&C. Memphis and Charleston
M.C.&L. Memphis, Clarksville, and Louisville

M.&O. Memphis and Ohio
M.&T. Mississippi and Tennessee
Mob.&O. Mobile and Ohio
N.&C. Nashville and Chattanooga
N.&N.W. Nashville and Northwestern
N.O.J.&G.N. New Orleans, Jackson, and Great Northern
N.O.&O. New Orleans and Ohio
N.&D. Nashville and Decatur
W.&A. Western and Atlantic

Tennessee's railroads in 1861. Tennessee Public Service Commission, Nashville.

East Tennessee by rail to Louisville and Charleston. West Tennesseans evinced nearly as much ardor as East Tennesseans; most Middle Tennesseans, however, seemed satisfied with their turnpikes and steamboats.

The state legislature chartered six railroad companies in 1831 and more in the following years. It also authorized the state to provide up to half the capital of any railroad or turnpike company by issuing bonds to be turned over to the company in exchange for stock. Even with this generous state aid, however, few railroad companies could raise sufficient capital. Hard times following the Panic of 1837 dried up Tennessee's reservoir of private investment funds, and eventually all the chartered railroad companies went bankrupt, leaving the state and some private investors holding worthless stock certificates. (The turnpike companies, however, especially those in Middle Tennessee, were more successful.) Only one railroad actually got under way; it operated in 1842 on a short track leading out of Memphis, until the sheriff seized its locomotive for debt.

These failures left a bad taste in the mouths of many, and railroad enthusiasm in Tennessee abated for a time. But in the late 1840s it swelled again, encouraged by the proliferation of railroads in neighboring states and by the publicity attending a railroad convention in Memphis in 1845. This gathering brought in hundreds of delegates from many states, including the famous South Carolinian John C. Calhoun. Once again the Tennessee legislature began chartering railroad companies and offering financial support. Local governments chipped in, too; and, with the return of prosperous times, private investors opened their wallets.

The result was the great Tennessee railroad boom of the 1850s and early 1860s. At the beginning of 1850, not a single mile of track in the state was operational; a dozen years later, twelve hundred miles existed. By then, even the complacent citizens of Middle Tennessee had been bitten by the railroad bug, and it was there that the state's first important railroad, the Nashville & Chattanooga, began running in 1851. By 1854, its track had been completed all the way to Chattanooga, where connections could be made to the Deep South. Middle Tennessee's other important interregional line, the Louisville & Nashville, linked those two cities by 1859. West Tennesseans gained rail connection to the Atlantic seaboard when the Memphis & Charleston was finished in 1857, and to the Midwest and Gulf of Mexico when the Mobile & Ohio opened in 1861. East Tennesseans got their long-desired interstate nexus when the East Tennessee & Georgia line was completed from Knoxville to Dalton in 1855 and the East Tennessee & Virginia from Knoxville to Bristol in 1858.

The economic effects of the railroads were tremendous, although their full impact would not be felt until after the Civil War. By providing a ubiquitous and cheap means of long-distance transportation, railroads encouraged more and more Tennessee farmers to grow a surplus for export—not least of all, the growers of East Tennessee, some of whom began producing wheat to help feed the cities of the Northeast and the South. The railroads also cut travel time between the different sections of the state and furthered the growth of the cities, towns, and villages they passed through. Knoxville and Chattanooga, in particular, were beneficiaries of the railroad.

One thing Tennessee's antebellum railroads did not do, however, was unify the state economically. All the important lines but one (the Memphis & Charleston) ran north and south, not east and west; they were built to link each grand division with out-of-state markets and suppliers, not with other parts of Tennessee. On the eve of the Civil War, one could not travel by train between Knoxville and Nashville, or between Memphis and Nashville, without taking a circuitous route out of the state.

Industry

Despite the state's economic fragmentation, both agriculture and commerce made great strides in antebellum Tennessee. But the same cannot be said for industry. To be sure, manufacturing establishments existed in Tennessee; the census takers counted 2,572 of them in 1860. The great majority of these, however, were neighborhood blacksmith shops, tanneries, grist mills, lumber mills, and the like; they were, in other words, two-, three-, or four-man operations that produced strictly for a local market.

Of the "true" industries in Tennessee—that is, those producing goods on a large scale for outside markets—five were of real significance. These were: tobacco processing, with 39 factories and 662 employees; coal and copper mining, with 8 mines and 804 employees; machinery and rail car manufacturing, with 12 factories and 835 employees; cotton textile manufacturing, with 30 mills and 899 employees; and iron manufacturing, with 71 establishments and 1,701 employees.

Iron-making, in particular, was a substantial industry in antebellum Tennessee. Some of it was carried on in upper East Tennessee; but most was done in the Western Highland Rim, where all the necessities—accessible ore deposits, limestone for smelting, wood for fuel, rivers for transportation—were found in abundance. Some of the iron operations, including the prominent Cumberland Iron Works of Stewart County, were quite large, comprising a community of one hundred or more workers and their families, centered around a great furnace that stayed "in blast" day and night, pouring out molten iron.

Despite the growing number of furnaces and factories, however, industry remained a very small part of antebellum Tennessee's economy. The amount of capital invested in industrial plants was dwarfed by that invested in farms, livestock, and agricultural equipment; and industrial laborers were but a tiny fraction of the state's workforce.

Tennessee was not alone in that respect. Compared to the North, all the southern states were industrially backward in the antebellum era. Some of the causes were economic—the South suffered from capital shortages, transportation deficiencies, and other problems—but others were ideological. Most southerners continued to champion the ideals of Jeffersonian agrarianism, which held farming to be the noblest calling and land ownership the true guarantor of freedom. Not until after the Civil War would a significant number of Tennesseans and other southerners embrace industrialization.

Social Divisions

It is not easy to describe the "typical" Tennessean of the antebellum era. It is in fact impossible, for there was no such thing. A realistic description of antebellum society must acknowledge important distinctions among people; it must show, among other things, the differences between men and women, between rich and poor, between free and enslaved.

Antebellum Tennesseans lived in a time when nearly all Americans believed that women and men had distinct, though mutually supportive, social roles and that they should confine themselves to their "separate spheres." A man's proper role was as husband and father, family provider, and participant in public life. A woman's proper role was as wife and mother, nurturer of the family, and guardian of domestic tranquillity. Although marriage by that time was seen as a more companionate institution than had been the case in earlier eras, a woman still was expected to defer to her husband as the head of the family. Women's subjection was embodied not only in custom but also in law: married women, for instance, could not (except in unusual circumstances) hold property in their own names. Moreover, women could not vote, hold political office, or serve on juries. Such duties and privileges were reserved for men; the duties and privileges of women were confined to the home.

In practice, though, there were many exceptions to the rule. A number of women, mostly widows, lived independently as heads of their own households. Some women, married as well as single, worked outside the home. These included nearly all slave women, who were put to work in their masters' fields or kitchens; and some white women, mostly very poor, who took jobs as domestics, seamstresses, laundresses, or even factory workers (nearly six hundred were employed in Tennessee's cotton mills, for example). Furthermore, rural white women, though they did not labor in the fields, played a key role in providing for the family with their spinning, weaving, sewing, poultry raising, and vegetable gardening—or, in the case of plantation mistresses, by overseeing the slaves who performed those chores. Nevertheless, the idea of "separate spheres" exerted a pervasive and powerful influence in antebellum Tennessee.

Traditional ideas about one's proper role also shaped relations among the social classes. By the antebellum era, Americans had come a long way from the strictly hierarchical society characteristic of the colonial era. For one thing, people of all classes now could vote and hold office (as long as they were white and male), and in many other respects society was more egalitarian than in the old days. Nevertheless, in Tennessee and the rest of the South—to a greater extent than in the North—class distinctions remained very apparent.

Among whites there were, broadly speaking, three social classes. At the top of the social order stood the aristocrats, few in number but great in influence. They were mostly planters, although some were wealthy professionals such as lawyers or merchants. They generally dominated the top political offices and wielded great economic power. Aristocratic families lived in large, expensively furnished houses, wore fashionable clothes, and rode in fancy carriages. They had many black servants to wait upon them, and they educated their children in private academies.

Just below the aristocrats, socially speaking, were the yeomen, who made up the great majority of white families. These were people who owned small to middling amounts of property, including, in some cases, a few slaves; most were farmers, some were herdsmen or artisans. The yeomen had a comfortable but by no means luxurious existence. Their houses were modest cabins, not the large frame dwellings of the aristocrats; and they rode in rough wagons pulled by balky mules, rather than in fine carriages pulled by blooded horses. Yeomen worked with their hands, unlike those above them socially;

A typical Tennessee yeoman's homestead in the antebellum era. East Tennessee Historical Society, Knoxville. *Harper's New Monthly Magazine*, November 1857.

and they did not enjoy much leisure time. Their children could go to school only when not needed on the family farm or in the family artisan shop, and they went to the common schools rather than the academies.

Below the yeomen were the poor whites. Having no productive property of their own, poor whites worked as tenant farmers or as hired hands on the farms or in the shops of the yeomen. They were desperately impoverished, lived in leaky hovels, made do with the crudest of furnishings and patched clothes, and had very little in the way of schooling; many were illiterate.

Despite the glaring social distinctions and the great inequalities of wealth and comfort, however, relations among the white classes generally were not hostile. Yeomen and poor whites sometimes griped about the snobbishness of the aristocrats, but on the whole they quietly accepted their own places in the social order. Still retaining traces of the traditional view that hierarchy was the natural condition of society and that aristocrats should lead while others followed, most yeomen and poor whites saw no contradiction in using their democratic political rights to elect aristocrats to high office.

East Tennessee was an exception to this rule, however. There, where plantations and aristocrats were very scarce, there existed a yeoman-dominated society unlike that in the rest of the state. The East Tennessee yeomanry scorned the pretensions of the aristocracy and favored men of their own kind in public office—men such as Andrew Johnson of Greeneville, a one-time tailor who, with the help of his East Tennessee constituency, rose to political prominence and devoted his career to promoting the interests of the common people against what he called the "damnable," "swaggering" aristocrats.

Racial Divisions

Whatever points of contention there might have been among aristocrats, yeomen, and poor whites, there was one issue on which they stood shoulder to shoulder. This was the matter of race. White Tennesseans in the antebellum era, with very few exceptions, were convinced that blacks were inferior and potentially dangerous people who must be subjugated and rigorously controlled. Only if blacks were enslaved, whites believed, could the two races coexist.

This racist consensus did not soften, but rather hardened, as the years went by. Early in the nineteenth century there had appeared in Tennessee, as in other states, an antislavery movement (to be discussed in the next section); but it never was widely supported in Tennessee and soon died out there. Meanwhile, as the state's economy expanded, slavery became more firmly entrenched. Farmers found the use of slave labor profitable, and most who could afford to do so bought slaves; the big plantations were worked entirely by slave labor. Slaves became a significant part of the manufacturing labor force, too, especially in the iron industry.

By 1860, slaves comprised 25 percent of Tennessee's population. They

Advertisement for a Nashville slave-trading firm. Artifact no. 81.30. Imprint from an envelope in the Tennessee State Museum, Nashville.

were not distributed evenly across the state, for they were most numerous where plantation agriculture was prevalent. Thus, slaves made up only 9 percent of East Tennessee's population, but made up 29 percent of Middle Tennessee's and 34 percent of West Tennessee's. In three counties—Williamson in Middle Tennessee and Fayette and Haywood in West Tennessee—slaves outnumbered whites. In the state as a whole, approximately one white family in four owned at least one slave. But in East Tennessee, the proportion was only one in nine, while in Middle and West it was nearly one in three.

As slavery expanded, whites became ever more determined to preserve and defend the institution. The bloody 1831 slave uprising in Virginia, led by Nat Turner, and the emergence of a radical abolitionist movement in the North at about the same time frightened white Tennesseans. They reacted by tightening the screws on the slave population and vigilantly guarding against "outside agitators." New local and state statutes imposed stricter regulations upon slaves and strengthened the system of citizen patrols, whose job was to watch for suspicious activities among the slaves. White fears of subversion were manifest in an episode in 1835, in which a Bible salesman from Ohio named Amos Dresser was apprehended in Nashville carrying antislavery pamphlets. A vigilance committee administered twenty lashes to Dresser on the public square before expelling him from the city. The next year the state legislature made it a felony to distribute abolitionist tracts or make abolitionist speeches; these "crimes" were punishable by a prison term of up to ten years for the first offense and twenty for the second.

As white Tennesseans cracked down on slaves and Yankee troublemakers, they persuaded themselves that slavery was not just a necessary evil but a "positive good"—good not only for whites but also for the slaves themselves, who were being "nurtured" and "civilized" by the superior white race. Most whites who owned slaves believed not only that slavery was right but also that they themselves were benevolent masters whose bondsmen were grateful, loyal, and contented (unless stirred up by outsiders). Nostalgically recalling the "scenes of jollity" he had witnessed in his plantation's slave quarters, one former slaveholder wrote after the Civil War, "When I contrast the lives of . . . master and slave . . . I am constrained to believe the slave must have been the happier."

The reality of slavery usually was otherwise. Not all masters were the indulgent paternalists they liked to think they were, and many slaves were forced to endure starvation diets, brutal beatings, or sexual abuse. Even for those slaves whose masters treated them well by the standards of the day, slavery meant constantly abasing themselves before white people, living in primitive conditions, working long hours at the most menial and arduous tasks, and being deprived of basic rights, such as the ability to move around freely, change jobs, own property, or get an education. Nor could slaves even count on keeping their families intact: slave sales took many a black

A Former Slave Remembers

In 1929 and 1930, a number of very elderly former slaves were interviewed by a Fisk University researcher in Nashville. One of them, a man named Reed who had grown up on a Middle Tennessee tobacco farm, told his story in these words:

> I was a boy in slavery. Now you talk about hard times, I have had hard times. I started plowing at eight years old. . . . The most barbarous thing I saw with these eyes . . . [was when] my oldest sister, she was fooling with the clock and broke it, and my old marster [i.e., master] taken her and tied a rope around her neck— just enough to keep it from choking her—and tied her up in the back yard and whipped her I don't know how long. There stood mother, there stood father, and there stood all the children and none could come to her rescue. . . . I know plenty of slaves (women) who went with the[ir] old marster. They had to do it or get a killing. They couldn't help it. Some of them would raise large families by their owner.

youngster from his or her parents and tore many a husband and wife apart. One who suffered such a heartbreaking loss was Millie Simkins of Middle Tennessee, who told an interviewer long after the Civil War about her experience as a slave: "My first mistress sold me because I was stubborn," she remembered. "She sent me to the 'slave yard' at Nashville. . . . I was sold away from my husband and I never saw him again."

Why did the slaves not rise up against such an inhumane system? The primary reason is that the white community had overwhelming power and was quite ready to kill any slave who resisted enslavement. Even the merest rumor of a slave revolt was enough to incite whites to murderous violence, as happened in the Middle Tennessee iron district in 1856, when word spread that slaves were plotting to revolt at Christmastime. White vigilantes lynched at least six slaves and mercilessly flogged dozens—perhaps hundreds—of others before the terror subsided.

Another reason slaves generally chose to accommodate themselves to slavery rather than rebel against it was the fact that they were not uniformly and unremittingly miserable. Despite slavery's harsh repressiveness, most slaves were able to establish a stable, rewarding family life that helped to ease the burdens of slavery. And, too, slaves managed to create a little community of their own in the slave quarters, where, after sundown and on Sundays, they could enjoy a respite from the woes of servitude and find fellowship and fulfillment in the company of their enslaved brethren. The "scenes of jollity" on the old plantation that former slaveowners liked to talk about were not necessarily products of wishful thinking; many former slaves, too, recalled such scenes.

Undoubtedly, though, most of the former slaves' memories were unhappy ones, for, even in the best of circumstances, slavery was a cruel institution. If slaves generally behaved as their masters wanted them to, it was only because they had no other choice; their seeming contentment and docility were, for the most part, but a mask. As the Civil War years would reveal, in their hearts slaves hated slavery and longed to be free.

A word must be said here about the small number of blacks in antebellum Tennessee—some 7,300 in 1860—who did not have to endure the travails of slavery. These free blacks were former slaves who had been emancipated by their master or by their master's will, or who were descended from slaves who had been thus freed. Released from the restraints of the slave code, free blacks could move around and seek economic opportunity, and in some cases they were able to acquire property and an education. A few, such as Peter Lowery, a successful Nashville businessman and minister, achieved a measure of prominence.

Although free blacks escaped the restrictions of slavery, they still had to confront white racism. As whites became more and more committed to slavery as the solution to the race problem, they grew correspondingly more suspicious of free blacks. Laws were passed making it harder for masters to free their slaves, requiring newly freed slaves to leave the state, and barring free blacks in other states from moving to Tennessee. Moreover, those free blacks who continued to live in the state witnessed the curtailment of many of their civil rights. Thus, Tennessee's free blacks lived in a kind of twilight zone—not enslaved, yet not wholly free.

Culture

The antebellum years witnessed significant cultural development in Tennessee, as the rawness of the frontier gave way to the refinement and decorum characteristic of Victorian America. It must be said, though, that, by the standards of the long-settled East Coast, Tennessee and the other western states seemed but partially tamed and civilized, even in the years just before the Civil War.

Eager to emulate sophisticated easterners, some Tennesseans set out to bring "high" culture to Tennessee. Intellectual clubs, known as lyceums, appeared in towns and cities. These organizations (one was the Tennessee Society for the Diffusion of Knowledge, founded in Nashville in the 1830s) held regular meetings at which their members discussed literature, the arts, and science. Bookstores appeared, too, and a number of private subscription libraries were established, including the Knoxville Library Company. Historically minded citizens in Knoxville established the East Tennessee Historical and Antiquarian Society in 1834, and those in Nashville followed suit in 1849, founding the Tennessee Historical Society. By the late antebellum era, moreover, every town with any claim to respectability had at least one theater.

Many Tennesseans believed that the true mark of culture was higher education. In the antebellum era, that meant not only colleges, which aimed primarily at preparing men for the professions (teaching, the ministry, law, and medicine), but also academies, which provided schooling for young people up to about eighteen years of age—that is, what we now would regard as a high-school education.

Academies and colleges could be found in Tennessee even during the frontier era, but they multiplied rapidly during the antebellum years. By 1860, there were 274 academies and 35 colleges in the state. Some of the academies, among them the Nashville Female Academy, were outstanding institutions with a national reputation for excellence. If none of the colleges achieved such prominence, some nevertheless were well regarded, including Stewart College in Clarksville, East Tennessee University (now the University of Tennessee at Knoxville), Cumberland University in Lebanon, and the University of Nashville. All the colleges were quite small by today's standards, for few people in those days felt the need of a college education; most professional men still learned their trade not in the classroom but at the side of an experienced mentor. Probably the largest college in the state was the University of Nashville, with 600 students. It included a law school and a medical school. East Tennessee University's student body numbered only 110 in 1860, and 73 of those were youngsters enrolled in a college preparatory program.

Whatever the extent of high culture may have been in antebellum Tennessee, it touched only a small minority of Tennesseans. The theaters, lyceums, and other institutions were available only to town and city folk, and in many cases only to the well-to-do (the libraries, for example, were open only to dues-paying members). The great mass of Tennesseans read nothing but popular literature (including newspapers, dozens of which were published in the state by mid-century) and enjoyed only the more rustic forms of entertainment, such as horse racing, fiddling, and storytelling. Nor did the masses often partake of higher education: the academies and colleges were available only to the elite minority who could afford them (and, in the case of colleges, only to men). Yeomen and poor whites generally had to settle for the rudimentary education offered in the primitive "old-field" subscription schools or the state-sponsored common schools; and blacks, of course, were denied even that.

The only truly inclusive element of antebellum culture was religion. Churches proliferated in town and country alike and included in their congregations blacks and whites; women and men; aristocrats, yeomen, and poor whites. At camp meetings and revivals, too, people of every sort came together. In antebellum Tennessee, religion was monopolized (as it continues to be, though to a lesser extent) by evangelical Protestantism. The three largest evangelical denominations accounted for 83 percent of the state's 2,311 churches in 1860. Building on their success in the Great Revival during the early years of the century, the Methodists outdistanced all their rivals. They claimed 43 percent of all churches, while the Baptists had 30 percent and the Cumberland Presbyterians 10 percent. Other denominations represented in the state included Presbyterians (8 percent) and Disciples of Christ (5 percent). There were, in addition, a few Episcopal, Lutheran, and Roman Catholic churches and two Jewish synagogues.

Among those who participated enthusiastically in the evangelical movement and other aspects of antebellum Tennessee's popular culture were many Cherokee Indians. Hoping that whites might relax their relentless pressure against the Cherokee Nation if the Cherokees became more like their antagonists, some Cherokee leaders began urging their people to take the "white man's road." Their appeals were seconded by white Protestant missionaries who established churches and schools among the Cherokees, most notably at the Brainerd Mission near Chattanooga. Many Cherokees heeded the call. Not only did they begin speaking English and worshipping in Protestant churches, but also they started wearing white-style clothes and living in white-style log cabins. They also gave up hunting and trapping for full-time farm agriculture, often aided by the labor of black slaves whom they had purchased. Furthermore, they abandoned the matrilineal clan system that had granted relatively high status to women and instead adopted the white system of patrilineal families and patriarchal households that confined women to their "separate sphere." No one knows how far Tennessee's Cherokees eventually might have traveled along the white man's road, for their journey was cut short when they were driven from the state in the late 1830s.

Reform

One of the distinguishing features of the antebellum era, in Tennessee and across the nation, was a broad-ranging spirit of reform. Although the reform impulse in Tennessee and the rest of the South never was comparable with that in the North, it nevertheless manifested itself in the Volunteer State in significant ways. Generally speaking, the reform movements were of three sorts: humanitarian, democratic, and geared to self-improvement.

The earliest—though ultimately the least effectual—humanitarian reform effort in Tennessee was the antislavery movement. Around the beginning of the nineteenth century, many Americans began to take a hard look at slavery in the light of their Christian beliefs and the ideals expressed in the Declaration of Independence. A number of local antislavery societies were established in East Tennessee, and in 1815 representatives of those societies met in Greene County and formed an umbrella organization, the Tennessee Manumission Society. Among its officers was a Jonesboro Quaker named Elihu Embree, who in 1819 began publishing one of the nation's first antislavery newspapers, the *Manumission Intelligencer* (he replaced it the following year with the *Emancipator*). Another Quaker, northern-born Benjamin Lundy, began publishing the *Genius of Universal Emancipation* in Greeneville in 1822.

Embree, Lundy, and Tennessee's other antislavery advocates were a moderate group, on the whole (at least in comparison with many of their northern counterparts). Their activities consisted mainly of urging the state legislature to adopt a gradual emancipation plan and using "moral suasion" to convince slaveholders that slavery was un-American and un-Christian. Believing that their cause would fare better if whites did not have to face the prospect of living with freed blacks, many antislavery Tennesseans urged that emancipated slaves be colonized in Liberia or Haiti. The Tennessee Colonization Society, founded in 1829, was devoted to that aim.

Even these modest proposals, however, won little support in Tennessee. At their peak in the 1820s, the local antislavery societies had no more than a thousand members. Moreover, nearly all the societies were in East Tennessee, where slavery was relatively unimportant; the other sections of the state were pretty much devoid of antislavery sentiment. The Tennessee Manumission Society, financially strapped from the beginning, was virtually defunct by 1830. The Tennessee Colonization Society never raised enough funds to transport an appreciable number of blacks. Elihu Embree's newspaper died with him in 1820. Benjamin Lundy published his for less than three years, then headed northward, following in the footsteps of a number of other Tennessee antislavery leaders who had lost hope for the movement in the Volunteer State. The failure of antislavery petitioners to influence the 1834 state constitutional convention already has been discussed; so, too, have the popular and legal pressures that subsequently silenced antislavery advocates and strengthened the slave system.

The most unusual—indeed, by the standards of the time, bizarre—antislavery effort in the state took place not in East but in West Tennessee. Those responsible were not Tennesseans but outsiders, led by a remarkable Scottish-born woman named Fanny Wright. Defying social convention, Wright crusaded publicly in Europe and America for a variety of causes, among them antislavery. Eventually she conceived the idea of a colony where slaves could be educated and prepared for freedom, and in 1825 she founded such a colony thirteen miles from Memphis, calling it Nashoba. There she brought a number of slaves she had purchased and a number of whites who were to "uplift" them. Wright herself stayed at Nashoba only a few months, but she continued to oversee the experiment from a distance and soon broadened its ideals and practices to include full racial equality, free love, and atheism. Nashoba collapsed from mismanagement within five years, and Wright transported the thirty-one blacks to Haiti. Even if Nashoba had been better managed, it could not long have survived the opposition of local whites, who were appalled by the Nashobans' blasphemous repudiation of God, marriage, and white supremacy.

Among humanitarian efforts, far more successful than the attempt to end slavery was the campaign to improve the treatment of criminals and the mentally ill. Prior to the 1820s, Tennessee's criminal code was a barbarous relic of ancient times. Its emphasis was on retribution by severe corporal punishment: the death penalty was decreed for many offenses, while lesser crimes were punished with branding, whipping, or pillorying. Moreover, the only places of detention in the state were squalid county jails, and among the wretched prisoners held there were people whose only crime was inability to pay their debts.

Reformers—the most prominent was Gov. William Carroll—argued that the penal system was cruel, ineffective, and intolerable in the enlightened nineteenth century. Eventually the state legislature responded. Imprisonment for debt was eliminated gradually between 1827 and 1842. The most significant reforms came in 1829, when the legislators abolished the death penalty, except for first-degree murder, and did away with the branding iron, the whip, and the pillory in favor of prison sentences. At the same time, they authorized the construction of a state penitentiary near Nashville, where criminals were to be not merely incarcerated but also rehabilitated. The penitentiary, completed in 1831, was hardly an exemplary institution by today's standards. At night prisoners were placed in solitary confinement in cells three and a half feet by seven and a half feet. During the day, they were forced to labor in total silence in prison workshops. But by the standards of the age, this was a humane and up-to-date facility where wrongdoers got decent food, clothing, and medical care; religious instruction; and plenty of time to contemplate their sins and repent.

Before the antebellum era, the treatment of the mentally ill, like the treatment of criminals, was abominable. Society simply did not know what to do with the mentally ill except confine them. Many were locked in attics or basements by their families; some wound up chained in poorhouses or immured in jails. Antebellum reformers, including Governor Carroll, sought to persuade the public and the lawmakers that insanity was a disease that could be cured by removing those afflicted from their unhealthy environment to a special treatment facility known as an asylum. In 1832, the Tennessee legislature approved the construction of a state asylum near Nashville. It was not completed until 1840, however, and proved poorly designed and unable to care for more than a few dozen patients at a time.

There matters stood until the arrival of the famous northern reformer, Dorothea Dix, who came to Nashville in December 1847 as part of her nationwide crusade on behalf of the mentally ill. She stayed several weeks, inspecting the state asylum and visiting many unfortunates confined elsewhere. Her written report, addressed to the legislature but also printed as a pamphlet and distributed throughout the state, was a shocking indictment. Dix found the asylum altogether inadequate and conditions elsewhere frightful. Many of the insane, she said, were "pining in cells and dungeons, pent in log cabins, bound with ropes, restrained by leathern thongs, burthened with chains." Her findings prodded the legislators into action, and they soon authorized a new asylum. It opened in the 1850s and offered healthful surroundings and enlightened medical care to a large number of patients.

Democratic reform in antebellum Tennessee grew out of the Jacksonian belief that everyone (at least every white male) was as good as everyone else and equally worthy of participating in public life. The political reforms that came about already have been discussed. The other important outgrowth of the democratic spirit—more inclusive than political reform, for it embraced women as well as men—was the campaign for public education. A truly democratic society, many insisted, must provide education not just for an elite few, but for all citizens.

Tennessee took large strides toward that goal. In the 1820s, the legislature created a common school fund with money from the sale of public land. In the 1830s, in obedience to the new state constitution's mandate to promote education, the legislators created a state board of common school commissioners to oversee the school fund and disburse the earnings from it. The most important step came in 1854, at the urging of Gov. Andrew Johnson, who thereafter was known as the "father of public education in Tennessee." In that year, the legislators authorized a state poll tax and property tax for educational purposes, which nearly doubled the amount of state money available for schools. These tax revenues, along with the interest on the common school fund, were to be distributed to the counties on the basis of their school-age free population. The results were soon apparent: the number of public schools, teachers, and pupils increased significantly, while the adult illiteracy rate fell.

Nevertheless, Tennessee's system of public education remained pitifully backward by later standards, and even by the standards of the antebellum northern states. Attendance was not mandatory, and the demands of farm work kept yeoman and poor white children at home most of the time. The number of pupils enrolled by 1860 was considerably less than half the state's school-age white population. Moreover, state funding remained inadequate (less than fifty cents per school-age child annually), and many counties were reluctant to supplement it with tax revenues of their own. Only in Nashville and Memphis, which had the financial wherewithal and the concentrated population to make mass education feasible, did really respectable local school systems appear—and only there was public education offered beyond the elementary level.

As they struggled to make Tennessee a more humane and democratic place to live, many antebellum reformers also preached the gospel of self-improvement and self-control. The evangelical movement, with its emphasis on conversion and living a Christian life, can be viewed as one aspect of this crusade. Another was the temperance movement.

Heavy drinking was a fact of life in early-nineteenth-century America. Taverns were popular social centers, politicians "treated" the voters at election times, and many men drank regularly on the job. Temperance advocates, pointing to the social and economic costs of drunkenness and particularly the violence, crime, and dissoluteness they associated with saloons, called upon drinkers to renounce the use of ardent spirits.

"Parson" Brownlow and the Temperance Cause

The temperance movement had no more zealous advocate than "Parson" William G. Brownlow of Knoxville, a minister and newspaper editor who crusaded for the movement as passionately as he did for his other pet causes, Methodism, Whiggery, and slavery. He joined the Sons of Temperance in 1850 and thereafter spoke out regularly on the subject, both on the podium and in his newspaper, the *Knoxville Whig*. Brownlow's colorful diatribes depicted alcohol as an "infernal demon": "His glaring eyes dart through the land, his hot breath poisons the air, and his relentless clutch is upon every thing good and beautiful." The Parson waxed especially eloquent on the subject of saloons, which he called the "breathing holes of Hell," responsible for "murders, man-slaughters, burglaries, riots, tumults, and all the other enormities with which the country abounds." He himself, he boasted, "never drank a dram of liquor" until middle age and then only as a medicine when very ill.

The movement gained some support in Tennessee. Local chapters of the national Sons of Temperance were established, and at least two temperance newspapers, including the *Maryville Temperance Banner*, were published in the state. Churches got into the act, too; the Holston Conference of the Methodist church, for example, required its ministers to preach at least one temperance sermon a year. Pressure from the temperance forces led the legislature to outlaw saloons in 1838, though it repealed that edict eight years later. Some temperance supporters called (unsuccessfully) for a total ban on the manufacture and sale of alcohol. That goal, however, was more characteristic of later prohibitionists than the antebellum temperance advocates, who, like the anti-slavery advocates, generally put their faith in "moral suasion."

By 1860, Tennessee in many respects had changed dramatically in the past forty-five years. Expansion, development, and reform had transfigured the state's social, economic, political, and cultural landscape. Increasingly, however, Tennesseans now found themselves distracted by another matter. Soon they would be forced to put aside all else to focus upon the great crisis of the Union.

Suggested Readings

Ash, Stephen V. *Middle Tennessee Society Transformed, 1860–1870: War and Peace in the Upper South*. Baton Rouge, La., 1988.

Atkins, Jonathan M. *Parties, Politics, and the Sectional Conflict in Tennessee, 1832–1861.* Knoxville, Tenn., 1997.

Bailey, Fred Arthur. *Class and Tennessee's Confederate Generation.* Chapel Hill, N.C., 1987.

Bergeron, Paul H. *Antebellum Politics in Tennessee.* Lexington, Ky., 1982.

Campbell, Mary E. R. *The Attitude of Tennesseans toward the Union, 1847–1861.* New York, 1961.

Clark, Blanche Henry. *The Tennessee Yeomen, 1840–1860.* Nashville, Tenn., 1942.

Coulter, E. Merton. *William G. Brownlow: Fighting Parson of the Southern Highlands.* 1937. Reprinted, Knoxville, Tenn., 1999.

Davenport, F. Garvin. *Cultural Life in Nashville on the Eve of the Civil War.* Chapel Hill, N.C., 1941.

Dunn, Durwood. *An Abolitionist in the Appalachian South: Ezekiel Birdseye on Slavery, Capitalism, and Separate Statehood in East Tennessee, 1841–1846.* Knoxville, Tenn., 1997.

Egerton, John. *Visions of Utopia: Nashoba, Rugby, Ruskin, and the "New Communities" in Tennessee's Past.* Knoxville, Tenn., 1977.

Goodstein, Anita Shafer. *Nashville, 1780–1860: From Frontier to City.* Gainesville, Fla., 1989.

Humphrey, Steve. *"That D— —d Brownlow," Being a Saucy & Malicious Description of Fighting Parson WILLIAM GANNAWAY BROWNLOW.* Boone, N.C. 1978.

Lamon, Lester C. *Blacks in Tennessee, 1791–1970.* Knoxville, Tenn., 1981.

McKenzie, Robert Tracy. *One South or Many? Plantation Belt and Upcountry in Civil War–Era Tennessee.* Cambridge, England, 1994.

Mooney, Chase C. *Slavery in Tennessee.* Bloomington, Ind., 1957.

Norton, Herman A. *Religion in Tennessee, 1777–1945.* Knoxville, Tenn., 1981.

Parks, Joseph H. *John Bell of Tennessee.* Baton Rouge, La., 1950.

Sellers, Charles G. *James K. Polk: Jacksonian, 1795–1843.* Princeton, N.J., 1957.

White, Robert H. *Development of the Tennessee State Education Organization, 1796–1929.* Nashville, Tenn., 1929.

Winters, Donald L. *Tennessee Farming, Tennessee Farmers: Antebellum Agriculture in the Upper South.* Knoxville, Tenn., 1994.

Wooster, Ralph A. *Politicians, Planters, and Plain Folk: Courthouse and Statehouse in the Upper South, 1850–1860.* Knoxville, Tenn., 1975.

6

The Civil War

No STATE WAS MORE RAVAGED or more divided by the war of the 1860s than Tennessee. Its location made it a hotly contested strategic prize and the scene of many battles between the armies of North and South. Divisions among its people, too, generated bitter internal conflicts that persisted even after the war ended.

Tennessee's experience as one of the southern states that seceded and formed the Confederacy was in many ways unique. The last state to leave the Union and the first to rejoin it, Tennessee also was the only one that seceded by legislative declaration rather than convention ordinance, the only one whose secessionist government collapsed before the war ended, the only one that experienced large-scale *Confederate* military occupation and martial law, the only one that came entirely under the control of the federal army before the war ended, the only one completely exempted from the Emancipation Proclamation, and the only one that, on its own, formally abolished slavery.

Secession

Tennessee was not in the forefront of the movement to form an independent southern nation. Indeed, until the Civil War actually broke out, Tennesseans on the whole took a very moderate stand, hoping against hope that some compromise might be worked out that would keep the South and North together in the Union.

It was not that Tennesseans were undisturbed by the controversies that in the 1850s turned more and more southerners toward the idea of secession. Like most other whites below the Mason-Dixon Line, those in Tennessee had begun to see the North as an alien culture whose people were hostile to the South. They came to believe, too, that the North's burgeoning economy and population threatened the South's traditionally strong influence in national affairs.

At the heart of the matter was slavery. White southerners feared that their "peculiar institution" was in danger. A small but growing radical abolitionist movement in the North was demanding an immediate end to slavery throughout the South. Some abolitionists were helping slaves to escape via an "underground railroad" to the North and were interfering with the efforts of slaveowners to reclaim them when apprehended. Perhaps even more disturbing, because it was more broadly supported in the North, was the campaign to keep slavery out of the western territories. This was both a symbolic and a substantive issue. White southerners felt insulted by the assertion that slavery was inimical to the American way of life and should be prohibited wherever it was not already established. At the same time, they recognized that the addition of new free states created from the territories would undercut slave-state power in Congress. Some feared, too, that bottling up the growing slave population in the South without a safety valve eventually would lead to a racial explosion.

Two events finally pushed many white southerners over the edge. In 1859, an armed band of radical abolitionists, led by John Brown, raided a federal arsenal in Harpers Ferry, Virginia, hoping to spark a slave revolt. The plot failed, but many southerners became convinced that this was merely the first skirmish of an all-out abolitionist war against slavery. They concluded that the South could no longer be safe in a nation where abolitionism was allowed to exist.

The second event was the momentous presidential election of 1860. Sectionalism by that time had so disrupted American politics that four candidates were in the field. The Democratic Party, torn apart by the slavery issue, could not agree on a candidate, and thus two Democrats ran. Stephen A. Douglas of Illinois was the favorite of northern and some moderate southern Democrats, while John C. Breckinridge of Kentucky was the favorite of most southern Democrats and especially the strong southern-rights advocates. The candidate of the Republican Party, whose key platform plank was opposition to slavery in the territories, was Abraham Lincoln of Illinois; for obvious reasons, the Republican Party had very little support outside the North and far West. The fourth hopeful was John Bell of Tennessee, who offered himself as a compromise candidate. The platform of his newly created Constitutional Union Party stressed sectional reconciliation, and his support came mostly from former Whigs, whose party had disintegrated as a national institution in the 1850s.

The campaign was an exciting one in Tennessee and across the nation. In the Volunteer State, favorite son Bell eked out a victory by plurality. He garnered a little less than 48 percent of the vote, while Breckinridge got just under 45 percent and Douglas less than 8 percent (Lincoln was not on the ballot in Tennessee). Nationally, however, Bell won only three states. Douglas fared even worse. Breckinridge did better, taking most of the South. But the efforts of all three were in vain, for Abraham Lincoln swept the North and far West, giving him a solid majority of the electoral vote and thus the election.

Lincoln's victory triggered the secession of the seven Deep South states, beginning with South Carolina on December 20, 1860. The majority of whites in those states could not abide living in a Union dominated by a Republican administration. Not only would slavery be threatened in the territories, they believed, but it might be threatened at home as well, for Lincoln, with his patronage power, could implant the Republican Party in the South. Moreover, because Lincoln had won without the electoral votes of a single southern state, it seemed that the South now was politically irrelevant and thus bereft of influence over federal policy. Secession seemed the only answer.

Some in Tennessee were swayed by such reasoning. One was Isham G. Harris, a West Tennessee lawyer, planter, and Democrat who had been governor since 1857. When the Deep South states began leaving the Union, Governor Harris wanted Tennessee to join them. Knowing that many Tennesseans would oppose him, however, he avoided calling openly for secession. He did, however, summon the legislators into special session on January 7, 1861. When they assembled, Harris sent them a fiery message denouncing the "aggressions of the Northern States" and requesting a popular referendum to decide whether to convene a special state convention "to take into consideration our federal relations." The legislators obliged, authorizing a referendum to be held February 9. Voters also would cast ballots that day for delegates to the convention, so that a second election would not be necessary if the convention was approved.

In the weeks leading up to the referendum, Tennessee was ablaze with political activity. Secessionists were vocal and well organized, but so were their unionist opponents. Many unionists, including John Bell, argued for a wait-and-see policy, pointing out that Lincoln had not overtly threatened slavery and that the South still had great influence in Congress and the Supreme Court. Unionist sentiment was especially strong in those parts of the state where slaves were few and in those parts where the Whig Party (which persisted in Tennessee as a state-level organization known as the Opposition Party) traditionally had dominated. Secessionism, on the other hand, was strongest in the plantation districts and in areas of Democratic dominance.

Unionism triumphed decisively on February 9. Voters rejected the proposed convention by 55 percent to 45 percent. These figures considerably understate the unionist majority, however, for many unionists voted in favor of a convention, hoping that it would resoundingly reject secession. The votes garnered by candidates for delegate, a better measure of voter sentiment, revealed overwhelming support for the Union: unionist candidates won more than three-quarters of the total.

Not surprisingly, given the demographic and partisan factors that influenced the electorate, there were sharp sectional differences in the February vote. West Tennessee, where slaves were numerous and the Democracy strong, cast 74 percent of its votes in favor of a convention. East Tennessee, where slaves were few and Whiggery strong, cast 81 percent of its votes *against* a convention. Middle Tennessee was almost evenly divided, with 51 percent against a convention. Overall, however, the unionists' victory was incontrovertible, and they were jubilant. "The mad waves of secession found an iron embankment around this proud commonwealth," wrote one, "which defied all their fury."

The other states of the Upper South likewise rejected secession during those winter months. Meanwhile, the Deep South states formed a provisional Confederate government in February. Lincoln was inaugurated on March 4. There matters stood until the spring. On April 12, South Carolina military forces opened fire on the federal army garrison inside Fort Sumter in Charleston harbor, which Lincoln had insisted on holding despite Confederate protests. Three days later, Lincoln called on the states of the Union to furnish troops to put down rebellion, in effect declaring war on the Confederacy.

Lincoln's proclamation was the final jolt that shook Tennessee loose from the Union. Most Tennessee unionists were "conditional" unionists: they sided with the North only so long as the federal government followed a hands-off policy toward the seceded states. But now they were being forced to choose sides in a war; for most, there could be only one response.

Secessionists of Franklin County

In no county of the state were secessionists more active than in Franklin County, which is in southeastern Middle Tennessee, on the Alabama line. Although Tennesseans as a whole decisively rejected the proposed secession convention in the referendum of February 9, 1861, Franklin Countians voted for it by a six-to-one margin (1,240 to 206).

On February 24, the citizens of Franklin held a mass meeting. Resolutions were passed expressing "mortification and regret" that Tennessee had rejected the convention and stating that the "hearts, sympathies and feelings" of the people of Franklin were with the seceded states. Another resolution lauded Jefferson Davis, president of the Confederate States of America, as "a Gentlemen, a scholar and a statesman" and denounced Abraham Lincoln as "a wag, a mental dwarf."

Not content with these resolutions, the citizens then declared themselves "out of the Union" and petitioned the Tennessee legislature to redraw the state line so that Franklin would become part of the seceded state of Alabama. The legislature never took any action on this unprecedented request, but that hardly mattered; before long, Tennessee declared its independence and joined the Confederacy.

Unwilling to wage war against their southern brethren, they chose to fight with them against the North.

Taking advantage of the sudden reversal of opinion among the conditional unionists—including John Bell, who now went over to the secessionist camp—Governor Harris informed President Lincoln that "Tennessee will not furnish a single man for purposes of coercion" and again called the legislature into special session. To avoid the delay that convening a secession convention would entail, he asked the legislators to adopt a declaration of Tennessee independence, based on the inherent right of revolution. This they did on May 6 by large majorities in both houses, though stipulating that their action be subject to a popular referendum to be held on June 8.

The June vote graphically revealed how sentiment had shifted in the Volunteer State. Tennesseans voted 69 percent to 31 percent to confirm the declaration of independence and thus to secede from the Union. The change since the February referendum was particularly striking in Middle Tennessee, where 88 percent of the voters now endorsed secession (in West Tennessee, 83 percent did so).

Whether Governor Harris had led the state out of the Union or merely surfed an irresistible tide is debatable, but in any event he was pleased. He could not, however, ignore the fact that some forty-seven thousand votes had been cast against his cause—the great majority of them in East Tennessee, which voted against the declaration by more than two to one (69 percent to 31 percent). The "unconditional" unionists who cast those ballots clearly were a force to be reckoned with. Tennesseans would not be going to war as a united people.

Confederate Tennessee

Outside East Tennessee, almost all the state's citizens rallied enthusiastically to the Confederate cause when the war began. Excited crowds gathered on courthouse lawns to hear patriotic speeches and cheer the raising of the Stars and Bars. Public confidence was high; few doubted that the war would be brief and the Confederacy triumphant.

Beneath the surface, however, flowed undercurrents of apprehension. Many Tennesseans feared that subversives, white and black, might stir up trouble on the home front. Thus authorities and citizens in Middle and West Tennessee took steps to secure their safety. Ruthlessly they persecuted anyone not fully committed to the Confederate cause. Those few still faithful to the Union were threatened with violence; some fled for their lives to the North, while the rest were cowed and silenced. The black population, long a source of white anxiety, now was supervised more closely and restrained more harshly. In some communities, citizens formed vigilante organizations to watch for suspicious activities. The Norris Creek Home Guards of Lincoln County, for example, pledged themselves to "the protection of our home from

Tennessee secessionists assaulting a Unionist. East Tennessee Historical Society, Knoxville. W. G. Brownlow, *Sketches of the Rise, Progress, and Decline of Secession* (Philadelphia, 1862), facing p. 169.

secret enemies, whether they be negro insurrectioners, abolition emissaries, or home traitors."

Meanwhile, without waiting for the June referendum, Governor Harris set about getting the state ready to join the fight against the North. On April 20, he dispatched a special envoy to act as liaison to the Confederate government. At the same time, he gave the Confederate army permission to build river fortifications at Memphis. On May 7, with the legislature's concurrence, he signed a formal military alliance with the Confederacy. Tennessee officially became a part of the Confederate States of America on July 22, joining the seven Deep South states and three other Upper South states that had seceded after the firing on Fort Sumter.

The state government's principal task that spring of 1861 was raising and equipping a military force and preparing defenses against the expected northern invasion. On May 6, at Harris's urging, the legislature passed the Provisional Army of Tennessee Act. This authorized the creation of a state army of fifty-five thousand men (twenty-five thousand active and the rest in reserve) and committed the state to a five-million-dollar war bond issue. The act also established a Military and Financial Board, headed by the governor, to oversee these matters. Harris appointed a Middle Tennessean and Mexican War veteran, Gideon J. Pillow, to command the Provisional Army.

Difficulties abounded. Recruiting was not one of them, for the men of the Volunteer State confirmed their reputation by flocking to the colors in large numbers (eventually some one hundred thousand Tennesseans would serve in the southern army). The problem was supplying them, especially with weapons. Harris had agents scour the state for private arms that could be readied for military use, and he purchased other weapons from out-of-state suppliers. But by July, when he tendered to the Confederacy the active Provisional Army forces—twenty-two infantry and two cavalry regiments, ten artillery companies, an engineer corps, and an ordnance bureau—they still were not adequately equipped. These units were, however, well organized, and they formed the core of what would become one of the Confederacy's two great armies, the Army of Tennessee.

Harris encountered other difficulties as well. He never managed to establish all the armories and powder mills needed for the war effort, mainly because the state was short on skilled workers and certain essential resources. Furthermore, the defensive fortifications Harris wanted never were completed—a failure that had disastrous results. Harris was not entirely at fault in this matter either, for he was handicapped by a lack of cooperation on the part of the state's slave owners, who coughed up only about one-tenth of the five

---

Confederate Women of Memphis

Women played a key role in military mobilization during Tennessee's brief experience as a Confederate state. Nowhere was this more true than in Memphis, an important Confederate military center. The demands of war created new opportunities for Memphis women to use their talents outside the home.

No sooner had the conflict begun than the women of the city began organizing voluntary associations to aid the war effort. The Military Sewing Society, for example, made soldiers' uniforms, while the Soldiers Aid Society staged concerts to raise money for a home for war widows and orphans. The shortage of men, great numbers of whom enlisted in the army, opened up jobs for women in the city's war-related industries. Many were employed in manufacturing gunpowder, percussion caps, and musket balls.

Perhaps the greatest contribution of the Memphis women was in the care of sick and wounded soldiers. Many women served as nurses in the Confederate army hospitals in the city, and one group of women organized their own facility, the Southern Mothers Hospital. Nursing was not a job for the frail or the weak-stomached: "The thought of a man having his leg or arm sawed from his body while living, was horrifying to our hearts," one Memphis woman recalled; "yet we had to get used to it[,] as well as all other distressing scenes attending a state of war."

thousand slaves Harris requested to work on the forts. On the whole, Harris proved to be an energetic and capable wartime governor, cooperating whole-heartedly with Confederate authorities and willingly setting aside his Democratic prejudices against activist government in order to do his duty.

As troublesome as the matter of military preparedness was, Harris had an even bigger headache as war governor: dealing with the East Tennessee unionists. The majority of East Tennesseans never reconciled themselves to secession, which they believed not only was illegal but actually formed part of a conspiracy by rich planters (whom the East Tennessee yeomanry long had detested) to consolidate their power over the common folk. East Tennesseans did not oppose secession out of any antipathy to the "peculiar institution," for they believed in slavery as devoutly as any other white southerners. They argued, though—correctly, as events would prove—that secession would not safeguard slavery but rather would endanger it, by eliminating the South's influence in Washington and inviting Yankee invasion.

Organized resistance to secession in East Tennessee began soon after the legislature passed the declaration of independence. In mid-May, a group of prominent Knoxvillians, including William G. "Parson" Brownlow and Oliver P. Temple, met in Temple's law office and agreed that East Tennessee unionists should present a united front. They then issued a call for a unionist convention. Brownlow spread the word in his newspaper, the *Whig*, and meetings were held all over the region to elect delegates. On May 30, four hundred men convened in Knoxville. For two days they heard passionate Union speeches by convention president T. A. R. Nelson, Sen. Andrew Johnson, and others. Then they approved resolutions condemning secession.

When the meeting adjourned, Johnson the Democrat and Nelson the old Whig resumed the joint speaking tour they had begun earlier that month, stumping the region to urge voters to reject secession in the upcoming referendum. People marveled at how the cause of the Union had brought together those two longtime political enemies, but that was not the only example of strange bedfellows that spring. Johnson also patched up old differences with Brownlow, whom he had once called a "vile miscreant." Brownlow, who previously had regarded Johnson as "a contemptible political prostitute" and an "unprincipled knave," now lauded the senator for his patriotism: "*Johnson is right*," he declared, "*and I will defend him to the last.*"

After the June referendum, 285 unionist delegates reconvened in Greeneville. (Andrew Johnson was not among them, for threats on his life by secessionists had persuaded him to leave the region on June 12; he headed northward to become the only senator from a seceded state to stay on at his post in Washington.) The Greeneville convention of June 17–20 not only denounced secession but also took the bold step of petitioning the legislature to allow separate statehood for East Tennessee. This request never was acted upon in Nashville. Nevertheless, the Greeneville convention and its predecessor in Knoxville were important. By rallying Union sentiment in East Tennessee, the conventions encouraged continued resistance to secession there, at a time when most unionists elsewhere in the Confederacy found themselves leaderless, disorganized, and impotent.

Governor Harris's initial response to the defiant East Tennesseans was a policy of "forbearance and conciliation," for he believed that they eventually would accept secession if treated with leniency. The indulgent governor even permitted Parson Brownlow to continue cranking out anti-Confederate editorials and flying his Union flag. The presence of Confederate troops in East Tennessee (needed to protect the vital railroad link between Virginia and the Gulf states) was a particularly sticky matter, for unionists regarded it as enemy occupation. To mollify them, Harris successfully urged Confederate authorities to appoint as regional commander a Tennessean, Gen. Felix Zollicoffer, who shared Harris's conciliatory goals. Harris also persuaded the Confederates to use Tennessee troops in the region insofar as possible and to keep those from other states in camps away from the main population centers.

Harris's forbearance was tested severely by the August 1861 state election. His gubernatorial opponent was William H. Polk, who accepted secession but gained favor among unionists by blasting Harris as a "dictator." Harris won the election by a large margin, but East Tennessee voted overwhelmingly against him. Furthermore, the East Tennessee voters elected United States congressmen in every district in the region, despite the governor's order to elect Confederate congressmen.

Harris was irked. Vowing to adopt a more "decided and energetic policy," he had some unionist leaders arrested and asked that more Confederate troops be assigned to East Tennessee, regardless of their origin. Parson Brownlow, learning of his imminent arrest for treason, shut down his newspaper on October 26 and hid out in the country. He later was arrested and jailed but eventually was allowed to go north.

State and Confederate authorities still acted with considerable restraint, however, until an incident in November. It had its genesis some weeks earlier, when an East Tennessee unionist named William B. Carter traveled to Washington and met with top federal officials, including President Lincoln. Carter presented, and received approval for, a plan to sabotage the strategic East Tennessee railroad. It was agreed that bands of unionists would strike simultaneously along the railroad and destroy nine key bridges. At the same time, a federal army would invade East Tennessee from Kentucky and a general uprising of unionists would begin.

On the night of November 8, Carter and his co-conspirators made their move, burning five of the bridges (though failing to burn four others that were heavily guarded). The expected Union army did not materialize, however, and the uprising fizzled.

This episode provoked a massive Confederate crackdown in East Tennessee. Hundreds of suspects were rounded up. Five of the bridge-burners were hanged, and two were left dangling for days beside the railroad track

Daniel Ellis and His "Thrilling Adventures"

To the Unionists of East Tennessee, Daniel Ellis was a hero. A native of Carter County, Ellis remained loyal to the United States after Tennessee seceded. He was among the bridge-burners of November 1861, but, unlike many of his co-conspirators, he eluded the subsequent Confederate dragnet by hiding in the mountains. Thereafter he waged a personal war against the Confederacy.

Familiar with every trail in his native region, Ellis served as a guide for people who wanted to escape from Confederate-held East Tennessee and go to Union-held Kentucky. Among those he daringly piloted to friendly territory were Unionists who wanted to join the federal army, men fleeing the Confederate draft, escaped Union prisoners of war, and escaped slaves. By the end of the war, those whom Ellis had helped numbered in the thousands. Some paid for his services, and these fees, along with money he received for carrying mail back and forth, and profits from his lucrative horse-stealing business (he targeted Confederate-owned horses only), allowed him to support his family during the war.

In January 1865, Ellis joined the Union army, was appointed captain of a cavalry company, and thereafter continued to operate in the mountains of East Tennessee. In 1867, he published a book about his wartime career, rather immodestly titled *Thrilling Adventures of Daniel Ellis, the Great Union Guide of East Tennessee.*

near Greeneville. Thereafter, the authorities abandoned conciliation, declared East Tennessee enemy territory, and suspended civil rights. Unionists were subjected to martial law, mass arrests and imprisonment, forced oath taking, and confiscation of property.

If the object of this get-tough approach was to bring the East Tennessee unionists to their knees, it failed miserably. What it did was embitter them more deeply and fuel their determination to resist. Many fled to Kentucky and joined the Union army (an estimated forty-two thousand white Tennesseans wore the blue during the war, the great majority of them East Tennesseans). Others formed guerrilla bands and harassed the Confederate occupation forces. Eventually, ten thousand Confederate troops were tied down in East Tennessee guarding strategic points and trying to subdue the hostile citizenry. The region remained a scene of violent anti-Confederate resistance until the Union army secured control of it in 1864.

Meanwhile, Tennessee's state government had ceased to exist. When federal forces invaded Middle Tennessee in February 1862, Governor Harris, the legislators, and other state officers abandoned Nashville and fled to Memphis. The legislature met there until March, then adjourned. Soon West Tennessee fell to the Yankees, too, and the state officials scattered. Harris joined the Army of Tennessee as a staff officer. He continued to hold the title of governor, however, and even went through the motions of calling a state election in 1863, though he himself declined to run again. Holding a real election was impossible, of course, but a few votes were cast by Tennessee troops in the Confederate army. They elected Robert Caruthers chief executive, but it was an empty honor, for he was a governor without a legislature or a bureaucracy—indeed, a governor without a state.

Tennessee as a Theater of War

It was perhaps inevitable that Tennessee would be the scene of many battles during the Civil War (more than any other state except Virginia), for strategically it was important to both sides. The Confederacy depended heavily upon the Volunteer State's material resources, which included East Tennessee's vital railroad; its wheat production; and its deposits of saltpeter, lead, and copper; as well as Middle Tennessee's iron furnaces and rich supplies of corn, hogs, cattle, horses, and mules. Moreover, Nashville was the leading military manufacturing center and storage depot in the western Confederacy, with Memphis a close second.

These facts alone no doubt would have persuaded the North to invade and occupy Tennessee, simply to deny its use to the Confederacy; but additional factors also led the Yankees to regard Tennessee as a prize worth having. For one thing, Chattanooga was a gateway to the Lower South; it had to be taken in order to capture Atlanta, one of the North's key strategic goals. Middle Tennessee provided the most direct invasion route from the North to Chattanooga, but the town also was accessible through East Tennessee, which furthermore contained vast human resources—the unionists—whom the North hoped to liberate and recruit as allies. The North also cast covetous eyes upon the Volunteer State's rivers—particularly the Tennessee and the Mississippi, which were veritable highways into the heart of the South. Control of the Mississippi was another of the North's primary strategic goals, and it could not be accomplished without holding West Tennessee.

For some months after the war broke out, responsibility for the state's defense lay with Governor Harris and General Pillow. They concentrated on defending the Mississippi, believing that Kentucky's declaration of neutrality (which for the time being was respected by the Lincoln administration) would safeguard the other parts of Tennessee from invasion. A string of forts was constructed along the Mississippi in West Tennessee, the north-

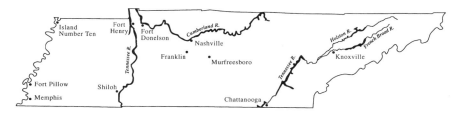

Civil War sites in Tennessee.

ernmost being at Island Number Ten. Less attention was devoted to protecting the Tennessee and Cumberland Rivers, although defensive works were built there, or at least started.

In early September 1861, the Confederate army commander in West Tennessee, a Middle Tennessean named Leonidas Polk, led a force into Kentucky and seized Columbus, where he built another fortification overlooking the Mississippi River. This violation of Kentucky's neutrality gave the North an excuse to send its own troops into that state.

Soon thereafter, Gen. Albert Sidney Johnston assumed responsibility for the defense of the entire Confederacy west of the Appalachians. With federal troops now pouring into Kentucky, Johnston had to decide how to defend the long northern border of Tennessee. He probably should have concentrated his greatly outnumbered forces somewhere to the south, but instead he chose to scatter them along the state line. In addition to Polk's troops and the garrisons at Fort Henry on the Tennessee and Fort Donelson on the Cumberland, Johnston had a small force under William Hardee, which he posted north of Nashville at Bowling Green, Kentucky, and another under General Zollicoffer, which took up a position in southeastern Kentucky to protect East Tennessee.

This thin line began disintegrating early in 1862. In January, Zollicoffer's force was routed by the Federals and fell back into East Tennessee; Zollicoffer was killed, and his troops were demoralized. The next month, the Union's Gen. Ulysses S. Grant led a combined army and navy expedition up the Tennessee River against Fort Henry. The fort—poorly designed, unfinished, and weakly garrisoned—surrendered on February 6. Grant then moved against Fort Donelson, twelve miles east of Fort Henry. Johnston reinforced Donelson's garrison. That proved to be a mistake, for the fort became a trap when Grant surrounded it with his army and shelled it with his gunboats. The fifteen thousand Confederate troops there surrendered to Grant on February 16.

The fall of Forts Henry and Donelson was the greatest disaster that yet had befallen the young Confederacy. A major portion of Johnston's force was now lost, the Tennessee River was open all the way to Alabama, and the Cumberland River was open to Nashville. Moreover, the rest of Johnston's defensive line had become untenable. He therefore ordered that Bowling Green and Columbus be evacuated (though the Mississippi River forts below Columbus were to be held). As the Confederates retreated southward, Grant moved in the same direction, up the Tennessee River. Another federal army under Don Carlos Buell marched from central Kentucky into Middle Tennessee, capturing Nashville in late February.

All the retreating Confederate units (save those in East Tennessee, which were not pursued by any Union army) gathered in northern Mississippi. There they were reinforced by units from other parts of the South and welded together into a real army (eventually called the Army of Tennessee), mainly through the exertions of Johnston's subordinate commanders, P. G. T. Beauregard and Braxton Bragg. So reinvigorated were the troops that their leaders soon began planning a counterattack.

Early in April 1862, Johnston's army moved northward to attack Grant, who had advanced almost to the Mississippi state line. The Confederates hoped to destroy Grant's army before Buell's arrived to reinforce it, and they almost succeeded. Surprised by an early morning assault on April 6, Grant's troops gave way; but some held their ground long enough to blunt the attack. The next day, with the arrival of Buell's troops, the Federals pushed the Army of Tennessee back. This battle (known as Shiloh, after a nearby church) was the biggest ever fought in America up to that time; when it was over, some twenty thousand men in blue and gray lay dead or wounded. Among the slain was Albert Sidney Johnston.

On the day the Battle of Shiloh ended, a federal force under Gen. John Pope captured Island Number Ten. In the succeeding weeks, the other Mississippi River forts in Tennessee fell one by one; and in June, northern troops occupied Memphis. Thus, by mid-1862, all of West and Middle Tennessee was in Union hands.

Johnston's successor, Braxton Bragg, thereupon decided to take the offensive again. Moving his army east and north, he joined with the Confederate force in East Tennessee, now under Edmund Kirby Smith, and together they invaded Kentucky. Buell's army followed him there, abandoning Middle Tennessee except for Nashville. In a battle in October, Buell managed to repulse the Confederate invaders. Smith then returned to East Tennessee, while Bragg pulled his army back to Middle Tennessee and took a position near Murfreesboro. There he faced the federal army, now commanded by Buell's successor, William S. Rosecrans. In the bloody Battle of Murfreesboro or Stones River (December 31, 1862, to January 2, 1863), Bragg unsuccessfully attempted to drive Rosecrans back toward Nashville. The Army of Tennessee then withdrew into the southeastern corner of Middle Tennessee for the winter.

The following summer, Rosecrans maneuvered Bragg out of the state al-

Wartime Chattanooga. East Tennessee Historical Society, Knoxville.

together, forcing him into northern Georgia and seizing Chattanooga. But with the aid of reinforcements from the Virginia front under Gen. James Longstreet, Bragg in September 1863 won a victory over Rosecrans (who had pursued him into Georgia) at the Battle of Chickamauga. The Federals retreated north to Chattanooga; Bragg followed and laid siege to the town.

Rosecrans was replaced in October by Ulysses S. Grant. Since Shiloh, Grant had been busy trying to secure control of the Mississippi River. Having accomplished that task with the capture of Vicksburg, Mississippi, in July, Grant now came to Chattanooga, along with some of his troops, and took the offensive against Bragg. In the battles of Lookout Mountain on November 24 and Missionary Ridge on November 25, Grant broke the siege of Chattanooga and sent the Army of Tennessee reeling back into Georgia.

Some weeks before Bragg encircled Rosecrans's army at Chattanooga, another Union army, under Ambrose Burnside, had invaded East Tennessee from Kentucky. The Confederate force defending the region fell back and joined Bragg. On November 4, Longstreet's command was detached from Bragg's army and sent to the northeast to stop Burnside. The Federals took up a defensive position around Knoxville and on November 29 repelled Longstreet's assault against a section of their works known as Fort Sanders. Longstreet and his troops thereupon withdrew into upper East Tennessee, where they spent the winter. With their return to Virginia in the spring of 1864, Tennessee was entirely under the control of the Union army.

Late in 1864, the Confederates made one last desperate attempt to retake

Sam Davis, Young Hero of the Confederacy

The son of a Rutherford County planter, Sam Davis enlisted in the Confederate army in May 1861; fought in campaigns in Virginia, Tennessee, and Kentucky; and was wounded at the battles of Shiloh and Perryville. In 1863, he took on a dangerous assignment carrying dispatches from a Confederate spy behind the Union lines in Tennessee. On November 20, not long after his twenty-first birthday, he was captured by federal soldiers in Giles County and taken to the headquarters of Union Gen. Grenville M. Dodge in Pulaski. Davis was acting as a messenger only, not as a spy, and he was wearing his Confederate army uniform; but he also wore a Federal army overcoat (dyed brown, a piece of apparel common in the poorly supplied Confederate army).

General Dodge, having read the dispatches Davis bore, told him he was being held as a spy and could be executed, but he would be shown leniency if he revealed the identity of the person who wrote the dispatches. Davis refused. Dodge thereupon convened a military commission that tried Davis and sentenced him to death. On the morning of his execution, November 27, a Union officer asked him why he did not accept Dodge's offer of leniency. Davis replied, "Do you suppose that I would betray a friend? No, sir, I would die a thousand times first!" Then he was led up the scaffold and hanged. A Union soldier who witnessed the event said, "He stood it like a man."

the state. Having failed to prevent the federal capture of Atlanta, which fell in September, the Army of Tennessee (now commanded by John B. Hood, and much weakened by hard fighting) marched through northern Alabama and into Middle Tennessee. There a federal army under George Thomas waited. On November 30, the Confederates suffered grievous casualties attacking a portion of Thomas's force at Franklin, but in bitterly cold weather pushed on to confront the main force entrenched around Nashville. At that point, Thomas took the offensive and in a two-day battle (December 15–16) decisively defeated Hood and sent the Army of Tennessee fleeing southward into Alabama, its ranks depleted and its days as an effective fighting force ended.

Tennessee contributed a number of outstanding leaders to the Confederate cause (and to the Union cause as well), but none achieved more fame than Nathan Bedford Forrest. Without any formal military training (he had been a businessman and planter before the war), Forrest emerged as a cavalry leader of true genius, rising from the rank of private to lieutenant general and bedeviling the Yankee army with daring behind-the-lines raids. One of his most celebrated exploits came in July 1862, when his thousand-man command surprised a larger force of Federals at Murfreesboro, capturing every one and seizing massive military stores. But Forrest's wartime career was marked by controversy (as his postwar career would be). There is strong evidence that, when his troops captured federal Fort Pillow (on the Mississippi River north of Memphis) in April 1864, they ruthlessly shot down some of the garrison troops—including many black soldiers—after they had surrendered.

The Military Governorship of Andrew Johnson

As federal commanders grappled with the military problem of invading and occupying Tennessee, President Lincoln grappled with the political problem of getting the state restored to the Union. He took a practical, *ad hoc* approach, as he did toward the other Confederate states where northern forces secured enough of a foothold to allow political reconstruction to get under way. Ignoring the debates over the precise legal status of the seceded states, Lincoln said simply that those states were "out of their proper practical relation with the Union" and should be brought back into a proper relation as quickly as possible.

The first step toward that goal would be to get loyal governments functioning in those states. The president decided to appoint a military governor to take charge of that task in Tennessee. The man he selected was Andrew Johnson.

Armed with a commission as brigadier general and broad authority to take whatever steps he deemed necessary to do his job, Johnson arrived in Nashville in March 1862. In some respects, he seemed a good choice for military governor. For one thing, he was devoted to the Union cause and determined to put down the southern "rebellion." Moreover, he was a Tennessean with long experience in state politics. Too, he saw eye to eye with President Lincoln on many matters, particularly on the nature of secessionism and the war aims of the Union. In that early stage of the war, both men believed that secessionism was not deeply rooted in the South and that there were only a few hard-core secessionists—mostly aristocrats and ambitious politicians—who had used deceit and demagoguery to trick the masses into supporting secession. All that was necessary was to allow the deluded citizens to see the truth, Lincoln and Johnson assumed, and they would voluntarily return to the Union. Furthermore, both men wanted to restore the South to the Union just as it was before the war, without any of the fundamental changes that some northern radicals were calling for.

On the other hand, certain factors rendered Johnson a less than ideal choice for military governor. First of all, he tended to be intransigent and undiplomatic, yet his job would require him to work smoothly with many sorts of people and to exercise a measure of tact and discretion. Moreover,

Johnson began his work deprived of his natural constituency—the East Tennessee unionists, who remained under Confederate control until the fall of 1863. Until then, the military governor could assert his authority only in Middle and West Tennessee, where unionists were few and those mostly old Whigs, some of whom found it hard to put aside their longtime enmity toward Johnson. The Democrats of Middle and West Tennessee were virtually all secessionists, and they despised Johnson as a traitor to his state.

Other problems, too, hindered Johnson's ability to carry out his duties. The division of authority between him and the federal army commanders in the state was vague, a fact that eventually led to jurisdictional squabbles. Although Lincoln generally sided with Johnson, the quarrels distracted the military governor from his work. Furthermore, not until the end of 1864 was Tennessee securely in federal hands. Until then, Confederate armies remained in the state, or at least threatened it, while Rebel cavalry raiders and guerrilla bands often disrupted federal control and encouraged secessionist citizens to defy Union authority.

Nevertheless, Johnson came to Nashville optimistic about the prospects for a speedy reconstruction of the state government. Based on his understanding of the situation, he devised a three-part program: he would bring the hard-core secessionists to heel, enlighten the deceived citizens and appease them with a conciliatory policy, and start holding elections to get the state's civil government functioning again.

In pursuit of the first part of his program, Johnson arrested a number of prominent secessionists in the Nashville area who refused to accede to his demands. The city's mayor, for example, spent six weeks in jail before agreeing to take an oath of allegiance to the Union. Johnson also incarcerated a number of ministers and newspaper editors who were known for their pro-Confederate sympathies. Secessionist aristocrats likewise felt the military governor's wrath, among them William G. Harding of Belle Meade plantation, who wound up in a northern penitentiary.

Meanwhile, Johnson issued proclamations and made speeches encouraging the wayward citizens to renounce the folly of secession and reembrace the Union. "The erring and misguided will be welcomed on their return," he assured them; "no . . . retaliatory or vindictive policy will be adopted." As a token of his benevolence, he even interceded with President Lincoln to obtain the release of "repentant" Tennessee soldiers who had been captured in battle and were being held in northern prison camps.

As the initial test of the third part of his policy, Johnson arranged an election for circuit court judge in Middle Tennessee in May 1862 and encouraged all the citizens to vote. His hand-picked candidate was a stalwart Nashville unionist named Manson M. Brien. Johnson was stunned and outraged, however, when the voters elected Brien's opponent, who was an outright secessionist. Johnson allowed the winner to take office, but then arrested him for disloyalty and appointed Brien in his place.

Thereafter, the military governor began to see the political situation in a different light and adjusted his policy accordingly. The Rebel citizens would not be easily dissuaded from their views, he concluded. He would not again try to hold an election until East Tennessee had been secured and the good unionists there could participate.

In fact, the continuing obstinacy of secessionist citizens in Tennessee led Johnson to rethink the whole matter of Union war aims. Lenient treatment of Rebels was counterproductive, he decided; it only encouraged resistance. Therefore he would replace the carrot with the stick. *"Treason must be made odious,"* he announced, *"traitors punished and impoverished."* Johnson furthermore came to believe that, even if the seceded states were forced back into the Union, sectional conflicts would continue unless the South was transformed—specifically by abolishing slavery. Although President Lincoln exempted Tennessee from the Emancipation Proclamation of January 1, 1863, Johnson subsequently came out in favor of freeing the state's slaves.

This led to a rift among the Tennessee unionists. On one side were Johnson and his fellow "radicals"; on the other were the "conservatives," who retained faith in a conciliatory policy toward secessionists and deplored the idea of revolutionizing the South. Among the conservatives was Emerson Etheridge of West Tennessee, who denounced emancipation as "treachery to the Union men of the South." This division in the unionist ranks impaired the Union cause in Tennessee and slowed the work of reconstruction.

In December 1863, President Lincoln issued a proclamation outlining a general plan of reconstruction. All citizens in the seceded states (except high-ranking Confederate officials) who took an "amnesty oath"—pledging only their future loyalty to the Union and acceptance of emancipation—would be allowed to participate in elections to restore their state government. If the number of citizens participating equaled at least 10 percent of the number who had voted in the 1860 national election, Lincoln would recognize the government they established and allow it to apply to Congress for readmission.

Johnson thought this plan too lenient. He no longer trusted erstwhile Rebels who claimed to have had a change of heart, and he was determined to exclude them from the reconstruction of Tennessee. Consequently, in preparation for the county elections he intended to hold in March 1864, Johnson announced that voters would have to take an oath of his own devising, swearing that they "ardently desire the suppression of the present insurrection" and would "heartily aid and assist all loyal people in the accomplishment of these results." This was too much for most of the former secessionists, and it was also too much for conservative unionists, who continued to believe that repentant Rebels should be encouraged to take part in reconstruction. The conservatives denounced Johnson's "damnesty oath" and appealed to Lincoln, but the president upheld the military governor. Many conservatives thereupon boycotted the March elections, result-ing in a minuscule turnout and embarrassment for Johnson.

Instead of compromising with the conservative unionists, Johnson turned against them and decided that they, too, must be barred from the work of reconstruction. This decision was influenced by the conservatives' support for Lincoln's Democratic opponent in the upcoming presidential election, Union Gen. George B. McClellan. Johnson, who was determined that Tennessee would vote in that election and would vote for Lincoln (and for himself, since he was Lincoln's running mate), imposed yet another oath on prospective voters. This one required that they "sincerely rejoice in the triumph of the armies and navies of the United States" and "oppose all ar-mistices or negotiations of peace." Conservatives, noting that the Demo-cratic platform called for peace negotiations with the Confederacy, cried foul. As one put it, "Andy will let us vote, if we swear to vote for him—not otherwise." Once again, however, Lincoln upheld Johnson. Most conserva-tives therefore boycotted the November 1864 election. The few ballots cast in Tennessee were almost all for Lincoln and Johnson, of course, but Con-gress disqualified the state's vote.

With the defeat of Hood's army in late 1864, no major obstacles to the re-vival of state government remained. Johnson therefore gave his blessing to a convention that would lay the groundwork. In January 1865, some five hun-dred Tennesseans—unionists all—gathered in Nashville. Some had been ap-pointed as delegates at local conventions, while some were self-appointed. The majority were federal soldiers, and nearly all were radicals, for most conser-vatives by then had decided to have nothing to do with Johnsonian reconstruc-tion. Not surprisingly, East Tennessee delegates outnumbered those from both Middle and West sections.

Most of the delegates went to Nashville under the impression that this convention would be only a preliminary step, to prepare for a real consti-tutional convention to meet later. Once assembled, however, the delegates assumed constituent power and approved a state constitutional amendment abolishing slavery, along with a series of resolutions repudiating Tennessee's declaration of independence; nullifying all acts of the state legislature after May 6, 1861; and calling for an election for governor and legislators (to be held after the voters had approved the amendment and resolutions in a ref-erendum). Then the convention in effect reconstituted itself as a political con-vention and nominated a slate of candidates, including Parson Brownlow for governor. (Brownlow had returned to Knoxville after the Union army oc-cupied the town; he revived his newspaper, renaming it the *Whig and Rebel Ventilator*, and resumed his editorial tirades against the Confederacy.) Just in case any conservative unionists or repentant Rebels were thinking about voting in the referendum and election, the convention specified that no one could do so who had not been qualified to vote in the 1864 presidential election.

On February 22, 1865, some twenty-five thousand Tennessee voters approved the constitutional amendment and the resolutions; only forty-eight voters cast negative ballots. On March 4—the same day Lincoln and Johnson were inaugurated in Washington—Brownlow and the radical slate of legislators were elected by a similar margin. These turnouts were small, but they met Lincoln's 10 percent stipulation. The state legislature assembled and inaugurated Brownlow on April 5, just as the war was about to come to an end.

Life under Federal Occupation

When the Union army invaded Tennessee in early 1862, the state's secessionist citizens panicked. Thousands hurriedly gathered as many of their belongings as they could carry off—including their slaves—and fled southward to Confederate-held territory, where they lived as refugees for the duration of the war. The great majority, however, remained at home to face the invaders, fearful of what was to come but hopeful that the retreating Confederate army soon would rally and return to liberate them.

Having heard many a rumor that the Yankees intended to murder, rape, and pillage their way through the South, the citizens were pleasantly surprised to find that the first enemy soldiers they met were, on the whole, well behaved and sometimes even friendly. Most northern military commanders in that early part of the war believed (as did Abraham Lincoln and Andrew Johnson) that the southern people had been hoodwinked into supporting secession and could be won back to the Union through a policy of conciliation. They therefore instructed their troops not to mistreat the citizens. General Buell, for one, scrupulously protected private property and declined to arrest or otherwise harass people simply for being secessionists. He also made it clear that he would not interfere with the institution of slavery, and he ordered that runaway slaves be returned to their masters.

Tennessee secessionists did not, however, respond to this lenient policy as the occupiers had hoped. Their Confederate patriotism was not superficial but rather was strong and deeply rooted, and they were determined to resist Yankee rule in every way they could—especially after they realized that the invaders were willing to indulge them. Brazenly they waved their Confederate flags and sang "Dixie" and "The Bonny Blue Flag" as Union troops marched by; some jeered the soldiers and shouted insults. Women (who comprised the large majority of whites in occupied Tennessee, because so many men were away in the army) were especially defiant, for they believed the Yankees would not dare retaliate against a female. Women in Nashville, for example, made a great show of holding their noses when passing Union soldiers on the street; and at least one mustered up the courage to spit on a federal officer.

The invaders were, for the time being at least, prepared to tolerate such

Rebel guerrillas attacking a train near Nashville. Special Collections, University of Tennessee, Knoxville. John Fitch, *Annals of the Army of the Cumberland* (Philadelphia, 1864), facing p. 642.

indignities in the hope that the conciliatory policy eventually would succeed. But they drew the line when it came to more serious forms of resistance: spying for the Rebel army, smuggling supplies to Confederate territory, and engaging in guerrilla warfare. As the months went by, these activities proliferated in occupied Tennessee. Guerrilla warfare, in particular, emerged as a serious threat to Union military control of the state. Operating in small, mounted bands in the rural areas, civilian men and boys would strike suddenly, cutting telegraph wires, tearing up railroad tracks, or ambushing isolated Union troop detachments, and then quickly disappear into the woods. Thoroughly acquainted with the terrain and secretly aided by their neighbors and kinsmen, these guerrillas easily eluded the troops sent to track them down.

Continuing civilian resistance in Tennessee eventually persuaded the Union army authorities (just as it persuaded Military Governor Johnson) to give up on conciliation and come down hard on the Rebel citizens. Federal commanders and provost marshals began jailing people—women and men alike—for the merest expression of Rebel sentiment. They furthermore began demanding that all citizens take an oath of allegiance and then arrested or banished those who refused. They also lifted restrictions on taking private property and thereafter seized whatever supplies they needed from the farmers. Where guerrilla attacks occurred, Union troops

A Plantation Despoiled

As military occupation continued, Union troops became more ruthless in foraging. One of their frequent targets was the splendid Belle Meade plantation just outside Nashville, which boasted a private park full of deer and buffalo. In a letter of September 14, 1862, plantation mistress Elizabeth M. Harding described her recent experiences:

There has been removed already from this place five hundred . . . waggon loads of hay, corn, oats, wheat, etc. . . . . [Soldiers] have taken every suitable horse I had except my carriage horses. . . . They broke [open] my dairy and removed therefrom every onion, potatoes, and winter vegetables which I had. . . . They come and demand of the servants to give them all the milk and butter on the place on penalty of having their brains blown out if they refuse. . . . They have wantonly shot—without even eating them—two Cashmere goats which . . . cost my Husband $1000 apiece. Three weeks ago we had 100 deer, and a herd of twelve or fourteen buffaloes, now we have about 40 deer left and not one buffalo. . . . And now, at this moment while I am writing . . . the premise is literally swarming with soldiers who are wandering all over the place plundering at will. At the same time there are thirty-seven wagons standing on the pike getting ready to load up with the small amount of hay and oats left on the place; and enstead of going through the gates they are knocking down the fences.

would retaliate by looting or burning nearby homes or by holding local residents hostage until the guerrillas desisted.

As their attitude toward the secessionists hardened, the northern occupiers also turned against slavery. Few were motivated by sympathy for the slaves; their real object was to punish Rebel slaveholders. Nevertheless, all were impressed by the increasingly evident desire of the slaves to be free. Even early on, when federal policy was conservative, numbers of Tennessee blacks ran off from their masters and sought refuge in the army camps. Eventually the army stopped returning these runaways (who were dubbed "contrabands") and instead put them to work as cooks, teamsters, and laborers. The trickle of runaways became a flood, as the military authorities began not only allowing but encouraging them to come in, adopting a de facto policy of emancipation even though Tennessee had been exempted from Lincoln's proclamation. By 1864, the army's general rule regarding slaves was, in the words of one officer, "Keep all we get, and get all we can."

As blacks grew restive and the northern occupiers turned radical, Tennessee slaveowners desperately tried to preserve their "peculiar institution." Many spread horror stories among their slaves about the abuse they would receive at the hands of the Yankees if they ran off. When that failed, some forcibly restrained their slaves and cruelly beat them. But the army eventually forbade such violence against blacks, and thereafter masters lost all control. They could only watch helplessly as their bondsmen deserted in droves or stayed on but refused to work without pay. Asked about the situation of blacks in Tennessee in late 1863, one northern official summed it up thus: "Slavery is dead."

Many of the slaves who left their masters found their way to "contraband camps" set up by the Union army, the first of which was established by order of General Grant at Grand Junction in West Tennessee in November 1862. Eventually there were some seventeen of these camps in Tennessee, all of them in the West and Middle portions of the state, where the black population was concentrated. Conditions in these facilities were not always ideal. One Union officer described the Grand Junction camp as "appalling." The Nashville camp was worse: it suffered from shortages of shelter tents, rations, clothing, blankets, firewood, and medicine, resulting in much sickness and death among the blacks there (one-sixth of the camp's population died during a single three-week period in the winter of 1865). Other camps, however, including those at Clarksville and Pulaski, were well managed and healthy; blacks there were provided not only the necessities of life, but also education, thanks to the efforts of northern missionaries (many of them women) who came south to help prepare the former slaves for freedom.

The contraband camps were intended as temporary shelters only. Young black men were encouraged to enlist in the Union army, and eventually some twenty thousand black Tennesseans did so. Army authorities put the black enlistees in segregated units under white officers and at first assigned them to support roles—guarding wagon trains, serving as garrison troops, etc. Eventually, however, they put some into the front lines. Tennessee's black soldiers distinguished themselves on a number of battlefields, most notably at Nashville in December 1864. Some sacrificed their lives. One was Henry Prince of Company A, Fourteenth U.S. Colored Infantry, whose regiment was ordered to attack the Confederate lines during a battle in northern Georgia in 1864. Warned by an officer that high casualties were likely, Prince replied, "Lieutenant, I am ready to die for Liberty." He then moved forward with his fellow soldiers until a bullet pierced his heart.

Contrabands unsuited for military service were encouraged to go to work for wages under contract with white employers—some of whom were northerners operating plantations abandoned by, or seized from, secessionist planters. Many blacks, however, shunned the contraband camps, the army, and the wage-labor plantations and instead crowded into the black shantytowns that sprang up in Memphis, Nashville, Murfreesboro, Clarksville,

Chattanooga, and other towns. There they got their first taste of real freedom from white control, and in some cases their first taste of politics. Contrabands in Nashville, for example, held rallies and mock elections, petitioned the authorities for formal emancipation, and in March 1865 held an enormous day-long festival celebrating the ratification of the state emancipation amendment, featuring parades, speeches, and band music.

White people in the cities and towns, by contrast, found little to celebrate (unless they were unionists), for they were constantly under the watchful eye of the Yankee occupiers and subject to strict military regulations. (All of Tennessee's cities and towns, and a number of villages as well, were held by garrison forces after the federal army took control.) Living conditions in these urban centers deteriorated badly as newcomers—contrabands, soldiers, northern civilians, and others—poured in. Memphis, for example, had had a prewar population of twenty-three thousand but by early 1863 had an estimated thirty-five thousand residents, not counting garrison troops. Military rule and overcrowding thoroughly disrupted the local economy: unemployment, inflation, and shortages of food and housing plagued the cities and towns. On the other hand, the presence of Union

---

Wartime Prostitution in Nashville

Even before the Civil War, Nashville had a large "red light" district—an eight-square-block area near the waterfront, known as "Smokey Row." But with the influx of Union soldiers following the capture of the city in 1862, the prostitute population multiplied. Venereal disease and other problems associated with the bordellos prompted the military authorities to try to rid the city of prostitutes entirely.

On July 8, 1863, the provost guards rounded up all they could find—some 150 women—and put them on a steamboat, the *Idahoe*, to be sent north. For the next several weeks, the boat went from port to port along the Cumberland and Ohio rivers, but at every stop the local authorities refused to let the passengers disembark. The *Idahoe* finally returned to Nashville on August 5, and the women went back to work.

The military authorities then tried a more realistic plan, in effect establishing America's first system of legalized prostitution. The women were allowed to pursue their careers, but each was required to obtain a license and undergo regular medical examinations. The system worked so well that it was copied in other cities garrisoned by the Union army, including Memphis.

troops did preserve order, and the occupation authorities generally permitted municipal governments and urban schools and churches to go on about their business as long as they did not promote secessionism. Furthermore, the army provided food to needy inhabitants of the cities and towns—partly for humanitarian reasons and partly to avoid bread riots.

People who lived in the countryside did not have to endure the constant presence of the Yankees, but in other respects they suffered far more than the urban folk. Army patrols and foraging parties periodically came by and often stripped the farmers of their livestock and provisions and took their fence rails for firewood, exposing their growing crops to destruction. As the war continued, many rural dwellers faced starvation. The Yankees did not feel obliged to offer relief supplies to people outside the cities and towns, nor were they concerned with preserving law and order there (except as necessary to suppress guerrillas). As a result, the countryside experienced not only famine but also anarchy. Bandit gangs appeared, preying ruthlessly on any man, woman, or child who ventured out on the roads. Travel became so dangerous that families would hole up fearfully at home for weeks or months on end. Thus, rural churches and schools ceased to function and community life disintegrated. Tormented by violence and starvation in this chaotic no-man's-land, thousands of the country folk sought refuge in the cities and towns, aggravating the overcrowding there.

A refugee family arriving at a Union Army post in Tennessee. LC-USZ62-33104. Library of Congress, Washington, D.C.

Confederate morale withered as military occupation continued, especially after Hood's defeat at Nashville ended all hope of redemption by the Rebel army. Confronted by overwhelming federal power and by the manifest collapse of slavery, the secessionist citizens of Tennessee—much sooner than those in regions behind Confederate lines—resigned themselves to northern victory and black emancipation. They did not, however, resign themselves to unionist political rule nor to black equality. Thus, as the war ended in the spring of 1865, the stage was set for the struggles of Tennessee's Reconstruction era.

Suggested Readings

Alexander, Thomas B. *Political Reconstruction in Tennessee*. Nashville, 1950.

Ash, Stephen V. *Middle Tennessee Society Transformed, 1860–1870: War and Peace in the Upper South*. Baton Rouge, La., 1988.

Atkins, Jonathan M. *Parties, Politics, and the Sectional Conflict in Tennessee, 1832–1861*. Knoxville, Tenn., 1997.

Cimprich, John. *Slavery's End in Tennessee, 1861–1865*. University, Ala., 1985.

Connelly, Thomas L. *Civil War Tennessee: Battles and Leaders*. Knoxville, Tenn., 1979.

Cooling, Benjamin Franklin. *Fort Donelson's Legacy: War and Society in Kentucky and Tennessee, 1862–1863*. Knoxville, Tenn., 1997.

Crofts, Daniel W. *Reluctant Confederates: Upper South Unionists in the Secession Crisis*. Chapel Hill, N.C., 1989.

Fisher, Noel. *War at Every Door: Partisan Politics and Guerrilla Violence in East Tennessee, 1860–1869*. Chapel Hill, N.C., 1997.

Hall, Kermit L. "Tennessee." In *The Confederate Governors*. Edited by W. Buck Yearns. 185–94. Athens, Ga., 1985.

Horn, Stanley. *The Decisive Battle of Nashville*. 1956. Reprinted, Knoxville, Tenn., 1968.

McDonough, James Lee. *Shiloh—In Hell before Night*. Knoxville, Tenn., 1977.

Maslowski, Peter. *Treason Must Be Made Odious: Military Occupation and Wartime Reconstruction in Nashville, Tennessee*. Millwood, N.Y., 1978.

Noe, Kenneth W., and Shannon H. Wilson, eds. *The Civil War in Appalachia: Collected Essays*. Knoxville, Tenn., 1997.

Temple, Oliver P. *East Tennessee and the Civil War*. 1899. Reprinted, Knoxville, Tenn., 1972.

Wyeth, John Allan. *That Devil Forrest: Life of General Nathan Bedford Forrest*. 1959. Reprinted, Baton Rouge, La., 1989.

7

Reconstruction

THE END OF THE CIVIL WAR did not bring an end to conflict and violence in Tennessee. The state's Reconstruction era, which lasted from 1865 to 1870, was marked by bitter strife over certain issues that the war left unresolved. It also was marked by hardship, as Tennesseans struggled to rebuild their war-ravaged economy and institutions.

Tennessee's Reconstruction experience differed in some ways from that of the other former Confederate states. The Volunteer State was readmitted to the Union well before any of the other southern states and thus avoided the Military Reconstruction program imposed by Congress in 1867. Furthermore, Tennessee saw few of the northern "carpetbaggers" who came south after the war and played a prominent role in southern politics. On the other hand, Tennessee's Reconstruction shared certain features with that of the other states, notably the battle between Radicals and Conservatives for control of state government and the quest of the "freedmen" (the former slaves) for political, economic, and social equality in the face of fierce white opposition.

Postwar Recovery

The most urgent task that Tennesseans faced in the spring and summer of 1865 was rebuilding their ruined homes and devastated communities. For many, the task was daunting. When former Confederate soldier Lee Billingsley returned to his Bledsoe County farm, he found that "the fences had all been burned [and] the negros [were] all gone except two." Some faced even bleaker circumstances. Edward Lee, for example, came home from the army to find "everything gone but the dirt." Most, however, set to work with a willing spirit. That spirit is exemplified by William Roach, who, as he recounted, "arrived home [from the Confederate army] Friday afternoon the 19th of May 1865 and Monday morning hitched a mule to a plow" and went to work.

Now that the federal occupiers no longer had to worry about Rebel cavalry raids and guerrilla attacks, they relaxed their strict military rule and turned their attention to restoring law and order in the countryside. With the aid of sheriffs and other civil officials elected or appointed under the revived state government, the Yankees wiped out the bandits who had terrorized the rural areas. Freed from danger, the country people now could travel freely on the roads. Thus the rural communities sprang to life after months or years dormant; and markets, churches, schools, and courthouses once again were crowded with country folk. In many cases, however, buildings needed extensive repair to undo the ravages of war.

Tennessee's cities and towns had remained vibrant throughout the war, thanks to the presence of Union garrison forces, and in the postwar period they seemed livelier than ever. The war precipitated an urban boom in Tennessee (though the state remained overwhelmingly rural). Nashville, for example, which had about seventeen thousand residents in 1860, had twenty-six thousand by 1870 (a 52 percent increase); Memphis, with twenty-three thousand in 1860, had forty thousand by 1870 (a 78 percent increase). This urban growth—which far outstripped the growth of the state's population as a whole (13 percent) over the decade—was in great part due to the influx of freedmen, who in the postwar years continued their exodus from the farms to the towns.

Civil authority gradually superseded the military, and eventually the northern occupation forces withdrew from Tennessee. With all vestiges of military rule removed, Tennesseans eagerly pursued their livelihoods and struggled to

---

A Refugee Returns, 1865

During the Civil War, minister William Eagleton and his wife left their home in Murfreesboro to seek refuge from the northern invaders. When they returned at the war's end, Eagleton surveyed what was left of his property and wrote this account:

[W]e found our home a desolation—enclosures all gone & the dwelling house from garret to cellar entirely empty—furniture, beds, bedding, library—all gone & the house itself dilapidated but not demolished. Some things have been found, but comparatively few & of little value. . . . Our house of worship where I had for so many years attempted to proclaim the glad tidings of salvation is an utter wreck, nothing standing but the cupola, & the graveyard is also a desolation. May we soon be permitted to witness the return of more auspicious times, & will the Lord in his mercy sanctify the present trial of this agitated land!

restore their state's blighted economy. In certain respects, they seemed remarkably successful. A glance at census statistics, for example, shows that by 1870, industrialization in Tennessee had reached a level that not only equaled but considerably surpassed that of 1860. Over the decade, the number of manufacturing establishments increased by 107 percent, the number of hands employed by 55 percent, and the value of products by 91 percent.

These figures should not, however, be taken as evidence that in the postwar era Tennessee's industrial economy was thriving. For one thing, the growth they represent was mostly in lumber mills, smithies, and similar enterprises—i.e., village artisan shops that produced goods on a small scale and strictly for the local market. The state's true industries, such as iron and tobacco manufacturing, were hard hit by the war and in most cases did not regain their antebellum status for decades, if ever. In Montgomery County, for example, which was a center of both iron and tobacco production before the war, the number of hands employed in the ironworks fell from 261 to 46 between 1860 and 1870, and capital investment declined 97 percent; while the number of hands employed in the tobacco factories fell from 344 to 6, and capital investment declined by 99 percent.

In any event, manufacturing remained but a minuscule part of Tennessee's economy in the immediate postwar years, as it had been in the prewar years. Agriculture remained the heart of the economy, but census statistics reveal that it had been grievously damaged by the war. Livestock production, for example, suffered terribly from the federal army's requisitioning and indiscriminate slaughter of animals. The number of horses in the state was 15 percent smaller in 1870 than in 1860, while the number of mules was 18 percent smaller, swine 22 percent, and oxen 37 percent.

One might think that crop production would recover rather more swiftly than stock raising, for all a farmer need do was rebuild his fences and sow his seed. But in fact corn output in Tennessee was 21 percent smaller in 1870 than in 1860, cotton 31 percent smaller, and tobacco down by 51 percent.

These crop declines were not due to the abandonment of farmland (the number of improved acres in the state actually increased slightly over the decade), but mainly reflected the derangement of the labor system. As freedmen flocked to the towns, farmers in many sections of the state experienced severe labor shortages. Moreover, the farmers found that they could not extract as much work from the black laborers whom they did manage to hire as they had extracted from their slaves in the old days, for the freedmen insisted upon the right to work as white people did. That is, they demanded Saturday afternoons off, refused to put women to work in the fields, and resisted the highly regimented gang system that had prevailed on the antebellum plantations.

Some freedmen even began to demand what long had been the ideal among whites: a farm of their own. Few had the money to buy land, but a good number did persuade white plantation owners to split up their estates

Sharecropper's cabin in post–Civil War Tennessee. *Scribner's Monthly*, May 1874. Special Collections, University of Tennessee, Knoxville.

into small plots, each of which then was farmed individually by a black family who paid the owner an annual rental fee in cash or, more often, crops. This "sharecropping" system satisfied the freedmen's desire for a degree of economic independence, but it was an inefficient method of production that hindered agriculture in Tennessee (and much of the rest of the South) for decades to come.

The Brownlow Government

While Tennesseans labored to rebuild their farms, shops, schools, and churches in the postwar era, they kept a watchful eye on events in Nashville. The new state government began operating in April 1865, a momentous time in American history. On the ninth of that month, Robert E. Lee surrendered his Confederate army, marking the end of the Civil War. Less than a week later, President Lincoln fell dead from an assassin's bullet, and Andrew Johnson ascended to the presidency.

Tennesseans scrutinized Governor Brownlow's first message to the legislature (delivered on April 6, the day after his inauguration) to see how he intended to deal with the important issues facing the state. Much of the message was unexceptionable. Hardly anyone could object to the governor's stated determination to quell the crime, violence, and anarchy that plagued the state; and few opposed his call for the ratification of the Thirteenth Amendment to the U.S. Constitution, which outlawed slavery throughout the nation. Tennessee, after all, already had abolished the institution within its own borders. The governor provoked enormous controversy, however, when he addressed the central issue of his administration: the question of who could vote and who could not.

In the February referendum, the voters had granted the first reconstructed legislature the power to set future voting qualifications. The Radical unionist Brownlow had no intention of letting former Rebels participate in politics, at least for the time being, and he made that clear in his message. "Guard the ballot box faithfully and effectually," he admonished the legislators, "against the approach of treason." The former Rebels naturally objected to this, and they were joined by Conservative unionists, who felt for-

---

A Price on Isham Harris's Head

One of the first actions of the Radical General Assembly that convened in 1865 was to offer a reward of five thousand dollars for the apprehension of the former governor and arch-secessionist, Isham G. Harris, who recently had surrendered with the Confederate army and had been paroled by Union authorities. In his official proclamation of the reward, Governor Brownlow drew upon his long experience in defamatory rhetoric, describing the "culprit Harris" thus:

> [He] is about five feet ten inches high, weighs about One hundred and forty-five pounds and is about fifty-five Years of Age. His complexion is sallow—his eyes are dark and penetrating—a perfect index to the heart of a traitor—with the scowl and frown of a demon resting upon his brow. . . . He chews tobacco rapidly, and is inordinately fond of liquor. In his moral structure he is an unscrupulous man—steeped to the chin in personal and political profligacy—now about lost to all sense of honor and shame—with a heart reckless of social duty, and fatally bent upon mischief.

Harris never was apprehended. He fled to Mexico and then England, where he bided his time until the legislature repealed the reward offer in 1867. Then he returned to Tennessee and, after the collapse of Radical Reconstruction, reentered politics. He served as U.S. senator from 1877 until his death in 1897.

giving toward the vanquished Confederates and also regarded them as potential political allies. But the legislature was dominated by Brownlow partisans, and in June 1865 it passed a franchise bill that barred former supporters of the Confederacy from voting for five years (fifteen years in the case of Confederate leaders). This act also set up a voter registration system—the state's first—administered by county court clerks, the purpose of which was to ensure that only eligible voters participated in elections.

Brownlow and his Radical Party faced a crucial test in the August 1865 congressional elections. By now the Conservative unionists had concluded that the best way to fight the Radicals was not to boycott elections, as they had done the previous November, February, and March, but instead to try to win the elections. They registered in large numbers and in August gave Brownlow a nasty surprise. Of the winning candidates for the state's eight congressional seats, only three were loyal to Brownlow. The governor managed to put a fourth ally into Congress by unfairly manipulating the returns from one district, but he could hardly deny that the overall result of the congressional races was a major disappointment to his cause. He was dealt another blow in March 1866, when the Conservatives swept the county elections in Middle and West Tennessee.

Brownlow thereupon decided that he must exercise stricter control over the ballot box. In April 1866, the compliant legislature amended the franchise law to give him the power he sought. The new law voided all previous voter registrations and decreed that voters must be reregistered by election commissioners appointed by the governor. These commissioners were given broad discretion in determining who was qualified to vote, and of course the governor expected them to examine very carefully anyone who seemed likely to vote Conservative. Moreover, the new law discarded the five- and fifteen-year clauses concerning former Rebels, and instead disfranchised them for life.

Meanwhile, the governor was working to get Tennessee restored to the Union—which meant, in practical terms, getting Congress to consent to seating the state's eight representatives and two senators (the latter having been elected by the legislature back in the spring of 1865). Had it been up to Andrew Johnson, this would have been done expeditiously. Since becoming president, he had come to favor the quick readmission of the former Confederate states and the enfranchisement of most ex-Rebels; when the war was over, he permitted those states (except for Tennessee and three others, where reconstructed governments already were functioning) to set up new governments dominated by former Confederates who had taken an oath of future allegiance to the United States. This brought Johnson into conflict with the Republicans who controlled Congress. The Republicans opposed returning the ex-Rebels (most of whom were Democrats) to power, and they were determined to oversee the revival of the southern state governments very closely.

William G. Brownlow, Reconstruction governor of Tennessee, c. 1865. East Tennessee Historical Society, Knoxville.

The battle shaping up in Washington affected politics in Tennessee and all the other former Confederate states. People began aligning themselves either with President Johnson and his mild Reconstruction program or with the congressional Republicans and their sterner program. Brownlow and his supporters naturally gravitated toward the Republicans, while the governor's Conservative opponents took up the standard of Andrew Johnson. In this contest Brownlow emerged victorious, for the congressional Republicans soon seized control of Reconstruction from President Johnson—and later nearly succeeded in removing him from office.

The fact that Tennessee's government was dominated in the immediate postwar years by a party friendly to the congressional Republicans—not the case in any other former Confederate state—meant that Tennessee's Reconstruction experience would be unique. In June 1866, Congress passed and submitted to the states the Fourteenth Amendment, which imposed strict terms on the southern states, aimed at protecting the freedmen and checking the power of the ex-Rebels. Brownlow and his party endorsed the amendment and in July the Tennessee legislature ratified it, despite a last-ditch attempt by Brownlow's legislative opponents to block ratification in the House by absenting themselves to prevent a quorum—an attempt the Radicals thwarted by having two absent members arrested, brought to the capitol, held in a room adjoining the House chamber, and then counted as "present but not voting."

Brownlow immediately telegraphed the U.S. Senate to announce Tennessee's ratification of the amendment (he could not resist adding to the message a gratuitous dig at President Johnson, who adamantly opposed the amendment: "My compliments," said the Parson, "to the 'dead dog' of the White House"). Congress repaid the favor that same month by seating Tennessee's senators and representatives. Moreover, when Congress in 1867 imposed military rule on the South, it exempted Tennessee.

The Volunteer State thus was back in the Union, but Brownlow and his Radical Party could not rest easy. The Conservative opposition was growing stronger, for Brownlow's high-handed rule was not only embittering his inveterate opponents but also alienating many of his erstwhile friends and driving them into the enemy camp. The Radicals' legislative majority was dwindling, and the Conservatives were preparing to mount a strong challenge to Brownlow himself in the next gubernatorial election. Eyeing these developments nervously, the governor proposed the most controversial measure yet: enabling Tennessee blacks to vote.

Brownlow's enemies denounced his conversion to the cause of black suffrage as purely self-serving, and doubtless they were correct. Previously he had not shown much enthusiasm for securing the freedmen's rights. However, as early as 1865, he had expressed his belief that "a loyal negro is more eminently entitled to suffrage than a disloyal white man" and had warned that if the ex-Rebels ever regained the vote, it would be necessary and proper to enfranchise the blacks. In order to justify his present advocacy of black voting, he now claimed that "a large number of disloyal persons" were voting, despite the stringent franchise law—which simply was not true. The truth was that the Radicals' support was diminishing among unionists; allowing blacks to vote seemed the only way to preserve the Radical majority—and it had to be done while the first Reconstruction legislature was still sitting (after that, it would require a state constitutional amendment, which Conservatives probably could block).

Brownlow faced considerable opposition on this issue even among his supporters, few of whom held any conviction of black equality. Nevertheless, swayed by the governor's reasoning on that point ("Think of some low white man in your community you would not dine with," he said; "does his casting a ballot make him your social equal?") and swayed even more by the manifest political necessity, Radical legislators in February 1867 enacted a law allowing adult black males to vote. Tennessee thus became the first southern state to enfranchise all black men.

That same month, in response to the governor's undoubtedly exaggerated claim that Conservatives were plotting to overthrow the state government by violence, the legislature created a military force, the State Guard, consisting of white and black troops loyal to the governor and under his command. Brownlow quickly activated this guard, calling up twenty-one companies not only to protect the government from the alleged Conservative coup, but also to protect the administration's interest in the upcoming August election.

Brownlow's challenger for the governor's chair was Emerson Etheridge of West Tennessee, who in April 1867 won the Conservative Party's nomination and then took to the hustings, calling for the enfranchisement of all white men and praising President Johnson. Brownlow was ill that spring and summer and could not travel the campaign trail and debate Etheridge, so he had to dispatch proxies to challenge Etheridge on the stump. The governor's absence made little difference, for his control of the registration machinery and State Guard and the nearly unanimous support of the well-organized black voters (thousands of whom enrolled in Radical-led political clubs called Union Leagues) spelled disaster for the Conservatives.

In the August 1 election—the first in American history in which blacks participated in large numbers—Brownlow received some 74,000 votes (about 40,000 of them from blacks), while Etheridge received fewer than 23,000. Furthermore, the Radicals captured all the congressional seats, all the state senate seats, and all but three of the state house seats. Radicalism, for the moment at least, not only reigned supreme but was virtually unchallengeable in Tennessee.

The Freedmen's Struggle for Equality

Tennessee's black men and women saw Reconstruction as a God-sent opportunity to repair the damage that slavery had done to them as a people and to secure for themselves all the rights and privileges that whites enjoyed. One of their first steps was to assert their claim to the self-identity and family integrity that to some degree had been denied them as slaves. They adopted surnames, for one thing; for another, they held legally sanctioned wedding ceremonies to formalize the marriages they had entered into as slaves. (In July 1865, for example, the Bedford County court issued 422 marriage licenses—406 of them to black couples.) Many freedmen also made desperate efforts to reunite their families, torn apart on the auction block in the days of slavery or separated in the chaos of war.

Once they were free, most blacks tried to remove themselves as far as possible from white supervision and control. They moved out of the old slave quarters and back rooms of whites' homes and built their own shanties or cabins. Furthermore, they withdrew from the white-dominated churches they had attended as slaves and founded their own all-black churches, led by black pastors. Most of these churches, like those of the whites, were Baptist or Methodist. But whatever the denomination, the black church emerged as a profoundly important institution among the Tennessee freedmen in the postwar era.

Many of the ex-slaves went so far as to segregate themselves in separate

---

A Freedman's Advice to His People, 1866

In September 1866, blacks in Giles County held a meeting to discuss the future of their race. Among those who addressed the crowd was a man named Aaron Shoat, who had some heartfelt words of advice for his listeners:

[F]ellow citizens you will permit me to say a few words in regard to our welfare, we want our colored race to be a people, we want our colored race to be able to do their own business. I want our colored race [to] rise and come up to the top of the Hill, let us make gentlemen and ladies of ourselves, let us not be pilgrims and hirelings all our days, we must come out and make men of ourselves. Let us educate our children. If we can't buy land, we must rent it in a way that we can make something, to bring our race out as a people. . . . [I]f we hire ourselves to any man white or black we have got to submit to his law and do his work as he wants it done, and stick up to our contract whether it may be good or bad. . . . [B]ut when you make a contract with any man be sure that you make a good one, and never go to work until you draw writing on the contract.

black communities. In the rural areas, there appeared all-black hamlets, such as "Mount Africa" in Maury County. In the cities and towns, which attracted blacks in great numbers in the postwar years, the freedmen tended to cluster in separate neighborhoods (later generations would call them ghettos). These urban neighborhoods—"Macedonia" on the outskirts of Columbia and "Hell's Half Acre" in Nashville were two of them—often were plagued by overcrowding, disease, and crime, but the blacks seemed willing to pay that price in order to distance themselves from whites and achieve a sense of community. Their communalism was bolstered not only by the black churches but also by the black fraternal organizations that were founded in the Reconstruction years, including such clubs as the Nashville Colored Benevolent Society and the Sons of Ham.

As they labored to bring forth a separate black community, the freedmen also labored to elevate themselves economically. Although, as noted earlier, few could afford to buy farms, many managed to achieve a sort of quasi-independence through sharecropping. And even the majority, who had to work as hired hands on a white man's farm or in his shop, found themselves far better off than in the prewar days, for freedom provided not only the right to wages but also the opportunity to move around, change jobs, negotiate with bosses, and wring concessions from them. One observer during the Reconstruction years in Tennessee noted that the freedmen had

A scene in the Memphis office of the Freedmen's Bureau. *Harper's Weekly,* June 2, 1866. Special Collections, University of Tennessee, Knoxville.

"learned by hard experience" and now were "shrewder in making bargains"; another pointed out that whites now "have to treat [blacks] well to get them to work for them."

In their dealings with white bosses and landlords, the black workers had help from a federal agency known as the Freedmen's Bureau, established by Congress in 1865. Though the bureau did not, as many blacks had hoped, confiscate the big plantations and parcel out their acreage to ex-slaves, bureau agents did oversee the signing of labor contracts between blacks and whites and operated informal courts where employer-employee disputes could be resolved. Although some of the agents were prejudiced in favor of whites, most were determined to see that blacks got a fair shake.

Some of Tennessee's freedmen managed to achieve true economic independence as artisans, businessmen, or professionals. By mid-1866, for example, there were in the town of Pulaski eight black-owned businesses (four stores, three restaurants, and a saloon), as well as ten black carpenters, eleven blacksmiths, two wagon makers, and ten bricklayers and plasterers. A Knoxville black, William F. Yardley, established himself as an agent for a New York life insurance company soon after the war. Knoxville also had a black doctor by 1870, while Memphis's large black community included at least one lawyer, admitted to the bar in 1868. A few freedmen were able to amass considerable wealth. Former slave Lewis Winters, for example, arrived in Nashville in 1865 with forty dollars worth of goods, established a grocery, and within five years was worth $3,500, a considerable sum in

---

A Young Black Student Displays Her Learning

In 1869, a northern missionary who was teaching at a school for black children in Gallatin asked her students to write thank-you notes to the missionary association that sponsored her. Among the notes that the association received was this one, dated June 1, from eleven-year-old Alice Tompkins:

Kind Friend: This is the first time I have ever tried to write to any of our northern friends. We have a pleasant school and good kind teachers and school mates. I feel very much interested in our school. It is true I am very small but the small can do something, I want to be useful while I am young, and when I grow up I hope to make a useful woman. I am trying to serve the Lord who is so good and kind to all. I want to see the day when our race will be educated. We are learning very fast and if we keep on will be able to teach others.

those days. Even more successful was Nashville hotel-keeper Henry Harding, whose fortune by 1870 amounted to $35,000.

Among the freedmen's most cherished goals was education, for they realized that, no matter how hard they worked, they never could achieve equality without some schooling. Many observers in the postwar years commented on the blacks' desire for knowledge. Former Union Gen. Clinton Fisk, the head of the Freedmen's Bureau in Tennessee, reported in 1866 that blacks were "hungering and thirsting" for education. Another northerner who visited Chattanooga soon after the war found that "the colored people are far more zealous in the cause of education than the whites. They will starve themselves and go without clothes, in order to send their children to school." Throughout the state, the freedmen eagerly went to work building schoolhouses and procuring teachers.

They had assistance in many cases from northern men and women, idealistic missionaries who came to the South during and after the war to help the newly freed blacks. One was the Reverend Ewing O. Tade of Illinois, an agent of the American Missionary Association, who arrived in Memphis in 1865. There he preached and conducted a school among what he sympathetically called the "poor, degraded, and despised" freedmen. The next year he moved to Chattanooga and founded the Howard School for black children. In 1867, that institution was taken under the wing of the Chattanooga board of aldermen and became the town's first public school. The most successful of Tennessee's missionary schools, however, was Fisk University. Founded in Nashville in 1866 by the American Missionary Association and the Western Freedmen's Aid Commission of Cincinnati, Fisk instituted a normal (i.e., teacher-training) program in 1867 and became one of the nation's preeminent black colleges.

View of Fisk University in 1868, two years after its founding. *Harper's Weekly,* October 3, 1868. Special Collections, University of Tennessee, Knoxville.

Whether run by missionaries or by freedmen themselves, the black schools were aided by the Freedmen's Bureau, and in some cases the bureau set up schools of its own. By September 1866, there were altogether forty-one schools for blacks in Tennessee, with 125 teachers and 9,400 pupils. These numbers swelled considerably in the years to follow, especially after the state legislature created a new public school system in 1867 and mandated that it be open to blacks (though the schools were to be segregated). Under Superintendent John Eaton Jr., a New Englander and former Union army officer and Freedmen's Bureau agent, the new state school system absorbed most of the existing black-run, missionary, and bureau schools and by 1869 could boast 498 black schools with almost 26,000 students.

Above all else, the Tennessee freedmen sought political rights, for they believed that, with the power of the ballot, they could secure all the other things they desired. Blacks began demanding political rights early, well before any white Radicals seriously considered granting them. In 1865, Nashville blacks petitioned the state government to enfranchise their people, declaring that the legislature could give "the colored man . . . a vote as safely as it trusted him with a bayonet." In that same city that year, black leaders from across the state gathered to discuss the condition of their race and to demand full rights; this State Colored Men's Convention thereafter became an annual event, continuing for many years. Nashville also was home to a black newspaper, the *Colored Tennessean*, whose editor, William B. Scott, crusaded tirelessly for equal rights.

One by one, the freedmen got many of the things they demanded, although in the state capital their speeches, editorials, parades, and petitions generally were less persuasive than the Radicals' self-interest. In 1866, probably with a view to pacifying the Republicans in Congress, the state legislature granted blacks all citizenship rights except voting, office holding, jury service, and marrying whites. In 1867, for reasons already discussed, the legislators enfranchised the freedmen. With the vote, however, the blacks gained real influence, and when the legislators in 1868 repealed the ban on black jury service and office holding, they acted, at least in part, in response to the freedmen's demands.

Although no black held state office in Tennessee during the Reconstruction years (in contrast to other southern states, where blacks held many high posts), a number of black political leaders did, with the help of their black constituents, win election to local office. Maryville merchant W. S. McTeer, for example, was elected to that town's board of aldermen in 1868; and several municipal posts in Nashville were held by blacks. One of the most notable black officeholders was Edward Shaw of Memphis. A saloon owner and eloquent orator, Shaw in 1869 was elected to the Shelby County Commission. Although he was, like virtually all his fellow blacks, a supporter of the Radical Party, Shaw did not hesitate to criticize the Radicals when he thought they were taking blacks for granted. "Teach them this," he told his followers, "that you have rights to be respected." To the Radicals themselves, he made it clear that "we are not to be 'led by the nose.'"

White Reaction

The great majority of white Tennesseans were former secessionists who, having accepted Confederate defeat and sworn allegiance to the United States, saw no reason why they should be denied political rights. They applauded the lenient Reconstruction policy of President Johnson—their wartime nemesis but now their hero—while they excoriated the Republicans whom Johnson was battling in Washington. Likewise, they praised the efforts of Tennessee's Conservative unionists to repeal the state franchise restrictions, while they denounced Governor Brownlow and his Radical Party as a despotic clique ruling by force and fraud.

Those of the ex-Rebels who lived in East Tennessee, where they were a minority, were even more embittered by the treatment they received after the war at the hands of vengeful unionists. Many former Confederate sympathizers, especially returned Rebel soldiers, were threatened, assaulted, and even murdered in the eastern counties in the postwar months. "Anarchy reigns throughout the country," wrote a Morristown man in June 1865. "Not a day passes but what some rebel receives his 400 lashes." Hundreds or perhaps thousands of men fled the region after receiving warnings such as that scrawled on a sign posted near New Market in July 1865: "All damed Rebels are hereby notified to lieve at wonce. . . . We are working by the order that you theving God forsaken helldeserving Rebels issued four years ago [saying] Union men and Rebels cannot live together."

More than anything else, it was the black quest for equality that stoked the burning resentment of Tennessee's ex-Confederates, for they remained as devoutly racist as they had been before the war. Acknowledging only that blacks no longer could legally be bought and sold, the former Rebels bristled at any suggestion that the freedmen might be entitled to social, economic, or political equality with whites. "The [white] people do all they can to degrade [the blacks]," a Freedmen's Bureau agent reported in 1866, "and keep them down to what they see fit to call their proper place." Another agent predicted that virulent racial hostility would persist as long as the freedmen asserted their rights: "The [white] people of the country will never be on good terms with the negroes," he said, "until they have got them in their power."

Such hostility extended to any whites who sided with the blacks or aided them in their struggle to uplift themselves. Freedmen's Bureau agents, northern missionaries, Radicals—all were vilified and ostracized by the ex-Confederates. The Pulaski Freedmen's Bureau agent, for example, was forced to live in his office with his wife and children because local whites refused to board them. A northern missionary who held religious services for blacks in Chattanooga lamented, "Here I must live a sort of dog's life—hated, shunned, and despised because I am a 'nigger preacher'!"

A Freedmen's Bureau Official Reports on Racial Conflict

J. R. Lewis, a northern-born man in charge of the Nashville area subdistrict of the Freedmen's Bureau, submitted this report to his superiors in August 1866:

> I do not think the best citizens are opposed to the Bureau, but unfortunately most of the planters . . . could not be classed as the best citizens. They are mostly rough and overbearing—hard to get along with. . . . The system of slavery has brutalized the [white] people until they feel as if they must kill the negro if he dares to speak in opposition to them. And in fact they act as if they would like to kill any man who hints that the negro has the same rights that they have. . . . I believe very little justice can be obtained for the colored people of this Sub District except by the agency of active and efficient Bureau Agents.

When verbal abuse and social excommunication failed to deter the freedmen and their white friends, the former Rebels resorted to threats. "We have determined to rid our community of Negro-loving fanatics," read an anonymous letter sent to a northern teacher in Memphis in 1866, ". . . You are one of the number." When threats failed, violence sometimes ensued. In Robertson County, angry whites burned down the cabin of a black man who had dared to quit wage labor and set himself up as an independent farmer. Black schoolhouses, too, felt the arsonist's torch: according to Eaton, the state school superintendent, sixty-one were burned down between 1867 and 1869. Persons as well as property were targeted by the wrathful ex-Confederates. In Hardeman County, for example, a white teacher of blacks was dragged from his dwelling by some neighborhood men, choked, beaten, tarred, and run out of the community.

Memphis was the scene of the worst outbreak of anti-black violence in Reconstruction Tennessee. Indeed, the Memphis Riot of May 1–2, 1866, was one of the bloodiest and most destructive race riots in American history. It began as a minor fracas between white policemen and some discharged black soldiers, but it escalated quickly, as white mobs seized weapons, invaded the black community of South Memphis, and went on a rampage. Federal troops finally restored order, but not before forty-six blacks and two whites were killed; five black women raped; and ninety-one homes, twelve schools, nine churches, and a Freedmen's Bureau office in the black community burned to the ground.

Random acts of racial violence continued throughout the Reconstruction period, but eventually they were overshadowed by the rise of organized violence, especially the activities of the Ku Klux Klan. Founded as a social fraternity in Pulaski in December 1865 by six young Confederate veterans, the Ku Klux Klan spread in clandestine fashion across the South and developed an elaborate hierarchy of local, district, and state officers. Its organization was formalized at a secret meeting in Nashville in 1867, and there Nathan Bedford Forrest was named supreme commander, or "Grand Wizard." The mysterious rituals and weird regalia of the Klan appealed to many, but even more attractive to some was the Klan's potential as a weapon against assertive blacks, Radical whites, and other "undesirables."

Incidents of intimidation by Tennessee's Klansmen multiplied after blacks gained the vote in 1867. Sometimes these were just shows of force: silent processions of robed and hooded horsemen in the dead of night. Sometimes there were more explicit threats, such as the posting of placards bearing Klan symbols and a warning: "Beware oh ye ungodly for the day of retribution is close at hand." Increasingly frequent, however, were episodes of brutal violence: surrounding an isolated cabin, Klansmen would drag their victim out to face at best a whipping, at worst an execution.

The approach of the November 1868 election saw a crescendo in Klan violence. In addition to the presidential contenders, Tennessee's congressional contenders also were on the ballot, for the legislature recently had decreed that congressional elections thenceforth would be held in conjunction with the presidential, rather than the state, elections. Determined to deny Tennessee's electoral votes to Republican Ulysses S. Grant and the state's congressional seats to the Radicals, the Klan instituted what one witness described as "a reign of terror." "No [Radical] union man or negro who attempts to take an active part in politics . . . is safe a single day," reported a Freedmen's Bureau agent in Middle Tennessee, "and all sleep with their arms."

Some of those targeted took to carrying their weapons during the day as well, ready to defend themselves if the Klan came after them. One was Edward Shaw, who had been marked for assassination by Memphis Klansmen. When they attacked a political rally Shaw was attending, he and other blacks drew their pistols, fired back, drove off the assailants, and then resumed their meeting.

Governor Brownlow was determined to fight back, too, in his own way. In July 1868, amid mounting Klan violence, he called a special session of the legislature and asked for more power to combat the hooded menace. Two months later, the legislators gave him what he wanted: an act (generally known as the Ku Klux Klan Act) providing stiff penalties for political terrorism, and another that gave the governor sweeping police powers, including command of the reactivated State Guard and authority to declare martial law in any county threatened by the Klan. Brownlow also requested and received from the U.S. government a regiment of federal troops, who were stationed in Middle Tennessee in preparation for the election.

These precautions, as well as the governor's continued control of voter registration, helped Grant carry Tennessee in November. Nevertheless, it was

Ku Klux Klansmen in disguise, 1868. *Harper's Weekly*, December 19, 1868. Special Collections, University of Tennessee, Knoxville.

clear that the Klan had had some success in dissuading blacks and Radical unionists from voting, at least in Middle and West Tennessee: the total vote for Grant in those two regions was only about two-thirds of that garnered by Brownlow fifteen months earlier. Moreover, in two congressional districts, Radical candidates failed to outpoll their Conservative opponents. (With yet another act of creative ballot counting, however, Brownlow was able to deny the Conservatives those two congressional seats.)

Alarmed by the election results, Brownlow declared war on the Klan. In January 1869 he mobilized the State Guard, and in February he imposed martial law in nine Middle and West Tennessee counties. Moreover, in an effort to obtain some convictions under the Ku Klux Klan Act, the governor hired a Cincinnati man named Seymour Barmore to infiltrate the Klan and obtain incriminating evidence. Barmore, who called himself the "greatest detective in the world," proved to be daring but woefully incompetent. The Klan quickly caught on to him and advised him to get back to Cincinnati, a warning he ignored. Early in 1869, Barmore disguised himself and managed to get into a Klan meeting in Pulaski; but he was recognized later as he boarded a train to head back to Nashville. A telegraph message raced ahead of the train to Columbia, where Klansmen boarded Barmore's car and removed him. Six weeks later, his lifeless body was pulled from the Duck River, a rope around his neck and a bullet through his brain.

Not long after Brownlow mobilized the State Guard, Grand Wizard Forrest formally ordered the members of the Ku Klux Klan to destroy their masks and costumes and desist from further public demonstrations. This may have been nothing more than a ploy, however, to avert a crackdown by Brownlow (and by state and federal authorities elsewhere in the South). In any event, organized violence against blacks and Radical unionists in Tennessee did not end. And with the 1869 state election approaching, there could be little doubt that more trouble was ahead.

Downfall of the Radicals

Governor Brownlow's resignation on February 25, 1869, set the stage for the final act of Reconstruction in Tennessee. The parson, having decided to try exercising his political talents in the national arena, had persuaded the legislature to elect him to the U.S. Senate. His departure for Washington left the governor's chair to the speaker of the state senate, an East Tennessean named DeWitt C. Senter.

Though known as a stalwart Radical and a friend of Brownlow, the new governor indicated that he would not be as uncompromisingly partisan as his predecessor. Not long after taking office, he relaxed martial law where Brownlow had imposed it, and then he demobilized the guard.

Meanwhile, the state was gearing up for the August 1869 election, and Governor Senter made it clear that he was interested in another term in office. This, however, provoked a crisis within the Radical Party. From the beginning of Reconstruction, the party had been troubled by campaign factionalism—i.e., two Radical candidates running for the same post, to the benefit of the Conservative candidate—but that factionalism had been confined to local, legislative, and congressional races. Now, with the powerful Brownlow no longer at the helm, factionalism threatened the Radicals' gubernatorial campaign. At the Radical state convention, held in Nashville in May, Senter was challenged by Middle Tennessean William B. Stokes. Supporters of the two rivals got into a shouting match that escalated into a brawl; the donnybrook ended only after police arrived. Thereafter, the two sides refused to compromise. They wound up holding separate meetings, and each nominated its favorite. Thus, both Senter and Stokes prepared to run for governor, each one claiming to be the legitimate Radical candidate.

The Conservatives, having watched these developments with great interest, shrewdly decided not to field a gubernatorial candidate. Their hope was that one of the Radical candidates would make a bid for Conservative support; in order to get it, of course, he would have to make some concessions—particularly on the key issue of franchise restrictions. The Conservatives' strategy succeeded beyond their expectations. On June 5, 1869, as Senter and Stokes began a series of joint campaign appearances, Senter stunned his opponent, the audience, his party, and indeed the whole state by boldly announcing his support for immediate repeal of all voting restrictions.

An important factor in Senter's apostasy was a state supreme court decision handed down just seven days earlier. The justices had ruled that the voiding of the 1865 voter registrations under the 1866 franchise law was unconstitutional. This meant that about thirty thousand men—Conservatives all—who had been registered by county court clerks in 1865 but subsequently barred from voting by Brownlow's hand-picked election commissioners now would be eligible to vote. This, along with the continued suppression of the black and Radical unionist vote by Klan violence, made it very likely that Conservative voters would equal or even outnumber Radical voters on election day. No doubt Senter figured that, however many votes he lost among the Radicals by coming out for the enfranchisement of former Rebels, he would gain even more among the Conservatives. Too, it must have been obvious to the governor that, in the long run, the Conservatives would triumph in Tennessee, if only because the sons of ex-Rebels, too young to have taken part in the war and thus not disfranchised under the law, were coming of age. Radicalism was doomed, and Senter saw advantages in ingratiating himself with the inevitable victors.

After Senter's announcement, the Conservatives enthusiastically endorsed him, even though he still was calling himself a Radical. (The Conservatives did run their own candidates for other offices.) Meanwhile, Senter decided to take an even more drastic step in order to ensure his election. Using his power as governor under the franchise law, he began removing the election commissioners appointed by Brownlow and replacing them with his own people, who were given to understand that no man was to be denied registration, no matter what the law said. In the weeks leading up to the election, ex-Confederates by the tens of thousands signed up.

The result was an enormous turnout on election day (175,000 voters, compared to 97,000 in 1867 and 83,000 in 1868) and an overwhelming victory for Senter and for the Conservative Party. Senter beat Stokes by 120,000 to 55,000 (Stokes's total was about the same as Grant's in 1868). The governor carried all three sections of the state; his margin was narrow in the East, but he outpolled Stokes by three to one in the Middle and West. The new state senate would have twenty Conservatives and only five Radicals; the house would have sixty-six Conservatives and seventeen Radicals.

The legislature assembled in October 1869 and immediately began undoing the work of the Radicals. The Ku Klux Klan Act and the State Guard Act were repealed and the whole state school system was swept away, leaving public education a matter of county option. The legislature also repealed laws (passed in the Brownlow years at the urging of blacks) that banned racial segregation in public transportation and protected the rights of laborers.

The work of demolition did not stop there. In response to widespread public complaints, the legislature reduced the citizens' tax burden. State taxes had quadrupled under Radical rule, in part because of the need to fund the new school system, but also because of the Brownlow regime's generous underwriting of railroad construction through the issuance of state bonds. This matter of the state debt became quite a scandal, for a good portion of the $14 million in bonds wound up in the pockets of corrupt railroad executives and their cronies in the legislature, or was turned over to mismanaged railroad companies which went bankrupt and left the state responsible for the debt. Along with its other actions, the new legislature repealed all laws granting state aid for internal improvements.

The legislature's single most significant act, however, was calling for a convention to write a new state constitution. An election was authorized, to be held in December 1869; the voters were to vote for or against a convention and elect delegates. Although technically the franchise restrictions were still in effect (they legally could be abolished only by state constitutional amendment), the legislature declared that voting would be open to all adult males. In December, the electorate approved the convention by a five-to-one margin and elected seventy-five delegates, of whom only four were Radicals and none was black.

The convention met in Nashville on January 10, 1870. John C. Brown of Middle Tennessee, a former Confederate general and Ku Klux Klan member, was elected chairman. Six weeks later the convention adjourned, having hammered out a new state constitution. The voters ratified it in March.

The constitution of 1870, which (with a few amendments) is still

Tennessee's governing document today, preserved the basic structure of government as set forth in the previous constitution, that of 1834. Most of the significant differences between the two documents reflect the Conservatives' desire to ensure that no regime ever again could exercise power as Brownlow and his Radical Party had. Under the new constitution, the governor's authority to use the militia and invoke martial law was restricted, the state was barred from underwriting any private business enterprises, and a limit was set on the number of days the legislators could collect per diem pay (an effort to prevent lengthy and expensive legislative sessions, a hallmark of the Brownlow years). Most importantly, the new constitution instituted universal manhood suffrage (though a poll tax was authorized) and forbade the legislature ever to tamper with that right. This left the door open to black voting, of course, but the framers of the constitution correctly assumed that the poll tax would reduce such voting to negligible proportions.

Shaken by the abrupt overthrow of Radical rule, blacks and Radical unionists appealed to the federal government. They sent petitions to Congress and to the president, claiming that the 1869 election had been a fraud; and a delegation of black leaders, headed by Nashvillian James C. Napier, went to Washington in March 1870 bearing a memorial that documented the violence against Radical voters in Tennessee. The object of these entreaties was to persuade the federal authorities to invalidate the election and the new constitution and put the state under military rule, as had been done with the other former Confederate states. But these efforts were fruitless. President Grant declined to get involved; Congress investigated the election but likewise decided not to intervene, after hearing testimony not only from the losers but also from the winners, including Governor Senter, who assured Congress that the election had been a fair one.

The Conservatives confirmed their triumph in the first elections under the new constitution (which decreed that state elections would be held in even-numbered years, along with federal elections). In August 1870, the voters elected six state supreme court justices, all Conservatives. In November they elected John C. Brown governor, put Conservative majorities in the state house and senate, and installed Conservatives in six of the eight congressional seats. These elections set the pattern that would characterize Tennessee politics for a long time to come: the Conservatives (by then generally calling themselves Democrats) were dominant in Middle and West Tennessee; the Radicals (calling themselves Republicans) were dominant in East Tennessee. As long as the Democrats remained united, they could count on controlling the post of governor and the legislature. The Republicans, however, could count on maintaining a strong minority in the legislature and holding two or three congressional seats.

While most whites in Tennessee cheered the downfall of Radicalism, blacks saw it as a disaster. The brief reign of the Radicals had inspired hope among the freedmen that eventually they might achieve equality, but it had not permanently secured their equality in any respect. They remained, on the whole, poor, illiterate, subjugated, and powerless. Nor could they expect any help from the federal government, which rapidly was losing interest in their fate (the Freedmen's Bureau was defunct in Tennessee even before the 1869 election). With their future now bleak, most Tennessee blacks simply resolved to do the best they could with what they had; but some, determined to continue the quest for equality, packed up their belongings and emigrated to more promising places. As time went by, thousands more would follow.

Tennessee's whites, meanwhile, ended their night riding and put the issues of Reconstruction behind them. Over the next few years, whites elsewhere in the South would do the same, as, one by one, the other Radical state regimes were overthrown. Thus the era of Reconstruction came to a close, and the era of the New South began.

Suggested Readings

Alexander, Thomas B. *Political Reconstruction in Tennessee*. Nashville, 1950.

Ash, Stephen V. *Middle Tennessee Society Transformed, 1860–1870: War and Peace in the Upper South*. Baton Rouge, La., 1988.

Bailey, Fred Arthur. *Class and Tennessee's Confederate Generation*. Chapel Hill, N.C., 1987.

Coulter, E. Merton. *William G. Brownlow: Fighting Parson of the Southern Highlands*. 1937. Reprinted, Knoxville, Tenn., 1999.

McKenzie, Robert Tracy. *One South or Many? Plantation Belt and Upcountry in Civil War–Era Tennessee*. Cambridge, England, 1994.

Patton, James W. *Unionism and Reconstruction in Tennessee, 1860–1869*. Chapel Hill, N.C., 1934.

Trelease, Allen W. *White Terror: The Ku Klux Klan Conspiracy and Southern Reconstruction*. 1971. Reprinted, Westport, Conn., 1979.

8

The New South

GOV. ROBERT LOVE TAYLOR surveyed the crowd. Sweltering before him in the heat of that day in June 1897 were sixteen thousand Confederate army veterans. Now aging men, they had been invited to come to Nashville to participate in celebrations marking Tennessee's first one hundred years of statehood in that same federal union they had fought to destroy. Around them, in the Centennial Exposition constructed by Nashville civic leaders, stood reminders of an idealized past—the Old South—and exhibits that promised a better life in the postbellum New South. A full-scale replica of the Parthenon recalled the Old South's claim to have united slavery and high culture, just as ancient Greece had done. A History Building featured displays honoring the men who fought on both sides in "the late war." But the Centennial Exposition balanced memories from the past against dreams for the future. Exhibits of farm machinery, telephones, and gasoline engines promised that technology would transform life in the New South. Joseph Killebrew, who for the past twenty years had promoted economic development for railroads and state government, filled the Nashville, Chattanooga and St. Louis (NC & St. L) Railroad's building with the fruits of his labors: ten thousand square feet exhibited Tennessee's natural and manufactured products. The Women's Building contrasted the old log cabin kitchen with a new, modern, model kitchen, packed with the latest domestic technology. The Negro Building, intended to showcase African American achievements and southern good will, featured exhibits from almost three hundred black schools and colleges, all created since the Civil War. The Centennial Exposition, like so many public occasions in the postwar South, was a conscious—and highly successful—attempt to show that southerners still revered the lost past, while they moved confidently into the future.

Standing before the veterans, on a stage bedecked with the Stars and Bars as well as the Stars and Stripes, Governor Taylor hit exactly the right note: "I doubt if the world will ever see another civilization as brilliant as that which perished in the South a third of a century ago. Its white-columned mansions under cool spreading groves . . . and its cotton-fields

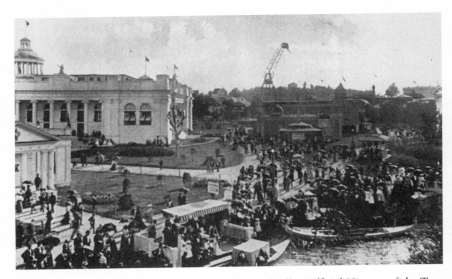

Crowd on Tennessee Day at Centennial Park, Nashville. *Official History of the Tennessee Centennial Exposition* (Nashville, 1898). Special Collections, University of Tennessee, Knoxville.

stretching away to the horizon, alive with toiling slaves . . . ; its pomp and pride and revelry; its splendid manhood and the dazzling beauty of its women, placed it as the high tide of earthly glory." While praising the past, Taylor promised a better future: "Look yonder at those flashing domes and glittering spires. . . . Look at what southern brains and southern hands have wrought. See the victories of peace we have won, all represented within the white columns of our great industrial exposition, and you will catch glimpses of her future glory." As the Confederate veterans and their families toured the exposition in the slowly fading summer twilight, thousands of electric lights came on, illuminating the architectural expressions of the state's traditions and its dreams of prosperity in a New South.

During the late nineteenth century, southern business boosters assured the nation that the "Old South" of slavery had been replaced by a bustling, industrious "New South," whose hard-working people looked to rival the Yankees in push and drive. Tennessee's New South promoters, men like Joseph Killebrew and entrepreneur Arthur Colyar, lured investors to the region by pointing out that the South's great natural resources of coal, iron, and timber awaited exploitation. To potential factory owners, the business boosters promised cheap, docile, native-born white laborers, willing to work long hours for low pay and uninfected with supposedly foreign ideas like trade unionism. New South boosters assured the nation that the South had no race problem—or, at least, none that money men need worry about. In short, New South promoters promised potential investors a capitalist's paradise, complete with very friendly state governments that would keep taxes low and turn a blind eye to safety violations and the exploitation of workers. To keep state governments sweet, business invested heavily in politics.

The New South ideal never was realized in Tennessee, despite decades of intense economic development. At the end of the century, most Tennesseans continued to make their living from farming, as their ancestors before them had done. Although some Tennesseans made fortunes in manufacturing, mining, and logging, most of the men and women who worked in the New South factories, mines, and mills earned no more than subsistence wages. Far from being docile, Tennesseans protested low wages and bad working conditions through strikes, riots, and small-scale guerrilla wars. Race remained a difficult and painful issue, as black Tennesseans fought in court and at the polls against the reestablishment of white supremacy throughout the state. State politics became an arena for competing economic interests. Yet the New South also brought with it a sense of movement, growth, and change that

Tennessee River packet *Edgar Cherry*, Christmas Eve, 1894. *Tennessee River Steamboats*, 1854–1901. Special Collections, University of Tennessee, Knoxville.

many Tennesseans found exciting. In the state, there could be no better symbol of the New South than the railroad.

Railroads

To recognize how important railroads were to Tennessee's postwar development, it helps to understand the transportation systems that railroads supplemented or replaced. Prior to the Civil War, most Tennessee commerce traveled up and down the rivers. Areas far from navigable rivers were isolated and undeveloped, accessible only by road. Tennessee roads were extremely bad. Rarely paved or even graveled, dirt roads dissolved into mud bogs during summer rains and froze into axle-breaking ruts in winter. With such means of transportation, commerce stalled.

Professionally engineered and constructed, railroads provided the first reliable and weatherproof means of transportation Tennesseans ever saw. Extensive railroad construction began in Tennessee in the 1850s, was interrupted by the Civil War, and took off in the late 1860s. By 1900, Tennessee had 3,137 miles of railroads. A traveler through the state could progress by rail from Bristol to Memphis and make connections to all the cities in the state. Railroads reached far up into the Cumberland Plateau, making possible the exploitation of coal and iron deposits. Because of the railroads, Tennessee cities grew into shipping and manufacturing centers. Even the smallest whistle-stop in the most rural county became part of regional, national, and international marketing networks. The impact was not always positive; while it became easier to sell Tennessee products, local producers found themselves facing competition from afar. Moreover, as merchants and farmers throughout the state complained, the railroads exerted too much power over local economies. Railroads seemed to set rates arbitrarily, with no regard to length of shipment. In addition, railroads could change rates without notice to the consumer. Tennesseans remembered that many of the railroads had been funded by state bonds, issued during Governor Brownlow's administration, and resented what they saw as the railroad's manipulative, price-gouging monopoly on commerce in the state.

For most Tennesseans, "the railroad" meant the Louisville and Nashville, or L&N. Formed before the Civil War, primarily by Louisville businessmen, the L&N served the Union as a shipping line. At the end of the war, the L&N began to build an empire that by 1880 ran southward from Louisville through Tennessee and into northern Alabama. From the 1880s through the 1930s, the L&N was one of the most powerful economic and political forces in the state. Although the railroad originally had been a "southern" line, by the 1880s the L&N's stock was owned primarily by northern and British investors; and a New York native, Milton Smith, ran the railroad upon which much of the commerce of the upper South depended. Smith was L&N president from 1884 until his death in 1921. Profoundly conservative, Smith believed that only the "fittest" companies would survive competition in the market, and he feared democracy: any state legislature might at any moment decide to confiscate the unpopular L&N, or at least regulate its shipping rates.

Historians use the term "political economy" to describe the interrelationship of political and economic forces. The L&N and the state of Tennessee can be viewed as a textbook case. To protect itself from regulation, the L&N invested in state politics, supporting several of the state's major newspapers and budgeting funds for bribes to public officials. This paid off when, in 1883, the General Assembly proposed a state regulatory commission to oversee railroad rates. Railroad lobbyists succeeded in getting the legislation watered down, so the commission created was ineffective; two years later, the commission was abolished outright. The railroad also bought influence by the simple expedient of letting public officials, from county sheriffs to state legislators, ride free.

This political influence, plus the L&N's great economic power, made the railroad a fierce competitor. In the 1870s, Nashville railroad entrepreneur Edmund "King" Cole built up the Nashville, Chattanooga and St. Louis (NC & St. L) railroad as a potential rival to the L&N. Cole's railroad threatened the L&N's monopoly over Nashville commerce. The larger railroad undercut Cole's control over the NC & St. L, buying a majority of the line's stock and forcing the Nashvillian out. In 1879, the NC & St. L became an L&N subsidary.

In the 1890s, Nashville native Jere Baxter, with widespread public support, attempted to free Nashville from L&N control by building a railroad east to Knoxville and northwest to Clarksville. The Tennessee Central (TC), as Baxter's railroad was named, opened up the Eastern Highland Rim and the Cumberland Plateau to economic development, and Baxter became a hero to people in that part of the state. However, Baxter failed in his ambition to break the L&N's monopoly. The older railroad's management fought him, denying the TC access to terminal facilities in Nashville and keeping up a barrage of criticism from the two capital-city newspapers under L&N control. After Baxter's death, the bankrupt TC passed into receivership; although it continued operation, it never posed a serious threat to L&N control.

Tennesseans complained about the railroads' arbitrary rates and political clout, but people in the state understood that the railroads brought economic development and the chance for prosperity. Building the lines boosted local economies: farmers hired on to work on the railroads, or sold timber for ties, while farm wives sold produce and food to railroad crews. Even while under construction, a railroad's payroll pumped more cash into the local economy than anyone had ever seen, creating a gold-rush effect. For generations of rural Tennesseans, the steel rails represented the road to prosperity.

Industrialization and Urbanization

With rail connections in place at the end of the 1880s, Tennessee experienced an amazing industrial boom. In 1890, the U.S. Census found 4,559 manufacturing plants in the state. Ten years later, there were 8,016. Much of the growth was concentrated in ten industries: flouring and grist mills, lumber and timber products, iron and steel, foundry and machine shops, textiles, railroad car construction, tobacco, cottonseed, leather, and planing mill products. These ten industries comprised 46 percent of the state's industry in 1900, and employed 56 percent of the state's non-agricultural workers.

In the late nineteenth century, Tennesseans were struck by the development of industries on a scale that never had been seen in the state before. The novelty of coal mines in the Cumberland Plateau and iron foundries belching smoke into the skies of Chattanooga attracted more attention than industries which had been there for years, or manufacturing plants producing mundane products like flour. At the turn of the century, however, the state's most profitable industry *was* the production of flour. Because the L&N Railroad's highly preferential shipping rates to and from Nashville made it possible to ship midwestern flour there for milling, during the 1890s the state capital became a major regional center for flour production.

Iron furnaces, Rockwood. *Scribner's Monthly* 8 (May–October 1874). Special Collections, University of Tennessee, Knoxville.

Table 8.1. Leading Tennessee Industries, 1900

Industry	Capital	Workers	Total Wages
Railroad cars and shops	1,319,628	2,817	1,459,319
Flouring and grist mills	5,931,037	1,154	544,722
Foundries, machine shops	3,768,565	3,283	1,185,211
Iron and steel	5,381,165	1,979	539,304
Leather	3,444,197	803	239,870
Lumber, timber products	12,900,595	11,192	3,424,510
Planing mill products	1,343,381	1,170	452,079
Oil, cottonseed, and cake	1,996,791	751	204,219
Textiles	6,384,194	4,251	790,031
Tobacco	1,852,511	1,237	311,514

SOURCE: U.S. Census, Manufactures, 1900.

The mills at Nashville, Knoxville, and Memphis, as well as others scattered throughout the state, contributed 20 percent of the total value of products in the state during the 1890s. Flour production lacked drama, but it produced home-grown fortunes and its profits stayed in the state.

Tennessee timber and wood products ranked second in number of plants but first in number of people employed. At the turn of the century, over eleven thousand Tennesseans worked in sawmills and other wood-product industries. This total omits the part-time loggers who spent part of each year harvesting the state's rich forests. In the late nineteenth century, loggers usually went into the woods after choice trees, such as walnut and cherry, which were in demand for fine furniture. Loggers cut trees selectively and "snaked" them out by mules to the nearest stream. The logs were tied into rafts from 200 to 250 feet long, then floated downstream to sawmills. This relatively simple method of logging changed as timber companies bought vast acreage, ran rail lines deep into the forests, clear-cut the forests, and processed the lumber in portable mills on site. Railroad connections made it possible to market Tennessee timber internationally. Trees cut from Tennessee hills might be shipped to Mexico or Canada, or to fine furniture manufacturers in Great Britain or France.

During the New South years, many southern states seriously encouraged the establishment of cotton mills, for social as well as economic reasons. Promoters argued that cotton mills would provide employment for poor southern whites in mountain districts and, at the same time, improve employees' morals by encouraging them to develop the work habits and discipline appropriate to the Machine Age. Throughout the South, local investors pooled their money to open mills, while elsewhere towns lured northern investment with the promise that mill workers were native white Protestants who had no radical ideas about unions: in short, mill workers in the South could be paid much less than similar workers in New England. The cotton-mill crusade never was as important in Tennessee as in neighboring states; but by the end of the century, textiles ranked second only to the timber industry in numbers of people employed. The mills provided work for over four thousand Tennesseans, many of them women and children, who could be paid less than men for doing the same work. In the new century, textile and clothing production would emerge as a major factor in the state's economy.

Table 8.2. Growth in Four Tennessee Cities, 1870 and 1900: Population and Manufacturing Establishments

	1870	1900	Increase (%)
State			
Population	1,258,520	2,020,616	60.6
Manufactures	5,317	8,016	50.8
Chattanooga			
County Population	17,241	61,695	257.8
City Population	6,093	30,154	394.9
Manufactures	58*	332	
Knoxville			
County Population	28,990	74,302	156.3
City Population	8,682	32,637	275.9
Manufactures	82*	218	
Memphis			
County Population	76,378	153,557	101.0
City Population	40,226	102,329	154.4
Manufactures	757*	659	
Nashville			
County Population	62,897	122,815	95.3
City Population	25,865	80,865	212.6
Manufactures	373*	489	

*The figures given here represent manufacturing establishments in Davidson, Hamilton, Knox, and Shelby Counties. Since the 1900 figures present manufactures within the cities listed, no valid comparisons may be made.

SOURCE: U.S. Census, Manufactures, 1870, 1900.

Entrepreneurs realized that the East Tennessee mountains and the Cumberland Plateau held veins of iron ore and good bituminous coal. John T. Wilder, for example, recognized Tennessee's mineral potential while stationed in the state as an officer in the Union army. After the war, the Yankee general came back to the South, bought up land containing coal and iron deposits, set up forges and foundries, and helped develop East Tennessee as a center of iron production.

Tennessee's cities grew rapidly during the late nineteenth century. Commercial centers before the war, the state's cities became centers of manufacturing as well; rural migrants, black and white, came to town in search of employment. As city populations outgrew city services, poor neighborhoods (black and white) became instant slums. Meanwhile, across town, aspiring members of a new middle class (black and white) created their own exclusive urban world.

Although Memphis in 1900 held its place as the state's biggest city, the river town's growth had been hampered by a series of deadly yellow-fever epidemics in the 1870s. Memphis began to regain her population and industrial strength in the 1880s. By 1900, Memphis's population had grown to 102,329. Between 1890 and 1900, the number of manufacturers in Memphis grew from 345 to 659, an increase of 91 percent, and the 1900 census showed 8,433 people employed in manufacturing. Shelby County specialized in the production of cottonseed byproducts, lumber, and timber products.

While maintaining its dominance of Middle Tennessee commerce, Nashville experienced steady industrial growth and, by the end of the century, ranked as the state's leading manufacturing city. In 1860, Nashville's population was 17,055. By 1900 it was 80,865. Between 1870 and 1900, the city's population increased by 212.6 percent. Good rail connections made Nashville a center of food processing and shipment. Nashville's flour mills ground out the city's most lucrative product, while the city's meat-packing plants dominated the mid-state market. In the 1890s, a Nashville entrepreneur, Joel Cheek, began marketing a premium coffee, which he named after the city's finest hotel: Maxwell House.

The New South transformed Knoxville and Chattanooga, bringing industry to what had been medium-sized mountain towns. Both cities grew dramatically in the last three decades of the century. Between 1860 and 1880, Knoxville's population more than doubled, from 3,704 to 9,693. Growth continued in the 1890s, with Knoxville's annexation of two adjacent small towns bringing the population to 32,637. Blessed with good rail connections, Knoxville drew aggressive merchants, many of them former Union soldiers, who built the city's wholesaling business into the third largest in the South by 1896. The mountain city also became a regional center for iron mills, machine shops, cloth mills, and furniture factories; during the 1880s alone, over one hundred new factories were built in Knoxville.

Although iron production was scattered throughout East Tennessee,

Chattanooga, which also had good rail connections, quickly became a regional iron center. The attitudes of Chattanooga's civic leaders, who favored development, probably helped, too. At one point, the local newspaper issued a "general invitation to all carpet-baggers to leave the bleak winds of the North and come to Chattanooga." The carpetbaggers took the city up on the offer. By 1880, there were six iron manufacturers in Hamilton County, employing 1,204 out of the 1,280 iron workers in the state. Briefly, in the late nineteenth century, Chattanooga appeared likely to become the South's premier rival to Pittsburgh, Pennsylvania. Ultimately Chattanooga lost out to Birmingham, Alabama, which was closer to better iron deposits and received preferential freight rates from the L&N, which owned large parcels of land there. By that time, however, other businesses had located in Chattanooga. Perhaps the best known was the Chattanooga Medicine Company, founded by two "carpetbagging" Union veterans after

---

Death Capital of the Mississippi

Memphis, Tennessee's largest city, was also its most deadly, a pest hole rife with filth-borne and tropical diseases. Typhoid and cholera visited Memphis repeatedly. In 1873 and 1878, Memphis experienced devastating yellow fever epidemics. The 1878 epidemic was so severe that most of the city's elected leaders either died or deserted their posts to flee into the countryside. The city's government collapsed, and Memphis briefly ceased to exist as a legal entity, being replaced by the "Taxing District of Shelby County."

Memphis's health problems derived from its poor drainage and sanitation: bayous along the city's edge collected the city's sewage, provided breeding grounds for mosquitoes, and contaminated the cisterns and wells from which most residents drew water. City cleanup efforts began in the 1880s, when sewers and drains were installed in districts inhabited by wealthy white people. Obtaining clean water proved harder. Finally the city dug deep wells. When the first one was completed and clean, pure water poured out, so many Memphians showed up with buckets that the police had to be summoned to maintain order.

By the 1890s, Memphis had made an impressive comeback. The city had an abundant supply of clean water, health officials no longer allowed hogs and cattle to wander through the streets, most streets were paved, and the death rate had been cut in half.

the war. The Chattanooga Medicine Company's products were famous throughout the New South: they made Wine of Cardui, a tonic for "female complaints"; and Black Draught, an extremely potent laxative.

In the 1880s, rural Tennesseans in search of work poured into Chattanooga, Knoxville, Memphis, and Nashville, crowding into low-rent districts and creating instant health hazards. Horrible yellow-fever epidemics almost destroyed Memphis in the 1870s. For a brief time the city lost its charter and was operated as the "Taxing District of Shelby County." Nashville had severe epidemics of cholera, a deadly water-borne disease, in the 1870s. During the 1880s, both Nashville and Memphis installed water and sewer lines, but many poor residents could not afford to install plumbing or run lines to the street—if the lines reached their streets. Gilded Age municipal projects often did not extend to districts where poor whites or blacks lived. Most of the traffic in Tennessee cities was horsedrawn, and horses made their own contributions to the pollution in city streets. Cities stank from open privies and horse manure. Water-borne diseases such as typhoid remained a hazard through the end of the century.

Concerned citizens cited the moral pollution of city life as well. In Nashville, the waterfront featured saloons and houses of prostitution; uphill from there was "Black Bottom," a district described in 1905 as full of "dives, brothels, second-hand clothing stores, filthy habitations . . . accompanied by the daily display of lewdness and drunkenness on the sidewalks

---

Mary Magdalene of Memphis

In 1872, Annie Cook came to Memphis, where she established a house of prostitution on Bayou Street. When a yellow fever epidemic broke out in 1878, most of the good citizens of Memphis fled. Annie Cook stayed, turning her house into a hospital and nursing yellow fever victims until she herself died of the disease.

Annie Cook was not the only self-sacrificing woman in Memphis. Four Episcopal and twelve Roman Catholic nuns also died caring for epidemic victims. Yet the prostitute's courage and compassion touched the public's heart. The *Memphis Appeal* eulogized her: "Annie Cook, the woman who, after a long life of shame, ventured all she had of life and prosperity for the sick, died September 11th of yellow fever . . . surely the sins of this woman must have been forgiven her, for her faith has made her whole— made her one with the loving Christ, whose example she followed in giving her life that others might live."

and redolent with the stench of every vile odor." Memphis's reputation as a regional center for prostitution, gambling, and general carousing had been earned before the Civil War and was enhanced in the late nineteenth century by the city's casual attitude toward violence. As the *Commercial Appeal* noted in 1909, "Killing is now the most thriving industry in this part of the country. They kill them next door to the city hall, and shoot them in the streets." In 1910, Memphis had the highest murder rate in the nation—47.1 homicides per 100,000 population, when the national average was 7.2. The chief statistician of the Prudential Insurance Company labeled Memphis the nation's "murder capital." As late as 1918, Memphis's murder rate was twice that of its nearest rival, Atlanta.

Middle-class Tennesseans blamed urban problems—poverty, vice, crime—on the moral deficiencies of city people. In Tennessee, as in much of the South, most people were evangelical Christians. Although many Catholics and Jews lived in Tennessee's cities, the overwhelming majority of churchgoers were Baptists, Methodists, Presbyterians, or members of the Disciples of Christ. Most churches, especially in rural areas, emphasized the necessity of individual repentance and salvation, and considered social problems to be consequences of the sinful nature of the world, which would endure until society as a whole experienced Christian conversion. This emphasis upon individual sin and salvation limited the impact of religion upon politics.

Sam Jones changed that. In the 1880s, Jones, a Methodist minister from Georgia, began a series of revivals in cities across the South. The message he brought to Tennessee's cities in 1884 and 1885 was old-fashioned fire and brimstone. He castigated Nashville's newly rich citizens for their indifference: "Hell is selfishness on fire, and the great wonder to me is that some of you don't catch fire and go straight to hell by spontaneous combustion . . . you love money more than your souls." He gave "men-only" sermons in sinful Memphis that reduced grown men to weeping "like whipped children." In Knoxville, he praised the Woman's Christian Temperance Union (WCTU), which many southern ministers condemned as too aggressive, political, and full of "masculine" women. In sum, Jones insisted that Christians had to do more than attend church on Sunday. He preached an activist religion that sent his converts into the world to do good, and philanthropy blossomed across the state.

Possessed by a new religious spirit, converts set out to fight sin in their communities, and they found the center of sin in the saloon. Jones, a reformed alcoholic, believed that drinking caused violence, crime, and poverty. A Methodist minister in Nashville summed up the new lack of tolerance for drinking in an 1886 sermon: "Christian Rum is the king of crime," he said, a "vampire which fans sanity to sleep while it sucks away the lifeblood. . . . It defies God, despises Jesus Christ . . . above all it murders humanity." Women especially opposed drinking, since drunken men abused and impoverished their families.

In 1885, temperance organizations in the state formed the Tennessee Temperance Alliance with the goal of prohibiting all alcohol in the state through a state constitutional amendment. In 1886, pro-referendum candidates won election to the General Assembly. A vote on the constitutional amendment was scheduled for September 1887. Sam Jones came to campaign for the amendment. The forces of "sin" fought back, ridiculing prohibitionists as "well-meaning but sentimental women" and "political Methodist priests." Conservative Democrats and Republicans alike mocked the forces of "ugly women, henpecked husbands . . . and $3 preachers," in the words of the Republican *National Review*. The amendment failed to pass, despite strong support in East Tennessee and in many rural counties.

Stunned, middle-class prohibitionists blamed the urban black vote. Although some blacks were prohibitionists (the WCTU had a "colored" branch in North Nashville), black political power derived from alliances made by black leaders with white urban politicians who were opposed to

---

Captain Ryman Gets Religion

When Sam Jones opened his 1885 revival in Nashville, no one scoffed more than "Steamboat Tom" Ryman, whose boats plied the river, well stocked with whisky and dancing girls. After days of hearing about Jones's preaching against liquor, Ryman decided to put a stop to it. He gathered his men and marched into Jones's revival, intending to beat Jones up. But he stopped long enough to listen to the sermon. Jones announced to the crowd that Ryman had come to assault him. Ryman stepped forward: "I came here for the purpose stated by Mr. Jones, and he has whipped me with the Gospel of Christ."

Ryman ended liquor service on his boats, converted his waterfront bars into mission halls, and hired a minister for the waterfront. For twenty years he funded a charity wagon distributing food and clothing to the poor, and a mission wagon which toured the business district on Sunday, complete with choir and organ. In 1888, Ryman helped fund construction of a Union Gospel Tabernacle on Fifth Avenue and Broad. After Ryman's death in 1904, the building was renamed Ryman Auditorium in his honor. The Ryman served Nashville as a gathering place for generations, hosting gospel shows and becoming, in the 1920s, the "mother church" of the Grand Ole Opry.

prohibition. The head of the Nashville WCTU, Mrs. J. D. Allen, charged that black voters were "under the lash of the liquor traffic" and had "marched to the polls shackled slaves, nothing more." Believing that reform was impossible as long as blacks had the franchise, prohibitionists supported the voting restrictions passed by the General Assembly in 1889 and 1890 and worked for local measures to curb black political power in Tennessee's cities.

Jim Crow: The New Racial Order

During the last quarter of the nineteenth century, African Americans in the South saw the rights they had won during Reconstruction denied, eroded, or legislated out of existence. Under the indifferent eye of the federal government, white southerners fought tenaciously against all moves toward racial equality or black political power. By the end of the century, most Deep South states had succeeded in denying blacks the right to vote. Cut out of the political system, blacks had no way to resist white-imposed segregation. "Jim Crow" laws, named after a supposedly comical dance tune that made fun of African Americans, mandated segregation in public schools and all public accommodations, from restrooms in the county courthouse to seating in the passenger cars on L&N trains. "Jim Crow" meant that all African Americans daily were forced to acknowledge publicly their lower racial status, while whites enjoyed the privileges of the master race: the best seats and accommodations everywhere.

Blacks in Tennessee did not escape the impact of segregation and of white racist violence. However, in race relations as in Reconstruction, Tennessee's history diverges from that of the rest of the South. During Reconstruction, black men in Tennessee never gained the political power that they held briefly in other southern states; conversely, when Reconstruction ended, black men in Tennessee did not lose all political power. In Tennessee, unlike other southern states, black men never completely lost the right to vote. (Black women, like white women, were denied the franchise.) Black voters were too useful, both to the Republican Party and to certain urban Democratic politicians, for either party to push for total disfranchisement. Thus black political leaders, such as Robert Church in Memphis and James Napier in Nashville, occasionally could negotiate better treatment for their people. Black people's chances for an education, for a job that paid a living wage, and for simple survival were better in Tennessee than in Mississippi or Alabama.

Despite these slight advantages, however, life for black Tennesseans was a hard and bitter struggle. Most black Tennesseans were farm laborers or tenant farmers, stuck in an economic dead end. When blacks migrated to Tennessee cities, as they did in increasing numbers throughout the late nineteenth century, they found most means of advancement closed to them. Whites would only hire black men to do the hardest, most menial, and lowest paid jobs. Black women worked as domestics, cooking and cleaning for whites. Yet, as difficult as life in the cities might be, it offered advantages as well, including better educational opportunities for children and a vibrant community life, often centered around churches. Segregation, by keeping blacks isolated, created the economic foundation for a black middle class of ministers, professionals, and businessmen. For African Americans born in slavery, the very existence of black businesses, black newspapers, black schools, and black colleges must have been a cause for optimism and hope.

Samuel A. McElwee. Special Collections, University of Tennessee, Knoxville.

As late as the 1880s, black Republican districts in West Tennessee sent black representatives to the state General Assembly. Even so, during the late nineteenth century, white Tennesseans gradually reduced black political power and passed laws segregating blacks. Black Tennesseans fought against these trends but lost. The combination of legal oppression, white violence, and the treachery of white political allies proved too powerful.

On the political front, black Tennesseans formed an essential element of the state's Republican Party. Yet white Republicans, mostly from the mountain districts of East Tennessee, had no commitment to black equality. They needed black votes to win statewide elections. To get those votes, they were willing to commit state funds to black schools, asylums, and other institutions. State politicians of both parties held paternalistic ideas about blacks and mouthed platitudes about their support for the uplift of the race. Neither party supported racial equality, as black Republican State Rep. Samuel McElwee found in 1887, when he introduced antilynching legislation into the General Assembly.

Whites used lynching to keep blacks "in their place." Most lynch mobs justified their actions by claiming that the men they killed had in some way threatened the virtue of white womanhood. Although illegal, lynching was so acceptable to whites that the Memphis newspapers sometimes announced the place and time at which black men would be killed by mobs. Yet investigators discovered that many lynching cases had nothing to do with sex.

Nor were all the victims male. In 1886, a white mob in Jackson killed a black woman, Eliza Wood, who was accused of poisoning a white woman. It was to her death that McElwee referred in his 1887 speech against lynching in the General Assembly: "The bell is rung, they enter the jail and strip her of every garment, and order her to march—buffeting, kicking, and spearing her with sharp sticks on the march. . . . She is swung up, her body riddled with bullets and orders issued not to interfere with her until 9 o'clock the next morning, in order that she might be seen." McElwee asked his listeners to imagine the victims of lynching in heaven "with united voices . . . asking the question, 'Great God, when will this Nation treat the Negro as an American citizen?'" He condemned the lynch mobs of three West Tennessee towns: "When the citizens . . . go to judgement with the blood . . . on their garments, it will be more tolerable for Sodom and Gomorrah in that day than it will be for Jackson, Dyersburg and McKenzie." Although McElwee's speech won national attention, his bill was tabled by the General Assembly. Before the end of the 1880s, McElwee himself would be driven from politics and would leave Tennessee in fear for his life, as conditions for blacks in Tennessee took a dramatic turn for the worse.

In 1888, the Democrats won control of state government and set out to consolidate that control by removing black votes as a factor in state politics. Over the next two years, the Democratic General Assembly passed legislation requiring that voters register twenty days in advance of the election

Crusade against Lynching

Born in slavery in Holly Springs, Mississippi, in 1862, Ida B. Wells became an internationally known investigative journalist, crusading for racial justice and women's rights. As a young woman, Wells moved to Memphis and secured a teaching job in a nearby town, commuting by train in the "ladies car." When a conductor tried to evict Wells from her first-class seat, she fought him and was thrown off the train. She sued the railroad company and won. Wells wrote about her lawsuit in the national black press, beginning her career in journalism. She later became co-owner of a Memphis newspaper.

After a friend was murdered by a white mob, Wells urged blacks to leave Memphis for the Oklahoma Territory and embarked upon her famous anti-lynching campaign. Whites justified lynching by claiming that black men raped white women. Investigating 728 lynchings, Wells found that, in most cases, sex was not even an issue. Blacks were lynched for political and economic reasons, she charged. In 1892, whites burned down her newspaper office and threatened to kill her. Fortunately, she was in New York at the time.

Wells settled in Chicago and married a prominent newspaper editor, Ferdinand Barnett. While raising five children, she founded a settlement house to help blacks adjust to urban life, and started the first suffrage club for black women in Illinois. Her reports on lynching, *A Red Record, Southern Horrors,* and *Mob Rule in New Orleans,* remain important documents for historians attempting to understand lynching and black resistance.

and present poll-tax receipts before being allowed to vote. Other legislation, aimed at preventing federal oversight of state elections, required separate ballot boxes for state and federal elections. However, the most devastating blow to black political power came in the guise of political reform: in 1889, Sen. Joseph H. Dortch of Fayette County proposed a bill requiring secret ballots for state elections. Traditionally parties had printed their own ballots—often brightly colored or printed with distinguishing pictures, and referred to as party tickets—which voters picked up at party headquarters and dropped into the ballot box. This meant that illiterates could easily vote the party ticket. The Dortch law's secret ballots required the voter to be literate: names were printed alphabetically and without party designation. This law functioned effectively to disfranchise illiterate blacks. However, many white Tennesseans, particularly in rural districts, also were illiterate. Therefore the Dortch bill exempted all rural areas and applied solely to Knox, Hamilton, Davidson, and Shelby Counties (later extended to towns with populations above 2,500). When the Democratic General Assembly, in 1890, passed an act requiring that all voters pay a poll tax, the Democratic plan for dominance was complete—and, not coincidentally, independent black political power in the state was ended. In the future, black voters would be a factor politically only when black votes could be used by powerful urban politicians. Black voters did not regain their rights until after World War II.

Republican politicians in Tennessee, never happy about being in a bira-cial party, withdrew support from black Republicans now that black vot-ing was blocked. Samuel McElwee, a delegate to the Republican national convention in 1888, received little support or protection from former Re-publican allies when white Democrats in his home county, Haywood, gave him five minutes to make his final political speech in the county—and five minutes to run for his life. McElwee, like many other refugees from Jim Crow, left Tennessee for Chicago.

Having removed black voters as an element in state politics, white poli-ticians now found it easier to complete the process of segregation. The his-tory of Jim Crow in Tennessee is hard to trace precisely and is rife with con-tradictions. For example, black leaders in the state at first accepted segregated primary schools—since the alternative was no schools at all for black children—but demanded black teachers for black children. In higher education, blacks were not allowed to go to state-supported schools such as the University of Tennessee, but received tuition grants to allow them to attend Fisk in Nashville or Knoxville College. Rarely did black Tennesse-ans challenge the de facto segregation that separated blacks from whites in public accommodations or housing. Instead, the railroads became the focus of white attempts to "draw the color line," and of black resistance. In 1883, the United States Supreme Court ruled that the Civil Rights Act of 1875, which had prohibited segregation, was unconstitutional. With the support of the courts, railroads in Tennessee and throughout the South began to segregate their passengers. Municipalities throughout the state followed by segregating streetcars. Black protests and boycotts failed.

The 1890s also saw an intensification of violence against blacks in the state. When three black men were lynched in Memphis, chiefly because they owned a grocery store that threatened to take business away from a white-owned store nearby, crusading journalist Ida B. Wells urged Memphis blacks to leave a town that would not protect their lives. Hundreds of Memphis blacks moved westward to Kansas, joining a movement of black southerners called the "Exodusters." In 1892, a white mob took from the Davidson County jail a black man accused of raping a white girl, and hanged him from the Cumberland River Bridge in the middle of Nashville. White political leaders, far from deploring violence, defended the right of white men to kill blacks who violated the racial code. Yet, despite disfranchisement and segregation, blacks, particularly in the cities, continued to struggle for individual and racial progress.

Exploitation and Resistance

Historians looking at the scope and the pace of industrial development in the New South have asked a very simple question: if the economy was booming, why did the region stay so poor? The answer historians traditionally have given is that most southern industries were extractive, exploitive, and colonial in nature. Extractive industries took raw resources and shipped them elsewhere for processing. Exploitive industries came to the South in the first place because labor costs were lower than elsewhere in the nation. The contention that the southern economy was "colonial" refers to the fact that southern railroads and industries often were owned by people from outside the South. Wealth produced in the South was not plowed back into further southern development, and wages stayed low. These special economic conditions led many Tennesseans to develop mixed feelings toward economic development: people wanted railroads and factories but resented the fact that their economic fates were in the hands of financiers on Wall Street.

Tennesseans did not automatically accept low wages and poor working conditions as their natural due. During the late nineteenth century, Tennesseans, like their counterparts throughout the nation, resisted, through strikes and armed mob violence, what they saw as economic injustice.

It is hard to determine what percentage of workers in Tennessee belonged to unions. Historians estimate that, during the late nineteenth century, the national union membership was about 8 percent of the workforce. The proportion of union men in Tennessee probably was lower, and probably was concentrated in urban areas. During the 1870s and 1880s, a national labor union, the Knights of Labor, attempted to organize workers across the country and across racial and gender lines. It had its greatest success among railroad workers. However, the Knights fell apart in the 1880s, and the organization was succeeded by the conservative American Federation of Labor, which organized skilled workers, such as machinists or printers, into craft unions. Unlike the Knights, the AFL showed no interest in unionizing women, blacks, or the unskilled. Despite the high percentage of black workers in Tennessee cities (by 1900, Memphis had the fourth largest urban black population in the country), black men usually were excluded from organized AFL activities. Since most Tennessee workers were unskilled, few belonged to AFL unions.

Tennessee workers often responded to perceived exploitation with unorganized, or "wildcat," strikes. Workers did not walk out for higher wages or better conditions; rather, they struck when employers threatened to cut wages or increase hours. When workers faced threats, not just to their pay, but also to their very right to have a job at all, strikes turned violent. Such was the background of the Coal Miners' War.

After the Civil War, the state government, deeply in debt, began renting out convict labor to New South industrialists. This saved the state the expense of building a new prison and paying for the upkeep of prisoners. The convict lease, common throughout the South, formed the basis of many New South fortunes. In Tennessee, as in other states, obtaining convict labor required careful manipulation of the state political system. A master of Tennessee's political economy, Arthur Colyar, a lawyer, newspaper publisher, industrialist, and Democratic power broker, joined with other industrialists and politicians in 1871 to form Cherry, O'Conner and Company, which obtained and held the state's convict lease through the 1890s. The leasing company rented out convicts at a profit to the companies of the men who had formed the firm. Although convicts were employed on plantations and in factories and helped to build the Tennessee Central Railroad and the Cincinnati Southern Railroad, most worked for a company founded by Colyar: the Tennessee Coal, Iron and Railroad Company (TCI). Using convict labor, TCI developed a New South industrial empire. TCI's Tennessee operations were small compared to their Alabama enterprises: TCI rented Alabama convicts until 1928, using them to develop the coal and iron fields of northern Alabama. Convicts had distinct advantages for TCI. First, they were cheap; second, they could be forced to work hard; and third, their very existence undercut free workers. As Colyar noted, "One of the chief reasons which induced the company to take up the system was the great chance it offered for overcoming strikes. . . . I don't mind saying that for many years the company found this an effective club to be held over the heads of free laborers."

Most convicts were black. In the New South, black men and women were sent to prison in greater numbers and for lesser offenses than whites. As a new generation of black men and women who had not been raised as slaves reached adulthood and refused to defer to old racial rules and manners, southern prison systems became agents of race control. Throughout the South, black male and female convicts slaved for New South industries. Tennessee convicts were shipped from the Nashville prison east to branch prison camps along the rail lines or into the hills to work in coal mines. In 1889, a state house committee called the system "a horror and a shame upon the state," noting that the branch prisons were "hell holes of rage, cruelty, despair, and vice." In 1893, a state investigating committee reported that convicts lived in filthy conditions: "The bedding was filthy to an extreme degree. . . . The convicts had no night-shirts or change of clothing, but slept two in a bed, close against each other and naked, or in the clothes in which they had worked. . . . The beds were without sheets or pillows and covered with grease, grime and coal dust." Convicts who failed to make their production quotas were routinely whipped. Residents of East Tennessee towns near branch prison camps remembered hearing convicts scream under the lash and in the 1930s could point to the convict burial grounds: "Nigger Hill."

The Coal Miners' War began when East Tennessee mining companies that had used free labor attempted to replace free workers with convicts. In July 1891, a Briceville mining company brought in convict labor to break a strike. On July 14, three hundred coal miners from around the county surrounded the convict stockade and demanded that the prison guards surrender. When they did so, the miners shipped the guards and prisoners back to Knoxville by rail. Gov. John P. Buchanan, at the head of the state militia, marched the convicts back to work. The miners refused to back down, and on July 20 shipped the convicts back to Knoxville again—along with the militia troop that was supposed to be guarding them. The miners then went to Coal Creek and did the same with the convicts there. They sent a message to Governor Buchanan: "We struggle for the right to earn bread by honest labor, and in principle are opposed to that system of labor that may be invoked to our degradation." Faced with this defiance of state authority, the governor sent in six hundred militiamen. The miners refused to stand down until a representative of the state promised them that a special session of the state legislature would be convened to repeal the convict lease. In August, the state legislature met. Not surprisingly, given the power of the TCI and the other companies whose profits depended on "state slaves," the legislature did not repeal the lease. Instead, it passed legislation making it illegal to interfere with the convict lease system.

The legal system had failed the miners, and they went to war. From 1891 to 1893, the miners liberated convicts, burned stockades, and fought running battles with the state militia. The miners' resistance presented a dilemma to the state. The convict lease was supposed to save tax dollars, but the convict war had cost much more than the state made on its deal with TCI and other companies. A Tennessee reformer estimated that the state made about $50,000 to $75,000 annually from the lease; but, during the Coal Miners' War, it had spent about $200,000 for the militia. In addition, while few white Tennesseans seemed to care about the abuse suffered by prisoners, many Tennesseans sympathized with the free miners in their struggle. Labor organizations demonstrated in Chattanooga, Memphis, and Nashville in favor of the miners. People from all over the state sent aid to the miners. By 1893, the convict lease had become expensive and unpopular, and the state legislature passed a bill abolishing the convict lease and authorizing the construction of a prison at Brushy Mountain, where convicts would mine coal directly for the state government. Prisoners continued to work for TCI until 1896, when the lease expired.

In the 1890s, when the nation slid into a major economic depression and employers tried to make up profits by cutting wages, workers walked out of Tennessee shops and coal mines. Throughout the state, skilled workers formed unions and created "Labor Councils" to represent the interests of working men. Tennessee employers rarely respected the legitimacy of unions, and most strikes in the 1890s failed. By the end of the nineteenth century, only the coal miners had developed a history of militant and successful labor struggle.

Back on the Farm

New South industrialization, while dramatic, directly touched the lives of only a small minority of Tennesseans. In the late nineteenth century, farmers outnumbered industrial workers six to one. In the Tennessee hills, far from rivers or rail lines, the purpose of farming was, as nineteenth-century farmers said, to "grow what you eat, and eat what you grow." Families worked the land to feed and clothe themselves, and they sold or bartered surplus. Making a living required the labor of all family members. Men cultivated fields and tended livestock. Before the turn of the century, much of the Tennessee hill country remained "open range," where cattle and hogs roamed free. Farmers periodically held roundups or simply went into the woods with a rifle to hunt down and kill a hog. Farm women tended chickens and milk cows, and they planted and harvested the gardens that provided much of the family's food. Tennesseans living on these small family farms were not indifferent to making money, but small family farms were oriented more toward survival than toward generating cash.

The New South industrial boom slowly transformed Tennessee's small farms. Many farmers took part-time jobs as loggers or railroad workers, leaving wives and children at home to work the farm. Others turned from harvesting corn to harvesting the forests on their own lands, gaining their livelihoods mostly from the sale of timber to small local sawmills. As Tennessee cities grew, so did the market for farm produce. Crossroads merchants traded coffee, sugar, tea, and manufactured goods for farm women's poultry, eggs, and butter, which they shipped to the cities. By the end of the century, farm families in general had more cash to spend and had become more dependent upon the market and upon part-time jobs off the farm for their support.

For the black and white Tennesseans in the state's plantation districts, the New South brought no better days. Instead, that era ushered in years of decline, as the sharecropping system became embedded in the southern economy. Sharecropping satisfied no one. Planters would have preferred to continue to work their large acreage with gangs of laborers and to control those laborers as they had their slaves. The freedmen rejected gang labor, preferring to work small plots of land without direct white supervision and to have small houses of their own. Although most former slaves wanted their own farms, their dreams of owning land rarely were realized: as late as 1910,

Tennessee Utopias

Throughout its history, Tennessee has been the site of many attempts to create a microcosm of the perfect society. In the antebellum period, Frances Wright, a British advocate of abolition and women's rights, attempted to build a biracial utopia at Nashoba in West Tennessee.

After the Civil War, British author Thomas Hughes founded Rugby, in Morgan County, as a refuge for the impoverished "second sons" of English gentry. Because English law usually required that an estate be given as a unit to the eldest son, second sons of the gentry did not inherit enough income to support them. By custom, however, they were forbidden to work at jobs that would lower their family's status, such as trade or manufacturing. Rugby flourished briefly as a tourist attraction but never got on its feet as a self-supporting colony.

In the 1890s, Socialists founded the Ruskin commune in Dickson County, hoping to build a small-scale model of the "cooperative commonwealth" proposed by Socialist and labor leaders as an alternative to industrial capitalism. Ironically, the commune was organized as a company, with settlers as stockholders. The colony suffered from poor leadership and internal controversies over politics, religion, and morality. In addition, most of the colonists lacked the farming experience needed to make a go of the communal farms and workshops. Ruskin ultimately disintegrated after colony members ousted the group's leader and sued each other for control of the colony's assets.

70 percent of the state's black farmers were tenants. The price of cotton—the crop most produced by West Tennessee sharecroppers—fell throughout the late nineteenth century, so that the more a sharecropper produced, the less he made at the end of the year. What profits accrued went to the landowner or, increasingly, to the merchant who supplied the cropper with fertilizer, farm supplies, and food for his family. Some sharecroppers got so deeply in debt that they owed landowners or merchants all their labor for the rest of their lives, a condition called "debt peonage." To escape debts, sharecroppers fled their farms for the cities, swelling the ranks of the urban poor.

Sharecropping never had been intended by any of the parties involved to be anything more than temporary. Once instituted, the system proved tenacious and eventually became biracial. White farmers who borrowed money to plant cotton faced the same market as their black neighbors and like them, slipped further and further into debt. Often they lost their land and became sharecroppers. Young farmers who lacked start-up capital also worked for shares. Sharecropping dominated the West Tennessee agricultural economy but was common throughout the state. In 1880, 34.5 percent of the state's farmers were tenants; thirty years later, the tenancy rate had risen to 41.1 percent of all farmers in the state. In 1910, the U.S. census noted that, of the native-born white farmers in the state, 35.5 percent were tenants; of the nonwhite farmers, 71.9 percent were tenants. Sharecropping maintained its hold upon the state's agricultural economy until the 1930s.

In the early twentieth century, Tennessee and Kentucky farmers joined together in the agricultural version of a strike against the emerging power of corporate agribusiness. In the 1890s, James Buchanan Duke put together a cartel of tobacco companies that set prices paid to farmers. When prices fell below production costs in 1905, farmers in the black-fired tobacco region, or Black Patch, of Middle Tennessee and Kentucky fought back, first through organizing cooperative marketing and then through violence. Farmers formed a Planter's Protective Association, pooled their crops, and held them off the market, demanding higher prices. In essence, the PPA called a tobacco farmers' strike. Wealthy planters led the PPA and coerced obedience to PPA rules from sharecroppers and tenants. Small farmers who attempted to sell directly to American Tobacco faced midnight visits from "night riders," who terrorized the strikebreakers. Night riders supposedly rode out to enforce the strike, but they also attacked black farmers, laborers, and workers in the pig-iron furnaces nearby, simply because they were black. Local authorities supported the PPA. In 1909, local juries, fed up with four years of violence and disorder, began convicting vigilantes; and the Night Rider raids gradually came to an end as tobacco prices rose and the federal government, pursing the Progressive policy of "trust-busting," broke up American Tobacco.

Politics, 1870–1890

In the late nineteenth century, Tennessee had two one-party systems, based upon loyalties formed during the Civil War and Reconstruction. Among whites, East Tennesseans voted Republican and West Tennesseans voted Democratic. In Middle Tennessee, most whites were Democrats, unless they came from a county that had supported the Union. On the local level, people often ignored party allegiances and voted for candidates they knew and liked, regardless of party. But when state or national elections rolled around, men lined up to vote as their fathers had lined up for combat. Usually Democrats won—as they had won the secession referendum in 1861. But if the Democrats divided, Republicans could win the post of governor and get enough seats in the legislature to pass bills with the cooperation of

Democratic factions. The Democratic Party's factions grew from conflicts over patronage and the benefits of office. Among these "perks" was the ability to do favors for one's friends, particularly those friends who ran railroads. Governors John Calvin Brown and James David Porter, both Democrats, became railroad executives after leaving office.

The issue that dominated Tennessee politics in the 1870s and early 1880s grew from the favors done for railroads by the Republicans in the 1860s. During Governor Brownlow's administration, the state had issued bonds to help defray the costs of railroad construction. Brownlow's critics charged that railroad companies had bribed members of his administration for access to this money; to add insult to injury, some of the "railroads" that acquired state funds in this manner proved to be fake companies, whose officers simply stole the money. Many taxpayers deeply resented paying higher taxes to fund bonds so tainted by corruption. These "low taxers" argued that the bonds should be either repudiated entirely or paid in part rather than in full. Opposing the "low taxers," the "state credit" faction argued that the state's credit must be upheld through payment in full. Although Governors Brown and Porter sided with the state credit faction, they were unable to win sufficient support in the General Assembly to pay off the bonds. Nor was the next Democratic governor, Albert Smith Marks, able to secure a settlement of this issue. During his term, the General Assembly proposed partial funding of the debt, but the voters rejected the settlement. In 1880, the Democratic Party split over the debt issue, and both factions nominated a candidate for governor. As a result, the Republicans elected Alvin Hawkins governor. Shocked by this defeat, the Democrats moved to reach a compromise under the leadership of Isham Harris, back in politics and then serving as a U.S. senator. Reunited with the "low taxers" dominant, the Democrats came back into office in 1882 with the election of William B. Bate. The 1883 General Assembly funded the bonds at 50 percent of face value and 3 percent interest, and the state debt controversy ended.

The election of Bate, and the reunification of the Democratic Party under Isham Harris's leadership, signaled the resurgence of former Confederates in state government. Bate had been a pro-secession "fire-eater," and Harris, as governor, had led Tennessee out of the Union. Historians have labeled these conservative Democrats "Bourbons" because, like the royal family of France, they resumed power after the revolution (in this case, the Civil War). Harris emphasized the necessity of unifying the party to stand against the Republicans. Harris aimed to maintain Bourbon power, and his faction was successful through 1884, when Bate was reelected.

In 1886, the Democratic Party could not unite behind any of the normal factions and turned to an "independent" Democrat from East Tennessee, Robert Love Taylor. The Republican Party nominated his brother, Alfred Alexander Taylor. (The Taylor family had divided during the Civil War,

War of the Roses. Robert E. Corlew, *Tennessee: A Short History,* 2d ed. (Knoxville: University of Tennessee Press, 1990), 379.

and the brothers had chosen different parties as a result.) The campaign that followed became famous in state political folklore as the "War of the Roses." Both Taylors were young, attractive representatives of a new generation in state politics. They toured the state, debating each other, playing fiddles, and telling jokes. Highly entertained, Tennessee's rural voters sent Bob to the governor's mansion.

While campaigning, Taylor had managed to obscure his actual political sentiments. Once in office, Taylor proved closer to the New South faction than to Harris's Bourbons. He supported federal aid to education (which the former Confederates considered treason to states' rights) and opposed railroad regulation. Despite their disappointment, conservative Democrats lined up behind Taylor again in 1888, and he won reelection. During his second term, Taylor endorsed legislation promoted by conservative Democrats to reduce African American voting power in the state, including the Dortch bill. When he left office in 1891, Taylor had done little to change the course of politics in the state.

American farmers, regardless of region or race, faced common problems in the late nineteenth century. As American agriculture became more integrated into the world economy, farmers found that prices for their crops depended on the international market. In an economy which was deflationary—the dollar was worth more every year—farmers who borrowed money to buy new equipment or land found that their debts went up in value annually, while farm prices dropped. Farmers everywhere complained about the ever-changing, unreliable rates railroads charged for shipping crops; the high tariffs that protected American industry from competition but raised the price of consumer goods for farmers; and tight-money policies that made it hard to obtain the credit farmers needed to operate. During the 1880s, farmers banded together to press for political change.

In the late 1880s, the Tennessee Farmers' Alliance was organized. In the South, the Farmers' Alliance called for railroad regulation, currency inflation through increased coinage of silver, and the Subtreasury, an ingenious scheme by which farmers could obtain easy credit using their crops as collateral. The Farmers' Alliance recruited black farmers as well as whites, although blacks were segregated into their own affiliated alliance. Throughout the South, conservatives regarded the Farmers' Alliance with fear. By organizing blacks and whites together, the alliance threatened to upset white supremacy. Moreover, the alliance's economic goals, if realized, would have undercut the power of landowners, merchants, and bankers.

Tennessee Bourbons were surprised and dismayed when the Farmers' Alliance leader, John Price Buchanan, won the Democratic Party nomination for governor in 1890. Fearing that failure to support Buchanan would split the party and lead to a Republican victory, Democrats of all factions lined up behind Buchanan, and he emerged victorious. In fact, Buchanan turned out to be much less radical than his position as Farmers' Alliance president had suggested. He did not support the Subtreasury, nor was he liberal on racial issues. (Alliancemen in the General Assembly supported the disfranchisement of African Americans.) Instead, he confined his platform to proposals that the Bourbons could support, including the free coinage of silver to inflate the currency.

In 1892, members of the National Farmers' Alliance formed a third party, the People's, or Populist, Party. The Populist Party adopted as its platform most of the Farmers' Alliance's economic proposals. Although the Tennessee Alliance did not endorse this new party, Bourbon and New South Democrats blasted Governor Buchanan and his faction as economic and racial liberals with suspicious ties to the Republican Party. Buchanan did not help himself by his actions during the Anderson County Coal Miners' War (discussed above). By the spring of 1892, the regular Democrats had made plans to dump Buchanan for Peter Turney in the coming election. Buchanan lost the Democratic nomination and ran as an independent with Populist support. Turney won by a large margin, after a campaign in which the Populists were accused of favoring racial equality (not true) and of having formed an alliance with the Republican Party (true.)

In 1893, Tennessee politics were firmly back under Bourbon control, with Turney as governor, Bate and Harris as senators, and Democrats in control of the General Assembly. With this amount of power, the Democratic Party could ignore the voters, as it did in 1894, when a Republican candidate won the gubernatorial election. The General Assembly simply threw out East Tennessee ballots on the grounds that the voters had not paid the poll tax (ignoring many similar Democratic ballots). Turney was reinstalled as governor for two more years.

In 1896, the state's Democrats, like Democrats throughout the nation, divided over inflation versus deflation, as symbolized by gold versus silver. Gold Democrats nominated a candidate. So did the Populists. Silver Democrats nominated "Our Bob" Taylor, whose popularity carried the election for the party. Despite Taylor's election, Bourbon Democrats remained in control of the state's politics and engineered the election of Benton McMillin in 1898.

Conservative Democrats maintained their popularity by appealing to rural voters. They proposed railroad regulation, inflation, and low taxes. Thus they adopted many of the Populist Party's economic goals, while maintaining a firm commitment to white supremacy and the ways of the Old South, for which many had fought thirty years before. At the same time, Bourbons were perfectly capable of advocating New South policies to gain voter approval. Canny political management allowed the generation which took Tennessee out of the Union in 1861 to dominate state politics in the 1880s and 1890s; with rare exceptions such as Robert Taylor, Bourbon leaders turned up as governor and as senators year after year. Bourbon leadership reflected Tennessee voters' desire for minimal governance.

Meanwhile, in Tennessee's cities, a younger generation grew increasingly discontented with the political economy as usual. After the turn of the century, Bourbons would fight another battle, one for which they were not prepared, against the forces of reform and modernization. The Progressive Movement in Tennessee was about to be born.

Suggested Readings

Ayers, Edward L. *The Promise of the New South: Life after Reconstruction*. New York 1992.

Cartwright, Joseph H. *The Triumph of Jim Crow: Tennessee Race Relations in the 1880s*. Knoxville, Tenn., 1976.

Couto, Richard A. *Lifting the Veil: A Political History of Struggles for Emancipation*. Knoxville, Tenn., 1993.

Doyle, Don Harrison. *Nashville in the New South, 1880–1930*. Knoxville, Tenn., 1985.

Eller, Ron. *Miners, Millhands, and Mountaineers: Industrialization of the Mountain South, 1880–1930*. Knoxville, Tenn., 1982.

Giddings, Paula. *When and Where I Enter: The Impact of Black Women on Race and Sex in America*. New York, 1984.

Honey, Michael K. *Southern Labor and Black Civil Rights: Organizing Memphis Workers*. Urbana, Ill., 1993.

Jones, Robert B. *Tennessee at the Crossroads: The State Debt Controversy, 1870–1883*. Knoxville, Tenn., 1977.

Keith, Jeanette. *Country People in the New South: Tennessee's Upper Cumberland*. Chapel Hill, N.C., 1995.

Klein, Maury. *History of the Louisville and Nashville Railroad*. New York, 1972.

MacArthur, William J. *Knoxville: Crossroads of the New South*. Knoxville, Tenn., 1982.

Majors, William R. *Change and Continuity: Tennessee Politics Since the Civil War*. Macon, Ga., 1986.

Mancini, Mathew J. *One Dies, Get Another: Convict Leasing in the American South, 1866–1928*. Columbia, S.C., 1996.

McDonald, Michael J., and William Bruce Wheeler. *Knoxville, Tennessee: Continuity and Change in an Appalachian City*. Knoxville, Tenn., 1983.

McKenzie, Robert Tracy. *One South or Many? Plantation Belt and Upcountry in Civil War–Era Tennessee*. Cambridge, England, 1994.

Shapiro, Karin A. *A New South Rebellion: The Battle against Convict Labor in the Tennessee Coalfields, 1871–1896*. Chapel Hill, N.C., 1998.

Waldrep, Christopher. *Night Riders: Defending Community in the Black Patch, 1890–1915*. Durham, N.C., 1993.

Woodward, C. Vann. *Origins of the New South, 1877–1913*. Baton Rouge, La., 1951.

9

The Era of Reform

ON NEW YEAR'S EVE, 1899, Tennesseans toasted the new century with optimism. The economic problems that plagued the nation in the 1890s had faded away, and even farmers enjoyed a new prosperity. Urban Tennesseans marveled at advances of science and technology, already visible in the electric lights that brightened city nights, the telephones that linked city and country, and the automobiles that rattled and backfired along the streets, frightening horses. Young Tennesseans believed in progress: life would get better for them, and even better for their children. Many wanted better schools; cleaner, safer cities; and more services from government at every level. They were prepared to make progress happen. To do so would require action on the part of state government, and forcing that action would mean confronting the state's political system, still dominated by entrenched conservative Democrats.

Many Tennesseans, discontented with "politics as usual," joined with others throughout the nation to form a loosely organized social and political movement called Progressivism. Tennessee Progressives participated in national campaigns to curb the power of big business, improve cities, build better highways, reform educational systems, and win for women the right to vote. Though a national movement, Progressivism took on a particular regional flavor in the South. Southern Progressives, Tennesseans among them, believed that alcohol caused most social problems, and they embarked on a prohibition crusade marked by high moral fervor. In Tennessee, this crusade deeply divided the Democratic Party and culminated in a gun battle between influential Democratic politicians on the streets of downtown Nashville. To the outside world, as a national magazine noted, Tennessee seemed "a state gone mad."

Prosperity

The first two decades of the twentieth century saw a continuation of economic and population trends begun in the New South era. As industrialization proceeded, the state's cities experienced rapid growth. Rural Tennesseans, black and white, continued to make their way to town in search of

Table 9.1. Tennessee's Total Population, 1900–1920, by Race, and with Major Cities

	1900	1920
State	2,020,616	2,337,885
Race by Percentage		
White	76.2	80.7
Black	23.8	19.3
Major Cities		
Chattanooga	30,154	57,895
Knoxville	32,637	77,818
Memphis	102,329	162,851
Nashville	80,865	118,342

SOURCE: U. S. Census, Population, 1900, 1920.

jobs. In search of better opportunities, more and more black Tennesseans left the state, and the South, for the northern states—a migration that began as a trickle and turned into a flood after World War I.

Still, these continuities masked some significant changes within the state. First, Tennessee farmers, and American farmers in general, experienced almost two decades of prosperity. The years from 1900 to 1918 were golden years for American agriculture: for farmers, things had never been so good before, nor would they ever be so good again. No longer scrabbling just to survive, Tennessee farmers could find the time, energy, and money to concern themselves with political and social reform. Second, prosperity on the farms translated into prosperity in Tennessee cities, which were centers of agricultural commerce. Tennessee cities began to modernize, paving roads, stringing up electric and telephone lines, and extending trolley lines out to the growing suburbs. Urban dwellers clamored for more: cheaper utilities, better services, better schools, cleaner neighborhoods, more law and order. The old politics, based as it was upon which side one's grandfather had been on during the Civil War, had nothing to say about paving streets or creating state school systems. Discontented with the status quo, Tennesseans were ripe for politics aimed at reform.

Sources of Tennessee Progressivism

Progressivism in Tennessee did not begin as a grassroots movement for reform. The major progressive reform initiatives began as goals articulated by religious, educational, business, social, or political leaders, who then embarked upon campaigns to educate the public about the need for the re-

The Search for Purity

While Progressives often were motivated by their faith to attempt to change the world, at the turn of the century many Tennesseans believed that the churches themselves had become too worldly. Educated ministers, beautiful buildings, choirs, stained-glass windows—to many Tennesseans from rural backgrounds, it all seemed too fancy. When asked why he did not go to church, one man replied that "he stayed away from such places out of respect for his deceased old mother, who was a deeply pious woman and who always taught him never to attend places of fashionable amusement on Sunday."

The search for purity led to splits in religious groups. Offended by musical instruments in churches, mission societies, and the practice of calling ministers "Reverend," many members of the Disciples of Christ in Tennessee withdrew from such churches. In 1906, the federal religious census listed them as "Churches of Christ."

The Methodist Church experienced its own defections, as the "holiness," or "sanctification," movement took hold. Holiness people believed that Christians could be sanctified, receiving a "second blessing" that made them spiritually whole. Initially cordial to the Holiness movement, mainstream Methodist leaders eventually turned against it, fearing that the Holiness people were taking over Methodism from within.

Holiness people set up their own congregations, where they scandalized their neighbors by accepting women preachers and using popular music in services. Eventually the movement found institutional stability in several different religious groups. One of the most powerful, the Church of God, began in the mountains along the Tennessee–North Carolina border, but moved in 1907 to Cleveland, Tennessee, from whence it grew to be the second largest Pentecostal denomination in the United States. The strongest black Pentecostal church in the world, the Church of God in Christ, established its headquarters in Memphis.

form. Progressivism in Tennessee, unlike the movement in other states, originated outside the normal political system. While Tennessee politicians sometimes supported progressive goals, very few Tennessee politicians were themselves Progressives. Once public support was aroused, progressive leaders could then ask professional politicians to support a designated reform as the will of the people.

Although many rural Tennesseans supported progressive reform, progressive leaders came from the middle class of Tennessee's cities and small towns. Yet the distinction between rural and urban should not be drawn too deeply in this case. Tennessee's cities grew rapidly in the late nineteenth century because of migration from the state's rural areas. Most city folk, whether factory workers, small businessmen, or professionals, were not far removed from rural roots. Ultimately, Progressivism did not derive from class status or place of origin. Progressivism was an attitude that evolved into a political stance. The attitude was one of discontent with conditions as they were in the state, and the political stance was to demand an active governmental response to those problems.

Progressive leaders tended to be prosperous, well-educated, often small businessmen or professionals—or their wives. Nineteenth-century concepts of gender divided the world into two "spheres." Men's sphere included politics and business, while women's was home, church, and child care. In fact, the number of women in the state employed outside the home increased every year. Women found new clerical jobs (as "typewriters"), worked in stores or factories, or taught school. But progressive women in Tennessee did not usually challenge conservative beliefs about woman's place. Instead, they astutely based their demand for a new political role for

Table 9.2. A Profile of Tennessee Workers, 1920: Percentage of Workers Employed in Selected Occupations, and Percentage of Workers in Each Occupation, by Sex

Occupation	Employed in This Occupation (% of All Workers)	Male	Female
Agriculture	48.2	90.9	9.1
Mining	2.1	99.8	0.2
Public Service	0.9	96.3	3.7
Manufacturing	18.2	85.0	15.0
Domestic Service	8.9	24.6	75.4
Trade	8.1	88.3	11.7
Transportation	6.2	94.7	5.3
Clerical	3.7	60.1	39.9
Professional	3.7	52.7	47.3
All Occupations	——	81.7	18.3

SOURCE: U.S. Census, Occupations, 1920.

Expanding Woman's Sphere: Fannie Battle

Fannie Battle, born in 1842 near Nashville to a comfortable middle-class family, was brought up to be a genteel southern lady living a quiet life at home. However, history intervened.

During the Civil War, Battle's two brothers were killed, and Fannie herself was sent to federal prison for spying on the Union troops occupying Nashville. After the war, Battle made plans to marry, but her fiancé was killed in a train accident on their wedding day. Left on her own, in 1870 she became a schoolteacher and began doing volunteer work for a Nashville Methodist church.

When the Cumberland River overflowed its banks in 1881, leaving over one thousand people homeless, Battle helped organize the Nashville Relief Society. In 1886, she left teaching to become the Relief Society's full-time director. By 1901, she had helped reorganize the society, renamed United Charities.

Under Battle's leadership, United Charities drew upon the volunteer work of wives and daughters of Nashville's wealthy to raise money for organizations that aided poor women and children, including day care centers and kindergartens. Fannie Battle, raised in the Old South to be a lady, became a pioneer in one of the New South's new professions: social worker.

women upon traditional notions about the nature of women. Conservatives believed that women, being mothers, naturally were more moral and nurturing than men. Since much of the progressive agenda had to do with either morals (prohibition), "social housekeeping" (cleaning up cities), or nurture (school reform), progressive women argued that their political activism derived from their role as homemakers. Indeed, Tennessee suffragists promoted votes for women as a way to purify the state's politics. For these women, and for many men in the state, supporting progressive causes was more than political activism; it was a Christian duty.

The forces opposing Progressivism had time, tradition, and public inertia on their side. Urban mayors defended their male constituents against reformers who wanted to shut down the working man's saloon. Tennessee's powerful liquor industry funded the opposition to prohibition and to woman suffrage. Ironically, the same rural folk who supported prohibition often proved indifferent or hostile to other progressive reforms, such as good roads and good schools, despite the efforts of progressive leaders to invest those causes with the same moral fervor as the prohibition campaign.

Prohibition in State Politics

After prohibitionists failed to obtain passage of a statewide referendum banning the sale of alcohol, they turned their efforts toward drying up the state county by county. They worked through local option laws, using the 1877 "Four-Mile Law," which prohibited saloons within four miles of schools outside incorporated towns. Since schools dotted the Tennessee countryside, it was almost impossible to locate a saloon anywhere outside a town without violating the law. Modifications to the Four-Mile Law allowed prohibition to be extended to municipalities if they chose to exercise this "local option." Gradually most small towns "went dry." In 1907, Knoxville prohibitionists won a vote on a new city charter prohibiting alcohol, despite opposition from Mayor Samuel Heiskell. After 1907, liquor was illegal everywhere in the state except for Nashville, Memphis, Chattanooga, and LaFollette—and available everywhere in the state, in illicit bars known as "blind tigers" or directly from moonshiners. Prohibitionists, facing the fact that local option had not been a resounding success, redoubled their efforts for statewide prohibition.

Conservative, or Bourbon, Democrats, used to taking turns in the state's highest offices and picking the next governor or senator behind closed doors, found prohibitionists annoying. The reformers refused to play the political game as usual and would not support a candidate who did not support prohibition. Nevertheless, needing support, Democrats moved cautiously to adopt political stances that would appeal to the prohibitionist vote. But prohibition proved too explosive to confine within politics as usual and ultimately destroyed Bourbon Democratic domination of the state's politics.

The agent of that destruction was Edward Ward Carmack, who had made his reputation as a newspaper editor in Nashville and Memphis, writing for papers owned or sponsored by Bourbon Democrats. (Most of the state's major papers existed to promote particular political factions, although a few were sponsored by corporations, such as the L&N Railroad.) Carmack stood out among Tennessee journalists for his viciousness and his tendency to personalize political conflict. Carmack also was racist beyond the norm. At one point in his career, Carmack proposed repealing the Fifteenth Amendment, a proposal not even fellow conservative Democrats took seriously.

In 1896, Carmack was elected to the U.S. Congress from the Tenth District, defeating Josiah Patterson in an election that focused on the issue of gold versus silver, with Carmack taking the popular pro-silver position. Patterson contested the election all the way to the U.S. House of Representatives but lost to Carmack. In the House, Carmack proved a consistent conservative: opposed to activist government, loyal to his southern roots, and a staunch proponent of white supremacy. In other words, he was a classic Bourbon Democrat. In 1901, the General Assembly made Carmack a U.S. senator.

In 1905, the state's other senator, William Brimage Bate, died unexpectedly only five days after taking office. In such a situation, the General As-

Edward Ward Carmack. McKellar, *Tennessee Senators* (Kingsport, Tennessee, 1942). Special Collections, University of Tennessee, Knoxville.

sembly appointed a replacement. Robert Taylor felt the office should be his. But, following the recommendation of a caucus of Democratic legislators, the General Assembly awarded the Senate seat to the current governor, and replaced him as governor with the speaker of the state senate, John Isaac Cox. Taylor charged that the "snap caucus" had denied him his chance at a Senate seat. Carmack was a political ally of the new senator and governor, so Taylor challenged Carmack for his Senate seat in 1906. After a hard-fought and bitter contest, Taylor won by carrying the cities against

Carmack's rural vote. Ironically, Governor Cox lost his own bid for the Democratic nomination to Malcolm "Ham" Patterson, son of Josiah Patterson, Carmack's old opponent. The victories of Patterson and Taylor indicated that the Bourbon faction had lost its ability to pick and choose the state's officeholders.

Carmack seized upon prohibition as the vehicle for his return to politics. Beginning a push for mandatory statewide prohibition, the temperance forces appealed to Carmack to challenge Patterson for the gubernatorial nomination in 1908. Carmack never had been noted as a temperance advocate, but political expediency led him to assume leadership of the prohibitionist movement.

As governor, Patterson supported legislation to improve public education, a state pure food and drug law, a new general election law, and creation of both a state highway commission and a state reformatory for boys. Carmack, a Bourbon Democrat, never had supported such progressive reforms but quickly adjusted his position to appeal to public sentiment, running on a platform similar to Patterson's. The only real difference between the two candidates was that Carmack stood for statewide prohibition, while Patterson supported local option. Ultimately, Patterson defeated Carmack, winning both the primary and the general election against his Republican opponent.

Carmack returned to journalism as editor of the new *Nashville Tennessean*, created by young Luke Lea, a rising Democratic power in Middle Tennessee. Carmack used the paper to attack Patterson and all his friends, singling out Col. Duncan Cooper, an elderly politician who had been one of Carmack's first political allies and even, at one point, his employer on a previous newspaper. In turn, Cooper threatened Carmack, and both men began carrying guns. One late afternoon in November 1908, Cooper and his son Robin ran into Carmack on a downtown Nashville street. Cooper charged toward the editor, pointing and shouting. Carmack drew his pistol and fired two shots, hitting Robin Cooper. The younger Cooper then drew his gun and killed Carmack.

In death, Carmack became a martyr for the prohibitionist cause. With Luke Lea's *Tennessean* leading the charge, prohibitionists claimed that the liquor forces had conspired to murder Carmack. By this time, many Tennesseans who had nothing against drinking had come to resent the power of the "liquor trust." Under intense public pressure, the General Assembly in 1909 approved statewide prohibition over Governor Patterson's veto.

Duncan and Robin Cooper were convicted of second-degree murder. In 1910, the state supreme court overturned Robin's conviction on a technicality. Governor Patterson issued a pardon for Duncan Cooper, saying, "In my opinion, neither of the defendants is guilty and they have not had a fair and impartial trial, but were convicted contrary to the law and evidence." Patterson said, "Right is right no matter what the public might think." As

Night Riders of Reelfoot Lake

In 1907, "night riders" terrorized Lake and Obion Counties in a conflict that grew from disputes over the ownership of Reelfoot Lake. Reelfoot had been formed early in the 1800s, when a massive earthquake rerouted the Mississippi River. The law held that navigable natural lakes and streams were common property, owned by all. For generations, the community around Reelfoot had lived off the lake's natural resources, developing profitable commercial fishing businesses. The community's livelihood was threatened when entrepreneurs bought the lake and announced plans to drain it and plant cotton.

Restrained by the courts from draining the lake, the owners demanded that all fish caught commercially be marketed through them. The courts upheld the land company. Then the residents of Reelfoot formed night rider groups and began a campaign of terror. When night riders horse-whipped a Lake County squire for criticizing them, Lake and Obion Counties approached a state of guerrilla war.

In 1908, Reelfoot night riders kidnapped two prominent attorneys and took them out to the lake to kill them. Public opinion was aroused, and Gov. Malcolm Patterson personally led the state militia to Samburg, where they rounded up night riders. Eight men were tried and convicted of murder, but the state supreme court overturned the convictions; eventually the defendants went free.

In 1913, the state supreme court held that the lake was navigable and as such was public property. The night riders had won. To middle-class Tennesseans, particularly those in the growing cities, however, the night rider incidents seemed frightening indications of a breakdown in law, a social order in decay, and a need for reform.

a firestorm of public criticism rained down on the governor, even the liquor industry began to withdraw its support from him.

In 1910, when Patterson announced his candidacy for a third term as governor, his foes boycotted the Democratic primary, and he won the nomination without opposition. The Republican Party nominated a temperance candidate, Ben Wade Hooper. As prohibitionist Democrats lined up to announce their support for Hooper, Patterson withdrew from the race. Democratic regulars then prevailed upon Sen. Bob Taylor to run, once again, for governor.

Despite Taylor's long-standing popularity, public anger against Patterson and his friends ran too high. Ben Hooper became governor, elected by a fusion of prohibitionist Democrats and Republicans, and was reelected two years later. The fusionists also sent Luke Lea to the U.S. Senate.

Throughout his four years in office, Hooper worked for better schools, prison reform, better regulation of the state's banks and insurance companies, and other reforms. As a Republican, he had to obtain bipartisan cooperation to enact legislation. To many Tennesseans, it seemed unnatural that Republicans and Democrats should work together. At one point, the speaker of the state house, a Democrat who had not joined the fusionists, referred to Hooper as "a political hermaphrodite . . . a whip-haired anarchist . . . an accident born of fanaticism and a disgrace to the state." Hooper focused most on the issue that got him elected, prohibition, saying in 1911 that the state had the right to stop a citizen from drinking "for the great and righteous purpose of protecting society." Hooper pushed for better enforcement of the liquor laws, which were being defied openly in the state's urban areas.

Urban Resistance to Prohibition

Knoxville was the only one of Tennessee's cities to vote itself "dry." Nashville, Chattanooga, and Memphis refused to pass local prohibition laws and, once state laws were passed, refused to enforce them within municipal boundaries. Nashville's Mayor Hilary Howse bragged that he did more than "protect" saloons: "I patronize 'em!" Howse realized that his working-class constituents did not want prohibition, and he addressed an open letter to the governor: "I have never given you credit for being overburdened with intelligence or possessing any patriotism at all."

The most defiant urban mayor, however, was Ed Crump of Memphis. In 1913, Crump was just beginning his long rise to become the state's most powerful politician; the time when he would be nationally famous as "Boss Crump" was still decades away. Crump, a Mississippi native whose flaming red hair and assertive attitude earned him the nickname "Red Snapper," had been elected mayor in 1910 as a progressive reformer. Under Crump, Memphis's famous red-light districts and wide-open saloons did not disappear but were tamed and confined into certain neighborhoods where they could continue to operate without bothering the city's middle-class citizens. Crump portrayed himself as a defender of the people against the "interests," pressing utilities for better service and attacking the power of railroads. He ruled Memphis like a benevolent despot, supplying public benefits—better schools, parks, and cleaner streets—to black as well as white constituents. His political power depended in large part on black votes. Knowing that his constituents did not support prohibition, Crump defied the state to enforce the law in Memphis.

Municipal Vice

When Progressives campaigned to clean up Tennessee cities, they had more in mind than sweeping the streets. They wanted to destroy the "men's districts" in Tennessee cities.

In 1900, the Nashville "men's district" was typical. In a one-block area, 4th Avenue between Church and Union, bars like the Climax Saloon and the Southern Turf shared space with lawyers offices, men's clothing stores, Turkish baths, and pawn shops. Journalists, lawyers, and politicians met in saloons, ate meals there, and used saloons as telephone, mail, and message centers. Decent women did not venture onto 4th Avenue, sit in hotel lobbies, or eat in hotel dining rooms. Prostitutes cruised the street in carriages but had their own red light district in Black Bottom and "Hell's Half Acre."

Nashville, however, paled beside Memphis, which had a reputation for sin second only to that of New Orleans. In the Progressive era, Memphis's Grace Stanley, the city's premiere madam, was one of the wealthiest women in a town where prostitution was practically an institution. In 1907, the *Commercial Appeal* noted, "Dives have been flourishing as they never have before. Hundreds of lewd women . . . have been imported. Streetwalkers have been as thick as wasps in summertime." Reformers noted in horror that opium and cocaine easily could be obtained in Memphis's red-light district, and they attributed violent crime to the effects of cocaine on African American users. In attacking liquor, Progressive reformers attacked prostitution, gambling, and drug abuse as well.

In 1914, the Anti-Saloon League obtained an injunction forcing Nashville's bars to close in observance of statewide prohibition. A year later, the city commission ordered the brothels closed, probably in response to pressure from the city's most prestigious women's club. In 1917, in an effort to lure a military base to town, Memphis shut down its red-light district, throwing about one thousand prostitutes out of work. Charities helped the women find shelter or supplied money for them to leave town.

All such "cleanups" were temporary. Progressives never succeeded in driving liquor, drugs, or prostitution out of Tennessee cities, but they did force municipal vice out of the cities' main business districts.

In 1913, Governor Hooper convened the General Assembly in a special session for the purpose of obtaining stronger prohibition enforcement legislation. Prohibitionists put on a major lobbying effort, and the governor's measures passed. However, Howse and Crump remained defiant, and the saloons stayed open in the state's urban areas. Yet the 1913 vote proved to die-hard Bourbon Democrats that most Tennesseans supported prohibition. Bowing to the public will, the Democratic Party in 1914 nominated a prohibition candidate for governor, Thomas Clark Rye. His Democratic allies deserting him, Hooper lost his bid for a third term, and Rye became governor.

In 1915, Rye obtained the passage of the "Ouster Law," a measure by which local officials could be removed from office for refusal to enforce prohibition. With this law, Ed Crump and Hilary Howse were thrown out of office. Crump was reelected in 1916 and immediately resigned in favor of one of his cronies on the city commission. Never again would Crump allow his control of Memphis to be endangered by the state government. From his position as city trustee—he was elected for four straight terms, beginning in 1916—Crump built a political machine through which he ran Memphis behind a series of figurehead mayors. In the years that followed, Crump became Tennessee's king-maker, leader of the most powerful faction of the Democratic Party.

W. C. Handy, Boss Crump, and the Blues

W. C. Handy was raised to be a gentleman of color. Born in Alabama in 1873 to middle-class parents whose life revolved around church, Handy grew up singing in the choir. As an adult, Handy taught music in college but became a traveling musician, touring the South with brass bands that played for black and white alike. In his travels, Handy heard kinds of music he had never been taught in school: raunchy dance music from Delta brothels, work songs, and a strange, haunting music that people would learn to call "the blues."

When Handy's band was hired to play for Boss Crump's election campaign in 1909, Handy tried to create a new style of campaign song, using the music he had heard in the Delta. "Mr. Crump" became a great hit in Memphis. The song later was published under the title "Memphis Blues." Handy never claimed to have invented the blues, but he was one of the first professional musicians to make black music accessible to a white public, helping to create the musical fusion that ultimately led to rock and roll.

Governor Rye easily won reelection in 1916. With the passage of even tougher prohibition laws in 1917, saloons in the cities finally closed. Progressives turned their attention to election reform. In 1917, the General Assembly passed legislation requiring primary elections for statewide offices. When the U.S. Constitution was amended to allow popular election of senators, Tennesseans could vote for their chosen representatives rather than for delegates to a party convention or primary. Having bested Luke Lea in the contest for the Democratic nomination, U.S. Rep. Kenneth McKellar of Memphis was elected U.S. senator in 1916, defeating Ben Hooper. Governor Rye won reelection, to be followed in 1918 by Albert Houston Roberts.

When the entire nation "went dry" with the ratification in 1919 of the Eighteenth Amendment prohibiting the manufacture and sale of alcohol in the United States, the Tennessee prohibition movement ceased to be a dominant factor in state politics. It did, however, leave behind a substantial legacy. Although prohibition never completely removed alcohol from Tennessee, it managed to criminalize the sale of alcohol and drive it underground. The fight over prohibition shattered Democratic Party unity. Out of the shambles arose a new generation of politicians; Crump, Lea, McKellar, Cordell Hull, and Austin Peay all began their political careers during these years. The alliances and hatreds formed during the fight over prohibition would dominate the state's politics until after World War II.

Good Roads and Good Schools

Campaigns for good roads and good schools, while less dramatic than the struggle for prohibition, had a more lasting impact on the state. Better roads and schools spurred economic development and brought rural Tennesseans closer to the American mainstream. Indeed, Tennessee Progressives saw good roads and good schools as being linked: without good roads, counties could not consolidate the many one-teacher schools into modern, centrally located buildings, nor could schools stay open in the winter. Yet progressive reformers faced a difficult fight. Most rural Tennesseans were quite content with the roads they had, which were good enough for wagon traffic; and they saw no need to reform the schools. Many white Tennesseans believed that education past basic literacy—enough to read the Bible and "cipher," or do simple arithmetic—was a waste of time for farmers and their wives, and outright dangerous for blacks, who might get ideas above their stations. To obtain good roads and good schools, progressive reformers embarked upon propaganda campaigns: first to convince the public that reforms were needed, and second to convince the state's politicians that reforms had public support. For two decades, reformers stumped the state, speaking for roads and schools.

The campaign for better roads began in 1901, when Tennesseans formed a state unit of the Southern Good Roads Association. To attract public attention, they established "named highway associations," such as the Memphis to Bristol Highway Association, which in 1910 dramatized conditions on the state's roads by driving automobiles from Memphis to Bristol. In 1916, the U.S. Congress passed the Federal Aid to Highways Act, which offered matching funds to states that built highways to federal specifications. Anticipating the passage of this act, the state government in 1915 created a Highway Department through which to funnel federal money to construction projects. In 1919, the state legislature authorized matching funds: for each county dollar spent, the state would supply two state or federal dollars. With this incentive, some counties built roads from the county seat to outlying communities. However, as long as farmers thought of cars as rich men's toys, they resisted paying higher taxes to build good roads. A true statewide highway system linking county to county would not be achieved until Gov. Austin Peay made road building a priority in the 1920s.

At the start of the twentieth century, the state did not control public education, but let each of the ninety-five counties run its own schools. Conditions in education thus varied from county to county, or even from district to district within counties. In cities and towns, middle-class parents demanded good schools and usually got them. But most Tennesseans learned basic literacy in one- or two-room country schools, often wooden shacks or old cabins heated by coal stoves and lacking indoor plumbing. School terms were short, on average ninety-six days, and attendance was optional: pupils came and went as they pleased, attending an average of forty-seven days a year. The state's illiteracy rate in 1902 was 14.2 percent for native whites over the age of ten. Of the state's voting age men, 21.7 percent could not read their ballots or sign their names.

School reform in Tennessee grew from two sources: northern philanthropists and a small, dedicated network of educators centered at the University of Tennessee and in the state education bureaucracy. Northern reformers' interest in southern schools dated back to Reconstruction, when northern missionaries staffed schools for the freedpeople. Realizing that improving conditions for blacks required a better-educated white population, northern philanthropists made grants for schools, sponsored teachers' institutes, and established a normal school, Peabody, in Nashville. Through the Southern Education Board (SEB) and the Rockefeller family's General Education Board (GEB), philanthropists sponsored data collection and provided funds to stimulate educational campaigns in southern states.

Knoxville emerged as the center of education reform in the state, with dynamic, energetic University of Tennessee (UT) Professor Philander P. Claxton as the cheerleader for reform. Claxton headed the GEB-funded Summer School of the South, which in 1902 began to bring teachers from across the region to UT each summer to discuss educational conditions in the South. Claxton's students, many of them Tennesseans, went home fired up for school reform. Claxton was the primary link between the northern philanthropic groups and the state, working with the SEB and the Peabody Foundation. Before he left Tennessee to become U.S. commissioner of education in 1911, Claxton built a network of pro-reform educators, including the state superintendents. Realizing that education reform could not be accomplished without public mobilization, Claxton and the state superintendents ran education crusades every two years. Claxton himself traveled the length and breadth of the state to speak at school-reform rallies in rural communities. These travels generated stacks of resolutions calling for better schools. The reformers then took their resolutions to the General Assembly as proof that the state's people wanted better schools. The resolutions were general, but Claxton's legislative plan was specific and highly successful. Between 1907 and 1917, the General Assembly passed legislation replacing district school directors with county school boards, increasing education's portion of the state's revenues, enacting a compulsory education bill, requiring teacher certification, and mandating that each county establish a high school. Education reformers had much of which to be proud. However, the reforms that existed on paper often failed to reach rural districts. The reformers did achieve a historically significant victory in transferring control over education from parents and local communities to the state, beginning to build a uniform state system of education that formed the foundations of Gov. Austin Peay's reforms in the 1920s.

World War I in Tennessee

When the United States entered World War I in 1917, the federal government faced two tasks: to raise an army and to mobilize public support for the war. America traditionally had raised an army by calling for volunteers. Tennessee's nickname, the Volunteer State, derived from the willingness of Tennesseans to serve in past wars. However, in 1917, the federal government decided to conscript troops. This was a controversial decision, since the draft had proven very unpopular during the Civil War. Proponents of the draft argued that conscription would be efficient; would allocate the burden of service equitably among all sections, classes, and ethnic groups; and would ensure that key industries were not stripped of workers.

The greatest opposition to the draft came from southern and western states, whose constituents felt that conscription was an unnecessary violation of personal liberty. Congressmen from farm states feared that the draft would take farm workers while exempting factory workers. White southerners worried that conscription would upset race relations: black soldiers would be difficult to keep "in their place." Tennessee's Sen. Kenneth McKellar pressured the head of the proposed Selective Service to develop regulations insuring that cotton planters would not lose their black laborers. McKellar also introduced legislation that would have mandated attempts to raise a volunteer army before using conscription. Supporters of conscription, mostly from northern urban states, argued that, without it, the sons of the "best people" would volunteer and be killed (as had happened in England), while working-class people, many of them recent immigrants, would not volunteer at all. Congress authorized conscription.

On June 5, 1917, Tennessee men aged twenty-one through thirty registered for the draft. Later registrations drew in men aged eighteen to forty-five. By the end of the war, 61,069 Tennesseans had been inducted, and approximately 19,000 more had volunteered. Conscription in the state did meet with resistance. Some men refused to register; when inducted, they refused to serve. Others deserted and hid out in the hills. These men probably were not motivated by pro-German sentiment. Deserters may have been motivated by worry over their families. Since rural Tennesseans, black and white, married young, most of the men aged twenty-one to thirty-one had wives and children. During the First World War, the federal government made no blanket exemptions for marriage or fatherhood. Many rural draft boards, faced with a scarcity of single men, sent married men to service, and some sent married men with children.

Once inducted, the vast majority of draftees, however reluctant, accepted their service. Among them was Alvin C. York, who became Tennessee's

Knoxville welcoming returned soldiers at the end of World War I. McClung Historical Collection, Knox County Public Library, Knoxville.

most famous World War I soldier. York, like many other Tennesseans, felt that killing people was un-Christian, but he was conscripted anyway. During training, York's officers convinced him that God would approve of fighting Germans. In 1918, York, separated from his detachment, attacked a German position, killed 20 Germans and captured 131 more, marching them to the American lines to surrender. York was one of six Tennesseans to be awarded the Congressional Medal of Honor, and in the 1930s he became the subject of a very popular film.

During World War I, Congress delegated home-front mobilization to state Councils of Defense. Tennessee's Council of Defense, headed by Rutledge Smith of Cookeville, was organized in May 1917, in time to supervise registration for the draft. (Smith also acted as the head of the Selective Service in Tennessee, in which position he carried the title of major.) The state council authorized the appointment of councils in each county and charged them with "enlisting" public support for the war and raising money through a series of war bonds. Some rural Tennesseans reacted with suspicion when, in October, the councils urged women to register for war work. Fearing that they would be drafted, most Tennessee women refused to sign up: of 662,013 women in the state, only 66,000 registered. The director of women's registration in the state complained to Washington that German sympathizers had discouraged registration by linking it to women's suffrage. In 1918, the focus of war mobilization shifted to the sale of war bonds, and Tennesseans were urged to buy bonds to support the boys in France.

All evidence indicates that Tennesseans willingly supported the war, donating time and money to the effort. However, home-front war mobilization, intended to be voluntary, quickly became coercive. Women denounced as traitors and German sympathizers other women who refused to register for war work. People who did not buy war bonds were threatened: their names would go on "slacker lists" and be sent to Rutledge Smith or to the Department of Justice. "Things will be made uncomfortable for them," the Smith County newspaper warned. Under the federal Espionage and Sedition Acts, people who criticized any aspect of the war effort, from President Woodrow Wilson's leadership to the activities of the Red Cross, were arrested for sedition. Most of these cases were dropped when the war ended by armistice in November 1918. But public resentment of heavy-handed war mobilization would have political repercussions in 1920.

Women's Suffrage in Tennessee

The fight for women's suffrage began in the North before the Civil War. Drawn into the abolitionist movement by the belief that slavery was a sin which all good Christian women must resist, abolitionist women found that, when they tried publicly to oppose slavery, they were told that woman's place was in the home, not speaking in public or meddling in politics. Incensed, abolitionist women began examining their own status in American society. At that time, under law, women were treated as minors or dependents; once married, they surrendered to their husbands control of their property and earnings. They were denied access to education and most employment opportunities, could not sit on juries, and could not vote. The early women's movement addressed all these concerns. The movement failed to win much support in the South, where most white men believed that equal rights for women was a concept as ridiculous as freedom for slaves.

After the Civil War, Tennesseans joined with sentimental middle-class Americans in general to exalt woman as "queen of the home," deeming her a creature of fragile purity who never should dirty herself with something so low as politics. As a Shelbyville paper said in 1897, "Women to vote! To scramble at the polls side by side with the toughs and the darkies! Pretty sight that would be." Woman's influence could be exerted in society through her husband and her sons. This attitude held through the end of the century, although by that time Tennessee women were employed outside the home in shops, factories, and schools, and worked long hours in the home and on the farm.

On the national level, the fight for women's suffrage suffered a setback when, in the 1860s, the movement split into two factions. One, the National Women's Suffrage Association, led by Elizabeth Cady Stanton and Susan B. Anthony, agitated for a national amendment giving the vote to women. The other, the American Women's Suffrage Association, believed that women's suffrage could best be achieved through state action: a position that appealed to southern women, since it echoed the region's states'-rights traditions. Although this division hurt the movement for women's suffrage, both NWSA and AWSA succeeded in educating the public about the issue and made women's suffrage increasingly respectable. In 1890, the two factions reunited as the National American Women's Suffrage Association.

The late nineteenth century saw gradual improvements in the legal and social conditions of white middle-class American women. Most states passed laws allowing married women to make contracts, sue in court, keep control over their property (including their earnings), and obtain custody of their children. (Tennessee did not pass a Married Woman's Property Law until 1913.) Educational opportunities became more widely available, as state-funded colleges and universities admitted women under "coeducational" programs. In some states, women obtained limited suffrage, being allowed to vote in school board or city elections. Other states, mostly in the West, gave women full suffrage—Wyoming and Utah in the late nineteenth century; Oregon, Arizona, Kansas, Nevada, and Montana by 1914.

The South proved most resistant to suffrage. Southern men and women opposed suffrage on many grounds. First, conservative southerners truly believed that a woman's place was in the home. Second, many religious men and women believed that the Bible upheld male supremacy, much as their ancestors had believed that the "Good Book" justified slavery (indeed, the same chapters, but different verses, were quoted in both cases). Third, and most significant, southern antisuffragists argued that allowing women to vote would reopen the issue of black participation in politics and draw national attention to the mechanisms by which black men had been disfranchised in the South. Although the latter argument was less prevalent in Tennessee, where black men never had been completely disfranchised, the equation of voting rights for women and voting rights for blacks convinced many conservative Tennesseans to oppose women's suffrage.

The demand for women's suffrage in Tennessee, like that for other progres-

---

Learning about Injustice

In the late 1860s, railroads offered first-class and "smoker" cars. The latter were filthy and full of drunks who cursed and spat on the floor. Respectable people, black or white, bought first-class tickets. The family of Robert Church, a black man who had made a fortune in Memphis real estate, certainly qualified as respectable. Mary Church, five years old, was riding in the first-class car when her father stepped into the smoker. The white conductor came by. Mary Church remembered, "As he pulled me roughly out of the seat, he turned to the man sitting across the aisle and said, 'Whose little nigger is that?' The man told him who my father was and advised him to let me alone. Seeing the conductor was about to remove me from the car, one of my father's white friends went into the smoker to tell him what was happening." Robert Church insisted that they had bought first-class tickets, and the conductor left them alone. Mary could not understand what she had done wrong: "I hadn't mussed my hair. I hadn't lost either of the two pieces of blue ribbon which tied the little braids on each side of my head. I hadn't soiled my dress a single bit. I was sitting up 'straight and proper.'"

Mary Church grew up to be an intellectual, a college professor, and the wife of a federal judge in Washington, D.C. As Mary Church Terrill, she founded the National Association of Colored Women, was a charter member of the NAACP, and wrote extensively on racial issues. With members of the Woman's Party, she picketed the White House for women's suffrage. Terrill demanded that America live up to its promise of government by the people, not just "all who are shrewd and wise enough to have themselves born boys instead of girls, and white instead of black."

sive reforms, came not from the grassroots, but from the state's well-educated urban middle class and upper class. In the postbellum period, middle-class women in Tennessee cities and towns began organizing clubs. For black and white women alike, women's clubs often began as places for self-education, with women reading and discussing works of literature. Club work, seemingly so innocuous, gave women organizational skills and practice in public speaking. By the end of the century, women's clubs had progressed from discussing Dante to discussing conditions in their own communities. Action followed upon discussion. Throughout the state, women's clubs founded libraries, created parks, sponsored orphanages, and instituted relief agencies. Thus women became involved in local politics. Although few Tennessee women joined NAWSA, many middle-class women of both races belonged to the Woman's Christian Temperance Union (WCTU), which gained many supporters during the long struggle over prohibition. The WCTU called for national women's suffrage as a weapon to defeat the "liquor trust." The WCTU helped to make women's suffrage respectable.

Serious suffrage work did not begin in Tennessee until the late 1800s. In 1889, Lide A. Meriwether formed the state's first women's suffrage league in Memphis. Through the 1890s, Meriwether traveled through the state, lecturing and organizing. Maryville organized a suffrage league in 1893 and Nashville in 1894. By 1897, suffrage had become so socially acceptable that the genteel women who ran the Women's Department of the Tennessee Centennial Exposition sponsored "Suffrage Day" at Centennial Park, and brought national feminist leaders Jane Addams, Susan B. Anthony, and Anna Shaw to speak at the Exposition. In that year, too, suffragists held a convention and formed the Tennessee Equal Rights Association (TERA), electing Meriwether president. The TERA was an affiliate of the National American Woman Suffrage Association, whose president, Carrie Chapman Catt, came to Memphis in 1900 to address the TERA convention.

Throughout the nation, women's suffrage received support from Progressives, who believed that women would "clean up" politics. This appeal to maternal virtues proved very effective with many Tennessee women and men, who, according to suffrage advocate Anne Dallas Dudley, had seen a vision: "A woman's home will be the whole world, and her children, all those whose feet are bare, and her sisters, all those who need a helping hand . . . when men will not only fight for women, but for the rights of women."

Despite much support from the state's urban elite, suffrage work in Tennessee proceeded slowly from 1900 to 1917, hampered by public suspicion and disapproval. Before statewide suffrage could be achieved, suffragists had to diminish the prejudices of their neighbors. Through local suffrage societies, suffragists educated the public by sponsoring meetings, debates, essay contests, teas, luncheons, and suffrage balls, and by handing out literature and sending information to local papers. The beautiful and rich Anne Dallas Dudley, with her two pretty children, led a Nashville suffrage parade to Centennial Park, a living refutation of the antisuffrage argument that women's rights advocates were unattractive man-haters. By 1917, more than seventy suffrage societies had been organized in communities throughout the state, united under the Tennessee Equal Suffrage Association, and the NAWSA held its convention in Nashville that year, with widespread public approval. Women's suffrage was becoming respectable in Tennessee. In 1917, when the U.S. entered World War I, women's suffrage advocates volunteered for home-front mobilization work, attempting to prove that women's exemption from military service did not prevent them from being useful citizens who deserved the vote.

Although the NAWSA dominated the Tennessee women's suffrage movement, the more radical National Woman's Party (NWP) also organized in the state, receiving much of its support from organized labor. The NWP originated as the Congressional Union, the NAWSA's congressional lobby. Led by Alice Paul, young women dissatisfied with NAWSA's methodical, diplomatic, and ladylike lobbying bolted NAWSA in 1916 and formed the NWP. Influenced by British suffragists, who used demonstrations, civil disobedience, and violence to dramatize their demands, the NWP staged demonstrations in Washington and picketed the White House during World War I. When NWP pickets appeared with signs comparing President Wilson, who did not support women's suffrage, to the German Kaiser, they were attacked by mobs and arrested. In jail, NWP members went on hunger strikes, and Alice Paul was force-fed. These tactics disgusted conservative suffragists like Dudley, but they appealed to younger women. Sue Shelton White, a young court reporter from Jackson, became state chair for the NWP in 1918. In 1919, White was arrested for burning an effigy of President Wilson in front of the White House and spent five days in jail.

As women's suffrage gained support in Tennessee, an antisuffrage opposition began to organize. Led by John J. Vertrees, a Nashville lawyer whose clients included railroads, manufacturers, and liquor interests, the antisuffragists made the traditional argument that woman's place was in the home, but they also accused Tennessee suffragists of endangering family life and white supremacy. Suffragists believed that the "antis" were funded by the L&N, manufacturers who wanted to continue using child labor, and the liquor trust—all interests threatened by woman suffrage. When a female antisuffragist, Josephine A. Pearson, wrote to a newspaper protesting that not all "antis" were influenced by the liquor trust, Vertrees made her president of the Tennessee branch of the National Association Opposed to Woman Suffrage.

Tennessee suffragists began their campaign for the vote by asking for an amendment to the state constitution in 1915. Despite support from Governor Hooper, this proved to be a laborious and difficult process. In 1917, suffragists changed their tactics and asked for a limited franchise which would enable them to vote in municipal elections and presidential elections.

Anne Dallas Dudley, suffragist and homemaker. *Women's Work in Tennessee* (Memphis, 1916). Special Collections, University of Tennessee, Knoxville.

This reform failed to pass the General Assembly in 1917, but it passed in 1919 and was signed by Governor Albert H. Roberts.

In Washington, the women's suffrage movement finally had obtained passage of the Nineteenth Amendment, which was sent to the states for ratification in 1919. Ratification required approval by thirty-six of the nation's forty-eight states. By March 22, 1920, thirty-five states had ratified. National attention focused on Tennessee, one of the few southern states where suffrage had a chance of passage. Suffragists urged Governor Roberts to call a special session for ratification. Roberts hesitated, since the state constitution required that any vote on a constitutional amendment be made by a legislature that had been elected after the amendment had been submitted to the states. However, the U.S. Supreme Court decision ruled unconstitutional a similar provision in the Ohio state constitution, and Roberts's legal advisors argued that he legally could call the special session. Roberts came under pressure from President Wilson. The president, long ambivalent or indifferent concerning women's rights, had decided to support suffrage. When Wilson urged Roberts to call the session as a service "to the party and to the nation," Roberts scheduled the special session for August 9.

Pro- and antisuffrage forces converged on Nashville. Suffragists and their friends wore yellow roses, while "antis" wore red roses. Carrie Chapman Catt, who checked into the Hermitage Hotel for the duration of the session, recalled that the lobby was a sea of red and yellow. Among the prosuffrage forces were the League of Women Voters, the Woman's Party, Democratic and Republican women's groups representing different factions of Tennessee's always divisive politics, and a Men's Ratification Committee, led by former Gov. Thomas Clark Rye. Vertrees, Pearson, and Tennessee "antis" were joined by representatives of the Southern Women's Rejection League, whose members argued against ratification on the basis of states' rights, white supremacy, and the family. Suffrage workers noted a steady stream of men, suffrage and "anti" alike, making their way to the eighth floor of the Hermitage Hotel, where the antisuffrage forces had set up an illegal bar: "As the evening grew late[,] legislators . . . were reeling through the hall in a state of advanced intoxication." When out-of-state suffrage workers asked why the prohibition law was not enforced, they were told, "In Tennessee whiskey and legislation go hand in hand, especially when controversial questions are urged."

The session opened on August 9, and the legislative battle began. Opponents of suffrage charged that the legislature's action was unconstitutional. One state senator attacked suffrage leaders personally, such a flagrant violation of good manners that it helped the suffrage cause. The senate approved suffrage, 25 to 4, on August 13. Attention then focused on the house. House Speaker Seth Walker had pledged his support but changed his mind just before the session and worked to impede passage by parliamentary maneuvers. Meanwhile, back at the Hermitage, the "anti" lobby cajoled, bribed, and poured drinks. The "antis" accused the suffragists of flirting with assembly members to win their votes. Finally, a vote was scheduled for August 18. The night before, Catt told suffrage supporters, "There is one thing more we can do, only one; we can pray."

After opening debates, Speaker Walker moved to table the resolution approving the amendment. Had the tabling motion carried, the amendment would have been dead. Much to the surprise of the audience packed into the gallery, the tabling motion tied, 48 to 48. A supposedly antisuffrage member had changed his mind. The legislature then voted on the amendment itself. It passed, 49 to 46. A twenty-four-year-old Republican from East Tennessee, Harry Burn, had changed his vote to favor suffrage. Burn later explained his reasons: "I believe in full suffrage as a right; second, I believe we had a moral and legal right to ratify; third . . . my mother wanted me to vote for ratification." Burns added that few men ever had such an opportunity to "free seventeen million women from political slavery," and said, "I desired that my party. . . might say that it was a Republican from the East mountains of Tennessee . . . who made national woman suffrage possible."

With Burn's vote, Tennessee ratified the Nineteenth Amendment, becom-

Southern chivalry. Carrie Chapman Catt Papers, Tennessee Historical Society Collection, Tennessee State Library and Archives, Nashville.

ing the "perfect thirty-sixth" vote necessary to allow women suffrage. Antisuffrage forces were outraged and for weeks thereafter carried on a desperate and ultimately futile battle to get the General Assembly's approval rescinded or declared illegal. Although the national Republican and Democratic parties both had supported women's suffrage, angry Tennessee voters blamed the Democrats, including Governor Roberts, for this progressive reform.

Suffragists had promised that women would clean up politics; antisuffragists had warned that allowing women to vote would destroy the home. Neither prophecy came true. As Tennessee politicians quickly discovered, women voted much as their fathers, brothers, and husbands did. Yet women's suffrage had a deeper symbolic meaning: it was a sign of approaching cultural changes that swept across the state in the 1920s. In the following decade, "woman's place" would be only one of the issues dividing traditionalists from conservatives, as Tennesseans learned to live in the modern era.

Suggested Readings

Chambers, John Whiteclay. *To Raise an Army: The Draft Comes to Modern America.* New York, 1987.

Doyle, Don Harrison. *Nashville in the New South, 1880–1930.* Knoxville, Tenn., 1985.

———. *New Men, New Cities, New South.* Chapel Hill, N.C., 1990.

Grantham, Dewey. *Southern Progressivism: The Reconciliation of Progress and Tradition.* Knoxville, Tenn., 1983.

Keith, Jeanette. *Country People in the New South: Tennessee's Upper Cumberland.* Chapel Hill, N.C., 1995.

Link, William A. *The Paradox of Southern Progressivism, 1880–1930.* Chapel Hill, N.C., 1992.

Majors, William R. *Editorial Wild Oats: Edward Ward Carmack and Tennessee Politics.* Macon, Ga., 1984.

Miller, William D. *Memphis during the Progressive Era, 1900–1917.* Memphis, Tenn., 1957.

Wheeler, Marjorie Spruill, ed. *Votes for Women! The Woman Suffrage Movement in Tennessee, the South, and the Nation.* Knoxville, Tenn., 1995.

10

Modern Times

DURING THE 1920s, Tennesseans struggled to reconcile modern-ism and tradition. Gov. Austin Peay brought modern management to state government, while pushing progressive reforms through the General Assem-bly. New roads and better schools brought modern culture to Tennessee's most isolated areas, while thousands of country people moved into the state's cities. Tennesseans joyfully embraced aspects of modern life: good roads, fast cars, better schools, radios, the bright lights of town. Even as they embraced the new, however, Tennesseans reaffirmed tradition. A new medium, radio, became the vehicle by which country and blues, the traditional music of the rural South, gained urban audiences. A modern Ku Klux Klan used violence to enforce traditional morality and keep women and blacks in their places. Most significantly, in 1925, the General Assembly gained inter-national attention when it passed legislation forbidding state schools to teach evolution. At the end of the decade, traditional patronage politics made a comeback in the administration of Gov. Henry Horton and his patron Luke Lea, whose mismanagement of state funds led to their political downfall and public disgrace.

Republican Landslide in 1920

Albert H. Roberts, elected governor in 1918, made himself so unpopular that irate voters swept him, and most of the rest of the state's Democrats, out of office in 1920. In that year, voters across the nation turned against the Democratic Party, which had presided over World War I. But Roberts's defeat was in part his own fault. He did receive public approval for his poli-cies favoring education, which included better pay for teachers, and for his "law and order" stance, which led him to support the creation of a state police force in 1919. But in supporting women's suffrage, he alienated con-servative Democrats. He angered liberal Democrats by his willingness to use state power against organized labor. Apparently Roberts, like many other Americans in 1919, believed that the United States was in danger of being taken over by Communists, and he feared that labor union activities would lead to revolution. He urged communities to organize Law and Order Leagues and used state troops (commanded by his son) to break a strike at a Nashville shoe factory. When Knoxville trolley-car workers went on strike, Roberts sent in the state guard, reinforced with federal troops from Camp Gordon, Georgia. Not surprisingly, labor voted against him in 1920.

Finally, Roberts alienated farmers, still the majority of the population in Tennessee, through a tax-reform plan that backfired. Roberts's plan required that taxes be placed on a sliding scale, while real property would be assessed at its true market value (not at a much lower value, as often had been the case for politically favored businesses). "Intangible" property, such as stocks and bonds, also would be taxed. Roberts assumed that the owners of intangible property would reveal their assets voluntarily. With this new tax source in place, land taxes could go down. As might have been expected, the owners of stocks and bonds did not step up voluntarily to be taxed. Meanwhile, tax assessments of real property, which farmers could not conceal, increased 260 percent, while assessments on lots in town went up 140 percent. When farmers got their tax assessments, Roberts's popularity plummeted. Luke Lea's faction of the Democratic Party backed another candidate, unsuccessfully, for the Democratic nomination, then gave Roberts less-than-enthusiastic support in the general election.

The Republican Party capitalized on this situation by nominating Alf Taylor for governor in 1920. "Uncle Alf," the Republican brother of "Our Bob," last had run for governor against his brother thirty-four years earlier. Seventy-two years old, Uncle Alf charmed crowds by playing his fiddle and telling hound-dog stories, but he also hit Roberts's tax plan hard, claiming that farmers were not businessmen and should not be taxed as such. Roberts hoped that the women's vote could swing the election for the Democrats, but the Republican Party also could claim credit (or blame) for women's suffrage, and the women's vote divided on party lines typical of the state. Uncle Alf became governor in 1920 but accomplished little, and in 1922 he faced a formidable opponent, Austin Peay.

Austin Peay: Progressive Traditionalist

Tennessee had more than its fair share of colorful politicians in the 1920s. There was Boss Crump in Memphis, Nashville's Hilary Howse, and former Gov. Malcolm Patterson (whose notoriety had only increased when he was caught in a brothel raid in 1913, repented, got religion, and became a prohibitionist). There was Luke Lea, former senator, real estate developer, and publisher of the *Nashville Tennessean*. Despite the plethora of flamboyant politicians available, the Democratic Party in 1922 nominated the colorless, boring Austin Peay. Historians remember him as the state's best governor in this century and perhaps in the state's entire history.

Peay had entered politics in 1908 as Patterson's campaign manager but after the Carmack affair had dropped out of the political scene to practice law. In 1918, he unsuccessfully contested for the Democratic gubernatorial nomination, losing to Roberts. In 1922, he defeated Alf Taylor and became governor. Reelected easily in 1924, in 1926 he became the first governor since the Civil War to win a third term. Peay's great political feat was to drag state government into the twentieth century. Unlike pre-war Progressives, Peay avoided moral issues such as prohibition. A "business Progressive," he promised efficiency and focused on creating a modern structure for government, building a statewide system of roads, and greatly improving the state's schools. Although he was elected with the support of urban voters, Peay's modernization program had its deepest impact on rural Tennesseans, who became his staunchest supporters.

Peay made reorganizing state government his first priority. Sixty-four separate agencies ran the state's business and reported to the General Assembly. In 1923, Peay proposed to the General Assembly the Administration Reorganization Bill, combining agencies into eight departments that reported to the governor rather than the legislature. Despite the fact that this bill reduced legislative power, the General Assembly approved it, thereby greatly increasing the efficiency of state government. The measure also greatly increased the governor's power. With control of state government now centered in the governor's office, Peay could use patronage to consolidate his power and win support for further reforms, such as good roads.

A State Highway System

In 1920, Tennessee had a grand total of five hundred miles of paved roads scattered across the state. Despite campaigns by advocates of good roads, the creation of a State Highway Commission in 1915, and the availability of federal matching funds, previous governors had not made road building a high priority. In 1920, Confederate pensions received more funds from the state than highways. The Tennessee Good Roads Association (TGRA), a lobbying group composed of members of the state's urban auto clubs, warned that Tennessee risked being scorned as a "detour state." The TGRA promised that roads would bring the blessings of civilization to rural Tennessee: "The progress of any country or community is dependent upon good roads. And the deplorable backwardness and illiteracy which exists in some parts of the South is due almost entirely to a lack of good roads[,] which makes impossible a free exchange of ideas and produce." Under the slogan, "Lift Tennessee Out of the Mud," the TGRA campaigned for a bond issue to build a state highway system. In April 1923, the General Assembly rejected the bond issue, with rural legislators voting against it. Rural voters who wrote to the governor to oppose the plan cited opposition to state debt, fear that the bond money would be squandered by corrupt state officials, and fear that the TGRA's road-building plan would benefit the cities at the expense of the countryside.

Cumberland County road commissioner inspecting Highway 28 from Pikeville. Bryan Stanley, *The Way It Was: Crossville—Cumberland County.*

Peay countered the TGRA with a proposal to build roads on a "pay as you go" basis, funded with gasoline taxes and vehicle registration fees and supplemented by short-term bonds. He vetoed a bill that would have given counties, especially wealthy urban ones, more control over the revenues raised by the new gas tax. The TGRA leadership, opposing the "pay as you go" plan, attacked the governor during his 1924 reelection campaign. Peay won reelection, and construction of the state highway system began, employing hundreds of men across the state. By the end of the decade, Tennessee had over six thousand miles of state highways. Peay's road-building program eventually cost $75 million, but it did not mire the state in long-term debt. Peay's popularity in rural areas increased, but his refusal to support a bond issue for roads cut into his urban support.

Peay's new good roads helped to create a new industry in Tennessee: tourism. Peay was instrumental in creating one of the state's first tourist attractions, the Great Smoky Mountains Park. For years, visitors to the mountains, impressed by the region's natural beauty, had argued that at least part of the Southern Appalachians should be protected as a national park. Timber companies with options on the last stands of uncut forest in the East disagreed, and attempts to create a park in the Smokies stalled. By the 1920s, Knoxville civic leaders, realizing that the park would be a great asset for their city, began serious efforts to promote its creation.

In February 1925, Congress passed legislation authorizing a national park in the Smokies but failed to appropriate money with which to buy the land. The park would have to be pieced together from lands donated and bought, and then given to the national government. In April 1925, Peay urged the state legislature to purchase 76,500 acres as the nucleus for the park. The Knoxville Chamber of Commerce chartered a train and brought the entire General Assembly from Nashville to see the proposed park site, but the bill failed to pass until Knoxville Mayor Ben A. Morton said that the city itself would pay one-third of the purchase price for the first acreage. Knoxvillians raised $500,000 in local funds, including over $1,000 in pennies contributed by schoolchildren in Knox and neighboring counties. Slowly, park boosters cobbled together tracts. With the help of the Laura Spellman Rockefeller Fund, Tennessee and North Carolina purchased more land in 1927. In the 1930s, the federal government began supplying funds for land purchases and took over management of the park.

In 1925, Peay turned his attention to school reform, pushing through the General Assembly a General Education Bill hailed by education reformers as the capstone of decades of effort. Any county that levied a fifty-cent tax for schools would receive enough funds for an eight-month school year. Schools had to comply with state school laws and follow the state curriculum, or lose their state funding. The bill also established a uniform pay scale for teachers throughout the state. Moreover, the bill increased funding for the University of Tennessee. Like Peay's other reforms, the bill increased the power of the governor over the state legislature by placing the schools under the control of the state superintendent, whom the governor appointed. The General Education Bill was controversial. As State Superintendent P. L. Harned noted, it "would necessarily conflict with the local interest of certain communities and the personal interest of many individuals." Conservatives opposed increased governmental spending, rural politicians resented the way the bill cut into their control of local institutions, and many rural people resented paying taxes to fund the state university. The bill passed after intense lobbying by the State Teachers' Association, who so packed the capitol building that exasperated legislators finally had to order them off the floor of the senate while it was in session. By using money collected statewide on tobacco sales to equalize the school year and teacher salaries throughout the state, Peay's administration essentially taxed the cities to pay for improvements in rural education.

Peay was Tennessee's ultimate Progressive, in the mid-1920s finally bringing long-sought reforms to fruition. It is a measure of his abilities that, while state expenditures increased from $15.6 to $26.2 million during his three terms as governor, the state government never ran in the red. Peay always balanced his budget; found new sources of revenue, such as gasoline and tobacco taxes; and kept land taxes low. Originally supported by the state's urban centers, in part because he promised efficient, businesslike government, Peay lost urban support as it became clear that much of the state's tax revenue would be spent on bringing better services to rural Ten-

Rutherford County school health class, 1929. Harry Mustard Photograph Album, Tennessee Historical Society Collections, Tennessee State Library and Archives, Nashville.

nesseans. As Peay's urban support eroded, he used his new patronage power to court rural political bosses and to reach out to East Tennessee Republicans. In 1926, when the Howse and Crump machines backed Hill McAlister against Peay in the Democratic primary, Peay ran as the rural candidate against the urban machines, winning by eight thousand votes.

In his third term, Peay's ability to lead the state legislature faltered. He already had antagonized urban delegations. While rural voters supported Peay, the rural political elite resented the ways in which his school and roads programs diminished their control over local institutions and patronage. In addition, the governor's health was failing. Having been reelected in November, Peay in January contracted a bad case of influenza, which was complicated by pneumonia. He never quite recovered and died in October 1927.

Country Comes to Town

During the 1920s, Tennesseans of both races continued to leave the farms to find jobs in town. After experiencing relative prosperity from the turn of the century through the First World War, agriculture in the state and in the nation plummeted into a postwar recession that presaged the Great Depression of the 1930s. As farm prices dropped, farmers found it increasingly hard to make a

Piggly Wiggly

The modern supermarket was invented in Memphis in 1916 by Clarence Saunders, a wholesale grocer. Before Saunders's innovation, grocery stores usually were small, dark places with merchandise stacked to the ceiling along the walls behind counters. A customer told a clerk what she wanted, and the clerk got it down for her. Customers had to wait until a clerk was available. Many groceries also sold liquor behind the counter.

Saunders thought he could do better. He offered clean stores without liquor and with cheaper merchandise. He provided scales so that customers could weigh their own produce, and gave them sales receipts. Most important of all, Saunders allowed customers to get the merchandise themselves. They could comparison shop, taking as much or as little time as they pleased. "Piggly Wiggly will be born not with a silver spoon in his mouth, but with a workshirt on his back," Saunders said.

The first Piggly Wiggly's immediate success prompted Saunders to offer franchises of the store. By 1923, he had 1,268 stores. With his profits, Saunders built a mansion called the "Pink Palace," now a Memphis museum.

living. Ironically, good roads and good schools, which were supposed to make rural life more attractive, had the opposite effect. Improved education made it easier for rural youth, particularly young women, to find jobs in town. Better roads allowed young people to visit cities and get a taste for urban life. Most of all, good roads and good schools gave rural areas glimpses of the developing national consumer economy, stimulating an appetite for consumer goods that a farmer's income never could supply.

In towns like Nashville, where thriving banking and insurance industries created a job market for clerks, typists, and secretaries (already stereotypically female occupations), the number of women migrants outnumbered men. Since the turn of the century, state educational reforms had created the best-educated and most independent generation of women the state had ever seen. In the nineteenth century, women had been more likely to be illiterate than men, but in the early twentieth century women were quick to take advantage of new opportunities for schooling. A white country girl with a high school education could get a job in town. In Nashville, banks and insurance companies recruited young women through networks that reached back into rural communities, often through country churches. One

Table 10.1. Tennessee's Urban Population, by Race and Sex, 1910 and 1920

Year	Male	Female
1910		
White	144,895	145,536
Black	70,375	80,131
1920		
White	215,209	225,464
Black	80,568	89,896

SOURCE: U.S. Census, Population, 1930.

Nashville businessman recalled that girls came to town in men's shoes, with their long hair in braids. With their first paychecks, they bought clothing, shoes, and makeup; then they had their hair cut into fashionable "bobs." Women migrants to the city often lived in dormitory-style boarding houses sponsored by their new employers, until they saved enough money to rent their own apartments. Years later, when comedienne Sarah Cannon created the character "Cousin Minnie Pearl," just come to town in her funny shoes and her hat with the tag still attached, formerly rural women laughed, recognizing themselves in the 1920s.

Black Tennesseans experienced the pull of city lights just as whites did, but they had other, more urgent reasons to leave the countryside for the city: a virulent resurgence of racism. Racist fears focused especially on black veterans of World War I. When conscription first was proposed, white supremacists throughout the South worried that black soldiers would return from military service unwilling to accept their subordinate roles any longer. Having fought for democracy abroad, they might demand some at home. Some politicians went so far as to suggest that blacks should be exempted from military service altogether. This kind of racism did not appeal to whites who were about to be drafted, however, and the idea was dropped. Black soldiers served with distinction in France. But when they came home, whites reminded them of their places with threats, violence, and riots throughout the South.

In August 1919, racial tension exploded in Knoxville, when police arrested an African American man who was accused of shooting a white woman in an attempted robbery. While the accused was transferred quickly to Chattanooga, whites in Knoxville stormed the city jail, freed white prisoners, cleaned out the confiscated whiskey stored in the jail, and tore down the jail and the sheriff's home. The mob then marched toward Knoxville's black neighborhood, stopping on the way to break into businesses and loot

Knoxville race riot, 1919. McClung Historical Collection, Knox County Public Library, Knoxville.

firearms. As the mob approached the black neighborhood, shooting broke out. Tennessee guardsmen, sent to keep order, joined the white mob in its assault, and several people were killed. Only the arrival of fresh troops the next day restored order.

From 1919 through the end of the 1920s, blacks left the state in the "Great Migration," seeking a better life in Chicago, Detroit, and other northern industrial centers where a man could get a job at decent wages.

Those who stayed increasingly moved into Tennessee's cities. The schools there, while not up to the standards set by Peay's new program for whites, nevertheless were better than those found in rural areas.

In town, black leaders sometimes attained a modicum of political power, due to the peculiar nature of the state's two-party system. Black leaders, as Republicans, had access to federal patronage that white Democratic city mayors wanted to tap into. In addition, mayors needed black votes. This enabled black leaders like James Napier in Nashville to rise to power as brokers standing between their people and the white political structure.

In Memphis, Robert Church became a leader of the "Black and Tan," or biracial, faction of the state's Republican Party, and he exerted considerable influence in national party councils. When Republicans were in the White House, as they were through the 1920s, Church could influence federal patronage in the city. Acting as de facto "boss" of Memphis's black community, Church formed an alliance with Boss Crump. The Crump machine paid the poll taxes for hundreds of black men, then on election day distributed the poll-tax receipts to the men and provided transportation to the polls. Crump's enemies charged that in Memphis black men did not vote, but "were voted," as Crump wished in municipal and state elections. However, in the 1920s, blacks in Memphis did benefit from the Crump machine's rule, getting better schools, better recreational facilities, and access to city jobs.

Blues and Country

In the 1920s, music born in the rural South gained its first national—and even international—audiences. Although blues was black music (or, as recording companies called it in the 1920s, "race" music) and country, or "hillbilly," music was assumed to be white people's music, the roots of both musical forms were similar. Rural southerners of both races listened to traveling medicine shows and string bands, and played fiddles, guitars, banjos, and harmonicas. Both sang gospel music at tent revivals. The musical forms of the rural South crossed racial boundaries. Thus, one of the fathers of country music, the railroad brakeman Jimmie Rodgers, who was white, recorded blues songs; while one of the stars of country radio in the 1920s was DeFord Bailey, a black harmonica player from Smith County, who explained that his family all had performed "black hillbilly music."

Southern music began to reach urban audiences in the 1920s, due to the new availability of record players and radios. Both had been invented earlier, but in that decade technological innovations and mass production made them accessible to a mass audience. Record players, referred to as "Victrolas" after the very popular RCA-Victor model, became a staple item in households throughout the South. Prior to the 1920s, radio was a hobby for young men, who tinkered with crystal sets and kept records of far-distant stations they had found. But in the 1920s, radio became a broadcast medium. Businesses often sponsored stations as a method of advertising: both of Nashville's pioneer radio stations, WSM and WLAC, were started by insurance companies; originally the stations broadcast from the company offices in downtown Nashville.

These new media created new demands for music—for records to be played on Victrolas and for musicians to perform on the radio—and this exposure created even more demand. Having listened to the music on the radio and purchased the record, people wanted to see their favorites perform live. Suddenly musicians who had played at barn dances, parties, bars, and dives found that they could quit their day jobs, go on tour, and actually make a living through their music.

Blues performers like Chattanooga native Bessie Smith, and Alberta Hunter, who was born in Memphis, honed their musical talents performing throughout the South but found prosperity performing in New York and Chicago. As black music moved northward with the Great Migration, blues attracted black and would-be hip white urban audiences. Smith's 1923 recording of Hunter's song, "Down Hearted Blues," sold over two million records, becoming one of the biggest hits of the decade.

Bessie Smith

Chattanooga native Bessie Smith made the blues popular nationally in the 1920s. Bessie was nine years old when she began singing for money on the streets. A violent, hard-drinking, pistol-carrying woman, Bessie lived the life she sang about in blues songs filled with sexual innuendo, bravado, and misery. By the 1920s, Smith had learned to combine her down-and-dirty repertoire with stage glamour: she wore elaborate beaded and sequined gowns and headdresses to sing lyrics no radio station of the time would play. (For example, in "Empty Bed Blues," Bessie lamented that, since her man had left, "my bedsprings are all rusty.")

In 1923, Smith cut her first record, "Down Hearted Blues," written by Memphis native Alberta Hunter. It sold more than two million copies and made her a nationally known figure, the "Empress of the Blues." Bessie's music introduced white urban audiences to the blues, and she became the top blues singer of the decade. The national vogue for blues faded at the end of the decade, and Smith stopped recording, but she continued to tour. She was killed in an auto accident in Mississippi in 1937, leaving behind a legend that continues to influence musicians today.

White hillbilly music did not receive national attention until the 1930s. But the origins of Nashville's current music business can be found in the 1920s, at radio station WSM. The station was owned by the National Life and Accident Insurance Company, which sold cheap life insurance to working-class blacks and whites. (The station's call letters signified We Serve Millions.) In 1925, WSM hired George Dewey Hay, a native of Memphis, as announcer and program director. Hay came to Nashville from Chicago, where he had hosted the WLS Barn Dance, a program featuring hillbilly music. Building on his success in Chicago, Hay began to program music designed to appeal to WSM's rural and working-class clientele. He hired local string bands and singers to perform "old-time" music and encouraged

The Carter Family

In July 1927, Ralph Peer, a talent scout for Victor, makers of Victrola record players, came to Bristol, on the Tennessee-Virginia border, in search of local talent. Peer's Bristol sessions rank among the most significant recordings in American musical history. At Bristol, he recorded the first country music star, Jimmie Rodgers of Mississippi, who had driven in for the occasion. Peer also found A. P., Sarah, and Maybelle Carter—the Carter Family from Maces Spring, Virginia. Sarah Carter, A. P.'s wife, played autoharp and sang lead, while sister-in-law Maybelle played guitar, using a method that became known as "Carter Picking." A. P. found songs for the group, sang harmony, and drove the car. Although they were dissatisfied with their work on the Bristol sessions, the Carters went on to become legends of country music.

Leaving the Appalachian Mountains for the Mexican border, the Carters worked for powerful "clear-channel" radio stations with signals that blanketed much of the country. People across the nation first heard traditional musical standards like "Wildwood Flower," "Keep on the Sunny Side," and "Will the Circle Be Unbroken" sung by Sarah and Maybelle Carter. Eventually, A. P. and Sarah divorced, and both retired from the music business. But Maybelle Carter formed another band with her daughters and in 1950 joined the Grand Ole Opry. By the 1960s, the Carter style of music was too hillbilly for Nashville, but "Mother Maybelle" went on the college folk-music circuit, where her authenticity in singing mournful ballads from the Appalachian Mountains made her a great popular success.

them to pretend to be bumpkins just off the farm, disguising the fact that many of them had performed for years in traveling shows.

In 1927, Hay's country show followed a program of classical music. Hay announced that, following the Grand Opera, he would present the "Grand Ole Opry." The Opry's format was not unusual; radio stations throughout the South programmed "barn dances" featuring country music. But the Opry provided a nucleus around which an industry would grow, much to the dismay of Nashville's cultural elite, who preferred that the city be known as the "Athens of the South," not the home of hillbilly music.

Reactions to Modernity

Nothing symbolizes Tennesseans' ambivalent attitudes toward modern times better than the image of an urban factory worker spending money to buy a Victrola, so that he could play records that reminded him of the music he had grown up hearing back on the farm. Tennesseans embraced technological change while mourning the loss of a (perhaps mythical) rural world of Christian faith and social harmony. Conservative ministers, black and white, thundered sermons against licentious music, dancing, wild young women with short skirts and bobbed hair, and young men who spent too much time running up and down the highways in fast cars. While parents on both side of the color line worried about their reckless children, racist whites also worried about blacks' getting "out of their place." During the 1920s, many Tennesseans made attempts to defend traditional social, racial, and gender roles. They used methods that ranged from reasoned public argument through political action to violence.

The Ku Klux Klan had disbanded at the end of Reconstruction. As the history of the "night riders" and of lynching in the state demonstrates, white people were perfectly capable of terrorizing their black neighbors without it. But in 1915, Hollywood director D. W. Griffith released the first truly modern motion picture, *The Birth of a Nation*, which was based on a historically inaccurate, racist novel about Reconstruction, *The Klansman*. As audiences flocked to see Griffith's movie, a Georgia salesman—a man who previously had made a living promoting fraternal orders like the Elks and the Woodmen of the World—saw a business opportunity. He formed a secret society he called the Ku Klux Klan and began to sell memberships in it. The reconstituted Klan remained small until the 1920s, when two publicity agents began to retail the organization with all the modern skills normally used to sell soap. The KKK's organization was, in essence, a pyramid scheme: from new members' dues, the Klan recruiter took a cut, and so did the person who recruited him, and so on up the ladder to headquarters. Using modern sales methods, Klan recruiters built up an organization that stood opposed to most aspects of modern life in the 1920s.

Although the new KKK was a white supremacist organization, that was

That old-time religion: baptizing at Errassmus, 1924. Bryan Stanley, *The Way It Was: Crossville—Cumberland County.*

not its strongest selling point. What the Klan offered recruits in the 1920s was a nativist, anti-immigrant, anti-Catholic, anti-Semitic version of "100 Percent Americanism," for which only white Protestants need apply. This anti-immigrant stance appealed to Protestants in states like Ohio, Indiana, and Pennsylvania, where Catholic votes wielded considerable political power. In states like Tennessee, where Catholics and Jews were a very small minority and where blacks, also a minority, were repressed by segregation and disfranchisement, the Klan's appeal was somewhat limited. However, the KKK appealed to conservative Tennesseans by opposing "immorality." Firmly in favor of prohibition, Klansmen broke up stills and whipped moonshiners. They hauled prostitutes to the authorities for arrest and terrorized divorced or "loose" women. In Knoxville, the KKK denounced "petting parties" and "wild dancing."

The KKK never attained the power in Tennessee that it mustered in some southern and midwestern states. Although individual ministers and church members joined the Klan, the leadership of Protestant denominations in the state did not support the organization. The Methodist and Presbyterian denominational papers denounced the Klan; the Presbyterian editor noted that the KKK violated "every basic precept of the religion of Jesus." The KKK failed to win active support from any significant political leader in the state. Instead, the Klan attracted as members working-class white men whose economic position placed them in competition with blacks for survival in Tennessee cities. The KKK found its greatest support in the northeastern and southwestern corners of the state, in Knoxville and Memphis.

In the early 1920s, the secret society enrolled over two thousand Knoxville men as members and held initiations and cross burnings on Sharp's Ridge. In 1923, the KKK held a large rally at Chilhowee Park and tried to influence local city elections by stationing members at all polling places. However, the Klan's power in Knoxville faded quickly, probably due to the exodus of whites from the integrated inner city and out to the growing all-white suburbs.

When the KKK organized in Memphis, it faced formidable opposition from Boss Crump. Crump later would brag about his stand against the Klan, writing that he had "fought the Klan from start to finish." His detractors suggested that Crump, unable to tolerate the Klan as a rival power within Memphis, sent out his organization men to rig the city elections in 1923 so that the Klan's candidate for mayor lost. Crump was as committed to white supremacy as any other politician in the state, but his machine depended upon the votes of blacks, Jews, and Irish and Italian Catholics. His attitude toward blacks was one of condescending patronage, not fear or aversion. He had no patience with either anti-Semitism or anti-Catholicism. In 1928, when Catholic Al Smith ran for the presidency on the Democratic ticket, the votes of Tennessee Protestants gave the state to the Republican candidate, Herbert Hoover. But Crump held the line for the Democrats in Memphis and denounced anti-Catholicism, reminding his constituents of the many contributions Catholics had made to their city. In other southern states, ambitious young politicians felt that they must join the KKK in order to further their careers. Crump's opposition made joining the KKK a pointless, and possibly dangerous, course for a would-be politician to take in Tennessee. While Tennessee politicians rarely condemned the Klan and many probably shared the Klan's attitudes, relatively few became dues-paying members.

In 1925, Tennessee became an international symbol of resistance to modernism when the state legislature passed a bill making it illegal to teach evolution in Tennessee public schools and the law was tested in a spectacular trial at the Rhea County Courthouse. The Dayton "Monkey Trial" was the culmination of years of controversy over supposed conflicts between religion and science. In the years since Charles Darwin's publication of *The Origin of Species* in 1859, most mainstream northern Protestant churches had made their peace with evolution. (Both Methodists and Baptists had split into northern and southern branches before the Civil War.) As one liberal churchman put it, evolution was how God worked. By 1900, influenced by Darwinism and by new methods of literary and historical analysis, many northern Protestants had come to believe that the Bible contained symbolic, not literal, truth. While this became the dominant view in some denominations, determined conservatives initiated a movement to counter such thinking. They insisted that Christians could not give up certain basic tenets of faith. In 1910, two California businessmen sponsored the publication of a series of pamphlets on theological issues. Called *The Fundamentals*, the series lent its name to the movement.

"Fundamentalists" insisted that the Bible was "inerrant," or without error, and most held that the Bible must be accepted as literal, not symbolic, truth. Fundamentalism became a divisive issue in many American denominations, causing fractures in churches and seminaries. But fundamentalism was not really a contested issue in most southern churches, where Darwinism never had been accepted in the first place and where theological liberals were hard to find. Operating outside the larger national fundamentalist movement, conservative Christians in the South shared with their northern counterparts concerns about the impact of modernism on young people: what happened to fundamental beliefs when they conflicted with science as taught in the public schools?

In 1925, resolutions to prohibit the teaching of evolution in the state's public schools were introduced in both houses of the General Assembly. The senate version was tabled in favor of the bill proposed by State Rep. John Washington Butler of Macon County. The Butler Act was designed to prohibit the teaching of "any theory that denies the story of the Divine Creation of man as taught in the Bible, and to teach instead that man descended from a lower order of animals." Butler was a somewhat unusual legislator. A farmer who operated a threshing machine, a Primitive Baptist, Butler had only eight years of education. But in the hills of Tennessee, that was more schooling than most people had, and Butler certainly was a literate and thoughtful man. He wrote columns for the local newspaper and had taught briefly in the public schools. As a legislator, Butler was assigned to a committee that supervised the state-run schools for the handicapped. In examining the books used, he found that Darwinism was being taught, and he decided to introduce legislation to prohibit the practice. He probably also was influenced by the anti-evolution campaign then being conducted by William Jennings Bryan, statesman and former Democratic presidential candidate, for whom the Democratic legislator had the greatest respect.

The Butler bill received widespread public support from most denominations in the state. The Baptist Pastors Council of Nashville supported the bill, as did individual ministers and congregations throughout the state. On the other hand, some religious leaders in the state sent messages to the General Assembly opposing passage. A Methodist minister in Columbia charged the legislators with "making monkeys of themselves." But such opposition was muted. The Butler Act passed both houses with ease, and Governor Peay signed it. In his message to the General Assembly concerning the Butler Act, Peay noted that the state had mandated Bible reading in public school classrooms since 1915. Peay pointed out that it would be inconsistent for the state to promote Bible reading while teaching a scientific theory that undermined belief in the Bible. The governor considered the Butler Act chiefly symbolic and publicly doubted that it ever would be enforced. However, he approved the symbolism behind the legislation, writing that the act was "a distinct protest against an irreligious tendency to exalt so-called science and deny the Bible in some schools and quarters—a tendency fundamentally wrong and fatally mischievous in its effects on our children, our institutions and our country."

The passage of the Butler Act aroused immediate national attention. The American Civil Liberties Union, which had been formed in 1920, announced that it would provide funding for any Tennessee teacher who wished to challenge the law. The challenge came from a young teacher from rural Rhea County in East Tennessee, John Thomas Scopes.

What happened in Dayton, Tennessee, in the summer of 1925 has been the subject of newspaper stories, magazine articles, books, plays, and movies. Many Americans base what they think they know about Dayton on *Inherit the Wind*, a play later made into a movie, that fictionalized the Scopes trial. The movie shows East Tennesseans as a howling mob out to injure the young high school teacher accused of teaching Darwinism. In real life, Scopes was not threatened or ostracized by the community of Dayton, nor

John Thomas Scopes meets Clarence Darrow. "Looking Back at Tennessee" Collection, Tennessee State Library and Archives, Nashville.

was he in danger of imprisonment; the penalty for violating the Butler Act was a small fine. In his willingness to be tried for violating the Butler Act, Scopes did Dayton a favor, and the leaders of the town knew it.

The Scopes trial, so often played as high drama, in reality was a comedy, although one with serious implications. The event grew out of a friendly debate around a drug-store soda fountain table between some Dayton merchants and an engineer who worked for one of the local coal-mining companies. The engineer contended that modern biology could not be taught without teaching evolution. Scopes happened to come in at this point. The twenty-two-year-old teacher did not normally teach biology at the high school, but he had been helping students review for tests. The men around the table asked him if he taught evolution. Scopes said that any teacher who followed the state-approved textbook taught evolution. The Dayton town leaders decided to take the ACLU up on its offer and had Scopes indicted by the Rhea County grand jury. (This put Scopes in a somewhat awkward position, as he was not sure that he ever had taught evolution, and he hoped that his students would not remember that he hadn't. The regular biology teacher, however, was a family man who did not want to face trial.) The local bigwigs hoped to get national publicity—to "put Dayton on the map." They succeeded beyond their wildest imagining.

William Jennings Bryan volunteered to try the case for the state, and Scopes accepted the offer of ACLU member Clarence Darrow to defend him. Darrow was the most famous trial lawyer of his generation. The prospect of courtroom combat between the two famous men brought scores of reporters to Dayton in the summer of 1925. Scopes's students testified that he had taught evolution, thus establishing that he had violated the Butler Act. (Scopes was relieved that he did not have to testify.) Darrow then requested permission to introduce his expert witnesses: Christian theologians, Hebrew scholars, geologists, biologists, and other scientific and linguistic experts. Darrow said that, since the Butler Act prohibiting teaching theories that contradicted the Creation story as told in the Bible, his expert witnesses were necessary to establish what the Bible said and what Darwinism said, in order to see if they contradicted. The judge ruled against this attempt to expand the case. Contending that some examination of Genesis was necessary for his case, Darrow then called Bryan to the stand as an expert witness on the Bible. The resulting exchange, while dramatic, did nothing to alter the course of the case. Scopes was convicted and fined. An appeals court overturned his conviction on a technicality but upheld the validity of the law.

Scopes went off to graduate school, courtesy of participants in the trial, including Darrow's expert witnesses. Bryan, exhausted by the trial, died a week after its conclusion. Dayton settled down to live with the consequences of being, historically, forever on the map. Ultimately, the trial changed nothing. The Butler Act remained on the books in Tennessee until

1967, despite repeated attempts by members of the Tennessee Academy of Science and the American Association of University Professors to persuade the state legislature to repeal it. Despite Darrow's contention that he had won a moral victory in Tennessee, the Scopes trial extended, rather than limited, the impact of the Butler Act. Fearful that they would lose sales, textbook publishers self-censored, purging Darwin from high-school biology books until the 1960s.

The trial was a profound embarrassment to intellectuals in the state. Newspaper reports from Dayton depicted rural Tennesseans as, at best, ignorant religious bigots and, at worst, subhuman "anthropoids." Baltimore journalist H. L. Mencken said that Dayton was "the bunghole of the United States, a cesspool of Baptists, a miasma of Methodism, snake-charmers, phony real-estate operators, and syphilitic evangelists." Chagrined at becoming a national joke, educated Tennesseans reacted in various ways. While the presidents of state-supported colleges maintained a politic silence, Vanderbilt University's chancellor raised money to build more science labs and a school of religion as an "answer to Dayton." But a group of young intellectuals affiliated with Vanderbilt decided to mount a counterattack. If the South was different, backward, not modern, then they would defend those attributes as positive, not negative. In 1930, "Twelve Southerners," most of them affiliated with Vanderbilt, published *I'll Take My Stand: The South and the Agrarian Tradition*. In essays on southern history, country life, education, race relations, and art, the "Nashville Agrarians" attacked modern industrial society and upheld the superiority of the agrarian way of life. Although their methods differed, the Agrarians shared with KKK members, fundamentalists, and fans of the Grand Ole Opry a nostalgia for rural worlds that even then were passing away.

Fall of the House of Lea

When Gov. Austin Peay died in the middle of his third term of office, he was succeeded by the speaker of the senate, Henry Horton. Horton lacked political or administrative experience. A lawyer, he had served one term in the state legislature (1907–9) as a prohibition Democrat. In 1927, he had been elected to the state senate and chosen as speaker. Upon succeeding Peay, Horton quickly turned for help and advice to Luke Lea, a powerful figure among midstate Democrats and a supporter of the late governor's reforms. Lea's forceful personality so overwhelmed Horton's that, critics charged, Lea became governor in all but name. Ultimately, Lea's involvement with Horton proved disastrous for both men, and for the state.

Luke Lea had been involved at every turn in state politics since 1906, when he supported Malcolm Patterson for governor. The scion of a wealthy Middle Tennessee family, Lea founded the *Nashville Tennessean* in 1907, using the paper to support prohibition and oppose the L&N. Lea broke with Patterson over prohibition and in 1907 allied with Carmack. When Carmack lost his gubernatorial bid, Lea gave him a job as editor of the *Tennessean*. After Carmack's death, Lea's was the loudest voice demanding vengeance against the Coopers. He became a leader of the prohibitionist Democrats and was elected to the U.S. Senate in 1911, at age thirty-two, serving one term. In 1917, Lea volunteered for the U.S. Army, becoming an officer in the 114th Tennessee. He earned international notoriety when, at the end of the war, he made a raid into neutral Holland in an unsuccessful attempt to capture the defeated German Kaiser, who was in exile there. Upon his return to Nashville, Lea resumed his political role and expanded his business interests. By the 1920s, Lea presided over a banking, publishing, and real estate empire, built through his alliance with Rogers Caldwell, whose investment bank, Caldwell and Company, specialized in handling bonds for southern states. By 1929, Caldwell controlled a variety of manufacturing, building supply, oil, and insurance companies; a chain of department stores; the Nashville Volunteers baseball team; and seventy-five banks in Tennessee and Arkansas. Lea and Caldwell together bought Holston National Bank in Knoxville and Union and Planters Bank in Memphis, and Lea went on in 1930 to acquire a controlling interest in a North Carolina bank. Caldwell, a businessman, was motivated primarily by profit. Lea wanted power and used his growing fortune to further his political ends. In 1927, Lea and Caldwell bought the *Memphis Commercial Appeal* and the *Knoxville Journal*, giving Lea a forum for his political views in each of the state's three largest cities.

Governor Peay's administrative reforms had placed control of patronage and state contracts in the hands of the governor. Peay had a reputation for scrupulous honesty, and no hint of political impropriety ever has been attached to him. However, in 1927, while Peay was still alive but ailing, Lea asked State Highway Commissioner C. Neil Bass to buy "Kyrock," a road-building material produced by Caldwell's Kentucky Rock and Asphalt Company, without competitive bidding. Bass refused. A month later Peay died, Horton became governor, and Lea became his most trusted advisor. Horton fired Bass, replacing him with one of Lea's friends, and state contracts began to flow to Caldwell's company. In 1928, Horton's connections with Lea and Caldwell became a campaign issue for his two opponents, Hill McAlister, who received the support of the Crump machine, and Lewis Pope, who had served as Peay's commissioner of institutions. Horton won reelection by only five thousand votes.

In truth, Horton's involvement with Lea and Caldwell went much deeper than the Kyrock scandal. Under Lea's direction, the state government began to operate as a virtual subsidiary of Caldwell and Company. What follows is a simple summary of very complex financial transactions. At the governor's insistence, and with the General Assembly's approval, the state in 1929 and 1930 issued about $45 million worth of bonds for highway construction. Banks which "handle" government bonds earn a commission for doing so. Banks usually submit bids for handling government bonds. In this case, the only bids were from Caldwell banks, and commissions for bond sales went to Caldwell and Company. The funds raised by these bonds were deposited in Caldwell banks, where Caldwell used them to cover his own financial shortfalls. Caldwell was able to do this because the state superintendent of banks, a Lea appointee, always informed Lea before the state auditors arrived at Caldwell's bank. Finally, the bonds raised money for road construction, and the state awarded contracts for supplies to Caldwell companies.

Tennessee politicians had a long history of using state government to feather their own nests, but the operations described above were on a scale not seen in the state since Reconstruction. To some extent, Caldwell and Lea were products of their times. During the economic boom of the late 1920s, many Americans borrowed money and otherwise overextended themselves to buy stocks and make investments, gambling that the "bull market" would continue. However, Lea also was capable of penny-ante dishonesty. He wanted the state to pave highways going to his supporters' houses and to his real estate holdings in West Nashville. When the state highway commissioner, appointed by Lea because he was willing to go along with the Kyrock scam, drew the line at this, Governor Horton fired him.

In October 1929, the stock market crashed. Caldwell and Company began to scramble to survive, with the state funds deposited in Caldwell's bank their only hedge against collapse. Lea and Caldwell frantically put together mergers and arranged loans to keep the company going until after the 1930 gubernatorial election.

Boss Crump hated Luke Lea, who, as a prohibitionist Democrat, had supported Crump's ouster as mayor in 1915. But Lea controlled the governor and could appoint Crump's enemies to positions of power in Memphis. To protect his control over his city, Crump cut a deal with Lea. Crump gained control over state appointments in Memphis. In return, the Shelby County delegation supported Horton in the General Assembly, voting to approve yet another bond issue for road construction; and Crump swung Memphis's votes behind Horton in the 1930 election, allowing him to win easily.

Three days after Horton won reelection, Caldwell and Company collapsed, setting off panic and bank failures throughout the South. Eventually 120 banks folded, causing untold financial hardship to thousands of people. Federal deposit insurance had not yet been enacted, so, when a bank failed, a depositor's money simply was gone. The state of Tennessee alone lost an estimated $7 million, which had been deposited in Caldwell banks. The fall of Caldwell and Company did not "cause" the Great Depression in the South. The Depression was an international economic crisis beyond the control of any one nation, let alone any one company. For many anguished investors, however, Lea and Caldwell had brought the Depression home, ushering in hard times.

As the extent of the debacle became clear, Lea's political enemies demanded blood. A "Public Emergency Committee," consisting of men whom Lea had fired, defeated in politics, or otherwise humiliated, held public meetings across the state, exposing Lea's malfeasance and demanding justice. Boss Crump led a drive to impeach Governor Horton. To save Horton, Lea called in his political markers, mobilizing support from contractors and state workers, who lobbied for the governor. Horton's supporters apparently convinced the General Assembly that Boss Crump was a greater threat to the state than the ineffectual governor, who was allowed to serve out the rest of his term. Caldwell managed to avoid jail, although he lost most of his property. Luke Lea bore the brunt of the public's vengeance. In 1931, a North Carolina court convicted Lea and his son of fraud in connection with the bank they owned there. Lea appealed the case all the way to the U.S. Supreme Court but lost. The Leas then fought extradition to North Carolina until the new governor, one of Lea's political enemies, issued a warrant for his arrest. Lea and his son ultimately were reduced to hiding out in the country, driving from town to town in an effort to avoid the state police. Finally, in 1934, the Leas surrendered. The former senator served two years in prison.

With Lea out of the way, Boss Crump emerged as the state's top politician. The nature of political power in the state had changed, however. As the New Deal remade relations between the federal government and the states, the politician most important for Tennessee was not Boss Crump, Senator McKellar, or Governor McAlister, but the man in the White House—Franklin D. Roosevelt.

Suggested Readings

Country Music Foundation. *From the Beginnings to the '90s: Country Music and the Musicians*. New York, 1994.

Doyle, Don Harrison. *Nashville in the New South, 1880–1930*. Knoxville, Tenn., 1985.

———. *Nashville Since the 1920s*. Knoxville, Tenn., 1985.

Frome, Michael. *Strangers in High Places: The Story of the Great Smoky Mountains*. Knoxville, Tenn., 1966.

Ginger, Ray. *Six Days or Forever? Tennessee v. John Thomas Scopes*. New York, 1958.

Lamon, Lester C. *Blacks in Tennessee, 1791–1970*. Knoxville, Tenn., 1981.

Majors, William R. *Change and Continuity: Tennessee Politics Since the Civil War*. Macon, Ga., 1986.

Malone, Bill C. *Singing Cowboys and Musical Mountaineers: Southern Culture and the Roots of Country Music*. Athens, Ga., 1993.

McDonald, Michael J., and William Bruce Wheeler. *Knoxville, Tennessee: Continuity and Change in an Appalachian City.* Knoxville, Tenn., 1983.

Miller, William D. *Mr. Crump of Memphis.* Baton Rouge, La., 1964.

Norton, Herman A. *Religion in Tennessee, 1777–1945.* Knoxville, Tenn., 1981.

Scopes, John Thomas, and James Presley. *Center of the Storm.* New York, 1967.

Tidwell, Mary Louise Lea. *Luke Lea of Tennessee.* Bowling Green, Oh., 1993.

Wills, Gary. *Under God: Religion and American Politics.* New York, 1990.

11

Depression and War

IN OCTOBER 1942, soldiers of the United States Army appeared at the doors of farmhouses in the hills of Roane and Anderson Counties, telling the residents that the federal government was confiscating their land. The soldiers would not tell the baffled farmers and miners why their property was being taken or what would replace their little communities: Elza, Scarboro, Robertsville, Wheat. As the residents left, construction began on roads, barracks, and mysterious giant buildings, all surrounded by a tall fence and guarded by soldiers. Soon the government began hiring workers for the secret project. Thousands of Tennesseans, many of them unskilled and totally in the dark as to the nature of the project, worked under the direction of scientists and technicians whose accents often betrayed origins half a world away from the Tennessee hills. By 1945, the compound held seventy-five thousand residents and had become the fifth largest city in the state. Army officers suggested that the new city be named Valhalla or Shangri-la, but employees of the project preferred the name "Oak Ridge."

The item produced by thousands of workers left Oak Ridge in 1945 in one small padded briefcase, chained to the wrist of one courier, who transported it to another secret installation in New Mexico. Oak Ridge produced the uranium isotope used to created "Little Boy," the first atomic bomb, which was dropped on Hiroshima, Japan, in 1945.

Oak Ridge was only the most spectacular example of the impact of federal action upon Tennessee during the Great Depression and World War II. The federal government became a part of everyday life in a way never seen before. In Tennessee as throughout the nation, federal programs fed the starving, provided work, restructured agriculture, and supported the rise of organized labor. In Tennessee, however, federal government intervention went much farther than elsewhere, as the state became the center of a major social experiment, the Tennessee Valley Authority.

Impact of the Depression

The Great Depression that began when the New York stock market crashed in the autumn of 1929 reached Tennessee in November 1930. When the

Oak Ridge under construction; ruins of Wheat in the foreground. Photograph by James E. Westcott. U.S. Department of Energy. *The Oak Ridge Community, 25th Anniversary Publication.*

Caldwell banking chain collapsed, people lost their savings. Their panicked neighbors rushed to their banks to withdraw their deposits, causing further bank failures. A number of prominent Tennessee businessmen committed suicide, preferring death to bankruptcy and disgrace. In all Tennessee cities and towns, businesses laid off workers, reduced wages, or closed outright. Charitable organizations fed the hungry with "bread lines" and "soup kitchens" on Knoxville's Gay Street. Beggars appeared on downtown Nashville streets, and homeless families built a shanty town on the river's banks. In many cities and towns, cash all but disappeared and a barter economy emerged.

Memphis was hit less severely than other large southern cities. When panic-stricken depositors began a "run" on Union Planters Bank, Boss Crump ordered the bank officers to pile up all the bank's cash on the counters so that people could see it, and he personally walked up and down the lines of anxious people, assuring them that the bank was sound. Union Planters stood. Memphis's diversified local economy and its status as a trading center for the region protected it from the worst effects of the Depression, but the city still lost almost one-third of its industrial jobs. The Crump machine tried to put people to work, even supplying boxes of apples that unemployed men could sell on downtown streets.

Throughout the state, desperate white workers took jobs, such as cooking and cleaning, that previously had been considered "colored"; blacks could find no work at all. Private charities could not supply enough food for the thousands thrown out of work in Tennessee's cities. By the winter of 1932–33, social workers in Tennessee cities reported that people were malnourished, and some were on the edge of starvation.

While the Depression devastated the cities, rural Tennesseans joked that they hardly noticed it, since times had been so hard for so long. Farm prices had fallen after the end of World War I and had remained low through the 1920s, before going lower in the early 1930s. Agribusinessmen (those people whom Tennesseans at the time called "big farmers") suffered when the market for cotton or tobacco fell. Tenant farmers lost what little chance they had to make a profit. But Tennesseans who owned their land survived the Depression using traditional "small farmer" methods; they grew all their own food, kept their purchases to a minimum, and "made do." Ironically, the Depression led to a reversal of the migration from farm to city that had been characteristic of the 1920s. Now sons and daughters, laid off from city jobs, came home, often bringing their families with them, to eke out a living on the old home place.

The New Deal

In 1932, Tennesseans voted overwhelmingly for the Democratic candidate for the presidency, Franklin Roosevelt. Roosevelt promised the country a "New Deal" and pushed through Congress a series of programs that, while combating the Depression, also transformed the relationship of the American citizen to the federal government. New Deal programs such as the Social Security Act of 1935 established the foundation for a national welfare state. From 1933 to the end of the decade, the New Deal reached into every community in the nation to supply "relief" (welfare) for the destitute and put the jobless to work.

Tennessee got its share of New Deal funds and more. While the leaders of some southern states feared the New Deal as an unwarranted intrusion into local affairs and a danger to state's rights, Tennessee's political leaders did everything they could to attract federal dollars to the state. In that they were successful, due in part to the nature of Tennessee politics. Unlike many other southern states, Tennessee had something approximating a two-party system and had the potential to go Republican in presidential elections, as it had in 1928. Roosevelt cemented Tennessee's loyalties to the Democratic Party by approving New Deal projects for the state. But the state's greatest advantage derived from the voters' habit of returning the same men to Washington over and over again. Having attained seniority, Tennesseans held positions of power in Congress. Joseph W. Byrns, whose Middle Tennessee district included Nashville, had been in the House of Representatives since 1909 and rose to be speaker before his death in 1936. Cordell Hull, formerly congressman from the Fourth District, was elected senator in 1930 and became Roosevelt's secretary of state in 1933, a job he held through World War II. Sen. Kenneth McKellar, who had been in office since 1916, headed the state's delegation. Roosevelt needed McKellar's support for New Deal legislation, and McKellar made sure that Tennessee received New Deal funds.

Throughout the state, thousands of men constructed roads, bridges, parks, public buildings, and the state's first housing projects, under such New Deal programs as the Public Works Administration (PWA), the Works Progress Administration (WPA), and the Civilian Conservation Corps (CCC). The PWA, headed by Secretary of the Interior Harold Ickes, specialized in substantial building projects. Many post offices and schools in the state still display PWA plaques in their front lobbies. In Nashville, the PWA built the state's Supreme Court Building and State Office Building, and remodeled the Capitol. The WPA provided work relief for adult men, and some small amount of work relief for women. (New Deal authorities shared with most Americans the belief that married women should not work outside the home—although, during the Depression, the number of married women workers actually increased.) While the WPA's critics charged that the agency's initials stood for "We Piddle Around," WPA workers throughout the state improved highways, schools, and hospitals. In Nashville alone, WPA workers paved the streets, built the city's first airport, and constructed public facilities at Percy Warner Park. WPA funds also employed artists who decorated public buildings, college students who preserved or transcribed old records (now extensively used by historians and genealogists), teachers for adult education programs, and public health workers. The CCC employed young single men to work on conservation projects, including improvements to state and federal parks, under the direction of the Department of the Interior, housing them in camps administered by the U.S. Army.

Although the entire state benefited from the New Deal, Memphis gained the most. Senator McKellar was from Shelby County and was affiliated with Boss Crump's machine. Crump firmly supported the New Deal, and in return Roosevelt's administration supported the Crump machine. Crump was allowed to pick the men who administered New Deal programs in Memphis. Thus the New Deal became another source of patronage for the Memphis boss. Historians of the New Deal agree that the Crump machine ran local relief programs fairly and efficiently, with only a small amount of political chicanery. (Members of Boss Crump's organization were criticized for asking relief workers for campaign contributions.) The PWA built John Gaston Hospital, several schools, and (with the Army Corps of Engineers) Riverside Drive. When the Tennessee Valley Authority made cheap, publicly-owned electrical power available, Memphis obtained $18 million in PWA funds to build distribution lines into the city. The city also used New Deal funds to build new public housing complexes. The Bluff City received more than its share of the state's WPA funds, using them to improve roads, hospitals, parks, and schools.

As the Roosevelt administration's accommodation to Boss Crump indicates, the New Deal did not threaten the local power bases of Tennessee Democrats. For blacks in Tennessee, that was not good news. The Roosevelt administration did not take any stands in support of civil rights.

To angry black leaders, FDR explained that he needed the support of southern congressmen to be able to pass New Deal legislation. FDR allowed local program administrators to discriminate on the basis of race, if that was the local custom—as it was through most of the nation. CCC camps had quotas limiting the admittance of young black men, and the camps were segregated. PWA jobs went to whites disproportionately. In Memphis, the PWA tore down middle-class black neighborhoods to build public housing for whites. Black leaders charged that the National Recovery Agency (NRA), which encouraged businesses to set wages and prices voluntarily, should be called the "Negro Removal Act" or "Negroes Ruined Again," since it led to displacement of black workers. When white employers had to pay blacks the same rates as whites, they simply fired blacks and hired white workers. Although officially the WPA imposed no quotas, historians note that in Memphis most jobs went to whites. The Memphis director of the National Youth Administration, one of the New Deal agencies that made a sincere effort to be fair to blacks, told the NAACP that he would not hire a black assistant: "So long as there are white people who need work I will not recommend a negro for the place." WPA training programs for black women in Memphis received praise from the local press as designed to train "a well-rounded servant." The New Deal's agricultural programs, discussed below, proved disastrous for black sharecroppers.

Even though New Deal programs reinforced the southern color line, federal relief nevertheless did supply the means of survival for many black families in Tennessee. Grateful for even these small favors, black voters, traditionally Republican, began switching their party affiliations to the Democrats.

Reforming Tennessee Agriculture

In the 1930s, most Tennesseans still made their living from agriculture. While WPA and CCC projects employed farmers and their sons, they did little to alleviate a crisis in agriculture that had been building since the Civil War. Farmers in the 1930s had many of the same problems as farmers in the late nineteenth century: overproduction, lack of access to credit, and high protective tariffs that hurt overseas markets for American produce. The Depression made the farm crisis worse but did not cause it.

The Roosevelt administration recognized that, while southern farmers shared concerns with farmers throughout the nation, they also had problems specific to the region. In 1938, President Roosevelt called the South "the Nation's No. 1 economic problem." In some southern states, the majority of farmers were tenants and sharecroppers, producing cotton or rice, and were locked into an economic situation so dire that it amounted to peonage. Tennessee's situation was different. As always, the conditions of farmers varied from the East Tennessee mountains to the West Tennessee delta.

In the state's hill-country districts, the agricultural crisis grew from

Table 11.1. Tennessee's Total Population, 1920–1950

Year	Total Population	Percentage Rural	Percentage Urban
1920	2,337,885	73.9	26.1
1930	2,616,556	65.7	34.3
1940	2,915,841	64.8	35.2
1950	3,291,718	*55.9	44.1*

*In 1950 the Bureau of the Census changed its definition of urban. The percentages above were calculated using the new definition. By the older definition, 61.6 percent of Tennesseans still lived in rural areas in 1950, with 38.4 percent residing in urban areas.
Source: U.S. Census, Population, 1950.

population pressure: there simply were too many people on the land. For generations, the fathers of Tennessee farm families had divided their farms so that each of their many children could have an inheritance. This system, while just and equitable for the heirs, proved disastrous for agriculture. By the 1920s, many Tennessee farmers owned no more than twenty acres of land, which they used to feed their families. Many farmers made the cash that paid their property taxes by working at jobs off the farm. New Deal economists took the view that marginal farmers would be better off leaving the land for jobs in the city and believed that programs to help twenty-acre farms were a waste of time. Instead, the Roosevelt administration's farm programs were designed to help "big farmers" become more productive businessmen. Programs such as the Agricultural Adjustment Administration had a profound impact on landowners and on the tenant farmers who worked for them in West Tennessee.

New Deal agricultural specialists argued that overproduction kept farm prices low. To raise prices, production must be cut. In 1933, the Roosevelt administration secured passage of legislation creating the Agricultural Adjustment Administration, which was authorized to pay farmers to reduce their acreage in seven crops, including tobacco and cotton, the two staple crops grown most often in Tennessee.

Tobacco was produced by larger commercial planters in western Middle Tennessee and by small family farmers throughout the eastern half of the state. In the early 1930s, small farmers reported that their profits on a year's crop of tobacco sometimes failed to pay the gasoline bill for hauling the crop to market. Tobacco farmers overwhelmingly supported the AAA's voluntary acreage limitations, which stabilized the market. Under the Kerr-Smith Tobacco Control Act of 1934, farmers who produced more than their quota had to pay prohibitive taxes. Domestic tobacco companies agreed to pay farmers an average price per pound, thus assuring farmers that at least some profit could be made. Tobacco farmers voluntarily signed up for AAA production quotas, produced less tobacco, and saw their profits rise. With government acreage quotas and price supports in place, tobacco farming became the most reliable source of cash for many small farmers.

In West Tennessee, farmers plowed up their cotton in exchange for the promise of federal subsidy checks. Recognizing that farmers needed better access to credit, the federal Commodity Credit Corporation began allowing cotton farmers to borrow against their crops. In 1934, Congress passed the Bankhead Cotton Control Act. Under this legislation, cotton farmers who planted more than their AAA allotments would have to pay in taxes 50 percent of the market price for their excess cotton. The effects of these enactments were not felt immediately, but in succeeding years cotton prices began to rise.

While cotton planters benefited from the New Deal, sharecroppers emerged as clear losers. When planters took land out of production, they effectively laid off tenant farmers, sometimes without notice, as a sharecropper's wife in

Cotton picking near Memphis. Philip M. Hamer, *Tennessee: A History, 1673–1932.*

Henry County recalled: the landlord "didn't say a word about our crops we was about middle ways of. The move jist came on us before we could plan for it." When tenant farmers stayed on the land and planted less cotton, the government subsidy checks went to the landowner, not to them. When tenants complained, their grievances were heard before AAA committees composed of landlords. Liberals within the federal Department of Agriculture protested and fought a long but useless battle on behalf of southern tenants, succeeding only in getting themselves fired by the Secretary of Agriculture.

In 1934, sharecroppers in Arkansas, encouraged by Socialist Party leader Norman Thomas, formed the Southern Tenant Farmers' Union (STFU) to protest layoffs and landlords' appropriation of government benefits. By 1935, the STFU had about thirty thousand members, including many West Tennessee farmers. The STFU was a biracial organization. As a black Arkansas organizer told white farmers, "The same chain that holds my people holds your people too. . . . It won't do no good for us to divide because that's what the trouble has been all the time." Faced with intense hostility from planters in Arkansas, the STFU located its headquarters in Memphis.

In 1935, the STFU called a sit-down strike during the cotton harvest, winning a 50-percent wage increase for cotton pickers. Planters retaliated with violence; hired guns frequently chased organizers from Arkansas across the bridge and into Memphis. Cotton planters looking for nonunion labor sent trucks into Memphis to carry day-laborers out to the fields. When the STFU put picket lines on the Harahan Bridge, Memphis police arrested the strikers. The STFU failed to win long-term concessions from landlords but did succeed in focusing national attention on the plight of southern tenant farmers. Although the Roosevelt administration offered some token programs for displaced farmers, they supplied very little help. Secretary of Agriculture Henry Wallace said that the cure for the farm situation was not "in making more farms and more farmers, but in making more city employment."

The Roosevelt administration's agricultural policies aimed at stabilizing agribusiness. New Deal agricultural specialists considered the resulting displacement of tenant farmers a necessary, if unfortunate, side-effect. Tenant farmer families who were thrown off the land had nowhere to go but the cities, at a time when urban employment opportunities for uneducated white farmers were scarce and for black farmers practically nonexistent. Many former tenants wound up on relief, beginning a multigenerational cycle of dependency. Some critics of the New Deal allege that the current deterioration of the nation's inner cities has its roots in New Deal cotton policy.

The New Deal and Tennessee Labor

New South promoters had lured industries to Tennessee and other southern states by promising investors a cheap, docile workforce. Despite sporadic wildcat strikes and occasional labor-related violence, the New South promise had been upheld. Southern workers were the least unionized in the nation, and Tennessee followed the regional norm. Most factory workers did not belong to unions. Skilled workers who had been through a union apprenticeship program often belonged to craft unions affiliated with the American Federation of Labor (AFL). AFL unions were segregated and predominantly white and male.

Throughout the 1920s, promoters of industry in Tennessee continued to promise businessmen that they would not be bothered with unions. Since northern investors associated unionization with immigrant labor, Tennessee industrial promoters emphasized the state's ethnic purity. In 1926, a Nashville paper noted, "It is Nashville's proud boast that more than 98 per cent of its population is native born." In 1929, the Memphis Chamber of Commerce reported that Memphis had "small likelihood of strike disturbances, because of Anglo-Saxon stock and the Negro. The latter is an excellent laborer when properly handled and is not prone to organize."

In 1929, young white native-born "Anglo-Saxon" women from the Tennessee mountains led one of the most violent strikes in the state's history when textile workers walked out of rayon plants at Elizabethton. Gov. Henry Horton sent in the National Guard to protect strikebreakers. The supposedly "docile" women workers screamed insults at guardsmen and "scabs," blocked the plant gates, and held out against National Guard tear-gas attacks. The Elizabethton strike, part of a larger general strike of southern textile workers, failed to produce lasting benefits for workers, but it foreshadowed the rise of labor militancy in the state in the 1930s.

Roosevelt's administration, unlike those of previous Republican presidents, was pro-union. Section 7(a) of the National Industrial Recovery Act (NIRA), passed in 1933, guaranteed the right of workers to organize and bargain collectively. However, union supporters argued that Section 7(a) was not enough. In 1935, Sen. Robert F. Wagner of New York introduced in Congress the National Labor Relations Act, which created a National Labor Relations Board (NLRB). The NLRB would supervise elections and intervene if management used coercive tactics against union organizers. Tennessee's senators and representatives supported the Wagner Act, probably out of loyalty to FDR, who moved to support the bill after the Supreme Court declared the earlier NIRA unconstitutional.

Meanwhile, a group of unions dissatisfied with the AFL's conservative policies, and in particular with the AFL's lack of enthusiasm for organizing industrial workers, split from the older union to form the Committee for Industrial Organization (later the Congress of Industrial Organizations, or CIO). The CIO's chief focus was unionizing the major industrial centers of the North and Midwest. But the organization's leaders knew that the South could not be written off; for years, northern factory owners had undercut union drives by threatening to move their plants south if workers instituted unions.

Elizabethton Strike, 1929

The Elizabethton textile strike of 1929 demonstrated the militancy of supposedly docile "Anglo-Saxon" workers and the independence of young rural women. Young women, many not out of their teens, led their coworkers out of two German-owned rayon mills in a strike for higher pay. The strikers affiliated with the United Textile Workers.

While Elizabethton civic boosters deplored the strike, many farmers and small-town merchants sided with the strikers. The county sheriff openly sided with the strikers, promising to protect property but not scabs. A local Baptist preacher told the strikers, "The hand of oppression is growing on our people. . . . You must come together and say that such things must cease to be." Women workers told reporters that, if they were fired, they simply would go back to the farm. "I haven't forgotten how to use a hoe," one woman said.

Governor Horton sent in the National Guard to protect strikebreakers and the rayon plants. While the Guard set up machine guns on rooftops, women workers blocked the access roads to the plants, and men dynamited the houses of "scabs" and the Elizabethton water main. About 1,250 people, including many young women, were arrested for confrontations with the National Guard. Women paraded past the Guard posts carrying American flags, forcing the Guardsmen to stand at attention and present arms to the strikers. Some local members of the National Guard resigned rather than face the jeering of young women they had known all their lives. Strikers flirted with the Guardsmen: "I told him he was too much of a man to shoot a lady." (Several marriages followed the strike.) Union organizers who came to Elizabethton were astonished at the courage and determination shown by the young mountain women, who walked the picket lines in their best modern dresses.

The organizers considered the Elizabethton strike a test case for textile organizing in the South. The result was negative: the strikers lost, and many were blacklisted. Yet labor militancy lingered on in Elizabethton. In the 1930s, Elizabethton rayon workers joined the CIO-affiliated Textile Workers Union of America, then switched to the AFL's United Textile Workers later in the decade. They formed the largest rayon workers' local in the nation.

CIO-affiliated unions began organizing in Tennessee in 1936, much to the dismay of Tennessee businessmen and politicians, who considered the new organization a Communist-dominated plot to destroy southern industrial advantages and white supremacy. In truth, the CIO *did* welcome Communists as members, *was* committed to integrated unions, and *did* threaten to end the state's low-wage advantage in recruiting industry, by raising the wages of southern workers. The CIO made Nashville and Memphis primary targets for its 1937 organizing drive. In Nashville, the CIO successfully organized publishing, meat packing, and textile factories, adding ten unions, with about seven thousand members, to its roster.

The CIO's gains in Nashville were balanced by defeats in Memphis, where the organizing drive met staunch opposition from city government. The Crump machine was not strictly anti-union. Leaders of the AFL were accepted into Crump's inner circle. The Memphis machine also allowed the CIO's International Ladies Garment Worker's Union to organize three small clothing manufacturing companies in the city. But Crump, Mayor Watkins Overton, and city police chief Will Lee publicly announced that they would not allow the CIO to organize large industrial plants in Memphis. Memphis's anti-union policy became a factor in luring businesses to the city. In 1936–37, just as the CIO's southern campaign began, the Memphis city government persuaded Firestone Tire and Rubber to open a Memphis plant that would employ 1,500 workers by promising to keep the CIO out. (Firestone moved to Memphis, and trucked workers to the polls on election day, with instructions to vote the Crump ticket.)

When the CIO-affiliated United Automobile Workers sent an organizer to Memphis in 1937 to unionize Ford and Fisher Body, Mayor Watkins Overton denounced the union as "communists and highly paid professional organizers. . . . They care nothing for Memphis—only to use us if they could. . . . Let them go elsewhere, if anyone wants them. We don't, and we won't tolerate them."

The Memphis police commissioner promised that "we will free Memphis of these unwanted people." The following night unidentified assailants beat the CIO man severely; when he got out of the hospital, he was attacked again. The UAW leadership and most of the nation thought the Memphis city government was behind the assaults. City, state, and federal authorities in Memphis refused to investigate the incident. Defeated, the UAW called its organizer home to Detroit. Crump wrote to Senator McKellar, "Everyone has forgotten about the CIO down this way. Don't hear anything about it." In 1940, efforts to organize the Firestone plant failed in a similar manner. Firestone finally was organized by an all-white AFL union, with the support of Memphis city officials. As Crump had promised, Memphis remained outside the influence of the CIO.

The CIO concentrated its efforts in the cities. But many Tennessee factories and mines were small and far from urban centers. During the 1930s, places

Highlander School

The Highlander Folk School staff rose to national prominence during the labor struggles of the 1930s. Founded in 1932 in Grundy County by Myles Horton and Don West, Highlander offered classes in union organizing and labor law. Zilphia Horton, Myles's wife, taught union songs to striking workers. Southern workers sang her adaptation of an old hymn, "We Shall Overcome," on picket lines in the 1930s, long before the song became a civil rights anthem.

In 1937, the CIO asked Highlander to manage the organization's southern education drive. By the 1940s, Highlander had become the CIO's center for worker education in the South. Grundy County authorities, and conservatives throughout the state, considered Highlander a center of Communist agitation and repeatedly threatened to either shut it down or blow it up. Highlander members denied connections with the Communist party but prided themselves on their opposition to class and racial oppression.

Much to the disgust of regional conservatives, Highlander had friends in high places. In 1940, Secretary of State Cordell Hull helped sponsor a fundraising concert for the school in Washington, attended by First Lady Eleanor Roosevelt.

After World War II, Highlander became a school for civil rights activists. Perhaps the most famous "graduate" was Rosa Parks, who had attended a Highlander class on resistance to segregation shortly before her arrest for violating segregation laws on Montgomery, Alabama, bus lines. Her action sparked the birth of the modern civil rights movement.

like the coal mines at Davidson-Wilder in Fentress County and the Richmond Hosiery Mills in Soddy-Daisy became literal battlegrounds, complete with gun battles, bombings, and midnight assassinations, as workers and management struggled for control. Generally management won. At the end of the 1930s, organized labor could point to only mixed success in Tennessee.

Tennessee Valley Authority

In most of the country, electricity is supplied by privately owned power companies, whose main objective (like that of any corporation) is to maximize profits. Such was the case in Tennessee before the 1930s. The result was that, while Tennessee cities and towns had electrical power, the majority of farms did not, since stringing lines far out into the countryside was not profitable. While urban Tennesseans enjoyed the benefits of modern technologies, the energy gap meant that most rural Tennesseans' way of life had not changed since the late nineteenth century.

Advocates of publicly owned utilities, ranging from Sen. George Norris of Nebraska to Boss Crump, argued that government should build and run utilities. Opponents held that power production was a business like any other and that power was best provided by private enterprise. For many, state-supplied electrical power smacked of socialism. However, during World War I, the Army Corps of Engineers began construction of Wilson Dam at Muscle Shoals, Alabama, to supply hydroelectric power for a government gunpowder plant. The plant was converted to fertilizer production after the war. Senator Norris quickly realized that the dam could be the nucleus of a government-run utility, providing a "yardstick" by which private utilities' claims about the costs of producing electrical power could be measured. This information could be used by authorities throughout the nation to regulate utility costs. During the 1920s, Norris led the battle in Congress to keep the Muscle Shoals installation from being sold or leased to private companies.

The Nebraska senator repeatedly introduced legislation in Congress that foreshadowed the eventual TVA, only to have his bills voted down or vetoed. By the early 1930s, most southern congressmen had come to support Norris's initiative, believing that cheap electrical power was essential for economic development in the region. Opposition came from northeastern Republicans, who were opposed to government competition with business. But when FDR was elected in 1932, Norris's prospects looked much better. FDR long had been a friend of public power. He visited Muscle Shoals with Norris in January 1933 and began to talk publicly about the potential for regional reform inherent in a Tennessee Valley project. Roosevelt envisioned TVA as an experiment in regional planning and development, to include "yardstick" electrical plants, flood control, reforestation, conservation, and general improvement in the situation of the valley's population, who numbered among the nation's poorest. Encouraged, Norris and his staff had a new Muscle Shoals bill ready to go before FDR officially took office in March 1933. Introduced in the House of Representatives by Rep. Lister Hill and strongly supported by Tennessee's congressional delegation, the Tennessee Valley Authority (TVA) Act of 1933 was passed by Congress and signed by FDR in May 1933. The new agency was headquartered in Knoxville.

The TVA's early development was hampered by controversy inside the agency and opposition without. The agency's chairman, Arthur Morgan, feuded with the other two members of the TVA board, David Lilienthal and Harcourt Morgan, formerly president of the University of Tennessee, until FDR fired him in 1938. A more serious threat was a series of lawsuits by

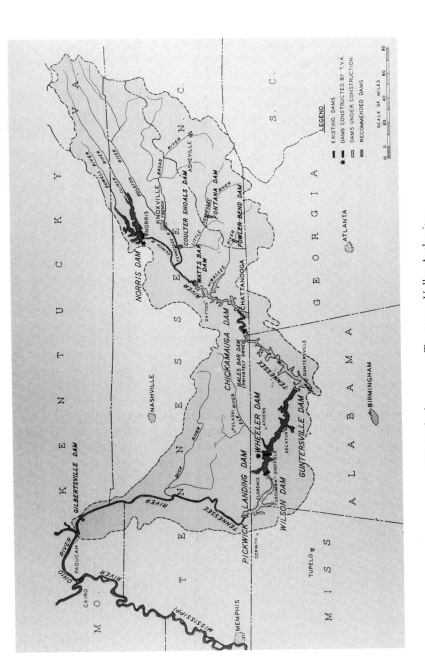

TVA in the late 1930s. Tennessee Valley Authority.

private power companies, including Tennessee Electric Power Company, which served Nashville and other Tennessee cities, and Memphis Power and Light. Through litigation, the private utilities wanted to prevent TVA from selling electricity in competition with them or, if that failed, to prevent the agency from expanding throughout the region. The private companies also hoped that their lawsuits ultimately might reach the Supreme Court, which might rule TVA unconstitutional. However, in 1936, the Supreme Court upheld a circuit court decision in favor of TVA's right to generate and sell power from Wilson Dam at Muscle Shoals; and in 1938, a federal court in Chattanooga ruled that the agency was constitutional and that its generation and sale of electrical power did not exceed its legislative mandate. By refusing to hear the private utilities' appeal of this case, the Supreme Court signaled that TVA would not be found unconstitutional. After 1938, private utility companies began to sell their properties to TVA or municipalities, and public power became the norm throughout the state.

Despite litigation and bureaucratic infighting, between 1933 and 1951, TVA built multiple dams on the Tennessee River and its tributaries, including Norris Dam on the Clinch River in East Tennessee and Pickwick Dam in West Tennessee. The new dams helped control flooding and improved navigation, and effectively eradicated malaria from the Tennessee River Valley. Construction employed thousands of men, the first clear economic benefit to the valley. Agency agricultural specialists gave valley farmers training in new methods and encouraged the use of cheap phosphate fertilizers developed at TVA research stations. TVA encouraged its employees to unionize and bargain collectively. The agency built "model villages" at dam construction sites and established rural libraries and bookmobiles, which it then turned over to local authorities. Tennessee's state park system benefited from TVA's donation of lakeshore lands, and the state's Conservation Department began with TVA support.

Tennessee cities and towns moved as quickly as possible to obtain cheap TVA electricity. Boss Crump, who had favored public power since his first term as Memphis's mayor, considered TVA a fulfillment of his lifelong dream. With the Crump machine's strong encouragement, Memphis residents voted seventeen to one in favor of switching the city's power from Memphis Power and Light to TVA, and Mayor Overton obtained a PWA grant to build or purchase transmission lines. Tennessee Electric Power Company sold its facilities in Nashville and Chattanooga to the municipal governments. Because cheap TVA power allowed poor people to afford electrical service, electric heat replaced coal stoves, and cities became much cleaner.

TVA's impact on rural Tennesseans was even greater. Through the Rural Electrification Agency, country people could form electrical cooperatives and purchase TVA power. Most farm families began by putting up lights (usually in the center of the room, and turned on by a long, dangling string) and purchasing their first electrical appliance: the electric iron, to replace the literal irons that had to be heated atop a stove. Electric radios, sewing machines, heaters, stoves, and refrigerators followed as the Depression ended in the 1940s. Electric pumps made indoor plumbing feasible. In sum, TVA electricity brought the valley's residents into the twentieth century. The agency provided the power behind the state's subsequent economic development.

The agency's achievements did not come without a cost. Building Norris Dam alone required the removal of thousands of people. In a pattern that would be repeated throughout the valley, the agency compensated landowners (but not tenant farmers) for the loss of their land, assisted in relocation, and moved churches and cemeteries. Despite all good-faith efforts by the agency, being evicted from family land embittered many East Tennesseans, some of whom maintain their hostility toward the agency to this day. Others mourned the loss of home and community but took consolation in TVA jobs. The TVA's ecological impact, while not of much interest to job-hungry Tennesseans in the 1930s, is of greater concern to conservationists now. The agency's dams made the Tennessee the nation's most controlled river. In the 1930s, no surveys of endangered species slowed dam construction. Finally, TVA, like other New Deal agencies, replicated the South's racial policies. Although the agency's policies promised equitable treatment, TVA failed to hire blacks in proportion to their presence in the population; employed those blacks hired only for the most menial, low-paying jobs; and failed to provide black workers with living quarters equal to those afforded whites, despite protests from black leaders in the valley and criticism by the NAACP.

Boss Crump and Governor Browning

By the 1930s, Edward Crump had become the king-maker of Tennessee politics. Crump's power derived from Tennessee voters' apathy, amplified by a poll tax that made voting expensive for poor people. During the 1920s, 1930s, and early 1940s, less than one-third of the state's eligible voters, or about 450,000 people, bothered to go to the polls. The Republican vote, concentrated in East Tennessee, was insufficient to threaten Democratic control of the governorship. The candidate who amassed the approximately 150,000 votes necessary to win the Democratic primary became governor of Tennessee. Boss Crump controlled Shelby County's 50,000 votes. Candidates with his support needed only 100,000 votes from elsewhere in the state to win; those without Crump's approval found it difficult to line up support or raise funds, since professionals considered their campaigns lost causes before they started.

Crump's drive for control of the state's politics grew from his desire to protect his fiefdom in Memphis from interference by a governor or state legislature. Crump never forgot how he had been deposed as mayor because he refused to enforce prohibition in Memphis, and he devoted his career to making sure that this could not happen again. By the 1930s, national newspapers found him an irresistibly gaudy anachronism. Born in 1874 in Holly Springs, Mississippi, to impoverished gentry, Crump by the 1930s had aged into the very model of an old-fashioned southern gentleman. Attired in custom-made suits, sporting a mane of snowy white hair, courtly in his demeanor, Crump loved a parade, took busloads of children and old people to the circus, and drove down to Holly Springs every Sunday to visit his mother. His loyalties were fierce, as were his hatreds, and he expressed them publicly in full-page ads purchased in Memphis papers. He gave Memphis clean, safe streets, parks, and public recreational facilities; kept city vice and crime under control; and created a pro-business, pro-development climate that excluded unions and included cheap TVA power. His enemies charged that he, or his cronies, also "voted" Memphis citizens, white and black, as if they were the subjects of a Caribbean "banana republic"; authorized the beating of union organizers; terrorized black leaders who got out of line; frightened political opponents so much that they were scared to campaign in Memphis; and demanded that everyone, from WPA workers to prostitutes and gamblers, contribute to the machine's campaign funds.

The controversy that Crump stirred up during his lifetime makes it hard even now to assess the man. Personally honest, Crump made a point of keeping his finances strictly separate from those of the city. His stand on national issues was that of a liberal, albeit tinged with paternalistic racism. In 1930 he was elected to Congress and served through the first years of the New Deal, supporting every measure introduced by the Roosevelt administration. Crump disliked giving speeches and preferred to exert influence behind the scene. Journalists who observed him in Washington described him as a polished, well-dressed man out to get his way with "smooth words and gentle hints." During the 1930s, Crump's opponents in Memphis seem to have been beaten up on a regular basis, but the violence cannot be traced directly to Crump himself. Like a monarch, he held himself aloof from the day-to-day workings of his kingdom. Crump always had "deniability."

Although the Memphis newspapers, particularly the *Press-Scimitar*, deplored Crump's control of Memphis, most people in Memphis did not seem to mind. By their willingness to line up behind Crump in election after election, Memphis residents attested that the machine gave them good value for their vote. Although members of the organization used brutality when necessary to maintain their control, most of the machine's success came from good organization. The machine dunned the business community for campaign contributions, paid poll taxes, supplied supporters with receipts so that they could vote, and transported its voters to the polls on election day. With deep pockets and good organization, the Shelby County machine carried election after election, to the consternation of politicians elsewhere in the state. After years of hearing Crump denounced as an evil political genius (no one doubted his skill), many rural Tennesseans saw him, and Memphis residents in general, as epitomes of urban wickedness: a bunch of drinking, gambling, carousing, corrupt river rats, many of whom were black, Jewish, or Catholic. For bigots throughout the state, the very fact that blacks were allowed to vote in Memphis was enough to condemn the Crump machine.

The 1932 gubernatorial election signaled Crump's ascendancy. In a three-man race among Hill McAlister; Lewis Pope, who had been a member of Austin Peay's administration; and former Gov. Malcolm Patterson, remembered chiefly for his pardon of Duncan Cooper after the Carmack shooting, Crump and Senator McKellar supported McAlister. Luke Lea backed his former enemy, Patterson. Crump denounced Patterson as "the same local and long-distance liar that he has been for years. . . . Drunk or sober, he is the same Patterson today as of old." Pope received no support from any faction of professional politicians. Although McAlister won the race, Pope came in a close second and would have won if not for Shelby County's votes. Pope charged that the Crump machine had defeated him by "voting" ineligible blacks and stuffing ballot boxes. The *Memphis Press-Scimitar* protested that to allow the votes of Memphis blacks to nullify "the vote of white Democrats in a score or more of the smaller counties in Tennessee, is a disgrace." Pope mounted an independent campaign against McAlister in the general election, but McAlister easily defeated both Pope and the Republican candidate. Seasoned political observers realized that, in coalition, Crump and McKellar now controlled a political organization that dominated the state.

McAlister proved a disappointment to Crump. Reformers, concerned that Austin Peay had concentrated power in the governor's office, making it possible for the Horton administration to loot the state, were pleased that McAlister supported measures transferring budgeting and accounting out of the governor's hands. However, McAlister did little to raise state revenues or diminish the state debt. Though displeased by the governor's lackadaisical administration and his 1934 announcement in favor of state-wide prohibition, Crump supported him for reelection because he lacked a viable alternative, and McAlister was reelected.

In 1934, a new player emerged on the Tennessee political scene. Gordon Browning, a six-term congressman from Carroll County, challenged the Crump machine's candidate for the Senate seat vacated by Cordell Hull, who had resigned to become FDR's secretary of state. Although Browning lost, the race gave him visibility throughout the state. Browning was most popular among veterans of World War I. He had commanded Battery A, a National Guard unit from Memphis, and he numbered among his friends veterans who supported opposing factions in state politics, including high-ranking members of the Memphis machine and Crump's greatest enemy, Luke Lea. Browning saw the post of governor as a stepping-stone to his ultimate goal, McKellar's seat in the Senate.

In 1936, Browning announced that he would run for governor. McAlister, knowing that his attempt to get the General Assembly to enact a sales tax had cost him Crump's support, decided not to run for reelection; and Crump indicated that the Memphis machine would be neutral in the race. But Senator McKellar, aware that Browning planned to oppose him in 1940, supported education commissioner Burgin Dossett for governor. Browning proved to be a highly effective campaigner. Realizing that McKellar's man was going to lose, Crump abandoned his long-term alliance with the senator to announce his last-minute support for Browning, who won the primary and the general election. Shelby County's votes increased his majority, but Browning would have won without Crump's support, making him the rare Tennessee politician who did not owe his victory to Crump. Nonetheless, Browning thanked Mayor Overton for the city's support: "More than sixty thousand reasons why I love Shelby County."

Browning's first months in office were a resounding success. With the General Assembly's enthusiastic support, Browning reorganized state government, creating a Department of Administration, including divisions of accounts, budget, personnel, and purchasing; a Department of Conservation, to oversee state parks, game management, and tourism; and a new Department of Institutions and Welfare, through which the new welfare programs mandated by the Social Security Act of 1935 would be administered. Browning named Wallace Edwards, who had been Governor Horton's secretary, as commissioner of the new Department of Administration.

During his campaign, Browning had promised to "clean up" state government. As governor, he created a commission to investigate corruption in all state institutions and departments, and placed former gubernatorial candidate Lewis Pope in charge. Browning also obtained passage of a bill creating a civil service merit system in hiring for state jobs.

As a candidate, Browning endorsed the Tennessee Education Association's "Eight Point Program" for improving schools and raising teachers' salaries. As governor, he submitted the TEA's proposal to the General Assembly and worked hard for its passage. The General Education Act of 1937 increased funding for schools, established a minimum term of eight months for elementary schools and nine months for secondary schools, and required the state board of education to set minimum pay standards for teachers, with increases to be based on education and experience, thus effectively raising teachers' salaries.

When the Depression began, Tennessee's state debt stood at $97 million. During the early thirties, as state revenues declined, the debt had not been retired, but instead refinanced with more bonds. By 1936, the debt was almost $129 million. As governor, Browning's task was twofold: to find more revenue for the state and to develop a plan for paying off the state debt. He took to the state legislature the first general revenue bill proposed since 1931. It included increases in existing taxes and new privilege taxes on over one hundred different kinds of businesses, ranging from restaurants to vending machines. After heated debate, the General Assembly passed the bill on March 5, 1937, and then recessed. During the break, Governor Browning and members of his cabinet consulted with New York financiers to put together a debt retirement plan that would satisfy the investors who held Tennessee bonds. The Browning plan consolidated all the outstanding debts into one package to be paid for with new consolidated bonds, which would be funded from specified tax revenues. While members of the business community praised the plan, the Shelby County delegation tried to block passage in the General Assembly. Browning prevailed, and the Debt-Reorganization Act passed the General Assembly in May 1937. Tennessee's credit rating soared. In Browning's view, getting the General Assembly to approve debt refinancing was the most outstanding achievement of his administration.

Browning took office in January 1937. By May, he had pushed through the General Assembly more important legislation than any governor since Austin Peay. But the popular and powerful governor proceeded to damage his political career in an ill-considered attack on his only rival in the state, Boss Crump. Although Crump had supported Browning in 1936, he began to turn against the governor when Browning appointed friends and allies of Luke Lea to important positions in his administration. Senator McKellar, Crump's long-time friend and ally, knew that Browning intended to challenge him for the Senate in 1940. He convinced Crump that Browning, as congressman, had not supported TVA. For his part, the governor charged that Crump tried to exert too much influence over appointments and over state government in general. Browning said that he told Crump, "You can ride if you want to but you can't drive. I'm driving this wagon. I'm governor of Tennessee."

After a summer of rumors and behind-the-scenes skirmishes, Browning opened hostilities in October 1937. He called the legislature into special session and pushed through two bills designed to destroy Crump's machine. One authorized the state government to go through the voter registration books in Shelby County and purge them of fraudulent voters. The other, and more serious, enacted a county unit voting system in the Democratic primary. Under such a system, the candidate who carried a county would get one vote, and the man who got a majority of counties would win. Shelby County's sixty thousand votes thus would weigh equally with the votes of the state's smallest rural county. Rural legislators supported Browning's measure, but many people who had opposed the Memphis machine for years were appalled that Browning would take an action that effectively disfranchised the voters of Memphis. When the measure passed, the trustee of Shelby County immediately obtained an injunction against its enforcement and began litigation that ultimately would reach the state supreme court. In November, Browning called the legislature into another special session to increase the membership of the State Board of Elections; Browning planned to pack the enlarged board with his supporters. In a radio address, Browning said, "My fellow citizens, a statement by the great apostle I verily believe to be fitting here, when he said: 'For we wrestle not against flesh and blood, but against principalities, against powers, against the rulers of the darkness of this world, against spiritual wickedness in high places.'" Browning's measure passed, and the Election Board was increased in size and authorized to appoint county election board members. More injunctions were filed.

In February 1938, the state supreme court ruled that the county unit system was unconstitutional. Citing the Fourteenth Amendment, the court in effect said that Memphis voters could not be denied the right to vote for no good reason. In March, however, the court upheld the legislative act that had enlarged the State Elections Board, a victory for Browning. Meanwhile, Crump and McKellar prepared to fight Browning's reelection at the polls that fall. Searching for a candidate to back, they settled on a state senator, Prentice Cooper of Shelbyville. Cooper, a veteran of World War I, was a lawyer without any ties to the Memphis machine. Crump supported him because he had a chance of beating Browning.

During the 1938 Democratic primary campaign, both sides fought hard and dirty. Browning called Crump a dictator, and Crump retaliated by calling the governor an ingrate. The governor's specially appointed "crime commission" came to Memphis to conduct hearings, during which the Memphis machine was accused of bribery and vote fraud. When the Browning administration made plans to send troops into Memphis on election day, the Memphis machine obtained a restraining order, and a federal marshal delivered it to Browning when he made a speech at the Memphis fairgrounds on August 1. Although the governor depicted his trip to Memphis as an act of courage, Crump was not so foolish as to use violence against Browning. Instead, he concentrated on getting out the vote for Cooper. On August 4, Browning was soundly defeated, losing to Cooper 238,000 to 150,000.

Having attempted to destroy Boss Crump, Browning had succeeded only in making the Memphis machine more dominant in state politics than ever before. Governor Cooper never took orders from Crump, but he maintained friendly relations with the Memphis boss and won reelection in 1940 and 1944 with his support. McKellar fought off all challenges to his continued tenure as senator, winning reelection to another six-year term in 1940 and again in 1946.

Back home in Memphis, Crump consolidated his power through attacks on the black community. During the 1920s, Crump had an arrangement with Robert Church Jr. and other black Republicans: blacks voted as Crump told them in local and state elections, Church channeled federal patronage to Memphis, and Crump supplied civic services to black neighborhoods. But in the 1930s, with a Democrat in the White House, Crump no longer needed Church's federal connections. Church's own Memphis power base began to crumble, as blacks began to leave the Republican Party to join the Democrats. The NAACP, which had withered under Church's control, was rejuvenated through the activities of younger and more radical black leaders affiliated with New Deal programs and the

CIO. Crump reacted with what one historian has called "a reign of terror" against blacks in Memphis. According to the NAACP, the Memphis machine withheld federal funds from public works projects in black districts, including Beale Street, arrested blacks on trumped-up charges, and threatened black ministers and journalists who supported the NAACP. In 1938, when Church protested machine control of Memphis politics, the city sent him a bill for $80,000 in back property taxes. The former "boss" of black Memphis had to liquidate his real-estate holdings in his native city to pay the bill. Defeated, Church moved to Chicago. During the 1940 election, druggist J. B. Martin attempted to revive support for the Republican Party in the black community. In retaliation, the Memphis machine stationed police outside Martin's store and those owned by his supporters, with orders to search every customer who entered. The police commissioner wrote letters to black leaders, accusing them of "presumptuous ingratitude" and warning, "This is white man's country, and always will be, and any negro who doesn't agree had better move on." But a new generation of black leaders already had begun to organize voter awareness groups in Memphis, in preparation for the ultimate demise of Crump's machine.

Moving Out: World War II in Tennessee

After the Japanese attack on Pearl Harbor on December 7, 1941, Tennesseans went back to work with a vengeance. As the nation shifted to wartime production, the economy boomed. Factories had trouble finding enough workers. As young men shipped out to war, women took their place on factory floors. Thousands of rural Tennesseans, black and white, moved to towns and cities to work in defense plants. White Tennesseans made their way north to industrial cities in Illinois, Michigan, and Ohio. Scorned as "hillbillies," hicks, and rubes by northern city folks, many white Tennesseans worked all week in Detroit and drove "back home" every weekend, while others settled in their own ethnic communities, "Little Appalachias" to match the "Little Italys" and "Chinatowns" that dotted American cities. Thousands of black Tennesseans left the state entirely to find jobs in the North and on the West Coast, continuing the migration out of the South that had begun in 1919. Although Tennesseans worried about family members in service and were irritated by wartime rationing of gasoline, sugar, and other commodities, for most, the war years were good times; after a decade of despair, jobs were plentiful, and the future looked bright.

In the state's urban centers, factories converted to wartime production, and new plants sprang up. Manufacturers moved to the state to take advantage of TVA power. In Memphis, about one hundred plants manufactured war-related materials. These firms ranged from Firestone, which switched from producing tires to producing life rafts, to a former Piggly-Wiggly store equipment plant that made tables upon which people folded parachutes. In Nashville, a

Cornelia Fort

On December 7, 1941, Cornelia Fort was doing what she loved best: flying. Born in Nashville in 1919 to upper-class parents and educated at Ward-Belmont and Sarah Lawrence College, Fort had walked away from a wealthy debutante's life to become an aviator. By the spring of 1941, she had obtained her commercial license and instructor's rating, and in October 1941, she moved to Hawaii. She was in the skies above Honolulu giving a flying lesson when the Japanese began their bombing run on Pearl Harbor. Although the Japanese shot at her small plane, Fort managed to land.

As military service drained away male pilots, the government called for women flyers to act as instructors and to fly missions within the United States. In 1942, Fort signed up for an all-female aircraft ferrying group. In 1943, Fort's group became part of the Women's Airforce Service Pilots (WASPs). Although the women's service could be hazardous—they flew new, untested planes from factory to airfield; trained male pilots; and occasionally towed dummy planes for novice gunners to practice shooting at—at first WASPs received no military status or benefits. Nonetheless, Fort wrote letters home indicating that she enjoyed her job.

In March 1943, Fort became the first American woman to die in service during World War II. A student pilot, attempting to show off, flew too close and hit her plane. Fort was buried in Nashville's Mount Olivet Cemetery. Cornelia Fort Airpark in Nashville was named in her honor.

new Vultee Aircraft plant opened in 1941, employing seven thousand Nashville workers, while older companies converted to wartime production.

Middle Tennesseans got used to seeing young men in uniform, passing through on their way to Camp Campbell near Clarksville, Camp Forrest in Tullahoma, and Smyrna Air Field; or on maneuvers. Because of its mild climate and varied terrain, Tennessee became a favorite site for military "war games" and other training exercises. Nashvillians scrambled to provide housing and "wholesome entertainment" for the soldiers who visited the capital city: one million during the first year of the war, over two million during maneuvers. The best efforts of concerned citizens were not enough; the town was so crowded with soldiers that they slept in the parks and streets. Honky-tonks thrived, and the hundreds of prostitutes who walked the streets around Capitol Hill, trolling for lonely soldiers, faced competi-

Vultee Aircraft Plant, Nashville. Department of Conservation Collection, Tennessee State Library and Archives, Nashville.

tion from amateur "khaki whackies," young women who loved men in uniforms. Venereal disease reached epidemic proportions.

The war transformed the economy of upper East Tennessee. Knoxville flourished as workers, drawn to East Tennessee to work in local factories, at Oak Ridge, and at TVA, poured into the mountain city in search of housing, shopping, and entertainment. In 1943, the per capita income of Knoxvillians was twice the state average and higher than the national average by over $200. Kingston experienced a similar boom, due to the Holston Ordnance Works.

Built from scratch during the 1940s, Oak Ridge owed its existence to the war. Gen. Leslie Groves, director of the secret Manhattan Project to build an atomic weapon, chose Oak Ridge as the project site for uranium isotope production. Groves wanted a place relatively isolated from major population centers, since no one knew how dangerous producing uranium isotopes might turn out to be, and close to electrical power. Work on the "Clinton Engineer Works" began in 1942. The government acquired a strip of land along the Clinch River seventeen miles long and seven miles wide, and surrounded it with fences and sentry posts. Inside the fences, the government built a gaseous diffusion plant, later operated by Union Carbide; a plant to house an atomic pile, operated by the Metallurgical Laboratory of the Uni-

Table 11.2. Tennessee Population, by Race, 1900–1940
(Percentage)

Year	White	Black
1900	76.2	23.8
1910	78.3	21.7
1920	80.7	19.3
1930	81.7	18.3
1940	82.5	17.4

SOURCE: U.S. Census, Population, 1940.

Table 11.3. Farmers: Owners, Managers, and Tenants,
1910–1935

	1910	1920	1925	1930	1935
Total Farms	246,012	252,774	252,669	245,657	273,783
Percent Owners	58.6	58.6	58.8	53.5	53.6
Percent Managers	0.3	0.3	0.1	0.2	0.2
Percent Tenants	41.1	41.1	41.0	46.2	46.2

SOURCE: U.S. Census, Agriculture, 1940.

versity of Chicago; a giant electromagnetic plant, operated by Tennessee Eastman Corporation; and a town to house workers.

By the end of the war, 75,000 people lived in Oak Ridge, and more commuted daily from Knoxville and other nearby towns to bring the peak workforce to over 89,000. Scientists and army officers lived in quickly constructed houses along instantly created tree-lined streets. Common female and male workers, mostly white southerners from Tennessee and adjacent states, lived in crowded, noisy barracks. Black workers, male and female, were housed in huts on the edge of the new town. Despite shortages, inconveniences, and constant reminders of being under military authority, worker morale was high: clearly, whatever they were making, it was important.

Oak Ridge got under way without the support, or even the knowledge, of state officials. When land appropriation began in 1942, Anderson County leaders went to Nashville to complain that the evicted families had been treated unfairly. They found that no one in the capital seemed to know anything about the "Clinton Engineer Works." Gov. Prentice Cooper was not

"To Hell with Roy Acuff"

According to legend, Japanese troops in the Pacific taunted American soldiers with a peculiar battle cry: "To hell with Roy Acuff!" While Japanese knowledge of American popular culture was limited, even these Asians had heard of the star of the Grand Old Opry.

In 1939, NBC radio began carrying the Opry, hosted by Acuff. Listeners nationwide were introduced to hillbilly music. During the war, country music performers played for soldiers in stateside army bases. Southern workers migrating to defense plant jobs in the North and West, too, crowded into bars to hear music that reminded them of home. The market for country music continued to expand.

Some of the most popular country songs of the 1940s reflected a sense of dislocation and alienation shared by many Americans in a decade of rapid social change. In addition to lauding the old folks back home in the mountains, the faithful sweetheart far away, and the American flag, country songs in the mid-forties began to explore unfaithful wives, cheating husbands, drinking, and wrecks on the highway. This tough new style of music, which came to be called "honky-tonk" after the bars in which it was first performed, gained national attention in the late 1940s through the performances and recordings of Hank Williams. After the war, recording studios began opening in Nashville to cash in on the new popularity of country music, and Nashville's current music industry began to develop.

briefed on the project until the summer of 1943, when a lowly army captain came to Nashville to tell the governor that a part of his state was about to be put off limits to all but authorized personnel. Cooper, who was noted for his hot temper, accused the army of stealing the farmers' land and of disguising a New Deal experiment in socialism as a war project. When the captain gave him Public Proclamation Number 2, which put the project under "total exclusion," Cooper refused to read it, tore up his copies, and threw them away. As the years passed, the military and project personnel at Oak Ridge became more adept in dealing with local and state authorities.

On August 6, 1945, the first atomic bomb, made with the uranium isotope U-235, was dropped on the Japanese city of Hiroshima. While some project workers expressed moral concern or sadness over the deaths of Japanese civilians, most were jubilant that the war was over. They crowded into the streets to cheer victory and their contribution to it. On January 1, 1947, the military

---

Outside the Fence

East Tennesseans watched in wonder, concern, and resentment as fences went up around Oak Ridge. Since the military could not explain the importance of the secret project, local folks did not understand why their lives were being disrupted. Some of the evicted families had been forced to move once or twice already, from lands taken for the Great Smoky Mountains National Park in the 1920s or Norris Dam in the 1930s. One local man said, "The only difference is when the Yankees came before, we could shoot at them."

Clinton, seat of Anderson County, was the gateway to Oak Ridge and bore the brunt of the Clinton Engineer Works (CEW), as the project was called. At first, the CEW's presence in Clinton was small: a telephone in a room above the Blue Moon Cafe. But as Oak Ridge grew, Clinton was swamped with strangers seeking housing. The town's football field and fairgrounds became trailer parks, and townspeople rented out any available living space, from attics to chicken coops. Prostitutes and bootleggers, realizing the business opportunities inherent in large numbers of young, single, male construction workers, swarmed into Clinton. Prohibitionist East Tennesseans disapproved of drinking; the young men and women at Oak Ridge wanted to party when their work was done. The city police force had to be increased, and arrests for public drunkenness jumped from one in 1940 to over two hundred in 1943. Oak Ridge employees speeding to work forced local residents off the road so often that, in 1943, twenty-one CEW guards were loaned to the county sheriff's department to keep order on the highways.

---

handed over control of the Oak Ridge facilities to the newly created Atomic Energy Commission, and Oak Ridge became a civilian town.

Portents of Things to Come

A Tennessee woman reminiscing about the years in which her friends and family scattered to military service and defense plant jobs from California to Oak Ridge recalled that her father waited impatiently for his sons to come home and take up farming. "Dad thought it would be just like it used to be. But of course it wasn't. The war changed everything." When her brothers came back from the army, they found jobs in town, becoming part of a migration of rural Tennesseans to urban areas that began in the 1940s and increased noticeably in the 1950s. Like young men and women throughout the state, they had no desire to see life return to "just like it used to be." Two very different sets of veterans signaled the younger generation's discontent most clearly in Athens and Columbia.

In McMinn County, returning veterans challenged the local Democratic machine, which for a decade had been accused of vote fraud and improper use of police power. Angered at the treatment they received from county sheriff's deputies, the GIs put together a political party and ran candidates for the 1946 election. The local machine prepared for the election by hiring three hundred deputies from outside the county. On election day, deputies arrested a GI poll watcher, held two others hostage, and shot an elderly black farmer when he tried to vote. At the end of the day, a small group of infuriated GIs broke into the National Guard Armory and the county's construction supplies; helped themselves to rifles, machine guns, and dynamite; and assaulted the courthouse, blowing up police cars and shooting several people. The machine's forces surrendered the ballot boxes, and the GI Party won the election.

Blacks well remembered that whites had used violence to reaffirm white supremacy after World War I. When, in February 1946, a black family got into an altercation with a clerk in a Columbia store, blacks in the town feared reprisals from whites. Black veterans took up arms, established a defensive perimeter around the town's black district, and shot out streetlights so that their rooftop sentries would not be seen. When Columbia city policemen trying to enter the area were shot, the county sheriff called the state for help but disapproved when the highway patrol's solution was to arm the white mob that had gathered in town. State authorities dispatched the National Guard to Columbia to restore order. Twenty-five black men were arrested. Due to public anger in Columbia, their trial was held in Lawrenceburg, where all but two were acquitted. The case received national attention and became a factor in the growth of the postwar civil rights movement.

The Battle of Athens symbolized the refusal of younger voters to submit any longer to machine political rule, while the Columbia race riot indicated that the black community's willingness to submit to political and social oppression was nearing an end. During the next decade, the generation that fought its country's enemies in Europe and the Pacific would fight for reforms in politics and race relations at home in Tennessee.

Suggested Readings

Biles, Roger. *Memphis in the Great Depression.* Knoxville, Tenn., 1986.
————. *The South and the New Deal.* Lexington, Ky., 1994.
Doyle, Don Harrison. *Nashville Since the 1920s.* Knoxville, Tenn., 1985.
Grant, Nancy. *TVA and Black Americans: Planning for the Status Quo.* Philadelphia, Pa., 1990.
Glen, John M. *Highlander: No Ordinary School.* 2nd ed. Knoxville, Tenn., 1996.
Hall, Jacquelyn Dowd. "Disorderly Women: Gender and Labor Militancy

in the Appalachian South." In *Unequal Sisters: A Multi-Cultural Reader in U.S. Women's History,* 2d ed. Edited by Vicki L. Ruiz and Ellen Carol DuBois, 348–71. New York, 1994.

Hargrove, Erwin C., and Paul Conkin. *TVA: Fifty Years of Grass-roots Bureaucracy.* Urbana, Ill., 1983.

Honey, Michael K. *Southern Labor and Black Civil Rights: Organizing Memphis Workers.* Urbana, Ill., 1993.

Horton, Myles. *The Long Haul.* New York, 1990.

Johnson, Charles W., and Charles O. Jackson. *City Behind a Fence: Oak Ridge, Tennessee, 1942–1946.* Knoxville, Tenn., 1981.

Lamon, Lester C. *Blacks in Tennessee, 1791–1970.* Knoxville, Tenn., 1981.

Majors, William R. *Change and Continuity: Tennessee Politics Since the Civil War.* Macon, Ga., 1986.

———. *The End of Arcadia: Gordon Browning and Tennessee Politics.* Memphis, Tenn., 1982.

McDonald, Michael J., and John Muldowny. *TVA and the Dispossessed: The Resettlement of Population in the Norris Dam Area.* Knoxville, Tenn., 1982.

McDonald, Michael J., and William Bruce Wheeler. *Knoxville, Tennessee: Continuity and Change in an Appalachian City.* Knoxville, Tenn., 1983.

Miller, William D. *Mr. Crump of Memphis.* Baton Rouge, La., 1964.

Smith, Douglas L. *The New Deal in the Urban South.* Baton Rouge, La., 1988.

I 2

The Civil Rights Era

THE POSTWAR WORLD BROUGHT change in abundance. Most Tennesseans experienced rapid demobilization and a quick adjustment to the new time of peace, after years of international warfare. In the years following 1945, much happened in the state, as well as in the nation and around the globe, to remind everyone that World War II had brought forth a different environment. Transformations occurred in economic life, in politics, in social and cultural life, and in race relations. Just as Americans were launching out into this new world of change, the United States became involved in international conflict once again. The location was Korea, torn by a tremendous civil war; this struggle had global ramifications, or so it seemed. American military forces fought on those foreign shores from 1950 until an uneasy truce ended overt hostilities in 1953. Yet this war did not appear to alter the changes ushered in by the completion of World War II.

The Political World

In Tennessee, the first elections held after the end of the war seemed to indicate politics as usual. In 1946, for example, Gov. James Nance McCord won reelection (he defeated Gordon Browning in the Democratic primary), and Kenneth McKellar secured yet another term in the U.S. Senate. But two years later, a "revolution" of sorts occurred.

The election year of 1948 centered on three different statewide races: gubernatorial, U.S. Senate, and presidential. In all these campaigns, "Boss" Crump of Memphis and his machine went down in defeat. If ever there was a representative of the old way of conducting politics in the state, Crump was the man.

In the governor's race, he saw no reason to alter his support for McCord, who sought a third consecutive term. But Browning, still smarting from the earlier defeat, mounted a strong effort to overthrow the Crump influence. McCord's support of the state sales tax in 1947 offered Browning a running start at his strategy. When the Democratic primary ended in August, Browning had swept 56 percent of the statewide vote in an impressive rejection of the Crump candidate.

The fall months which followed proved to be entertaining, if nothing else, because the Republicans ran Roy Acuff, the renowned country music singer, against Browning. Acuff offered numerous renditions of his most famous songs, but the voters decided to keep him at the Grand Ole Opry. Browning trounced Acuff in November, capturing 67 percent of the total vote.

The senatorial race was quite complicated and was made more so by Crump's early decision not to support Sen. Tom Stewart, the incumbent and a longtime Crump favorite. By 1948, Stewart had several liabilities: a lackluster career in the Senate, lukewarm support of TVA, and serious charges of nepotism (fourteen family members served on his staff at one time or another). Although denied Crump's backing, Stewart nonetheless decided to seek reelection. Meanwhile, the Crump leaders endorsed John Mitchell of Cookeville, whom they admitted they had never seen or met.

Estes Kefauver, a U.S. representative from Chattanooga, made it a three-way Democratic race when he entered the contest. Kefauver conducted an amazing campaign: he emphasized support for TVA and for world peace, but

Estes Kefauver and his famous coonskin hat, in the 1948 campaign. Nancy Kefauver is seated at right. Special Collections, University of Tennessee, Knoxville.

he gained his greatest strength by his attacks upon Boss Crump. Soon the campaign developed into a battle between Kefauver and Crump; Stewart and Mitchell were left to fend for themselves. When Crump complained that Kefauver, whom he tried to taint with the Communist label, reminded him of a pet coon, he inadvertently gave his antagonist a great campaign symbol: the coonskin cap. Voters responded in August by giving Kefauver 42 percent of the statewide vote, Stewart 32 percent; and Mitchell only 24 percent. What an incredible change in Tennessee politics! In November, Kefauver easily defeated his Republican opponent, Rep. B. Carroll Reece.

The presidential race of 1948 was not without excitement and turmoil either. The national Democratic Party split, as disgruntled southerners protested Harry Truman's stance on civil rights. They formed the States' Rights (or Dixiecrat) Party, with Strom Thurmond of South Carolina as their presidential nominee. Crump immediately threw his support to Thurmond and denounced Truman. On election day in November, however, Tennesseans gave 49 percent of their vote to Truman, who thereby carried the state; 37 percent to Republican Thomas Dewey; and only 14 percent to Thurmond. Again Crump's plans had been defeated.

The next important installment in the story occurred in 1952, when two new challengers emerged to overthrow entrenched power. In the governor's race, Browning, the incumbent who sought reelection, represented the old guard. Frank G. Clement challenged him in an exciting campaign, eventually defeating Browning (who was tainted by charges of corruption) in the Democratic primary. Clement had no problem winning the November general election.

McKellar, who had been in the U.S. Senate since the early part of the century, once again sought reelection. But Albert Gore Sr., a congressman, called for a change and took on this last vestige of the old Crump machine. On election day in August and in November, the voters agreed with Gore and sent him to take McKellar's seat in the Senate.

The presidential race of 1952 was of more than passing interest. Senator Kefauver sought and received endorsements in several presidential primaries that year. But he was not able to secure the Democratic nomination, which eventually went to Adlai Stevenson of Illinois. Tennessee voters switched party allegiances by going for the Republican standard-bearer, Gen. Dwight Eisenhower. This was the first time since 1928 that Tennessee had voted Republican in a presidential election, and it marked the beginning of a new tradition—namely, Republican support in presidential politics.

In the 1956 national contest, Tennessee Democratic leaders were everywhere to be seen. By the time of the national convention, at which Governor Clement was the keynote speaker, three Tennesseans had the possibility of being named the party's candidate: Clement, Kefauver, and Gore. The convention settled on Stevenson, however, but then staged a wide-open competition for the vice-presidential nomination. All three Tennesseans received votes in the balloting, with Kefauver finally emerging as the nominee. But his presence on the national ticket was insufficient to swing Tennessee back into the Democratic column; instead, the state voted again for Eisenhower. Undoubtedly, the political world was changing, and more changes were waiting in the wings. Even so, at times Tennessee politics in the post-1945 period looked remarkably like its former self.

Economics and Demographics, 1945–1970

A Tennessean did not have to look very far to ascertain postwar transformations in economics, population growth, and population movement. The state's overall population grew slowly but steadily over the decades, increasing about 300,000 every ten years. For instance, in 1940 the population was 2.9 million; by 1970 it had reached 3.9 million. But the truly significant development occurred by the time of the 1960 census, when, for the very first time in Tennessee history, the urban population constituted a majority (52.3 percent) of the state's citizenry. The trend had been visible for some time, but it arrived in 1960 and since then has never changed.

The move to the cities naturally was reflected in a declining number of farms. Whereas Tennessee had nearly 235,000 farms in 1945, that figure dropped to nearly 122,000 by the end of the 1960s. Although the farms dwindled in number, productivity continued to rise. Part of the explanation was the mechanization of farms. No better indicator can be found than the statistics on tractors. In 1940 there were slightly under 12,000 tractors on Tennessee farms; that number doubled by 1945. The figure more than tripled by 1955 and finally reached 100,000 tractors in 1960—truly astounding growth over a twenty-year period. Cotton was still king during the 1950s, but in the next decade it yielded its position to tobacco, soybeans, and corn, which became the three most important cash crops. Indeed, in 1967, the state produced the smallest cotton crop in over a hundred years.

Whether one lived on a farm or in a city, the question of personal income always was crucial. Data on per capita personal income reveal that the war years were prosperous ones for Tennesseans; consider that the figure stood at $337 in 1940 but had soared to $910 by 1945. Such dramatic growth was not replicated subsequently; suffice it to say that, during the twenty years from 1950 to 1970, per capita personal income tripled, rising from $1,016 to $3,151. It should be noted, however, that Tennessee always lagged slightly behind the averages for the southeastern region and considerably behind the figures for the United States as a whole. Nonetheless, rising income brought greater hope of well-being.

Closely associated with the declining number of farms and rising incomes was the growth experienced in the manufacturing sector of the state's economy. Although the figures on manufacturing establishments are not startling (their number increased from 3,300 in 1947 to 4,800 in 1963), the data on value added by manufacturing are quite impressive. This figure more than tripled, going from $962 million in 1947 to $3.3 billion in 1963. Unquestionably, Tennessee was shifting more and more to a reliance upon its industrial economy.

Certainly one of the readily noticed changes was the growth of state government. A simple fact should suffice: between 1950 and 1960, state government revenues more than doubled, from $239 million to $517 million; and in the following decade, from 1960 to 1970, the figures more than doubled again, from $517 million to $1.3 billion. The new world demanded more from government at all levels—local, state, and federal.

Social and Cultural World

Indicative of the insecurities which marked the postwar period, much attention focused upon the question of one's loyalty to the United States. Indeed, beginning in the late 1940s, the Truman administration required federal workers to sign a loyalty oath. Out of this climate emerged Sen. Joseph McCarthy of Wisconsin, who in February 1950 startled everyone with his announcement that he had a list of Communists who worked in the State Department. From that point until his formal censure by the Senate in December 1954, McCarthy and other political leaders implemented something of a "reign of terror" as they attempted to expose and root out all subversives.

Tennessee mostly avoided being targeted in the McCarthy witch hunt, although the Communist or subversive label was readily applied to persons active in desegregation endeavors. In early 1953, the state legislature established a special committee, chaired by Sen. Sterling Roberts, to investigate textbooks used in public schools, colleges, and universities. The committee staged a one-day hearing at the University of Tennessee (UT). Shortly thereafter, the legislative committee reported that it had uncovered no evidence of subversive teachings in the various textbooks being used throughout the state's schools.

Judd Acuff, a legislator from Knoxville, immediately expressed his dissatisfaction with the committee report. With no regard for truth, Acuff attacked a UT history instructor, Sam Baron, as a native-born Russian who was teaching Communism to university students. Acuff expanded his charges to include the accusation that a group of professors was engaged in teaching various foreign "isms." Senator Roberts defended the work of his committee and decried Acuff's attacks, and the UT chapter of the American Association of University Professors passed a resolution upholding the loyalty of the UT faculty. Meanwhile, the timid university administration promised to look into Acuff's accusations. With that, the matter more or less blew over, and there were no further problems until the civil rights crusade began in earnest.

Among the changes that Tennesseans witnessed in the twenty years after World War II were transformations in the world of country music. During this period, Tennessee achieved even greater recognition in the field of music, particularly country music. Much of the focus continued to be on Nashville as the true mecca of such music, but both Knoxville and Memphis made claims for special kinds of music. In the late 1940s and 1950s, for example, Nashville experienced the importation from Texas of the so-called "honky-tonk" style, with Ernest Tubb and Carl Smith leading the way. Probably no one had more influence and popularity, albeit fleeting, than Hank Williams, who arrived in Nashville in the late 1940s as a songwriter but quickly became an outstanding performer at the Grand Ole Opry. These singers and songwriters promoted a new version of country music.

Concurrently, there was a move to cross over from country to popular music. Eddy Arnold, by 1947 considered country music's most outstanding performer, made the shift to popular music in the 1950s. He became the epitome of the black-tie-and-tuxedos movement, although he seemed to retain a foot in both camps.

In a sort of rebellion against such changes in the country music world, the bluegrass movement emerged in the 1950s. It was anticipated by Bill Monroe's style change in 1945, when Lester Flatt and Earl Scruggs joined his band. Three years later, however, that pair left Monroe's band to form their own groups, and they moved to Knoxville. For a time that city became the locale of this new back-to-roots country music movement. Two radio stations there, WNOX and WROL, were the leaders in promoting bluegrass music. Many prominent musicians and others later to become famous performed on those Knoxville stations in the 1950s.

Meanwhile, some four hundred miles away to the west, yet another variant of country music emerged. Memphis served as the center of so-called "rockabilly" music, especially in the 1950s. This trend was fostered by Sam Phillips, who launched his Sun Records there. He recorded such new stars as Carl Perkins, Johnny Cash, and Jerry Lee Lewis. Without question, however, his most famous "discovery" was Elvis Presley, who first recorded with Sun Records in 1954. The rest, as they say, is history.

The country music "industry" became a tremendously profitable enterprise, bringing with it tourists who made pilgrimages to Nashville. The Ryman Auditorium (an old gospel tabernacle), which hosted the weekly Grand Ole Opry shows in this period, functioned as the "mother church" of country music. Despite obvious successes, however, the world of country music experienced some of the insecurities and changes of the postwar world.

Harbinger of Change: A Court Decision

On Monday, May 17, 1954, the world began to change in ways unanticipated by most Tennesseans. On that day, the U.S. Supreme Court rendered its landmark decision, *Brown v. Board of Education of Topeka*. The case involved a suit by black parents in Topeka, Kansas, who sought the admission of their child into an all-white public school of that city. Finding in favor of the parents, the high court ruled that the long-established legal tradition of "separate but equal" was unconstitutional. The unmistakable implication was that public schools everywhere soon would have to desegregate their racially separated classrooms.

Like all southern states, Tennessee maintained a rigidly segregated society. Simply stated, a caste system based upon race existed. Both by law and by custom, blacks were separated from whites. They were excluded completely from schools that had all-white student bodies; they did not enjoy equal access to housing; they had fewer rights than whites on public transportation; and separate public facilities (parks, restrooms, swimming pools) were provided for blacks. Moreover, Tennessee blacks had extremely limited access to the political world. In a word, Jim Crow was alive and well in Tennessee—and throughout the South.

It was a hopeful sign that the initial reaction to the *Brown* decision, as reflected in the state's newspapers, was surprisingly supportive. Of the eight daily newspapers in the four major cities, only one, the *Chattanooga News–Free Press*, castigated the Court for its ruling, declaring it a regrettable and unwise decision. The dominant sentiment expressed in the other seven newspapers was that the South would have to learn to live with the ramifications of the case. The press urged a calm and reasonable approach to the looming challenge of desegregation of public schools. Some editors admitted that the decision was not unexpected (in light of some earlier rulings by the Court regarding higher education). All in all, the newspapers set a healthy tone for the state.

Tennessee, as a government and as a people, never adopted the "massive resistance" approach embraced by such states as Virginia, South Carolina, and the states of the Deep South. To say this is not, however, to pretend that there were few difficulties with dismantling the segregated public school system or the racially separated society. The state had its share of violence and discord, but seldom was there any real question that, some day in the near future, white Tennesseans would welcome black Tennesseans into parts of their world.

It is possible to view the atmosphere of the 1950s as a monumental struggle between the Tenth Amendment (states' rights and sovereignty) and the Fourteenth Amendment (rights of citizens). Certainly many Tennesseans saw the conflict in these terms. When the dust settled from the period of change and confusion, however, the Fourteenth Amendment prevailed.

Schools of the 1950s: Agents of Change

Even before the 1954 court decision, there were hints that the entrenched and stultifying biracial society might be under evolving pressure to change. For example, in 1950, four black students sought admission to the law and graduate schools at the University of Tennessee. When the university resisted, they brought suit in the federal district court in Knoxville, where Judge Robert L. Taylor, no trailblazer on racial matters, ruled in their favor but declined to issue an order compelling the university to enroll the students. When these courageous black men took their plea to the U.S. Supreme Court, the university's Board of Trustees capitulated by deciding that, beginning in January 1952, blacks could enroll in the graduate and law schools. Of the original four students, only two ever attended the university. Gene M. Gray, who took classes for one year before transferring elsewhere, was the first black to enter the previously all-white state university. His friend, Lincoln A. Blakeney, attended the law school for only one quarter before withdrawing. Two years later, however, in 1954, a black woman, Lillian Jenkins, received a master's degree from the University of Tennessee, becoming the first of her race to graduate from that institution. These achievements indicated that the wall of segregation had been fractured.

Private colleges became involved also. In the fall of 1952, for example, Scarritt College in Nashville admitted two black students. A month or two later, the faculty at Vanderbilt University's Divinity School asked the university's Board of Trust to permit black admissions, but the board postponed action. At its May 1953 meeting, however, the board agreed to allow blacks from the local region to enroll in the Divinity School. The School of Theology at the University of the South in Sewanee accepted one black student for the summer of 1953. Thus a few small steps were taken on the road to desegregation.

The Clinton Story

The saga of the desegregation of the Clinton public schools is a tragic but ultimately triumphant one. The story had its roots in long-established discrimination against black students in Anderson County. Simply stated, the county provided no high school educational opportunities for blacks, other than the opportunity to ride a bus to Knoxville each day to attend the all-black Austin High there. As early as 1951, three years before the *Brown* ruling, blacks in Anderson County sought access to Clinton High. Eventually a suit against the county school board was taken under review by Judge Taylor in 1955. He ordered the school board to prepare to admit black students to Clinton High in the 1956–57 academic year. The scene thus shifted from the courts back to the schools.

In preparation for fall classes, fifteen blacks registered at Clinton High, a school of some eight hundred students. The new school year began without much disturbance, but the arrival of John Kasper, who operated out of Washington, D.C., changed things dramatically. Kasper appeared on the scene for the avowed purpose of blocking desegregation at Clinton High; accordingly, he went through the community stirring racial antagonisms. Kasper even attempted to force the school principal, D. J. Brittain, to resign, but students and parents rallied to Brittain's side in the dispute. Nevertheless, by the Labor Day weekend, the overall situation in the town was worsening steadily—so much so that Judge Taylor issued a restraining order against Kasper, barring his activities. Local officials, worried by the increasing levels of violence and destruction of property, entreated Gov. Frank Clement to provide police protection. The governor agreed and first dispatched one hundred highway patrolmen to Clinton; the following day, he sent six hundred National Guardsmen. Kasper, aided by others, had succeeded in driving a wedge of hostility between the two races in Clinton. But the appearance of troops immediately calmed the situation, and classes resumed at the high school.

The story did not end there, however, for harassment of black students at Clinton High continued. Moreover, in November, a jury in Anderson County acquitted Kasper of charges of inciting a riot. Meanwhile, Judge Taylor already had cited Kasper, *in absentia,* for contempt of the federal court for disobeying the injunction. Later in the fall term, frightened black students asked school officials for additional protection, a request that was denied. Therefore, certain white citizens agreed to escort the few black students from their homes to the school building each morning. The most prominent of these was the Rev. Paul Turner, pastor of the all-white Baptist church in Clinton. On the morning of December 4, Turner safely escorted the students to their classes, but immediately thereafter a group of whites attacked the minister as he departed from the school grounds and left him lying beaten and bloody on the sidewalk. News of this vicious assault upon the Baptist pastor stunned the community and helped bring about an almost immediate cessation of overt hostilities there.

In May 1957, at the conclusion of the school year, Bobby Cain received his diploma from Clinton High, the first black in Tennessee to graduate from a desegregated public school. In July, Judge Taylor presided over the trial of John Kasper and others accused of violating the federal injunction at Clinton. The jury found Kasper and several others guilty of the violation, whereupon Judge Taylor sentenced Kasper to a year's imprisonment at the federal penitentiary. This action seemed to signal the end of desegregation disturbances and difficulties in Anderson County. However, in October 1958, in a grim reminder of lingering hostilities, dynamite blasts reduced Clinton High to rubble. The community immediately rallied in support of the school, and there were no additional problems. Thus a small East Tennessee town with a minuscule black population weathered the somewhat surprising storms of racial unrest and tentatively opened the doors of desegregated education in the state.

The Nashville Story

The city schools of Nashville represented a much more formidable challenge to the desegregation movement. A black teenager, Bobby Kelley, wanted to attend nearby East High, but law and custom dictated that he be bussed across town to the all-black Pearl High. Consequently, his father, A. Z. Kelley, in 1955 brought a class action lawsuit against the school board to seek admission of black students to any school in the city. The federal district judge in Nashville, William E. Miller, agreed to hear the case the following year. After doing so, the judge ordered the school board to submit a desegregation plan by January 1957.

At that time, the board informed Judge Miller of its intention to desegregate only the first grade in the forthcoming fall of 1957. The plan had ample provision for pupil transfer, a fundamentally significant clause. The federal judge accepted the proposal, with the stipulation that the board subsequently (by December) must submit an agenda for admitting blacks to the other eleven grades.

Immediately the school board set about the task of preparing for the fall term, with desegregation of the first grade. It busily drew and redrew school zone lines with such skill that, of the potential group of 1,400 black first-graders, only 115 of them would be likely to attend previously all-white elementary schools. The board naturally allowed parents of these 115 pupils to opt for transfers to all-black schools; 96 requested such shifts. Therefore, desegregation in September actually would involve only *nineteen* black first-graders, spread among six different schools.

Despite this very small number of children, during the summer white Nashvillians began to have second thoughts. Some organized themselves to thwart the modest desegregation of city schools. By September, therefore, the atmosphere was tense. But the chief of police warned that persons attempting to interfere with peaceful desegregation would be arrested immediately. The police had not reckoned upon the sudden arrival in town of John Kasper, out on bond while awaiting an appeal of his earlier conviction in Judge Taylor's court. Kasper hoped to foment trouble, much as he had done the year before in Clinton. Nashville police, however, had other plans; very shortly they arrested Kasper on four charges. He posted bond on those counts, and then the police arrested him for illegal parking! Thereafter, Davidson County law enforcement officials arrested Kasper for having incited a riot with his speech of September 8. So it went for this much-harassed outside agitator. Meanwhile, Judge Miller issued an injunction against anyone who interfered with school desegregation. After this initial flurry of activity, including the nighttime bombing of one of the newly desegregated elementary schools, an uneasy truce descended upon Nashville. The situation here contrasted quite markedly with the one developing at the same time at Central High School in Little Rock, Arkansas. Indeed, one is tempted to argue that Nashville exemplified compliance, while Little Rock epitomized defiance.

A few months later, the school board submitted its overall plan. It called for desegregating one grade per year, until eventually all twelve grades would be included. When Judge Miller accepted this extended desegrega-

KEEP OUR WHITE SCHOOLS WHITE

HEAR SEGREGATION LEADERS:

Ace Carter
Bill Hendrix
Rev. Fred Stroud

Rev. John Mercurio
Dr. Ed Fields
John Kasper

and Others

TELL WHY Nashville has been sacrificed as the first major Southern city to mix White and Nigra children in public schools.

FIND OUT what can be done to stop the horrors of race mixing and the race riots, murders, hangings and race hatred that is certain to come if the School Board, Ben West, Frank Clement, and the Federal Courts go through with their evil plans to destroy all races in Nashville.

ALL CHRISTIANS Bring Your Friends.

TIME: 2:00 P.M., Sunday, August 11th

PLACE: Robertson Road and Croley Drive
(In West Nashville, off Charlotte Ave.)

SPONSOR: TENNESSEE WHITE CITIZENS COUNCILS.

HONOR---PRIDE---FIGHT SAVE THE WHITES

Handbill distributed in Nashville in 1957. Broadside Collection, Tennessee State Library and Archives, Nashville.

tion plan, black plaintiffs almost immediately challenged it. The case went to the Sixth Circuit Court of Appeals, which in 1959 upheld Judge Miller's decision. Eventually, in 1963, the U.S. Supreme Court heard a different case involving Nashville and Davidson County schools and struck down the grade-a-year plan. Unfortunately for Bobby Kelley, the passage of time meant that he graduated from all-black Pearl High.

Antedating the evolutionary progress of Nashville's public schools, two previously all-white Catholic schools in Nashville desegregated in the fall of 1954, when they admitted some fifty black students. Thus the first desegregation to occur in any Tennessee schools, other than colleges, was in the parochial schools of Nashville.

Desegregation Elsewhere

Other major school systems across the state experienced either partial or no desegregation by the end of the 1950s. For example, in Knoxville black students and their parents in January 1957 petitioned Judge Taylor to enjoin the school board from prohibiting them from enrolling in any all-white city schools. Curiously, Judge Taylor repeatedly postponed ruling on the case. In fact, he waited until Nashville's grade-a-year plan was upheld by the higher federal courts. Finally, in August 1960, Taylor approved a similar plan for the Knoxville and Knox County schools.

Although the Chattanooga school board in 1955 voted to begin mapping plans for desegregating the public schools there, it later (in the face of much local segregationist pressure) backed away from any consideration of the issue. It was the early 1960s before Chattanooga blacks brought suit to force desegregation of the public schools there.

Strangely enough, Memphis blacks made no overt efforts in the 1950s to push for the opening of all public schools to persons of all races. Instead, they focused upon desegregating buses, public libraries, and the zoo before the public schools. The schools finally were desegregated in 1961 in a swift and quasi-secret movement, as thirteen blacks enrolled in four different Memphis schools. Surprisingly, no overt protests over school desegregation occurred there.

What about the colleges and universities? As discussed previously, modest gains in desegregation already had been made in several institutions in the early 1950s. Securing admission of black undergraduates to the University of Tennessee, however, was more difficult than gaining admission of graduate or professional students had been. In 1954, shortly after the *Brown* case, the U.S. Supreme Court had ruled that racial segregation was unconstitutional in colleges and universities. Tennessee ignored that decision. In late 1955, local black attorneys in Knoxville appealed to the university's board to admit blacks to the undergraduate programs, but to no avail. The board agreed, in an April 1956 meeting, to adopt the step-by-step plan embraced by the state board of education, but then reversed itself. A few months later, the state supreme court ruled, in *Roy v. Brittain*, that all state laws requiring segregation were invalid. Despite this new ruling, the University of Tennessee board still refused to budge. Finally, finding itself under pressure from a recent black graduate of Austin High, Theotis Robinson, who threatened a lawsuit, the board yielded and in November 1960 decreed that there should be no racial discrimination in the admission of students. Thus, in January 1961, Robinson and two other blacks enrolled as undergraduates at UT.

Changes in racial policies at the state-supported colleges occurred rather easily. As early as May 1955, five college-age blacks sued the state in the federal district court in Memphis, seeking the right to attend Memphis State. The state board of education convened and worked out a plan whereby the state colleges would desegregate in five years, beginning the first year with graduate students and then a lower rank each succeeding year. Thus, by the fall term of 1959, all levels of student enrollment would be desegregated. Judge Marion Boyd of the federal district court refused to admit the five Memphis blacks who wished to enroll at Memphis State; instead, he accepted the state board's gradual plan of desegregation.

Among the private colleges, as noted above, several had begun admitting black graduate and professional students by the mid-1950s. Not until May 1962, however, did the Vanderbilt University board finally consent to the admission of blacks as undergraduates there. With all these developments in the various schools and colleges, Tennessee blacks gained some limited access to equal educational opportunities.

Desegregation of Collegiate Sports

With the recruitment in 1966 of Perry Wallace, a star black basketball player at Nashville's Pearl High, Vanderbilt broke the color barrier. The University of Tennessee (UT) followed suit the next year, with the highly touted recruitment and signing of two football players: Albert Davis of Alcoa and Lester McClain of Nashville. Unfortunately, controversy surrounding the admission of Davis caused UT to rescind its offer. (He subsequently enjoyed a successful football career at Tennessee A&I.) McClain thus became the person to break the racial barrier in college football in Tennessee. The track program at UT also recruited two black athletes in 1967: James Craig and Audry Hardy. By Hardy's senior year (1971), UT had seventeen black athletes—seven in football and ten in track. They soon were joined by star basketball players.

Desegregation Politics

As was indicated previously, Tennessee did not endorse the "massive resistance" response to racial desegregation. One reason for this restraint was political leaders who championed a moderate course. The four principal ones, though not the only ones, were Frank Clement and Buford Ellington, who served as governor during the 1950s and 1960s; and Estes Kefauver and Albert Gore, U.S. senators during this same era. Their beliefs and style of leadership offered no support for the rabid segregationist rhetoric and actions of southern political leaders in adjoining states.

Each of these four officeholders was challenged in campaigns during these two decades, to be sure; but they successfully (and in some instances overwhelmingly) defeated their opponents. In 1954, for example, Clement ran for reelection as governor and Kefauver for reelection as senator. Although this campaign came just months after the *Brown* ruling, the issue of school desegregation had not yet become prominent in Tennessee. Former governor Gordon Browning challenged Clement in the Democratic primary, vowing that he would never permit racial mixing in the public schools. The issue, however, never caught on, and Clement swamped Browning on election day in August. Pat Sutton fought Kefauver's reelection bid but confined most of his attack to charges that the senator was "soft on Communism." Kefauver had no trouble defeating Sutton. Since this was still the period of statewide Democratic Party hegemony, the general election in November was scarcely contested.

Four years later, in 1958, the race question had become a more volatile topic, given the experiences in Tennessee and elsewhere with school desegregation. Since Clement could not seek reelection, he pushed his political ally and cabinet member, Buford Ellington, to compete for the office of governor. Ellington ran into stiff opposition, primarily in the form of the state circuit court's Judge Andrew Tip Taylor, a staunch segregationist and conservative. Three other contenders campaigned for the governor's chair, the most important of whom was Mayor Edmund Orgill of Memphis, a moderate on race issues. In any event, as Taylor put pressure on Ellington, the latter began to hedge on the race question and eventually declared himself to be "an old-fashioned segregationist." Election-day results in August revealed an extremely tight contest: Ellington emerged on top, but only 8,700 votes ahead of Taylor, in second place. Racial issues seem to have altered the political climate somewhat.

Meanwhile, Senator Gore sought election for a second term in 1958, with former governor Prentice Cooper challenging him. Cooper launched attacks upon Gore, based almost exclusively upon fears of civil rights, desegregation, and the like. His was a blatantly racist campaign. But on election day, Gore defeated Cooper in the Democratic primary by 125,000 votes.

Two years later, in 1960, Kefauver faced a tremendous campaign with Andrew Tip Taylor. Sad to say, Taylor fought on the issue of race; it was perhaps his only hope for victory. Without doubt, this contest was an extremely difficult one for Kefauver, and few analysts offered his camp much encouragement. To his credit, the senator took a bold, unapologetic stand on behalf of his civil rights record. When the ballots were counted, Kefauver had trounced Taylor by over 230,000 votes, capturing almost 65 percent of the Democratic primary's vote. It was a great senatorial victory for Kefauver.

By the time of the 1962 gubernatorial campaign, all three Democratic contenders—Frank Clement, William Farris, and P. R. Olgiati—openly courted the increasingly important black vote, clearly indicating that the days of race baiting in statewide campaigns were over. Clement had no difficulty winning his third gubernatorial election. The challenge now rising on the state's political horizon was not civil rights or race, but a revitalized Republican Party.

Legislative Strategies

During their combined years as governor, both Clement and Ellington confronted legislative challenges over the question of desegregation of the public schools. Each managed to head off extreme measures by offering their own ambiguous proposals. In 1955, state senator Charles Stainback, representing Fayette and Haywood Counties (both of which had majority black populations), got the jump on the school segregation question. He offered a bill that allowed boards of education wide latitude in the assignment of pupils. Although the bill avoided the language of race or segregation, its intent clearly was to provide for the continuation of segregation in schools statewide. The Clement legislative forces bottled the bill up in committee, however, and it never came to a vote in the senate. Stainback then presented local bills to provide for maintenance of segregation in the schools of Fayette and Haywood Counties. He was joined in this questionable endeavor by proponents of bills for Tipton and Sumner Counties. By tradition, local bills always cleared the legislature and rarely were vetoed by the governor. But Clement, worried about the ramifications of these particular local bills, bravely vetoed them and checkmated segregationist forces in the legislature.

Two years later, in January 1957, in the wake of the Clinton desegregation experience, Clement opted to take the initiative. Addressing the legislature, he staked out a position in support of civil rights for black citizens. In his message, he outlined a five-bill package of proposals to deal with school matters. Two of these were most important. First was a "parents' preference law," which permitted local school boards to maintain racially separate schools for the children of parents who voluntarily sought such. Second was a "pupil assignment law," which stipulated that school boards could assign students to certain schools based upon several different criteria. Clement's lieutenants pushed his package through without difficulty and thereby enabled the governor to preempt the field of school legislation. The ambiguity of these laws, later invalidated by court rulings, allowed both sides to claim some measure of victory.

Ellington, who, as one of Clement's cabinet members, had helped secure the passage of this legislation, had to deal with a similar situation when he occupied the governor's chair. In early 1959, Ralph Kelley, a legislator from Hamilton County, introduced three bills which would have had serious negative consequences for public education. He proposed that the state attendance requirement be suspended, if parents were required to send their children to desegregated schools; that state funds should be prorated for children whose parents sent them to private schools; and, finally, that counties should hold referendums on the question of whether to abolish public schools. Either shrewdly or out of genuine ignorance, Ellington initially expressed support for the Kelley bills. Shortly thereafter, however, he began to hedge. Eventually the governor offered a three-part package of his own: parents could withdraw their children from public schools for "any good and substantial reason," but first they had to receive permission from the local school board, and then within thirty days they had to enroll their children in another public school or in a private school. Ellington, much like Clement, prevailed; and these remarkably vague bills cleared the legislature. So hazy were these proposals that not a single newspaper in the state published an editorial about them. Both governors, heading off the possibility of more dangerous legislation, proved that a little ambiguity goes a long way.

Resistance Organizations

Part of the explanation for the moderate approach taken by both Clement and Ellington is that they never felt pressured by a large, vigorous statewide segregationist group. There simply was not one, whereas in most other southern states one existed. Several different organizations vied for public support, to be sure, but they were unsuccessful.

The first of these, organized in June 1955, went by the daunting name of the Tennessee Federation for Constitutional Government (TFCG). Its founder was Donald Davidson, professor at Vanderbilt University; joining him were professional people, as well as some university colleagues. The TFCG emphasized states' rights, rather than focusing simply on school segregation. The organization was, as Mississippi newspaper editor Hodding Carter once said of similar groups, an "uptown Klan."

The TFCG published and distributed pamphlets and staged rallies, but it never enlisted a widespread following. Davidson boasted in 1957 that the federation had members in seventy-five of the state's ninety-five counties, but he failed to give exact membership numbers. The organization claimed *chapters* in only fourteen counties, primarily in West Tennessee. In 1956, the TFCG mailed questionnaires to 308 legislative candidates in an attempt to ascertain their views on the "southern way of life." Only one hundred persons bothered to respond; of that number, at least twenty expressed disagreement with the federation's program.

A somewhat more visible but no more successful organization was the Citizens Council. Headquartered in Mississippi, it attempted in 1961 to establish a strong chapter in Memphis, where very limited school desegregation had just begun. The council staged a large rally there in the spring of 1962, led by Gov. Ross Barnett of Mississippi. Thereafter the group systematically recruited members throughout the city. Although the council bragged about a large membership in the Memphis chapter, it steadfastly refused to reveal actual figures.

Eventually the council could claim organized chapters elsewhere in the state—Chattanooga, Jackson, Knoxville, and Murfreesboro, for example. But its greatest desire was to establish a vibrant chapter in Nashville, "the very citadel of carpetbag liberalism." Accordingly, in April 1962, the council held an organizational rally in a downtown Nashville hotel. Through that effort, the TFCG largely merged with the council; even so, the council's leadership was quite disappointed with its Nashville endeavors. In exasperation, one of its leaders denounced Nashville as "the worst city in the world."

While a few other segregationist groups existed around the state, none had any influence or stamina. Tennessee proved inhospitable to such organizations, although, ironically, there was plenty of segregationist sentiment in the state.

Civil Rights School: Highlander

Since its establishment in 1932 by Myles Horton, the Highlander Folk School, located near Monteagle, had offered adult education workshops and classes on a variety of topics. More important, it offered hope to people of the region. During its first twenty years of existence, the school's major emphasis was labor organizing activities. But as the 1950s commenced, Horton and his staff moved away from that focus and toward issues of race, racial prejudice, and the South's segregated institutions. Indeed, Highlander held its first workshop on these topics in 1953, a full year before the landmark *Brown* decision.

Throughout the decade of the 1950s, this folk school played a key role in the development of strategy and leaders, both white and black, for the push toward racial integration. In a real sense, Highlander was not a Tennessee school, for it belonged to the entire South. From its earliest days, Highlander held racially integrated classes and workshops, an aspect that would increase in the 1950s, eliciting threats and harassment by local and state authorities.

Not surprisingly, Highlander's first workshops in the decade focused on public school desegregation, for that was the immediate challenge facing the racially divided South. About a month after the *Brown* ruling, Highlander held a seminar on the prospects for desegregation of the public schools. Similar workshops followed at Highlander in 1955 and 1956; they attracted participants, black and white, from all parts of the South. Staff members also worked quietly behind the scenes with the Clinton High desegregation situation. The successful Montgomery, Alabama, bus boycott of 1955, initiated by the actions of Rosa Parks, who had attended Highlander workshops, stimulated Horton and others to embrace a concept larger than merely the desegregation of schools. Highlander determined that it really needed to deal with *racial integration*, not just school desegregation. Thus, in the latter half of the 1950s, the workshops shifted to broader concerns—transportation, public accommodations, voting rights, and the dismantling of the biracial society.

To help commemorate its twenty-fifth anniversary in 1957, Highlander hosted a large workshop and celebration on Labor Day weekend. Nearly two hundred persons of varying degrees of prominence in the civil rights

In the 1960s, billboards appeared that showed Martin Luther King Jr. attending a meeting at Highlander School, Labor Day weekend, 1957. Archives, Highlander Research and Education Center, New Market, Tennessee.

movement, including Martin Luther King Jr., gathered there. Two special guests, however, contributed to a subsequent nationwide controversy. One was Abner Berry, a reporter for the Communist Party's *Daily Worker*, who had come to cover the event and write a story for his paper. Unfortunately, he failed to identify himself properly and honestly to Horton. The other self-invited guest was Edwin Friend, an investigator for the Georgia Commission on Education, a segregation watchdog unit of that state's government. Like Berry, Friend concealed his true purposes from Horton: he came to spy and take pictures. A few months later, the Georgia agency issued Friend's work in a dramatic publication, *Highlander Folk School: Communist Training School*. The report created a sensation throughout the South, with more than a million copies eventually published and circulated. The twenty-fifth birthday event was not one that Highlander would soon forget or perhaps even recover from fully.

Two years later, Tennessee launched an effort to close Highlander down. Encouraged by Arkansas Attorney General Bruce Bennett, who allegedly had investigated Highlander and discovered that it "was a gathering place for Communists and fellow travelers," some Tennessee legislators in January 1959 pushed through a request for their own inquiry. The *Nashville Banner* and the *Chattanooga News–Free Press* led the editorial crusade on behalf of the proposed scrutiny, whereas other newspapers were skeptical of the whole enterprise. The legislative committee held hearings in Grundy County, site of the Highlander School, and then in Nashville. As a result of its investigation, the committee recommended that the school's charter be revoked.

On July 31, local law enforcement officials took matters into their own hands. Conducting a clandestine night raid on Highlander, they disrupted a racially integrated community workshop. (Horton was out of the country at the time.) Employing Gestapo-like tactics, the police made arrests, searched without warrants, planted "evidence," and confiscated "evidence." In the aftermath of the raid, the district attorney sought to padlock the school as a public nuisance. So-called hearings, presided over by Judge Chester Chattin, followed. The judge made his final ruling in February 1960, identifying three reasons for revoking Highlander's charter: Horton had operated the school for his own financial benefit, the school sold beer without a license, and its classes were racially integrated. On appeal, Chattin's decision went to the state supreme court, which, in April 1961, upheld his ruling but eliminated the charge concerning racially mixed classes. By excising this part from the verdict, the higher court eliminated the possibility that the case could be transferred to the federal court system.

Horton and his staff, sensing the futility of a continuing legal struggle, simply applied for a new state charter as the Highlander Research and Education Center and opened headquarters in Knoxville late in the summer of 1961. A few months later, the state auctioned off Highlander's furnishings and equipment at the old site and in 1962 followed with the final auction of the property and buildings. But, as Horton earlier had noted, the state could not put Highlander out of business by disposing of its property, for it was more than just a school, "it's an idea." He and his staff took that idea with them to their new location and continued to work for racial integration. During its Knoxville years, the school was subjected to abuse, harassment, vandalism, and extremely adverse publicity in the *Knoxville Journal*. Despite all these tribulations, the reconstituted school persisted throughout the 1960s—as did its vision of a South without a racial caste system.

Sit-in Demonstrations: Nashville and Elsewhere

The small steps taken in Tennessee to begin the desegregation of schools in the late 1950s fed the desire to push further. Thus, in the decade of the 1960s, civil rights leaders ventured beyond the schools and the courts. Blacks, with some assistance from whites, engaged in direct activities in the streets, in the marketplace, and elsewhere to break down the segregation walls. A story of tragedy and triumph unfolded.

The tactic of a sit-in demonstration by blacks was not new; it had been utilized in far-flung places before 1960. But events beginning early that year in the southern states had a tremendous impact on the whole civil rights struggle. The sit-in by a small group of black college students at Greensboro, North Carolina, on February 1 ignited a response throughout the South. This simple yet defiant (given the laws and customs) act—sitting at a lunch counter designated for whites only—sparked the strategy. Nashville reacted quickly; black leaders were ready for action. The presence of four black colleges assured the movement of a solid corps of brave and dedicated advocates of civil rights. Moreover, Nashville was fortunate in having highly effective black leaders, particularly clergy and attorneys.

As early as 1958, these leaders had organized the Nashville Christian Leadership Council (NCLC), in effect a local branch of Martin Luther King Jr.'s Southern Christian Leadership Conference. Almost immediately it sponsored a workshop on nonviolence, a program led by Rev. James Lawson, graduate student at Vanderbilt University, that continued throughout 1958–59. Early in 1959, the NCLC adopted as one of its goals the desegregation of downtown lunch counters. The group proceeded to negotiate with merchants, to no avail. Late in the year, the NCLC staged "test" sit-ins at two different department stores, the results of which confirmed that the stores would not serve blacks at the segregated lunch counters. In short, all that was needed to launch the Nashville movement was a catalyst; the Greensboro sit-ins provided one.

Before the month of February 1960 ended, Nashville blacks had participated in four different sit-in demonstrations at downtown stores, each drawing more participants than the one before. Not until the February 27 demonstration, however, did violence, as well as arrests, occur. Although the police arrested seventy-five students, they did not seize any of the white agitators

Lunch counter sit-in demonstration at Woolworth's, Nashville, February 1960. *Nashville Banner*; photograph by Bill Goodman. Reprinted by permission.

who had assaulted the demonstrators. In this sit-in, as in the others, black students did a remarkable job of adhering to the principles of nonviolence. They carried with them the following mimeographed instructions, written by student leader John Lewis.

DO show yourself friendly at the counter at all times.
DO sit straight and always face the counter.
DO refer all information to your leader in a polite manner.

DO remember the teachings of Jesus Christ, Mohandas K. Gandhi and Martin Luther King.
DON'T strike back, or curse back, if attacked.
DON'T laugh out.
DON'T hold conversations with floor-walkers.
DON'T leave your seat until your leader has given you permission.
DON'T block entrances to the stores and the aisles.
Remember love and non-violence, may God bless each of you.

After a sit-in on March 2, 1960, Mayor Ben West appointed a special biracial committee to work out solutions to the segregation problems. For a time thereafter, there was a lull in the demonstrations, as the students and their leaders waited for this new committee to report. In the meantime, because of pressure from the Interstate Commerce Commission, the Greyhound Bus station's previously segregated lunch counter served four black students. Finally, on March 25, the sit-ins resumed, largely because of lack of progress by the mayor's committee. Governor Ellington criticized this particular demonstration, alleging that the Columbia Broadcasting System had instigated the sit-in in order to film it for television.

A few days later, the mayor's committee offered its recommendation for partial desegregation of the downtown lunch counters, a proposal immediately rejected by black leaders. Students then took the initiative and commenced direct negotiations with merchants. No further sit-ins occurred for a period of some three weeks; meanwhile, black leaders launched a highly effective boycott of downtown stores. Given that black customers normally poured about $7 million annually into purchases at these stores, merchants simply could not ignore the boycott.

The final shock in the civil rights struggle that spring came in the early morning hours of April 19, 1960, when the home of a prominent black attorney, Z. Alexander Looby, was bombed. Fortunately, no one was killed or injured. In response to this incident, however, some three thousand demonstrators, black and white, marched to the courthouse in protest. Mayor West addressed the crowd and urged all citizens to end discrimination, including at lunch counters. During the first week of May, the merchants and black negotiators reached an agreement. It provided that, with advance notice, small groups of students would enter the downtown stores and patronize the lunch counters, where they would be served. After a trial of two weeks, all restrictions on the sit-ins would be lifted. The experiment began on May 10; from that date forward, there were no more segregated lunch counters in downtown stores. Another small victory had been won.

The Nashville sit-ins stand out for several reasons. First, they were the most successful, in that the goal of desegregating lunch counters was accomplished more quickly than anywhere else. Second, these sit-ins were the best organized and most disciplined of any seen throughout the South. In his visit to Nashville on April 20, 1960, Martin Luther King Jr. praised these aspects of the local demonstrations. Third, as a consequence of the sit-ins, Nashville produced a disproportionate number of civil rights leaders (including two chairmen of the Student Nonviolent Coordinating Committee). Finally, Nashville's emphasis on nonviolence set the tone for the whole student civil rights movement in the 1960s.

Naturally, Nashville was not the only Tennessee city to experience sit-in demonstrations. There were similarities, yet differences, among events in various cities. With the exception of Chattanooga, where initially high school students were involved, the pattern everywhere was for college students to serve as demonstrators. Chattanooga's first lunch counter sit-in, which took place on February 22, 1960, led to a race riot there. Knoxville experienced a slow and difficult period of demonstrations that stretched from March through early July 1960, before merchants capitulated to the demand for desegregated downtown lunch counters. Knoxville civil rights advocates participated in months of futile negotiations with government and business leaders before launching almost daily demonstrations.

In Memphis, black college students began sit-ins in March 1960 at two public libraries, art galleries, museums, and the Overton Park and Zoo. By the fall months, all of these had been desegregated. Black students in Memphis also engaged in demonstrations at downtown lunch counters and on city buses. Although the latter were desegregated in September 1960, it was not

---

Carmichael's Nashville Visit, 1967

In response to an invitation from a student group at Vanderbilt University, Stokely Carmichael, Black Power advocate and chairman of the Student Nonviolent Coordinating Committee, agreed to speak there on April 8. Two weeks prior to that date, he spoke at Fisk and Tennessee A&I universities, actions that sparked controversy in the Nashville community. Vanderbilt Board of Trust members questioned sponsoring the forthcoming speech by Carmichael, and the state senate passed a resolution condemning him. Despite such pressures, the almost anticlimactic address went forward as planned.

That night, a riot broke out at the Fisk campus between black students and Nashville police. A similar riot developed the next day at Tennessee A&I. Fortunately, no one was killed in either disturbance, although several people were wounded. Some blamed Carmichael's speech, others the police, and still others Vanderbilt University.

until early 1962 that Memphis merchants finally opened their previously seg-regated lunch counters to blacks. Interestingly, also in 1962, blacks succeeded in quietly and peacefully desegregating Memphis movie theaters. Thus, by the time of the famous 1964 Civil Rights Law, the four major Tennessee communi-ties already had dismantled important barriers to integration.

Voting Rights

For Americans, there is hardly a more cherished or fundamental civil right than the right to vote. In Tennessee, intimidation of black voters never matched that found in Deep South states. Yet, with the voting restrictions enacted late in the nineteenth century, including the poll tax, blacks never had been able to vote in numbers commensurate with their share of the population. The Crump machine in Memphis, of course, encouraged black voting, so that it could manipulate that sizable bloc of voters on election day. The introduction of the white primary in 1901 restricted black par-ticipation in elections. Although the state courts ruled that primary uncon-stitutional in the 1940s, the decree was not always adhered to throughout the state. With the repeal of the poll tax by the state's constitutional con-vention of 1953, it looked as if there was new hope for potential black voters. At that point, approximately 29 percent of the black voting-age population was registered to vote.

The two counties with black majorities, Fayette and Haywood, had shockingly poor records on voting rights. Intimidation there worked to

---

Viola McFerren of Fayette County

Viola McFerren and her husband, John, black landowners in Fayette County, thrust themselves into leadership roles. In 1959, John helped launch a voter registration campaign; his wife soon joined him. When local whites retaliated by evicting hundreds of black tenants, Viola McFerren, along with the Fayette County Civic and Welfare League, acquired ten large army surplus tents and established a "tent city" for the needy black families. This move elicited nationwide publicity and support. Viola McFerren then traveled to Washington to obtain aid from two federal agencies. Later she was instrumental in securing antipoverty funds for Fayette. With other parents, she filed a successful suit against the school board to force desegregation. Viola McFerren subsequently helped organize a black boycott of local businesses protesting continuing discrimination and inequality.

keep blacks in check. Of the 17,000 voters registered in Haywood, for example, only 17 were black! In Fayette, the situation was equally dismal; only 420 blacks were registered, out of 10,000 blacks eligible. Thanks in part to the impact of the Civil Rights Law of 1957, which established the Civil Rights Commission and authorized the U.S. attorney general to take action by injunction against registrars suspected of voting rights violations, several courageous black leaders in Fayette and Haywood were able to launch a voter registration drive in 1959. They organized the Civic and Welfare League in both counties to spearhead the new movement.

The campaign moved into high gear early in 1960, with actual registration of a limited number of voters and active intervention by the U.S. Justice Department. The new Civil Rights Law of that year authorized suits by the federal government on behalf of blacks who were prevented from registering, as well as the appointment of special federal registrars if this was deemed necessary. In June, representatives of the Civil Rights Commission investigated the situation in Haywood, and the following month John Doar of the Civil Rights Division of the Justice Department arrived. Doar quickly

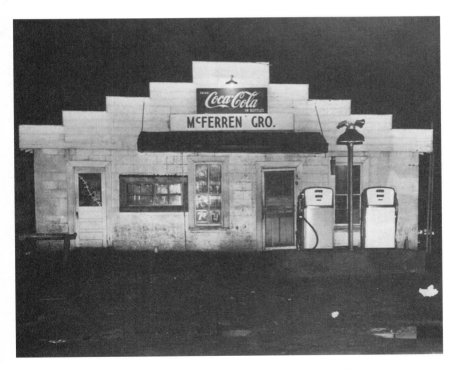

McFerren Grocery Store and Gas Station, Fayette County, headquarters for assistance to blacks in "Tent City." Photograph by *Memphis Press-Scimitar*. In Mississippi Valley Collection, University of Memphis Libraries.

agreed that attempts to block registration of blacks were both pervasive and harsh. But the presence and potential threat of the federal government seemed to encourage whites to new levels of retaliation against those blacks who sought to register. They evicted hundreds of black tenant families from the land, refused their cotton at the gins, withheld services and goods, cut off crop loans, and engaged in many other reprisals.

But this time blacks fought back. The Civic and Welfare Leagues in both counties, but particularly in Fayette, organized a "tent city" to provide temporary shelter for the evicted families. This action attracted national publicity and thereby stirred sympathy and support. Black leaders succeeded in securing federal monies and further Justice Department action, including injunctions against the white government officials in both counties, to prevent interference with voter registration. The story had a bittersweet ending: hundreds, even thousands, of blacks registered, yet white discrimination and intimidation, although diminished, persisted. Even so, by 1964, a year *before* passage of the 1965 Voting Rights Act, Tennessee had achieved voter registration for approximately 69 percent of the statewide black voting population.

The political process immediately opened up dramatically. A. W. Willis of Memphis, elected in 1964 to the state legislature, became the first black legislator since the late nineteenth century. Others soon followed. Moreover, at the local level across the state, increased numbers of blacks were elected to government posts. Important in changing the political scene was

---

Black Legislators, 1960s

In the 1960s, for the first time since the 1880s, blacks served in the Tennessee legislature. Elected in 1964, A. W. Willis Jr., a Memphis attorney, became the first of the black legislators. Willis was reelected in 1966 and was joined by five other blacks. Two of them were fellow Memphis attorneys: James O. Patterson, elected first to the house and then, in 1968, to the state senate; and Russell B. Sugarmon Jr., who after one term returned to his law practice and eventually became a sessions court judge.

In 1966, Nashville elected two blacks: M. G. Blakemore, a dentist and an attorney, who served four years in the house; and Dorothy L. Brown, a physician, the first black woman ever to serve in the legislature. Knoxville sent Robert J. Booker to the lower house, where he served for six years. The only new black legislator elected in 1968 was the prominent civil rights lawyer, Avon N. Williams Jr., who represented Nashville in the state senate for more than twenty years.

the 1962 *Baker v. Carr* decision by the U.S. Supreme Court. This case emerged out of a Tennessee lawsuit and concerned the failure of the legislature to reapportion itself. It had not done so since 1901, although required by the state constitution to reapportion its districts every ten years. Needless to say, rural districts were greatly overrepresented and urban districts woefully underrepresented. The Court's landmark decision enunciated the "one man, one vote" rule, requiring equity in legislative districts and even authorizing the federal courts to redraw district lines. As a result of this ruling, the balance of power shifted to the cities, where more and more blacks resided. This decision therefore opened more political opportunities for cities and also for blacks.

Memphis Garbage Strike

Despite many signs of progress achieved by blacks in their quest for long-denied civil rights, problems persisted. Memphis, despite surprising accomplishments in diminishing segregation, still experienced much racial discrimination. The plight of 1,300 black sanitation workers—extremely low wages and poor working conditions—was notorious. T. O. Jones, union organizer for the American Federation of State, County, and Municipal Employees (AFSCME),

Memphis sanitation workers' protest march, February 1968. Photograph by *Memphis Commercial Appeal*. In Mississippi Valley Collection, University of Memphis Libraries.

looked for an opportunity to galvanize the garbage workers. In February 1968, twenty-two black employees were sent home on account of bad weather and thus were paid for only two hours' work that day, whereas their white supervisors received a full day's pay. In addition, two workers accidentally were crushed in a garbage compressor. Jones seized upon these events and rallied sanitation workers to walk off their jobs. On Monday morning, more than 1,100 workers stayed home, and thus the strike began. Mayor Henry Loeb vigorously opposed it and all the demands of the union.

The garbage workers' strike acquired considerably more leverage and meaning when it was transformed from a mere labor dispute into a civil rights struggle. The local chapter of the NAACP announced that it would join the picket lines in support of the striking workers. On February 23, an unfortunate confrontation between the protesters and the Memphis police took place. Black clergy now assumed direction of the strike and also organized an economic boycott of downtown stores and the two Memphis newspapers. Meanwhile, the Memphis Committee on Community Relations attempted to convince the mayor to reach some sort of compromise with the labor union and with the entire black community, but to no avail.

The strike moved to new levels of intensity when black clergy invited Roy Wilkins, executive secretary of the NAACP, to visit Memphis. He addressed an enthusiastic rally of some nine thousand people on the night of March 14. Four days later, Martin Luther King Jr. arrived in Memphis and spoke to an even larger rally. On that occasion, he urged a general one-day strike by all black Memphians and promised to lead it. Eventually, March 28 was set as the date for the general strike. Certain white leaders once more attempted to get the mayor and city council to make concessions to the striking sanitation workers, but again they failed. Therefore, the general one-day strike commenced.

A crowd of at least five thousand peaceful marchers, led by King, paraded through the downtown streets. But a group of Black Power advocates, the Invaders, intent upon violence and destruction of property, joined the demonstration. Hardly had the peaceful march begun than the Invaders started smashing store windows; looting and a general riot quickly followed. Vigorous response by the police resulted in one dead black youth, at least sixty injured, and three hundred arrested. So much for a nonviolent demonstration.

Criticism of King's leadership erupted across the nation, for it was obvious that he did not have control of the march that day in Memphis. Partly in an effort to regain his standing, King decided to plan a second demonstration. On the evening of April 4, an assassin's bullet killed King on the balcony of the Lorraine Motel. It was a shot heard around the world; America's greatest civil rights leader was dead. In anger and frustration, blacks in Tennessee cities and elsewhere went on a rampage of rioting and violence.

In an almost anticlimactic gesture several days later, Mayor Loeb agreed to make concessions to the black garbage workers: a slight increase in pay and nominal recognition of the labor union. With that, the strike ended on April 16. But great damage had been done to the city's reputation; racial harmony and mutual respect remained elusive goals.

Nonetheless, in Memphis and in other Tennessee communities, the 1950s and 1960s had brought about great transformation. The old racially-based caste system had all but disappeared, certainly insofar as its legal aspects were concerned. The walls of segregation came tumbling down, but rubble remained. In the early 1970s, court-ordered busing to achieve racial balance in the public schools stirred new antagonisms or revived old ones. At the end of the 1960s, however, any observant visitor to Tennessee, or almost anywhere else in the South, had to admit that, on the racial front, the situation had changed remarkably. The civil rights struggle, although not completed, had wrought wondrous things.

Suggested Readings

Bartley, Numan V. *The New South, 1945–1980.* Baton Rouge, La., 1995.

Couto, Richard A., *Lifting the Veil: A Political History of Struggles for Emancipation.* Knoxville, Tenn., 1993.

Glen, John M. *Highlander: No Ordinary School, 1932–1962.* 2nd ed. Knoxville, Tenn., 1996.

Graham, Hugh Davis. *Crisis in Print: Desegregation and the Press in Tennessee.* Nashville, Tenn., 1967.

Lamon, Lester C. *Blacks in Tennessee, 1791–1970.* Knoxville, Tenn., 1981.

McMillen, Neil R. *The Citizens' Council: Organized Resistance to the Second Reconstruction, 1954–64.* Urbana, Ill., 1971.

Peirce, Neal R. *The Border South States: People, Politics and Power in the Five States of the Border South.* New York, 1975.

Tucker, David. *Memphis Since Crump: Bossism, Blacks, and Civil Reformers, 1948–1968.* Knoxville, Tenn., 1980.

13

The 1960s to Century's End

IN THE LAST THREE DECADES, Tennesseans have become more and more a part of a broad national culture and a complex national (and even international) economy. But they have not thereby lost all their distinctiveness. Even when touched by the same winds and currents that have swept across the rest of America and the world, Tennesseans have responded in ways that set them apart from others. Thus they have preserved and underscored their state's unique identity.

Since the mid-1960s, Tennessee has experienced wrenching changes and bitter conflicts. The civil rights revolution, discussed in the previous chapter, has been responsible for some of these. Others, perhaps less dramatic but no less far-reaching, will be discussed in this chapter. Although these changes and conflicts have been tempered by generous measures of continuity and consensus, they have made Tennessee a state very different from that which previous generations knew. Nor can there be any doubt that more profound transformations are in store for the next generation of Tennesseans.

A Changing Population

Since 1960, Tennessee's population has grown considerably. In that year, the census takers counted 3,567,089 Tennesseans. The population increased by 10 percent in the subsequent decade, another 17 percent in the 1970s, and another 6 percent in the 1980s. By 1990, the number of Tennesseans stood at 4,877,185. The overall growth rate for population in the 1960–90 period was nearly 37 percent, only slightly below that of the United States as a whole. Tennessee now is the seventeenth most populous state in the union, home to one American in every fifty.

The population boom of the past few decades was due not only to the fertility of the native population, but also to the state's attractiveness to those born elsewhere. Tennessee has welcomed many in-migrants who are drawn by the scenic beauty, climatic amenities, and burgeoning economy of the Volunteer State. A 1980 survey found that over 9 percent of the people living in Tennessee had moved there from another state within the last five years; by 1990 that figure was 11 percent. Although the majority of these in-migrants came from other southern states, a significant number traveled southward from colder climes, especially Illinois, Ohio, and Michigan.

By 1960, Tennesseans had become (by the U.S. Census Bureau's definition) a predominantly urban people; in that year, a little over 52 percent of the population lived in incorporated areas of 2,500 people or more. The trend toward urbanization has continued since then: by 1990, 61 percent of the state's population was urban. To use another measure of urbanization: in 1960, there were twenty-four towns and cities in Tennessee with a population of more than ten thousand; by 1990, there were thirty-seven.

The ranking of Tennessee's four largest cities has not changed since 1960. Memphis remains the state's largest; it grew from 497,524 residents in 1960 to 610,337 in 1990. Nashville grew much faster but remains second largest, its population expanding from 154,563 to 487,973 in the three decades. Next is Knoxville, boasting 111,827 inhabitants in 1960 and 165,121 in 1990. Not far behind is Chattanooga, with 130,009 people in 1960 and 152,466 in 1990. (These figures reflect annexations as well as natural population increase.)

Despite the fact that West and Middle Tennessee claim the two largest cities, East Tennessee has emerged as the most populous grand division of the

---

Memphis Soul

All Tennesseans are familiar with Nashville's role as the nation's country music capital, but not all know about Memphis's role in creating soul music, a distinctive style of black music popular in the 1960s. Soul derived from the rhythm-and-blues music popular among blacks in the 1940s and 1950s, but it added some gospel elements and a sense of assertiveness and black pride that grew out of the civil rights revolution.

The beating heart of Memphis soul music was the studios of Stax Records, where the greatest of the soul singers—including Wilson Pickett, Sam and Dave, and the legendary Otis Redding—all recorded at one time or another. Stax was unusual in that it was a biracial organization. Its owner was white, its singers were black, and its stable of studio musicians, writers, and arrangers included people of both races. Among the latter were white guitarists Steve Cropper and Donald "Duck" Dunn, black keyboardist Booker T. Jones, and black writer-arranger Isaac Hayes. Stax's integrated staff distinguished it from nearly all other record companies of that era, including its main rival in the soul-music genre, all-black Motown Records in Detroit.

state (with 37 percent of the whole, compared to 35 for Middle Tennessee and 28 for West Tennessee). This is because East Tennessee contains not only the third- and fourth-ranked places but also the Tri-Cities (Bristol, Johnson City, Kingsport) and a number of other fast-growing municipalities.

The most spectacular urban growth in recent years has been not in the cities proper but in their suburbs. Indeed, three of the four major cities actually lost population during the 1980s. Memphis and Knoxville lost nearly 6 percent, Chattanooga more than 10 percent; Nashville grew by 7 percent. Meanwhile, a number of formerly rural areas near the cities have become rapidly expanding bedroom communities—most notably, Williamson County, south of Nashville, whose population grew by 69 percent during the 1970s and another 39 percent during the 1980s.

Although Tennessee's population has changed remarkably in recent years, in some respects it has not kept pace with demographic transformations in the United States as a whole. Despite the growth of cities and suburbs in the state, Tennessee remains less urbanized than most other states. And, despite substantial out- and in-migration, the proportion of Tennessee residents who are natives of the state is considerably higher than the proportion of Americans as a whole who are natives of their state of residence. Moreover, Tennessee has been insulated somewhat from the waves of foreign immigration (primarily from Latin America and Asia) that in recent years have changed the demographic face of America. The number of foreign-born Tennessee residents has multiplied rapidly; but, as of 1990, it was still only a little over 1 percent of the population. In the United States as a whole, that figure was nearly 8 percent. Meanwhile, the proportion of blacks in the Tennessee population has remained steady (at about 16 percent) since 1960, although the proportion in the national population has grown.

An Evolving Economy

The industrial boom in Tennessee that was precipitated by World War II and had continued through the 1950s picked up even more steam in the 1960s. By 1972, the state could boast 5,647 manufacturing establishments, a 25 percent increase since 1958. The total value added by manufacture in 1972 was almost $8 billion, a figure three and a half times that for 1958. The number of Tennesseans employed in manufacturing increased by nearly 5 percent annually during the 1960s, a rate of growth even faster than that experienced in the 1940s and 1950s, and well over twice that of the United States as a whole in the 1960s. By 1969, some 456,000 Tennesseans were employed in manufacturing. This number comprised about 27 percent of the state's workforce, a proportion higher than in the nation at large.

Much of the state's industrial growth in the 1960s came from the establishment of branch manufacturing facilities by large northern industrial firms. Most of these were built not in the major metropolitan areas, but in rural sections of the state. In fact, as the years went by, manufacturing, as a sector of the economy, became more important in rural areas than in metropolitan ones.

The spectacular industrial growth rate of the 1960s could not be sustained indefinitely. Manufacturing employment has experienced a proportional decline since that decade and a numerical decline since the late 1970s, when it peaked at about 524,000. By 1991, only 501,000 Tennesseans worked in manufacturing (about 23 percent of the workforce). Such figures do not indicate that the state is "deindustrializing," however; rather, machines have replaced workers in many instances. Industrial output continued to expand through the 1970s, 1980s, and early 1990s, albeit at a pace slower than before; at the end of the twentieth century, industry's share of the state's gross product remained higher than in the 1960s. By 1990, there were nearly seven thousand manufacturing plants in the state, and the value added per year exceeded $30 billion. Moreover, Tennessee's economy and workforce have remained considerably more industrial than those of the nation as a whole.

In recent years, the state has continued to attract outside manufacturing investment, not only by U.S. firms but increasingly by overseas firms. Two huge automotive plants in the Nashville area, one established by General Motors and the other by the Japanese-owned Nissan Corporation, are among the state's most notable recent acquisitions. Even so, chemical production continues to be the state's leading manufacturing activity, as it has been since World War II.

Tennessee's impressive industrial development of the last few decades resulted from a number of factors, most of which were at work not just in Tennessee but throughout the South. For one thing, state and municipal governments, together with local boosters such as Chambers of Commerce, continued to court outside investors as aggressively as they had in the past. Those investors, for their part, became more and more interested in seeing what Tennessee and other "Sunbelt" states of the Southeast (and Southwest) had to offer, as the long-industrialized areas of the Northeast and Midwest grew less and less appealing as places to invest.

Among Tennessee's attractions were plentiful natural resources, a mild climate, and an expanding and increasingly affluent population that offered a ready market for manufactured products. The per capita income of Tennesseans, which stood at $1,575 in 1960, climbed steadily in the succeeding years, reaching $15,880 in 1990. At the same time, the proportion of Tennesseans living below the poverty line declined dramatically, from 39 percent in 1959 to less than 16 percent in 1989.

Another of the state's enticements was its increasingly sophisticated infrastructure. The federally sponsored interstate highway system, begun in the 1950s, eventually brought modern high-speed thoroughfares to all of Tennessee's major cities and many smaller ones, linking them to one another and the rest of the nation. In addition to the more than 1,000 miles of interstate highways that the state now boasts, there are over 12,000 miles of state highways, thanks to the state government's continued commitment to good roads (state expenditures for highway construction and maintenance rose sevenfold between 1960 and 1990). Moreover, a combination of federal, state, and local funding has provided modern airports for all of Tennessee's major cities.

The importance of the Tennessee Valley Authority (TVA) in modernizing the state's infrastructure and in luring industry cannot be overestimated. The agency's flood control and river navigation improvements turned the Tennessee River into an efficient artery of commerce whose barge traffic now is measured in billions of ton-miles annually and whose banks are lined with factories. (The river's usefulness has been enhanced by the completion in 1985 of the Tennessee-Tombigbee Waterway, a U.S. Army Corps of Engineers project that links the Tennessee River directly with the Gulf of Mexico.) Even more important was the cheap and abundant electric power that TVA offered. In response to growing demand (and in some cases to internal bureaucratic pressure), TVA continued to build new generating plants in the 1960s and beyond. At the end of the twentieth century, it was operating twenty-two hydroelectric, eight steam, and two nuclear facilities in Tennessee. The agency provided, and continues to provide, advice and assistance to local economic development organizations. Moreover, it boosted the state's attractiveness as a market by raising the standard of living throughout the vast valley.

Another key element in Tennessee's appeal to outside investors has been the low cost of doing business in the state. Local and state taxes have remained low by northern standards, and local governments in many cases have "sweetened the pot" by offering special tax breaks and other incentives to new industries. Even more important, at least to labor-intensive industries, are the relatively low wage levels that have prevailed in Tennessee and the weakness of organized labor in the state.

The union weakness can be accounted for in great part by the traditional antipathy of conservative, individualistic Tennesseans toward labor unions and by the generally anti-union attitude of state and local governments. (Tennessee, like most southern states, is a "right-to-work" state whose laws forbid closed-shop agreements between employers and workers.) Although the Volunteer State by the 1970s led the South in the proportion of unionized workers (21 percent of the nonagricultural workforce), that proportion was far below the average of states outside the South. Moreover, the figure has declined in recent years, by 1989 being less than 13 percent (in the U.S. as a whole that year, the portion was nearly 24 percent). In 1990, Tennessee's factory workers earned, on the average, $9.55 per hour, while those in the nation as a whole earned $10.83.

While industry remains a vital component of Tennessee's economy, it has been overshadowed in recent decades by the rapidly growing service sector—i.e., businesses that produce not goods but services, such as retail stores, hotels and restaurants, advertising and insurance firms, auto repair shops, movie theaters, hospitals, and nursing homes. The declining number of manufacturing jobs since the 1970s has been more than offset by the proliferation of service jobs.

The same factors that lured industry to the state also lured some major service businesses, but probably the single most important catalyst for the service-sector boom in Tennessee has been the remarkable growth of tourism. The state is singularly blessed (some would say cursed) with attractions that draw visitors from every corner of the nation and indeed the globe, bringing approximately $8 billion a year into the state's economy and providing jobs for 140,000 Tennesseans. These attractions include Elvis Presley's Graceland mansion in Memphis (600,000 visitors per year) and the Dollywood amusement park in Pigeon Forge (1,900,000). The crown

---

Death of the King

The whole nation was stunned on August 16, 1977, by news of the sudden death of Tennessee's most famous resident, rock-'n'-roll superstar Elvis Presley. He was found lying face down on the bathroom floor of his Graceland mansion in Memphis about 2:15 P.M. An autopsy by the Shelby County medical examiner identified the cause of death as coronary arrhythmia, an irregular heartbeat brought about by either hypertension or a heart attack. What came out much later was Presley's serious problem with prescription drug abuse; his doctor said that he was a "walking drugstore. He was drugged to the limit."

Presley was buried on August 18 in Forest Hill Cemetery in Memphis, following a funeral ceremony at Graceland. Those in attendance included Gov. Ray Blanton, who declared it an official day of mourning in Tennessee and ordered state flags to fly at half-mast.

Presley's adoring fans have not forgotten him since his death. Indeed, the cult that honors him probably is at least as large and devoted now as during his life. Graceland, opened to the public in 1982, is a veritable shrine, the scene of candlelight vigils held by the faithful each year on the anniversary of Presley's death. Numerous Elvis impersonators pay homage to the King on stages across the country. Many of his followers refuse to believe that their idol really is dead; sightings of him are reported regularly.

jewel of Tennessee's attractions, of course, is the Great Smoky Mountains National Park, which draws some 8,500,000 people annually and is by far the most visited of the country's national parks.

The retail trade also has been an important aspect of the service-sector boom in Tennessee. In common with the rest of the nation, Tennessee has seen an explosion of consumption in the last few decades. At the same time, the geography of the retail business has evolved. Suburban shopping centers and malls, made possible by the ubiquitous automobile and by highway improvements, have replaced traditional downtown shopping districts. In cities and smaller towns alike, once-vibrant Main Streets now stand deserted, while shopping centers and malls on the urban periphery buzz with activity.

The labor pool available for both services and manufacturing has been enlarged by the steep decline in agricultural employment over the years. The number of Tennesseans living on farms, which in 1960 stood at 587,000 (over 16 percent of population), fell in 1980 to 176,000 (less than 4 percent) and has continued to fall since. At the same time, the number of farms and the acreage under cultivation were dwindling, too, from about 158,000 farms and 16 million acres in 1959 to 80,000 farms and less than 12 million acres in 1987.

Even as the number of farmers, farms, and acres declined, however, agricultural production increased, thanks to the adoption of modern technology such as tractors and harvesters, improved fertilizers, chemical herbicides and insecticides, hybrid seed, scientific animal breeding, and improved feeds. There was, moreover, an increase in the average size of farms and thus in their economic efficiency. Sharecropping and tenant farming virtually disappeared. In fact, the number of family-operated farms, whether owned or rented, has dwindled to relative insignificance since 1960, as "agribusiness" has expanded.

Changing patterns of state, national, and international supply and demand have helped to transform Tennessee agriculture in the last few decades. Livestock production soared relative to crop production, and now livestock products (meat animals, dairy produce, poultry, and eggs) account for well over half of agricultural cash receipts. Tobacco superseded cotton as the top-earning crop in 1966, but in 1972 tobacco was superseded in turn by soybeans. Soy remains the king of crops in Tennessee (at least insofar as official statistics show—recent years have witnessed an untabulated but clearly enormous increase in the furtive cultivation of marijuana, which in fact now may be the state's leading money crop).

Despite the increased crop and livestock output, agriculture's role in Tennessee's economy has shrunk drastically. By the late 1980s, agriculture accounted for less than 2 percent of the gross state product (compared to nearly 29 percent for industry and over 69 percent for services), while the number of persons employed in agriculture amounted to less than 3 percent of the workforce. It should be noted that these statistics somewhat understate the importance of agriculture, for many of Tennessee's industries and services are agriculture-related. Nevertheless, it is clear that the days when agriculture was the heart and soul of the state's economy are long past.

Tennessee's agriculture, industry, and services all have been stimulated greatly by federal spending and development programs. A number of important federal installations—among them the Oak Ridge National Laboratory, the U.S. Army's Fort Campbell near Clarksville, and the state's nine national parks and historic sites—contribute directly to the Tennessee economy. Moreover, a host of federal agencies contribute indirectly by funding research at public and private institutions, most notably the University of Tennessee; and by tendering grants to state and local governments for a myriad of purposes, from highways and schools to public housing and environmental improvement. Dozens of federal agencies oversee one aspect or another of the state's economic development, including TVA, the Appalachian Regional Commission, the Department of Agriculture, the National Park Service, and the Department of Energy, to name only a few of the most important.

Politics and Government

The years 1960 to 1990 witnessed a virtual revolution in Tennessee politics. Traditional patterns of party affiliation, voter behavior, and interest-group predominance began unraveling in the 1960s, and new patterns have taken shape. The main beneficiary of these transformations has been the Republican Party, long overshadowed by the Democrats but now a powerful and frequently successful contender in statewide political contests.

The remarkable resurgence of the Republicans has its origins in a number of developments in the years after World War II. For one thing, the GOP benefited from the influx of in-migrants to Tennessee from outside the South, many of whom were Republicans. The growing affluence of many Tennesseans, natives and newcomers alike, encouraged them to take a new look at the Republican Party, whose fiscal conservatism was appealing to the upwardly mobile. At century's end, the party's strongest support in the Volunteer State was among the prosperous and well educated, and the suburbs where they live had become bastions of Republican strength. Even so, the GOP's most formidable bastion remained East Tennessee, which was as strongly and dependably Republican in 1999 as it was during Reconstruction and in every period since.

Certain national political developments also helped broaden the Republicans' support in Tennessee. In the 1960s, the Democratic Party emerged as the champion of black civil rights. Disturbed by the increasing political activism of blacks and by their growing influence in the Democratic Party, many conservative southern whites forsook that party and joined the ranks of the Republicans. Many more did so in the early 1970s, when Americans were bitterly divided over the Vietnam War. As the Democratic Party came

Alex Haley. Alex Haley Papers, Special Collections, University of Tennessee, Knoxville. Used by permission of estate of Alexander P. Haley.

under the control of liberal "doves," the Republican Party tenaciously defended the "hawk" position.

Signs of change were evident as early as the 1952–60 period, when Tennessee three times voted Republican in presidential contests. But the real turning point probably was 1966, when Republican Howard Baker Jr. defeated Gov. Frank Clement by a sizable majority (56 percent) in a U.S. Senate race. Baker thus became the state's first Republican senator since Reconstruction. In another significant contest that year, a Republican won the Ninth District congressional seat in West Tennessee; his Democratic opponent was a black man, the first in Tennessee history to win nomination for a congressional race. By no means did the 1966 election signal the demise of the Democrats, however, for Buford Ellington won a second term as governor that year (with 81 percent of the vote), and the Democrats retained their usual large majority in the General Assembly.

The Republicans scored more successes two years later, in 1968, when they won control of the lower house of the legislature for the first time in modern history. They were helped that year by the popularity of Republican presidential candidate Richard Nixon, whose plurality in Tennessee (38 percent) doubtless would have been a large majority but for the presence on the ballot of a third-party candidate, ultraconservative George Wallace, who attracted 34 percent of the vote. The Democratic candidate, Hubert

Alex Haley, 1921–1992

Tennessee has been home to a number of highly regarded writers in this century, among them novelists James Agee and Cormac McCarthy, short story writer Peter Taylor, and poet Nikki Giovanni. But none has achieved more popular renown than Alex Haley. Born in New York State, Haley was raised from infancy in the small West Tennessee town of Henning. He joined the Coast Guard in 1939, at the age of eighteen, and began writing stories in his spare time aboard ship. Retiring from the Coast Guard in 1959, he started a new career as a freelance writer.

Haley's first book, *The Autobiography of Malcolm X* (1965), based on Haley's interviews with that black leader for *Playboy* magazine, brought critical acclaim. But it was *Roots: The Saga of an American Family* (1976) that brought Haley a Pulitzer Prize and made him a literary superstar. A blend of fact and fiction, *Roots* tells the story of Haley's family all the way back to Kunta Kinte, who came to America from West Africa as a slave in 1767. The book captured the imagination of the public. As of this writing, it has sold six million copies and has been translated into more than three dozen languages. A twelve-part television miniseries based on it, broadcast in 1977, was watched by the largest television audience in history up to that time. In his later years, Haley lived in East Tennessee, but he is buried at his old home in Henning, now a state historical site and museum.

Humphrey, finished a poor third, with 28 percent. Nixon won reelection in 1972, again with the help of Tennessee, where this time he racked up a landslide margin of 68 percent; his Democratic opponent that year, George McGovern, was tarnished (in the eyes of most Tennesseans) with ultraliberalism and opposition to the Vietnam War. Nixon's subsequent disgrace in the Watergate scandal contributed to the 1976 victory of Democratic presidential candidate Jimmy Carter over Republican Gerald Ford, who had succeeded to the presidency in 1974, upon Nixon's resignation. A majority of Tennesseans (56 percent) gave their votes to Carter, partly out of revulsion toward Nixon, but also because the Georgia-born Carter was a fellow southerner.

In gubernatorial politics, the Republican resurgence began in 1970. Governor Ellington being constitutionally barred from succeeding himself, the Democrats nominated Nashvillian John J. Hooker. Hooker went down to defeat at the hands of Republican Winfield Dunn, a Memphis dentist virtually unknown in politics up to that time. Dunn, who garnered 53 percent of the vote, was the first GOP governor elected since 1920. He faced a General Assembly controlled by the Democrats, for the Republicans lost the narrow control of the lower house that they had won two years earlier. In 1974, the Democrats, aided no doubt by the Watergate backlash, regained the governor's office. West Tennessee Democrat Ray Blanton defeated East Tennessee Republican Lamar Alexander that year with 56 percent of the vote, and the Democrats extended their control of the legislature.

The U.S. Senate races of the 1970s confirmed that, in Tennessee politics, the Republicans now were a force to be reckoned with. In 1970, three-term Democratic Sen. Albert Gore Sr. ran for reelection but lost to William E. Brock III, a Republican congressman from East Tennessee. Brock capitalized on the growing public disenchantment with Gore, who was seen as liberal, dovish, and out of touch with his constituents. With Brock's victory and that of Dunn at the same time, Tennessee Republicans were riding high, simultaneously controlling both Senate seats and the governors' office. Two years later, in 1972, Howard Baker had no trouble defending his Senate seat against Democratic challenger Ray Blanton. In 1976, however, Senator Brock lost his seat to Democrat James Sasser.

In the late 1970s, Tennesseans paused between political campaigns to consider amendments to the state constitution. Initial impetus for this latest constitutional convention came from bankers and lesser money lenders who objected to the constitution's 10 percent cap on loan interest rates. By the time the convention met in 1977, however, a number of other issues also were on the table. Sitting through the summer and fall, the delegates hammered out thirteen proposed amendments, only one of which (a sweeping reform of the state judicial system) was rejected by the voters in the March 1978 referendum.

Among the approved amendments was one that allowed the governor to serve two consecutive terms. Another amendment removed the 10 percent ceiling on interest rates and authorized (in fact, required) the General Assembly to set an appropriate maximum. A third provision prohibited deficit spending by the state government, though still permitting issuance of state bonds, with certain limitations. Other amendments made changes in legislative procedures and modernized the county governments. A number of the remaining amendments amounted to constitutional housekeeping—i.e., repealing or revising provisions that had been invalidated by federal law. Mandatory segregation of schools and the ban on interracial marriage were repealed, and the voting age was lowered from twenty-one to eighteen.

Having brought their constitution up to date, Tennesseans turned their attention once again to electoral campaigns. Governor Blanton, though now eligible to succeed himself, chose not to run in 1978. He undoubtedly realized that he could not win, for his administration had been tainted by scandals, and his popularity was at rock bottom. The Democratic nomination for governor went to Jake Butcher of Knoxville, a multimillionaire banker; his Republican opponent was Lamar Alexander. Though Butcher's deep pockets allowed him to outspend his opponent, Alexander won handily, with 56 percent of the vote. Like his fellow Republican Dunn before him, however, he would face a Democratically controlled legislature.

Alexander's tenure as governor began most dramatically. In the waning days of Blanton's term, the outgoing governor (who already was under heavy criticism for his pardoning policy) suddenly pardoned fifty-two state penitentiary inmates, one of whom—a convicted murderer—was the son of one of Blanton's close political allies. Fearing further such actions, Alexander, in cooperation with the General Assembly and with the legal blessing of the state's attorney general, had himself hurriedly sworn in as governor on January 18, 1979, two days before his scheduled inauguration. Later investigations showed that Blanton was deeply involved in the corruption that had marred his administration, and eventually he went to prison.

Scandal and prison likewise ended the political career of Jake Butcher. After the 1978 campaign, he kept a high profile, overseeing his banking empire and playing a leading role in bringing the 1982 World's Fair to Knoxville. Clearly he had further political and business ambitions, but in 1983 everything came apart. State and federal bank examiners uncovered financial problems in the Butcher banks, a number of which eventually were declared insolvent. Butcher was forced to step down as head of the empire. Further investigations disclosed illegal banking practices by Butcher and a number of his associates. In 1985, Butcher pleaded guilty to federal bank fraud charges and served nearly seven years in prison.

Lamar Alexander proved a popular governor and easily won reelection in 1982, with 60 percent of the vote. (His Democratic challenger that year was Knoxville's Mayor Randy Tyree.) The Democrats, however, held onto their solid legislative majority throughout Alexander's second term, as they had during the first. Tennessee Republicans likely would have been glad to nominate the Maryvillian for a third term in 1986, but, since a third term was precluded by law, they turned to their earlier gubernatorial winner, Winfield Dunn. But Dunn lacked Alexander's appeal, and in the general election he was beaten by a West Tennessee Democrat, Ned Ray McWherter, longtime speaker of the state's house, who got 54 percent of the vote. McWherter proved to be at least as popular a governor as Alexander, and in 1990 he won 62 percent of the vote and a second term, defeating Republican Dwight Henry. Democratic majorities persisted in the legislature throughout the eight years of McWherter's tenure as governor.

Seesaw Republican-Democratic triumphs also characterized the U.S. Senate races during the period. Howard Baker easily won a third term in 1978, beating Democrat Jane Eskind with 58 percent of the vote. Four years later, Jim Sasser won a second term even more impressively, taking 62 percent of the vote in a race against Republican Robin Beard. In 1984,

The Sunsphere, centerpiece of the 1982 Knoxville World's Fair. University of Tennessee *Volunteer* yearbook, 1983. University Archives, University of Tennessee, Knoxville.

Baker announced his retirement, much to the sorrow of Tennessee Republicans, who saw their replacement candidate (a state senator, Victor Ashe of Knoxville) overwhelmed by Democrat Albert Gore Jr., a Middle Tennessee congressman raised in politics, who won 61 percent of the vote. Gore's victory put both Tennessee Senate seats back in Democratic hands for the first time in eighteen years. Gore and Sasser proved unbeatable in their next races as well. In 1988, Sasser took 65 percent of the vote against Republican Bill Andersen; in 1990, Gore took 68 percent of the vote against Republican William Hawkins.

The presidential races of the 1980s gave the Republicans much to cheer about. Tennessee contributed to the defeat of incumbent Jimmy Carter in 1980, giving his Republican challenger, Ronald Reagan, a plurality (49 percent). Four years later, the state helped Reagan gain a second term, giving him 59 percent in his race against Democrat Walter Mondale. The Volunteer State voted for a Republican and a winner again in 1988, when George Bush got 58 percent of the state's vote in his contest against Democrat Michael Dukakis.

Tennessee Democrats were heartened in 1992, however, when Bill Clinton took the state by a plurality (47 percent) and also won the presidency, denying Bush a second term. At that point, Tennessee's Republicans must have wondered if their resurgence had petered out, for the post of governor, both Senate seats, and a majority of legislative seats all were in Democratic hands. But 1994 brought a remarkable reversal of fortunes. McWherter being barred from succeeding himself, Democrats nominated Nashville's Mayor Phil Bredesen for the governorship. He was defeated, however, by the Republican nominee, Don Sundquist, a six-term West Tennessee congressman who took 55 percent of the vote. At the same time, in a U.S. Senate race necessitated by the resignation of Al Gore Jr. (who became Clinton's vice-president), Democratic congressman Jim Cooper was bested by his Republican opponent, lawyer-turned-Hollywood-actor Fred Thompson, who won 61 percent of the vote. The Democrats' biggest shock, however, was the resounding defeat of Sen. Jim Sasser in his bid for a fourth term; his Republican challenger, a Nashville surgeon and political neophyte named Bill Frist, took 57 percent of the vote. The Republicans also took control of the state senate, although the house stayed in Democratic hands.

The 1996 campaigns brought mixed results. Republicans celebrated Fred Thompson's easy victory in the race for a full-term U.S. Senate seat. But Democrats celebrated President Clinton's 48-percent plurality in Tennessee, which helped him to victory over Republican presidential contender Bob Dole. The Democrats also regained control of the state senate and retained control of the house.

Many political issues have stirred public debate and absorbed the attention of governors and lawmakers in Tennessee over the last few decades. But three issues in particular have been persistent sources of controversy and remain unresolved at the end of the twentieth century. One is tax reform. Pressure for better public services and facilities—especially schools, highways, and health and social services—has led to an enormous increase in state government expenditures over the years. In 1965, the state spent $702 million. Four years later, expenditures exceeded $1 billion. By 1975, that figure had more than doubled, and over the next nine years doubled again. By 1990, annual spending had doubled again, reaching $8.403 billion. Some of this increase was covered by transfer payments from the federal government, but most of it had to be covered by the state. Deficit financing being forbidden by the Tennessee constitution, the state government has had to rely on tax revenues.

Many other states, as well as the federal government, have found an income tax to be a fair and productive source of revenue. So far, however, determined opposition has prevented enactment of a comprehensive income tax in Tennessee. (Contrary to popular belief, Tennessee does have an income tax, but it is imposed only on selected unearned income—dividends and interest from out-of-state sources—and not on earned income, such as wages and salaries.) Opposition has come from all directions but has been particularly strong among the well-heeled and those desirous of attracting investment to the state. (These latter boosters also have lobbied hard to keep the state tax on corporate profits at its current low level.) Governors Blanton, McWherter, and Sundquist all advocated a state tax on earned income during their terms, but none succeeded in getting one.

In the absence of a comprehensive income tax, the state has relied on an ever-increasing sales tax, a singularly regressive levy but far more palatable politically than an income tax. Tennessee's sales tax is now among the highest in the nation. In recent years, calls have been heard to legalize gambling in the state. Proponents point out how much revenue other states have gained from legalizing and taxing such things as bingo, lotteries, horse and dog races, and riverboat gambling. Opposition to this has been loud and strong, particularly from fundamentalist religious leaders. So far the legislature has rejected every legalized gambling bill.

A second major issue over the years has been legislative apportionment. Throughout most of the twentieth century, the General Assembly was apportioned on the basis of the 1900 census, despite the state constitution's requirement of reapportionment each decade. This kept rural-district majorities in place in both houses of the legislature even after Tennessee became a predominantly urban state. The situation was reminiscent of the "rotten boroughs" of England. Moore County, for example, with a population of less than four thousand in the 1950s, had exactly as much representation in the state's lower house as Shelby and Fayette Counties combined, with a population of over half a million. Both houses were dominated by rural and small-town legislators from Middle and West Tennessee, who not only refused to consider reapportionment but also made sure that a more-than-generous share of state spending was routed into their districts and away from the cities and East Tennessee. The state courts declined to intervene.

In 1959, a Tennessean filed a class-action suit in federal court challenging the state's apportionment. Three years later, the U.S. Supreme Court handed down a decision in this case (*Baker v. Carr*) that was to have an enormous impact, not only in the Volunteer State but across the nation. The Court ruled that states must apportion their legislatures fairly, on the basis of "one man, one vote," and that the federal courts could step in to make sure that this was done. The Tennessee General Assembly then went to work on reapportionment but could not please the U.S. district court, which finally, in 1968, imposed its own plan.

The immediate result was a huge increase in urban representation and a corresponding decrease in rural representation, in line with the state's true demographic makeup. In the years since, court-supervised reapportionment has ensured that not only urbanites (and more recently suburbanites) are fairly represented, but also East Tennesseans, whose region's population has grown faster than that of the rest of the state. It also has helped to ensure that the hard-won political rights of blacks are not gerrymandered into impotence. Several black state representatives—the first since the 1880s—were elected in the 1960s, and as the century ends, about 10 percent of the General Assembly's members are black. The federal courts also have overseen the legislature's reapportionment of congressional seats; Tennessee sent its first black congressman, Memphian Harold Ford, to Washington in 1974.

The problem, of course, is that the battle over apportionment must be refought every ten years. With each new census comes another free-for-all in the legislature, as various factions endeavor to arrange the state's political map in their favor, followed by another round with the federal court to get the new plan approved.

The third persistent issue of recent years is the power struggle between the governor and the legislature. From the time of Austin Peay until the 1960s, the legislature was pretty much under the governor's thumb. For example, the governor usually dictated the choice of not only state comptroller, treasurer, and secretary of state, but even house and senate speakers and legislative committee chairmen. Fiscal policy also was basically in the hands of the governor. The legislature, enervated by complacency and enfeebled by high turnover and inadequate staff, rarely asserted itself against the chief executive.

This began to change in the 1960s, for a number of reasons. For one thing, the civil rights movement, reapportionment, and the Republican resurgence brought more blacks and Republicans into the legislature, many of them disinclined to go along with business as usual. Too, the election of three Republican governors since 1970 has stirred the Democratic legislative majority to declare its independence. Moreover, thanks to a state constitutional amendment of 1965, the General Assembly now meets annually rather than biennially. Consequently, legislators now are in a better position to monitor the state government, an ability they have further enhanced by funding larger legislative staffs and better office facilities and by creating (in 1967) a fiscal review committee. They also have given themselves a series of salary increases (another 1965 amendment replaced legislative per diem pay with salaries); this has encouraged more members to make legislative service a career, reducing turnover and nurturing a cadre of experienced lawmakers.

The General Assembly now no longer automatically bows to the governor's wishes. It has reasserted its constitutional prerogatives regarding appointments and fiscal policy and is quite ready to challenge the governor on all sorts of other issues. The attitude of many legislators is exemplified by the remark of one who, in the 1970s, stated that he had voted against a bill favored by the governor even though he had no particular objection to it, simply "to send Blanton the message that he can't run over us." While the governor remains the single most powerful figure in state government, the house and senate speakers have emerged as strong figures in their own right. Nashville has become an arena of executive-legislative combat on a scale unknown to previous generations of Tennesseans.

Society in Flux

The last three decades have witnessed not only important demographic, economic, and political changes in Tennessee, but also important social and ideological changes. Today's typical Tennessean (if there is such a thing) is, in certain ways, a fundamentally different person from the typical Tennessean of a generation ago.

For one thing, the modern Tennessean is better educated, owing to vast improvement in the state's educational system. Prodded not only by the demand for a better-trained workforce in an increasingly "high-tech" world, but also by the lobbying of powerful pressure groups such as the Tennessee Education Association and by the desire to make the state more attractive to outsiders who have money or talent to invest, the General Assembly steadily has increased educational funding over the years. Generous federal grants have added to the money available for public schools. The figures are striking: in 1965, the state spent $276 million ($336 per pupil) on public education; in 1990, it spent $2.842 billion ($3,730 per pupil).

The increased funding has brought about major improvements. The state began offering kindergarten instruction in the early 1970s. Furthermore, instruction at all grade levels has benefited from the increased number and improved quality of teachers. These improvements can be ascribed in part to significant salary increases for teachers over the years, most notably those instituted in the 1980s as part of Governor Alexander's Better Schools Program. In 1965, the state employed 34,231 teachers, of whom 6,981 had a master's degree or higher; in 1990, there were 50,009 teachers, of whom

26,107 had a master's degree or higher. The student-teacher ratio in 1965 was 26:1; in 1990, it was 17:1. In the meantime, the educational level of the Tennessee populace has climbed. In 1960, the median amount of schooling completed by persons above age twenty-five was less than nine years; at century's end, it is well over twelve.

Public higher education, too, has seen boom times since the 1960s, fueled by the same factors that boosted K-12 schooling. Funding for higher education has multiplied, and facilities have expanded enormously. In 1965, the state took the first steps to establish a network of community colleges, of which there are now ten. In 1967, the legislature created the Tennessee Higher Education Commission as a broad oversight and planning agency. The following year, the University of Tennessee was reorganized as a university system headed by a president, with a separate administration (under a chancellor) for each campus. These campuses are: UT-Knoxville (the "flagship" campus, housing the UT system's administration), UT-Chattanooga (created in 1969

The Farm: A Hippie Commune in Tennessee

Among the interesting social developments of the late 1960s and early 1970s was the "hippie" movement. Hippies were young people who condemned the materialism, repressiveness, and status-consciousness of American society and created an alternative culture marked by deliberately outrageous clothing and hairstyles, religious mysticism, psychedelic drugs, and casual sex. Some hippies went so far as to establish communes where they could withdraw altogether from the "straight" world.

One of the most successful of these was the Farm, near Summertown, Lewis County. Founded by a California hippie "guru" named Stephen Gaskin and 270 followers who migrated to Tennessee in 1971, the Farm was a collective whose residents turned over all personal property to the group and lived— without running water or electricity—according to the spiritual precepts of their leader. The people of the Farm experienced many travails in the early years of their experiment, including swarms of sightseers and freeloaders, as well as the arrest and three-year jail sentence of Gaskin for marijuana possession. But the Farm nevertheless has endured. At century's end, it is thriving, although it has abandoned collectivism and the primitive lifestyle—one of the few communes that survived the 1970s.

by the merger of the private University of Chattanooga with UT), UT-Martin, the UT Center for Health Sciences in Memphis, and the UT Space Institute in Tullahoma. In 1972, a Board of Regents was created to oversee the state's other institutions of higher learning, which include (besides the community colleges and the four state technical institutes) East Tennessee State University in Johnson City, Tennessee Technological University in Cookeville, Tennessee State University in Nashville, Middle Tennessee State University in Murfreesboro, Austin Peay State University in Clarksville, and the University of Memphis.

Enrollment in the state colleges and universities has mushroomed over the years. By 1990, the community colleges enrolled 40,955 students, the technical institutes 23,512, the Board of Regents universities 69,021, and the UT system 40,928 (25,579 of those at UT-Knoxville, the state's biggest school). At the same time, Tennessee's thirty-five private colleges and universities enrolled 44,454 students; the largest of these schools, Vanderbilt University in Nashville, had 9,236 students.

As Tennessee society was becoming better educated, it also was becoming more liberal, in the sense of loosening restrictions on personal freedom. Although this shift formed part of a national trend in that era, it was particularly striking in Tennessee and the other southern states, traditionally bastions of social conservatism. Signs of Tennessee's liberalization included the legalization of liquor by the drink in many municipalities; the repeal of local "blue laws" that forbade certain business and recreational activities on Sundays; the proliferation of sexually explicit books, magazines, and movies formerly prohibited; and the growing number of unmarried couples living together without fear of social ostracism or legal prosecution. Although without substantive impact, because the law had gone unenforced since the 1920s, the legislature's 1967 repeal of the infamous Butler Act (which banned the teaching of evolution in public schools) was a notable symbol of the growing liberalization.

The liberal reforms that had most impact were those attacking traditional role restrictions. The civil rights revolution, discussed in the preceding chapter, was one aspect of that assault. Another was the women's rights movement. In the 1960s and 1970s, many women, influenced in part by the example of African Americans, began to protest what they perceived as their own second-class citizenship. They saw themselves as victims of deep-rooted prejudice and discrimination that restricted their career opportunities and hindered their personal fulfillment. Such prejudice and discrimination were particularly entrenched, many believed, in Tennessee and the other southern states, where old ideas about a woman's "proper" place persisted tenaciously.

With the passage of the federal Civil Rights Act of 1964, which applied to women as well as blacks, women in Tennessee and elsewhere gained a powerful weapon with which to attack discrimination of many sorts. The Tennessee state government's immediate response was to establish a Commission on the Status of Women to investigate and make recommendations. In the following years, governors and legislators abolished some of the most blatant forms of discrimination; but more important, perhaps, were the state and federal courts, which struck down numerous discriminatory laws and practices in lawsuits brought by Tennessee women. These suits involved such issues as the right of married women to hold title to property and to use their maiden names, maternity leave and seniority rules for female employees, and the funding of girls' sports in high schools.

One measure of the success of the women's movement was the increasing number of women in the workforce, not just in the clerical, teaching, and nursing jobs traditionally open to them, but also in professional and technical positions long monopolized by men. Even more visible were the

---

Antiwar Protest in Knoxville, May 1970

The most notable Tennessee protest against the Vietnam War took place at the University of Tennessee in Knoxville on May 28, 1970. The occasion was a religious revival led by evangelist Billy Graham in Neyland Stadium. Such an event normally would not have provoked protest, except that Graham had invited his good friend, President Richard Nixon, to address the crowd. Nixon was the American most hated by antiwar activists at that time, given the recent U.S. military invasion of Cambodia and the killing of four student protesters at Kent State University in Ohio on May 4. Nixon's appearance at the Billy Graham Crusade in Knoxville was to be his first public appearance since the Kent State tragedy. He considered it safe to appear because the UT-Knoxville campus had a reputation for conservatism. He misjudged the mood of the campus, however.

Antiwar students and faculty, enraged that Nixon seemed to be using a religious meeting for political purposes, were determined to stage a demonstration. Several hundred gathered at the Student Center as the revival began, then marched to the stadium. There they were allowed in, but their protest signs were confiscated. Once inside, they pulled out other signs hidden in their clothes and yelled obscenities and antiwar slogans. Some attempted to move down onto the field and toward the podium but were prevented by police and Secret Service agents. Only nine demonstrators were arrested at the time, but police took photographs of the crowd and later identified the protesters and arrested nearly forty more in their homes or offices. A number eventually were convicted on charges of disrupting a religious ceremony.

Antiwar protester at Billy Graham rally, University of Tennessee, Knoxville, May 1970. University Historian's Files, University Archives, University of Tennessee, Knoxville.

increasing numbers of women in public life. In 1974, East Tennessean Marilyn Lloyd became Tennessee's first congresswoman. In 1978, Democrat Jane Eskind became the state's first major-party female candidate for the U.S. Senate; although she lost the general election to the popular Howard Baker, she polled nearly half a million votes. Furthermore, over the years women have been present in increasing numbers in the General Assembly and the upper reaches of the state bureaucracy.

Among the most vocal of Tennessee's women's rights advocates have been college women. In the 1960s, female students at many schools began protesting the differential treatment of the sexes that long had prevailed on college campuses, and eventually they were rewarded by the abolition of such rules as curfews and mandatory on-campus residence for women. They also succeeded, at some institutions, in getting women's studies courses added to the curriculum, just as blacks had secured black studies courses.

The women's protests on Tennessee's college campuses in the late 1960s and early 1970s were part of a broad student protest movement that was one of the most publicized social developments of that era. Although colleges in Tennessee and the rest of the South generally were quieter than colleges in other parts of the nation in those years, they were noisy and contentious by comparison with their earlier complacency. Taking their cue from peers at such schools as Columbia and the University of California at Berkeley, many Tennessee college students began demanding an end to administrative censorship of student publications and administrative veto power over student-invited speakers. They insisted that students must have a say in governing their colleges. When those battles were won, some students (joined by some of the younger faculty) moved in more radical directions, condemning America's entire government and society as corrupt, and in particular denouncing the Vietnam War. With the end of the war, however, peace returned to the campuses, which have remained relatively quiescent ever since.

It must be pointed out that the liberalizing tendencies of the last three decades never were endorsed unanimously by Tennesseans. Traditionalism remained strong in the Volunteer State, particularly in its small towns and rural areas. Even those Tennesseans who favored some degree of change in many cases were revolted by what they saw as the excesses of the more ardent activists, especially college radicals and women's liberationists. In some instances, a backlash against liberal reform arose, epitomized by the General Assembly's attempt in 1974 (disallowed by the federal courts) to repeal its ratification of the feminist-sponsored Equal Rights Amendment to the U.S. Constitution, which it had endorsed two years earlier with little dissension.

Balance Sheet of Modernization

There is no denying that the enormous changes of the last few decades have made Tennessee in many ways a better place to live. Tennesseans now are, on the whole, more affluent, better educated, and healthier than their parents and grandparents. They are surrounded by a vast array of modern conveniences and public facilities unknown to earlier generations, and they live in a society that allows them more opportunity for achievement and self-expression than their forebears enjoyed.

These are laudable accomplishments indeed, justifiable sources of pride for the Volunteer State. But Tennessee cannot be judged only against its old self. It must be judged also in the context of an American nation that like-wise has experienced rapid modernization. In such a perspective, Tennessee in some respects lags behind.

Consider, for example, prosperity. Despite the state's burgeoning wealth, per capita income in Tennessee was, at the end of the 1980s, only about 85 percent of that of the United States as a whole; Tennessee ranked thirty-sixth among the states in that regard. At that point, some 168,000 Tennessee families were living below the poverty line, or well over 12 percent of all families. The comparable figure for the nation was 10 percent. Poverty is particularly acute in the urban ghettos of the state and in many very rural counties.

Education presents an even more glaring contrast. Despite huge increases in funding for schools, Tennessee in 1991 ranked forty-fourth among the states in per-pupil expenditures. Of Tennessee's adult population, the pro-portion who are high school graduates, though it has climbed steadily over the years, ranked forty-fifth among the states in 1990. The state's propor-tion of college graduates ranked forty-third. Again, ghetto and rural resi-dents are poorest served. Public education in rural counties is especially dis-advantaged, because of the weak tax base there.

Another dilemma that Tennesseans must confront is one of the basic paradoxes of modernization—the fact that, in some cases, progress solves old problems only to create new ones. To cite one of the most obvious ex-amples, widespread adoption of the automobile has brought untold ben-efits, yet it also has brought anguish: in the last three decades alone, some forty thousand Tennesseans have been killed in traffic accidents, and hun-dreds of thousands more have been injured. Likewise, industrialization has been a boon in countless ways, yet it has caused great damage to the state's environment, in such forms as air and water pollution, strip mining, haz-ardous waste dumps, and other serious threats.

The reforms of the civil rights era also exemplify the paradox. The aboli-tion of formal racial discrimination opened up new worlds of opportunity for black Tennesseans. Yet the determination to wipe out every trace of racial dis-tinction, including residential segregation and black poverty, led to certain remedial measures—including school busing and "affirmative action" pro-grams—that have provoked a new wave of racially charged disputes in recent years.

So, too, with many of the other liberalizing developments since the 1960s. The women's movement and the new sexual freedom, for example, emanci-pated Tennesseans from old prejudices and constraints, but they have brought in their wake rising rates of divorce, a boom in single-parent families, and rampant venereal disease. Bitter conflicts have arisen between modernists and traditionalists over such issues as pornography, abortion, and gay rights.

As Tennesseans enter their third century of statehood, they can celebrate their state's accomplishments proudly. But they would do well not to ignore the state's difficulties and disgraces, both past and present. If the history of the Volunteer State teaches us anything, it is that there is no progress without pain, no triumph without tragedy.

Suggested Readings

Bartlett, Richard A. *Troubled Waters: Champion International and the Pigeon River Controversy.* Knoxville, Tenn., 1995.

Doyle, Don Harrison. *Nashville Since the 1920s.* Knoxville, Tenn., 1985.

Greene, Lee Seifert, David H. Grubbs, and Victor C. Hobday. *Government in Tennessee.* 4th ed. Knoxville, Tenn., 1982.

Johnson, Leland, and Daniel Schaffer. *Oak Ridge National Laboratory: The First Fifty Years.* Knoxville, Tenn., 1994.

McDonald, Michael J., and William Bruce Wheeler. *Knoxville, Tennessee: Continuity and Change in an Appalachian City.* Knoxville, Tenn., 1983.

Majors, William R. *Change and Continuity: Tennessee Politics since the Civil War.* Macon, Ga., 1976.

Wheeler, William Bruce, and Michael J. McDonald. *TVA and the Tellico Dam, 1936–1979: A Bureaucratic Crisis in Post-Industrial America.* Knoxville, Tenn., 1986.

Whisnant, David E. *Modernizing the Mountaineer: People, Power, and Planning in Appalachia.* 1980. Reprinted, Knoxville, Tenn., 1994.

Wolfe, Charles K. *Tennessee Strings: The Story of Country Music in Tennessee.* Knoxville, Tenn., 1977.

Young, Thomas Daniel. *Tennessee Writers.* Knoxville, Tenn., 1981.

Index

Tennesseans and Their History was designed and typeset on a Macintosh computer system using PageMaker software. The text and chapter titles are set in Sabon. This book was designed by Kay Jursik, composed by Kimberly Scarbrough, and manufactured by Thomson-Shore, Inc. The recycled paper used in this book is designed for an effective life of at least three hundred years.